Cybercrimes: A Multidisciplinary Analysis

Sumit Ghosh • Elliot Turrini
Editors

Cybercrimes:
A Multidisciplinary Analysis

Springer

Editors
Prof. Sumit Ghosh
917 Joel Drive
Tyler, Texas 75703
USA
sumit.ghosh@ieee.org

Elliot Turrini
10 Babbit Road
Mendham, New Jersey 07945
USA
elliot@collaborativehealth.net

ISBN 978-3-642-13546-0 e-ISBN 978-3-642-13547-7
DOI 10.1007/978-3-642-13547-7
Springer Heidelberg Dordrecht London New York

Library of Congress Control Number: 2010936441

Cover design: WMX Design GmbH, Heidelberg, Germany

Printed on acid-free paper

Springer is part of Springer Science+Business Media (www.springer.com)

Preface

What's so important about cybercrime? Isn't it just another form of crime – like a violent or financial crime? The answer is both yes and no. Yes, in this way that any crime is a violation of a criminal law. But no in three important ways. First, a single cybercriminal with just one computer, right knowledge, and Internet access can cause immense social harm that was previously considered impossible. Second, the potential harm from cybercrime increases every second of every day, as computing technologies become more ubiquitous in our lives. Third, cybercriminals are often much more difficult to apprehend than traditional criminals, rendering the enforcement of cybercrime laws even less effective at crime prevention than the general enforcement of criminals laws.

Today, computers are everywhere, starting from cash registers in the grocery stores to running our cars, medical instruments that automatically read our temperature and blood pressure, routine banking, navigating airlines, and directing electricity to our homes and businesses. Consider the future of biotechnology, where tiny computers in the form of smart devices will be implanted inside our bodies – similar to, but more powerful than a pace maker. These devices will interact with our bodies in some profoundly important ways, and send and receive wireless communications from our doctors. Today, and even more so tomorrow, virtually all of these computers are interlinked through computer networks. Increasingly, computers and networks will entrench literally every aspect of our civilization without exception.

For the first time in our civilization, computers and networks, together, constitute an amplifier of the human mind, where the amplification factor is at a billion and growing fast with no upper bound in sight. With such formidable potential and power, computers and networks are destined to fundamentally alter our world – even beyond what we can reasonably imagine.

To an ordinary citizen, cybercrimes may logically appear to be defined as crimes that involve computers in any role or capacity. In fact, governments, civil and criminal justice systems, and law enforcement agencies, worldwide, choose to use this broad, working definition to help guide them in their crafting of the laws of the land, legal thinking, and the development of law enforcement tactics. This understanding of cybercrimes is very useful; however, it is of limited depth and may impede our ability to adequately address the large and growing cybercrime problem.

The potential for cybercrimes to evolve into innumerable radically new forms at incredible speed, orders of magnitude faster than the mutation rate of biological bacteria and viruses, is very real. Unchecked and unabated, they can easily overwhelm societies and nations.

What prompted us, contributing authors, to come together and organize this book? We fear the almost unlimited harm that cybercriminals can impose in the future. While filmed long after this book began, the movie, "Live Free or Die Hard," is not science fiction. Parts of it represent real and growing threats. But, more importantly, the authors believe that a multi-discipline, holistic approach to cybercrime prevention is essential.

Overall, this book is a collaborative effort of all of the contributing authors, characterized by great mutual admiration and deep respect for each other. Specifically, this book represents a coalescence of three motivating factors. First, each of the authors had independently arrived at the same exact realization that cybercrimes pose a formidable challenge to the fast approaching cyberage and that the important underlying issues must be addressed to ensure a bright future. Second, in the course of his prosecutorial work at the US DOJ, co-author Elliot Turrini had become deeply convinced that cybercrime is an intellectually rich, multidimensional problem, which requires a unique multidisciplinary approach. Third, in the course of his interdisciplinary research spanning computer hardware description languages to networking, network security, computer architecture, programming languages, algorithms, banking, biology, genetics, medicine, business, financial services, and modeling and simulation, co-author Sumit Ghosh experienced a profound revelation that, as an amplifier of the human mind, the underlying principle of computers represents the seed of virtually every known discipline of knowledge, law included.

The co-authors passionately hope that this book will serve to raise a general awareness among everyone of what lies ahead in our future. From a pessimistic perspective, unless we as a society are very careful, we risk being drowned literally, not metaphorically, in cybercrimes. Being not too proud to borrow twice from contemporary cinema, consider the Matrix movies as the ultimate cybercrimes – which, by the way, are far more science fiction than "Live Free or Die Hard." From an optimistic perspective, with diligent prevention/security and effective investigation and prosecution of cybercrimes, we will be able to enjoy the wonderful benefits of computers without suffering the horrific potential harms from cybercrimes.

A better understanding of how perpetrators may hatch sinister plans, today and in the future, will help us preempt most of the destructive cybercrimes and foster greater advancement and fulfillment for all humanity. Computers and networks encapsulate amazing and incredible power, not the thermo-nuclear weapon kind, but grounded in thought and imagination with which we can shape our future for centuries, millennia, and beyond. As explained in Chap. 1, our optimism should be tempered by a recently coined economic principle called, "convenience overshoot," which shows that under America's form of capitalism, the economics of bringing new technologies to the market and the difficulties of predicting safety and security issues often lead to the commercial distribution of unsafe or insecure products. This is an important principle, which should guide our thinking about cybercrime and security.

The underlying theme of the book rests on three pillars. The first is that cybercrime is a severe societal threat. The endemic vulnerability of computing as seen through the constant battle to control the CPU; future changes in computing technology; continued expansion of computing throughout our lives; and our proven track record of the "convenience overshoot" all coalesce into a severe societal risk. Second, criminal prosecution is important but, by itself, it is not nearly a sufficient response to the threat. Third, we need a multi-disciplinary, holistic approach to cybercrime prevention and mitigation with a three-prong focus: raise attack cost; increase attack risk, and reduce attack motivation.

What sets this book apart is its unique and simultaneous blend of pragmatic practice and fundamental scientific analysis. This tone permeates the entire book and reflects the origin and genesis of the collaboration between Sumit Ghosh and Elliot Turrini. In 2001, the USA DOJ was anxious to find a way to trace an Internet Protocol (IP) packet back to its origin, so they could tag and track suspect IP data packets involved in money laundering and terrorism and subsequently apprehend the perpetrators. A number of very well known networking companies were eager to explore this urgent USA DOJ need and were willing to modify or alter the IP router technology. From fundamental analysis of networking, however, it followed that IP packets could never be traced back to the launch point with any degree of certainty. Today, it has become mainstream knowledge that the design of the store-and-forward IP protocol is fundamentally incompatible with security. Through the many, many discussions, the co-authors became thoroughly motivated not only to synergize their ideas but to extend the collaboration to include researchers and practitioners from related disciplines. Inspired by this project, co-author Sumit Ghosh had co-organized a USA National Science Foundation-sponsored workshop titled, "Secure Ultra Large Networks: Capturing User Requirements with Advanced Modeling and Simulation Tools," in 2003. The interdisciplinary approach of the workshop was very well received and some of the far-reaching presentation material have been incorporated in this book.

This book is organized into nine major parts, each addressing a specific area that bear direct and undeniable relationship to cybercrimes. Part I serves as introduction and presents a working definition of cybercrimes; Part II focuses on the computing and networking technology as it relates to cybercrimes and the technical and people challenges encountered by the cyberdefenders; Part III explains how to compute the economic impact of a cybercrime and develop security risk management strategies; Part IV addresses the vulnerabilities of our critical infrastructures and notes that the possibilities of Pearl Harbor-type and Katrina-type cyberattacks are very real, which may be accompanied by catastrophic consequences; Part V describes the psycho-social aspect of cybercrimes; Part VI focuses on efforts and challenges to regulate cybercrimes directly, through criminal penalties, as well as indirectly; Part VII explains how cybercrimes easily transcend national and other boundaries and lists specific disciplines that face formidable challenges from cybercrimes, worldwide; Part VIII elaborates on techniques to mitigate cybercrimes and stresses on a multi-prong approach; and Part IX concludes the book with a scientific, engineering, and technological analysis of the future of cybercrimes. Each of these nine parts are elaborated through a number of self-contained chapters, totaling twenty chapters contributed by a total of 14 authors. Co-author/co-editor Sumit Ghosh has edited all of the chapters in an effort to ensure uniformity, continuity, and a smooth flow throughout the entire book.

Although the book has been primarily organized to serve as a reference for legal scholars, computer scientists, military personnel involved in cyberwarfare, national-level policy makers entrusted to protect the country's critical infrastructure, national and international intelligence communities, economic analysts, psychologists, and social scientists whose interests in cybercrimes are both specific and holistic, it is written to appeal to a much wider audience. The book may be read by anyone in the legal community or peripherally related disciplines who plans to specialize in cybercrimes, cyberattacks, and cyberlaws and their enforcement; front-line police officers; computer forensics specialists; law students; law makers at the State and Federal (Central) levels; judges; practicing lawyers; technical personnel involved in patent litigation; patent lawyers; product liability lawyers, economic analysts; central bankers, finance ministers, monetary policy makers, Interpol, and insurance company personnel involved in risk and actuarial analysis and in underwriting policies for data security. The book will also serve network and computer security specialists as well as those who wish to redesign products to withstand product liability lawsuits, grounded on a fundamental understanding of the nature of computers, networking, and cybercrimes. Even ordinary citizens who may be called from time to time to serve in the jury in litigations involving cybercrimes, especially in the USA, may find themselves well educated by reading this book so they can blend their wisdom along with technology to protect society and our collective future.

The co-authors/co-editors feel deeply honored and grateful to all of the contributing chapter authors, namely, Alan Boulanger, Paul Schneck, Richard Stanley, Michael Erbschloe, Michael Caloyannides, Emily Freeman, Dan Geer, Marc Rogers, Stewart Baker, Melanie Schneck-Teplinsky, Marc Goodman, and Jessica Herrera-Flanigan. A very special gratitude is due to Carey Nachenberg, Fellow at Symantec Corporation; and Leonard Bailey, senior counselor to the Assistant Attorney General for National Security at the US Department of Justice for selflessly giving their time and sharing their concerns, knowledge, and wisdom. Co-author Sumit Ghosh is indebted, beyond description, to Elliot Turrini for introducing him to the world of cyberlaw and to Leonard Bailey for mentoring, guiding, and advising him through the complex issues of critical infrastructure protection and criminal regulations. We also thank many others for their time. We are especially grateful to Anke Seyfried of Springer-Verlag (Law division) for her incredible enthusiasm and patience relative to this book project and the entire editorial and production staff at Springer-Verlag.

March 2010

Sumit Ghosh
Elliot Turrini

Contents

Part VII International Character of Cybercrimes

Part VIII Mitigation of Cybercrimes

Part IX Future of Cybercrimes: Who Will Have the Last Word?

List of Tables

List of Figures

Part I
Introducing Cybercrimes

Chapter 1
A Pragmatic, Experiential Definition of Computer Crimes

Elliot Turrini and Sumit Ghosh

1.1 Introducing Computer Crimes

1.1.1 The Melissa Virus: The Turning Point

1.1.1.1 The David Smith Prosecution

Although the first known virus for a personal computer has been traced to 1980 and a systematic study had been undertaken at Bell Labs in 1984 [1,2], the world really did not take notice until the Melissa virus began to infect millions of computers in late March 1999. After the Melissa virus struck, Elliot Turrini was assigned as the lead prosecutor for the Department of Justice's criminal investigation into Melissa's disseminator. This also marked the conception of this book. Elliot had little to do with the physical investigation that led to the perpetrator's apprehension. With valuable assistance from America Online (AOL) investigators, the New Jersey State Police and the Federal Bureau of Investigation caught the perpetrator, David Smith, within days. It soon became clear that apprehending the perpetrator was the relatively easy part. AOL had provided a report stating that the Melissa Virus had been posted on a Usenet group hosted under AOL by an individual who had accessed an AOL account from a small ISP in Monmouth County, New Jersey. The caller identification information in the call record from this small ISP, revealed that the virus was launched from David Smith's apartment. The remaining steps associated with proving that David Smith had launched the virus involved classic police work, including search warrants and interviews, which the New Jersey State Police and the FBI conducted very well.

The more difficult part of the prosecution involved assessing the economic damage caused by the virus. This was very important because David Smith's penalty would correlate directly with the economic damage he had either intended or actually caused. In general, for all US federal economic crimes at the time, including malicious code dissemination, the greater the economic damage caused or intended, the more severe the punishment. The prosecution bears the burden of proving the damages. Thus, upon a federal conviction, the sentence of a computer virus

S. Ghosh and E. Turrini (eds.), *Cybercrimes: A Multidisciplinary Analysis*,
DOI 10.1007/978-3-642-13547-7_1, © Springer-Verlag Berlin Heidelberg 2010

disseminator will depend almost exclusively on the United States' ability to prove the actual or intended economic damage.

To assess the damage in a systematic manner, it was necessary to first define how the Melissa virus worked and what it did. Upon successful infection of a computer, the "Melissa" virus caused the following:

- It lowered the security components of certain word processing programs, making the infected computer more vulnerable to computer virus infection.
- It altered certain word processing programs in such a way that any subsequent document created using the program would be infected with the "Melissa" virus.
- It caused most computers using Microsoft Word and Outlook to transmit electronic mails to the first 50 e-mail addresses in the computer user's address book. Associated with each electronic mail was an attachment that was infected with the "Melissa" virus.

Where the infected attachment was opened on a different computer, say Y, using certain word processing programs, then Y was immediately infected with the "Melissa" virus and the cycle would repeat for Y. In the course of assessing the damage, Elliot Turrini interviewed a number of information security professionals and economists, searching for experts who could assist in computing precisely or even estimating the Melissa virus' economic damage. He quickly learned two important lessons.

First, cybercriminals felt immune from apprehension since they believed that (1) law enforcement could never apprehend them, and (2) in the rare event that they were caught, the punishment would be minor. This belief in minor penalty, according to the information security professionals, stemmed from the perception that in 1988, insignificant punishment was inflicted on Robert Morris for disseminating the Morris Worm. According to Professor Gene Spafford, the Morris Worm "exploited flaws in utility programs in systems based on BSD-derived versions of UNIX [, which] ...allowed the program to break into those machines and copy itself, thus infecting those systems. This infection eventually spread to thousands of machines, and disrupted normal activities and Internet connectivity for many days." According to the GAO, while the impact of the Morris Worm was difficult to assess, it likely infected "between 1,000 and 3,000 computers...." And, the GAO noted that while "[e]stimated losses from individual sites [were] ...generally not available[,] ...NASA's Ames Research Center and Department of Energy's Lawrence Livermore National Laboratory, two major government sites, estimated their dollar losses at $72,500 and $100,000, respectively" [3]. Despite this harm, Robert Morris was sentenced to 3 years probation, $10,000 fine, 400 h community service, and no restitution.

Second, Elliot observed that very few people were thinking about, and even fewer were working on assessing the economic consequences of computer crimes. At the time, the major source of information was the Computer Security Institute's annual computer crime survey. This was of little interest to the federal government, since the GAO report on the Morris Worm had already confirmed that "[n]o official estimates have been made of how many computers the [Morris Worm] ...infected, in part because no one organization is responsible for obtaining such information." However, "ICSA.Net," at the time a division of CyberTrust, was one of the few entities working on the economic consequences of a portion of malicious code. ICSA.Net's fortuitous efforts proved invaluable to the successful prosecution of David Smith. In March 1999, ICSA.Net had launched a "General Virus Prevalence Survey," a telephone survey spanning 300 randomly selected companies in North America with 500 or more computers. In one question, the survey had asked the respondents to identify any computer viruses that had infiltrated their networks and to quantify the damage caused. Following the Melissa virus's dissemination, 139 respondents provided their damage estimate data to ICSA.Net, which yielded a net damage between $77 million and $300 million. Although ICSA.Net's action was fortuitous, it was clear that few people in the United States of American comprehended the potential economic harm from malicious code.

The $77 million lower bound estimate became the foundation for David Smith's eventual guilty plea. Mr. Smith himself admitted that his crime had caused over $80 million in damage and, based on this guilty plea, the Federal Sentencing Guidelines required that Smith receive a sentence between 46 and 57 months of imprisonment. However, since Smith had cooperated extensively with the United States government following his guilty plea by aiding the investigation and prosecution of other malicious code writers, the judge expressed leniency by departing from the Federal Sentencing Guidelines and sentenced Smith to a mere 20-month imprisonment.

1.1.1.2 Lessons from the David Smith Prosecution

The David Smith prosecution brought into focus a number of important observations in the discipline of computer crimes.

First, it revealed the ongoing battle for control of the computers between the owners and cybercriminals. The Melissa Virus had acquired and exercised unauthorized control over each of the computers it had infected, by lowering their security settings and compelling them to send out infected e-mails to the first 50 addresses stored in each of the infected computer's Microsoft Outlook address book. The recipients of the virus-infected e-mails were equally defenseless, in that the infection was virtually automatic. While it was not obvious to all of us on the prosecution's side, this vulnerability was inherent in the design of our computing platform. Our computers "blindly" execute instructions and are highly mutable, i.e., susceptible to changes in their programming. This blind and total obedience and mutability drastically reduces the time and effort required for cybercriminals to acquire and execute unauthorized control over computers.

Second, the prosecution exposed the cybercriminal's unique and unprecedented advantages in this battle to control computers. The most glaring advantage was the virtually unlimited strike capability, fostered by the computer and the Internet and the homogeneity of the computers, both in terms of the hardware and software components and the overall design. The Internet enables millions of computers, worldwide, to communicate with each other through a uniform and common suite of well-publicized protocols, which, in essence, greatly reduces the time and money involved in attacking many cybercrime victims. With very little physical effort, and using only a single computer with Internet access, David Smith successfully attacked millions of computers. In the brick and mortar world, this feat would have required orders of magnitude more time, money, and energy.

The prosecution also exposed the cybercriminal's stealth advantage. While David Smith chose not to exploit it, the stealth advantage is staggering. Had Smith chose to launch the virus from a computer whose IP address could not be readily traced back to him, such as at a public library or a university (instead of his own apartment), it would have been very difficult, if not impossible, to locate and apprehend him. The combination of the Internet and the configuration of our computers provided and continues to offer even semi-sophisticated cybercriminals the cover of near perfect stealth. The stealth advantage is of overwhelming importance because the primary method to deter computer crimes is the criminal justice system, which, in turn, only works well only when the perpetrators can be identified and brought to trial. In cyberspace, stealth leads to anonymity, which can constrain the criminal justice system from correctly identifying, apprehending, and punishing the cybercriminals.

Additionally, the prosecution revealed the cybercriminal's communication and cooperation advantages in that they tend to communicate over the Internet and share their knowledge of how to attack and exploit other computers, unlike the ordinary computer owners, both in the private and public sectors, who have barely begun to share information. The Internet and the stealth advantage combine to allow cybercriminals unprecedented ability to share criminal insights and techniques. Consider how difficult it is for the bank robber to talk shop with thousands of peer bank robbers.

Third, the prosecution revealed that the criminal's risks in attacking other computers were very low. Unlike the traditional brick and mortar crime, attacking computers did not involve any risk of physical injury. No dogs would bite, no victim would retaliate, and no police would give chase. Also, given the cover of anonymity, the risk of being apprehended and punished was very low. This low risk, elaborated in the subsequent chapters of this book, greatly undermines the criminal justice system's ability to prevent and mitigate computer crimes. The criminal justice system is based on the concept of general deterrence, referred to herein as "traditional deterrence." Traditional deterrence is founded on the belief that fear of punishment deters crime. That is, ordinary people refrain from crime to avoid the negative consequences of criminal justice punishment. Clearly, traditional deterrence cannot and does not work when the potential perpetrators have little fear of being apprehended.

Fourth, and probably most important, the prosecution revealed that the stakes in the battle for control for other computers are very high. In particular, the prosecution highlighted that the potential economic and social harm from malicious code and related crime was astronomical. Some experts had pointed out that if the Melissa virus had otherwise contained a destructive payload that deleted information on the infected computers' hard drives, the attack would have destroyed a minimum of 5% of all of the digital information in United States businesses. The extent of the destruction would probably be much higher, given the absence of adequate backup facilities at the time. The ExploreZip worm, a malicious code, contemporary of the Melissa Virus, contained instructions to delete files from a computer's hard drive.

Overall, the David Smith prosecution was an eye-opener in terms of the reach and extent of computer crimes. It is worth noting that the Federal government had recognized this potential threat more than 10 years earlier, when the GAO report on the Morris Worm had reported the following:

> "although the Morris Worm is described as benign because apparently no permanent damage was done, a few changes to the virus program could have resulted in widespread damage and compromise, according to computer experts. For example, these experts said that with a slightly enhanced program, the virus could have erased files on infected computers or remained undetected for weeks, surreptitiously changing information on computer files."

Fifth, the prosecution revealed a related lesson that a multi-disciplinary, holistic approach involving expertise in law, technology, psychology and economics was needed to address the computer crime problem. The need for criminal law expertise is obvious, given that, presently, criminal justice system is our primary method to address crime. However, the criminal justice system is inadequately prepared to handle the problem alone, because (1) there are substantial impediments to identifying, apprehending, and punishing cybercriminals; (2) recent research has revealed that traditional deterrence is unlikely to be as effective as once believed in preventing computer crime; and (3) the criminal justice system is ill-suited at implementing alternative crime prevention strategies. This lesson was subsequently presented to US Congress in 2003 [4].

This deficiency had led Elliot and others to explore and examine alternative solutions to the criminal justice system, which revealed two insights: (1) the importance of social norms in controlling behavior and (2) the relationship between economics and crime mitigation. Many sociologists agree that social norms represent the strongest behavioral control. This fact, combined with the deficiency of the criminal justice system, highlighted the need to better understand the attacker's state of mind, i.e., his or her psychology, given that the ultimate goal is to dissuade potential cybercrimals from launching attacks. Thus, expertise in psychology is needed to mitigate computer crime. The need for technological expertise was evident because recent crime prevention research into alternatives to traditional deterrence revealed that raising attack costs, i.e., requiring more time, money, and energy to execute an attack, can lower the potential for crime, including computer attacks. Thus, by raising attack costs, we can persuade potential attackers that the perpetration is simply not worth the effort. The examination also revealed that both public, i.e., government, and private efforts, i.e., individuals, groups, and companies, must combine forces to mitigate computer crime.

Consider physical burglary as an example. Private efforts to mitigate burglary come in many forms, including door locks, alarm systems, watch dogs, and community watch groups. Public efforts also come in many forms and include traditional deterrence, civil penalties, police patrols, and public awareness campaigns. This joint mitigation approach must be forcefully applied to cybercrimes – as this book notes throughout.

It is well known that the degree of economic distress a type of harm inflicts substantially influences the amount of money that the private sector spends on mitigating and preventing it. For the example of physical burglary, we collect substantial information about the economic harm. Indeed, the insurance industry collects this information so that it can profitably sell insurance against burglary. Armed with this information, the insurance industry plays an important role by dictating the types of burglary prevention devices that home owners must employ in order to reduce their insurance premiums. Thus, by determining the economic harm from a particular type of crime, the insurance industry guides the private sector mitigate crime with greater efficiency. As a corollary to this theory, when the private sector is unable to accurately determine the economic harm from a specific type of crime, the corresponding crime mitigation effort suffers. The David Smith prosecution revealed how little we knew about the actual economic harm inflicted by malicious code and other cybercrimes. The need for economic expertise when attempting to mitigate cybercrime cannot be emphasized more strongly.

While not obvious at first sight, the David Smith prosecution also revealed the need to reexamine how civil laws, especially civil liability, can be used to mitigate cybercrime. The Melissa Virus exploited software flaws, which theoretically were product deficiencies. According to the product liability laws in the United States, the software manufacturers could in theory be held liable for such deficiencies. This fact led us to examine how civil liability can be used to create the proper incentives for IT manufacturers to develop and distribute more secure products. The more secure our IT products, the greater the cost of attacking, which would serve as a deterrence.

1.1.2 Cybercrimes in Early 2001

In early 2001, a strong effort was launched to bring together experts in law, technology, psychology, and economics to analyze and help mitigate the cybercrime problem. The United States Department of Justice (DOJ) has defined computer crime as "any violation of criminal law that involved the knowledge of computer technology for its perpetration, investigation, or prosecution" [5]. Thus, this definition extends computer crime to any crime where a computer is either the target, a tool, or a storage device [6]. Thus, computer crime included and includes a vast array of crimes, including hacking; virus writing; digital piracy; cyberstalking; e-mail piracy; and theft of any digital information, which extends to identity theft, bank fraud, credit card fraud, trade secret theft, international espionage, etc. Initiated in March 2007 and in effect today, March 2010, the DOJ [7] classifies, for the purpose of working prosecutors in real world practice, crimes that use or target computer networks as "computer crimes," "cybercrimes," and "network crimes," interchangeably.

By 2001, we started to observe that hacking, denial of service attacks, and insider abuse were rampant in the industry and elsewhere. Cybercrime was growing and posing a significant challenge. While analyzing the vast array of cybercrimes, we found ourselves driven to classify them, which, we believed would help us clarify issues and further our mitigation efforts. Initially, we organized cybercrimes into five basic categories, namely, intrusion, malicious code, denial of service attacks, digital piracy, and all others. Next, we began to distinguish between those cybercrimes that required the attacker to use technical expertise and often exploited what is commonly referred to as a computer "vulnerability" from those labeled non-technical cybercrimes such as cyberstalking and limited forms of copyright infringement for which little technical expertise was required. Exceptions notwithstanding, non-technical cybercrimes are limited in the scope and depth of damage they can inflict.

In contrast, technical cybercrimes can inflict astronomical amounts of harm. Technical cybercrimes generally fell into four categories, namely, hacking, malicious code, denial of service, and defeating anti-circumvention devices employed to protect copyrighted works. In these crimes, the attacker acquired and exercised unauthorized control over a computer system either by exploiting technical flaws or through social engineering. Denial of service attacks differed slightly, in that the unauthorized control was realized by overloading the victim computer so that the legitimate owner was denied the use of his or her computer. As long as the computer owner retained exclusive control over the computer system, the attacks failed. Where the cybercriminal gained some form of control over a different computer, attacks succeeded. Furthermore, the greater the control acquired by the attacker, the greater the potential for damage.

The core issue in technical cybercrimes is one of unauthorized control over the computing process, where the process encompasses the incessant activities of one or more of the millions of computers and computing devices, worldwide. A technical cybercrime is determined to have been committed when a single attacker or a group of cybercriminals succeeds in wrestling away from the legitimate owner control over the target computer or computing device in a way that violates a criminal law. While there may be scenarios when unauthorized control over the computing process does not violate a criminal law, the vast majority of such instances are technical cybercrimes.

1.1.3 Defining Technical Cybercrime

A technical cybercrime has been committed when the attacker has successfully wrestled away and extended some form of unauthorized control over the "computing process." The computing process represents the brain-waves inside our computers, which manifest in terms of arithmetic and logic operations on information at high speed. In general, the computing process involves the following steps. (1) First, information is fed into the computing process, which in general comprises a microprocessor and firmware. (2) Second, the computing process interprets the information. (3) Third, following interpretation, the process obediently executes the instructions in the information by sending instructions to other parts of the computer such as the hard drive and the monitor, which in turn obediently follows these instructions. The process occurs incessantly in the millions of microprocessor-powered computers operating worldwide. Thus, when one is in control of the computing process, one can successfully control the computer and any function that it can perform.

The computing process is similar to the common household light switch in that, when working properly, they both obediently follow instructions, produce measurable outputs, i.e., direct results, and have indirect consequences. The light switch follows the instructions imposed on it by anyone who has the ability to flip it up or down. When it is flipped, it either completes or interrupts a circuit, thereby turning a light ON or OFF. The direct result, i.e., the measurable output, is the effect on the light bulb. It is either illuminated or shut off and dark. The indirect consequences depend on the context, namely, the role the light plays. This could either be as routine as providing light to locate the glass of water at night to as critical as enabling one to read the instructions on one's heart medicine bottle.

The computing process essentially operates in the same way. The computing process obediently follows the instructions imposed on it by anyone or anything that has the ability to provide it with the instructions. The direct results, i.e., measurable output, however, may be vastly different from merely turning a light ON or OFF. The direct results from the computing process depend on the computer's configuration and its context i.e., how it is being used and what it controls. For example, when the typical computer user double clicks on the Internet Explorer icon, unbeknownst to him or her, the user is feeding instructions and exercising control over the computing process. The direct result of this control and the instructions fed to the computing process is that the Internet Explorer application is drawn into the computer's working memory, termed RAM, and displayed on the monitor, thereby enabling the user to browse the Internet. This is, of course, assuming that the computer has Internet access. While the actions behind the scenes are much more complex than what occurs when a light switch is flipped, the results are basically similar. The computer obediently follows the instructions.

As with the light switch, the indirect consequences of the computing process also depend on the context in which the computer is used. The indirect consequences can be mundane, such as when we use a computer and the Internet to check our Facebook page, or highly critical, such as when a NASA computer adjusts the trajectory of the shuttle, while en-route to the Space station. The indirect consequences can be immense in scope and highly critical to our well being. Consider the role our computers play in our critical infrastructure, ranging from water supply to gas, electricity, and telephone. Maintaining exclusive and precise control over computers that run our infrastructure is extremely important at all times. The same is true when computers run CAT scans or three-dimensional X-rays. Loss of control over the computing process can result in severe injury to the patient. The trend toward embedded computing, i.e., incorporating small computers in other products such as cars, ovens, pace makers, garage door openers, etc., pose a formidable challenge. Embedded computers are characterized by the same traits of blind obedience and mutability. By extending computers more widely, the practice of embedded computing opens up the possibility for potential cybercriminals to exercise even greater control and cause untold damage.

1.2 The Battle to Control the Computing Process

1.2.1 The Nature of the Battle

The control over the computing process is essentially a cyberbattle between the cybercriminal and the cyberdefender. While the owner is constantly expending effort to maintain full control over the computer at all times, the attacker is engaged in trying to wrestle away and exercise unauthorized control over the computing process.

Clearly, analysis of the cyberbattle requires careful examination of the cyberbattlefield, where the battle is waged. In the subsequent subsections, we will examine the constituent components and tactics used in the cyberbattlefield, utilizing rough analogies to military concepts, including reconnaissance, strike capability, stealth, and communications. We believe the rough analogies will help illuminate the subtle intricacies of the cyberbattle.

1.2.2 The Cyberbattlefield

The technical cybercrime battlefield, termed cyberbattlefield in this book, is an environment represented by the confluence of three key elements, namely, general-purpose computers, software, and the Internet. It also includes the economic and social forces creating, influencing, and constraining our use of technology. Although the physical world encompasses the cyberworld, its influence is significantly less than the intrinsic components of the cyberbattlefield.

1.2.2.1 The Key Elements of the Cyberbattlefield

- General-purpose computers include personal computers, such as desktops and laptops, mainframes, Blackberry devices, and iPhones. They were designed to perform basic information functions, namely, creation, storage, manipulation, and distribution, more easily, quickly, and inexpensively. They also form the core of the Internet. The computer, in turn, is comprised of four basic elements – hardware, firmware, operating systems, and applications. The hardware generally consists of the microprocessor, short-term memory such as the RAM and cache, long-term memory such as the hard drive, and input–output devices including the mouse, keyboard, DVD drive, CD-ROM drive, floppy drive, tape drive, monitor, etc. Each of the hardware element usually comes with a related computer program called a driver, which is a set of instructions that help the microprocessor and the operating system communicate with and control the device. Additional hardware elements include the motherboard, video cards, sound cards, etc. Firmware is an integrated circuit that is manufactured with persistent memory that contains the instructions that the microprocessor invokes to initiate the computing process.

Operating systems are software programs that define the computer experience by organizing and controlling the hardware and the applications and by providing a visual user interface. Operating systems transform a collection of hardware and applications onto a powerful computing tool, which users can control through the user interface provided by the operating system. Applications are computer programs designed to perform specific functions. When a user utilizes an application, such as a word processor, the corresponding program is executed by the microprocessor and it interacts with the individual through the operating system and user interface. By executing the application's instructions, the microprocessor performs the essential functions of the application such as saving a document on the hard drive.

Microprocessors are self-contained computational engines made primarily from silicon chips that behave as the heart and brain of the computer. Deep inside the microprocessors are logic gates that execute the computing process. To enable it to function, a microprocessor must be fed instructions. The permanent instructions built into firmware are the first sequence of instructions that the microprocessor executes when the computer is turned on. Usually, the firmware first instructs the microprocessor to ensure the computer's hardware is working properly. This is often referred to as the power-on self-test. When successful, the firmware instructs the microprocessor to activate the operating system, which the microprocessor complies by reading the boot information from the hard drive and loading the operating system onto RAM. The random access memory (RAM) acts as the microprocessor's short term memory, providing the microprocessor a convenient and fast workspace to store applications and data files to be utilized soon. In contrast, the hard drive is a storage location where applications and related data files are stored permanently. Behind the scenes, the operating system manages the hardware and related drivers to display the graphic user interface. Three of the most common operating systems include Microsoft Windows (Vista, XP, NT) Apple OS/X, and GNU Linux.

- Software comprises any computer program that is executed on a computer. It comes in two basic forms, namely, operating systems such as Linux and applications such as a word processor. At the lower level, software consists of a set of written instructions designed to perform a specific function. Software comes in an infinite variety of forms, ranging from the word processing and e-mail programs we use daily to the complex programs that are composed to launch the space shuttle. The common trait is that software begins with instructions written in a computer programming language, known as source code, that are compiled into object code so that the program can function on a specific computer and operating system. The operating system provides the graphic interface that enables users to communicate with and control the operating system, which in turn allows the users to control the applications. The operating system acts as the intermediary among the user, applications, and the hardware – enabling the user to perform the combined functions of the applications and hardware. The applications are sets of instructions that enable the user to perform the application's specific functions. Examples of applications include word processing programs, such as Microsoft Word; spread sheets, such as Excel and Lotus Notes; digital photograph manipulation programs, such as Adobe Photoshop and GIMP; and web-servers, such as Microsoft IIS and Apache. Only the designers' creativity and the hardware's capabilities limit the information processing functions that the applications can provide. When an application such as a word processor is in use, it sends instructions through the operating system to the microprocessor, which executes them blindly. For example, when a user double clicks on the Microsoft Word icon on the graphic user interface, the user causes the operating system to instruct the microprocessor to direct the hard drive to load the Word application onto RAM so that the microprocessor can easily and quickly execute Word's instructions. When the user begins to use Word's functions by opening an existing document, referred to herein as a data file, the user causes the Word application to send instructions to the microprocessor through the operating system, which cause the microprocessor to direct the hard drive to load the data file into RAM, so that the microprocessor can easily manipulate the data file. Thus, when an application is being used, both the operating system and the application feed instructions into the microprocessor to perform the application's functions.

- The Internet, in a nut shell, is a network of computers that, through a common language called protocols, permits each participating computer to communicate with each other. The Internet backbone is the Internet's core and is made up of large, privately owned computer networks known as backbone providers. The backbone providers consist of companies such as Sprint, AT&T, Verizon, and MCIWorldcom 2000 that own large and extremely fast computer networks that use fast fiber optic cables and powerful special-purpose computers, termed routers or switches. Each provider owns the cables and routers that comprise their part of the Internet backbone. The individual backbone networks are connected to each through Network Access Points ("NAPs") and Private Exchange Points ("PEPs"). NAPs and PEPs are the gateways between the backbone providers, which allow individual backbone providers to send each other electronic information. Because gateways connect all providers to each other, a single computer user with access to any one of the backbone provider's networks can transmit electronic information to all users within the networks of other providers. Generally, individuals are not provided access to the backbone providers directly; instead, they are offered access through smaller companies known as Internet Service Providers (ISPs).

The communications among computers over the Internet come in the form of data packets or cells. Each data packet or cell contains a part of a message, the sender's address, the recipient's address, and limited routing directives. Upon receipt of all of the data packets at the destination, a computer re-unites them, i.e., pieces together the parts of the messages to constitute the original contiguous message. The sender's and recipient's address come in the form of an Internet Protocol address ("IP address"), with the sender's address being the source IP address and the recipient's address being the destination IP address. The routers that comprise the Internet use the IP address to transmit the data packets to the appropriate recipient. The Internet permits users to send any information that can be organized into data packets. There is virtually no limit to the types of information that can be processed into data packets or cells. We can convert audio, video, text, and graphics into packets, all of which the Internet can transmit around the world and beyond the earth at amazing speeds. The only limits on the speed are the processing power of the routers and the capacity of the transmission media such as fiber optic cable.

1.2.2.2 The Artificial and Highly Mutable Nature of the Cyberbattlefield

Unlike conventional battlefields, where human beings face each other in deathly combat, the cyberbattlefield is artificial, i.e., not naturally found, and highly mutable. All of the components in the cyberbattlefield are human-made. Therefore, it follows that the components and the cyberbattlefield may be altered by human beings. Thus, some researchers argue that computers may be redesigned with biometric data built into the basic configuration to strengthen authentication and defeat intrusion by cybercriminals, while software may be made more secure through improved code writing practices and verification tools, and the Internet may be replaced with ATM protocols in which data cells may be traced to their point of origin, exceptions notwithstanding. In practice, however, modifying the cyberbattlefield may prove much more difficult, given the presence of powerful economic and social forces that have shaped this battlefield and wish to maintain status quo [8]. For example, privacy concerns have limited the use of biometric and other authentication technologies, evident in the backlash over Intel Corporation's disclosure that the Pentium processor chip contained a unique identifier that could trace an attack to the computer(s) that was involved in the perpetration. As a second example, economics have rewarded software manufacturers who have quickly brought products to the market, even when they were riddled with flaws and vulnerabilities. Clearly, to acquire a true understanding of the battle, it is important to identify all of the forces influencing its scope, shape, contours, rules, and laws.

Historically, in the traditional battlefields, combatants have always sought strategic advantages against the enemy. For example, during the American Civil War in Gettysburg, Union forces raced to encamp the hills at Cemetery Ridge and Culp's hill, which aided their victory. Despite a 3-to-1 superiority in numbers, the Confederate forces suffered heavy casualties in frontal attacks up the hill and could not dislodge the Union forces. This proved to be a turning point in the Civil War. The outcome might have been very different if powerful missiles had been available. Union forces occupying a small area on top of the hill would be easy targets, unlike the Confederate forces which could have been distributed thin over a much larger area. The issue of differential advantages hold true in the cyberbattlefield, as elaborated in the subsequent subsection.

1.2.2.3 Strategic Advantages and Disadvantages in the Cyberbattlefield

As in a traditional battlefield, the key strategic criteria in the battle to control the computing process includes reconnaissance, strike capability, stealth, and communications. We will first explain these terms as understood in the traditional military and then review their manifestations in the cyberbattlefield.

Reconnaissance refers to an exploration-based effort to gather information about the number, strength, and positioning of the enemy forces over a given limited area [9]. Strike capability encapsulates the ability to implement an attack and may be organized into three principal components, namely, speed, reach, and payload. While speed refers to the rate of progress into the enemy ranks as a function of time, reach is a measure of how deep and wide into enemy territory can force be projected, and payload implies the destructive power of the attack. Stealth is the ability to conceal an attack from the enemy until it is too late, while communications permit one to gather and disseminate relevant information timely and coordinate attacks for a favorable outcome. Although reconnaissance is a subset of communications, it has proven vital to many battles in history and is, therefore, assigned special status.

- *Reconnaissance*: In the cyberbattlefield, the attacker seeks out information about a target computer, its computing technology, platform, Internet access mechanism, and vulnerabilities, using web searches, worms, and other automated tools. Next, the information and vulnerabilities are analyzed and a method of attack formulated and launched. For the defenders, information about attackers is sparse and difficult to locate. Although firewalls, anti-virus software, honey-pots, and intrusion detection systems may offer information about the attackers, it is generally very limited. Attackers will generally conceal their identity by masking their true IP addresses or, worse, use someone else's IP address to misdirect any investigation. Even if IP hiding techniques were not readily available, current laws prevent private individuals and groups from obtaining information necessary to identify attackers. In the United States today, only law enforcement officials are authorized to gather information necessary to identify an attacker based on the IP address involved in the attack. Furthermore, there appears to be inadequate economic incentives for defenders to gather information about attackers. The key impediments include the low probability of correctly identifying the attacker and the greater likelihood that the attacker will lack sufficient funds to compensate the defender for the harm inflicted. Thus, efforts to identify the attacker appear to be a waste of energy, time, and money although, in theory, such efforts could increase the rate of apprehending the cybercriminals. This dilemma represents a classic collective action/free rider problem, because most individual defenders do not want to expend the resources without assurances that other defenders will do the same [10]. In summary, as to reconnaissance, the current configuration of the cyberbattlefield appears to favor the attackers over the defenders.

- *Strike capability*: Current US law prohibits defenders, with the exception of the US military, from striking back at an attacker, leaving them the options of either reporting an attack to law enforcement or seeking civil penalties (assuming the attacker can be identified). A defender, therefore, is inhibited from counterattacking at those suspected of attempting to attack him or her. The problem is aggravated by the fact that attackers generally deploy stealth tactics and they typically lack monetary resources to pay for the penalties.

  By its very nature, the cyberbattlefield allows an attacker to launch an attack with exceptional speed. While the computers execute in nanoseconds, optical fibers carry information at GB/s, causing very fast actions. The extensive reach of the attackers is enabled by the Internet that connects millions of computers around the world, and by the homogeneity of the computing hardware and the software platform. Thus, the Internet enables attackers to reach every computer's defenses very quickly from anywhere in the world. Although this does not automatically mean a capitulation of the target computer, the mere arrival of an attack at the defense perimeter can successfully restrict freedom, thereby constituting a denial of service attack. Since an attacker can strike from anywhere in the world and at any time, the defender is at a significant disadvantage. Massing defensive resources at every entry point is prohibitively expensive. In conclusion, as to strike capability, the current cyberbattlefield appears to favor the attacker over the defender.
- *Stealth*: The design of the Internet provides significant "stealth" advantages to attackers, allowing them to conceal their IP addresses with relative ease. In contrast, most defenders lack stealth; their location in cyberspace, i.e., their IP addresses and website domain names are publicly available. As a result, attackers can reach defenders anywhere in the world, causing defenders to face an almost limitless number and variety of attackers. Furthermore, most of the current defensive measures including firewalls, anti-virus software, and intrusion detection schemes focus on preventing the attacker from successfully delivering the destructive payload and taking over control – not on hiding a defender's location. For obvious reasons, defenders can neither conceal their location nor identity, often making them the proverbial, "sitting duck."

  In contrast, the cyberbattlefield enables even semi-skilled attackers to make it virtually impossible for defenders and law enforcement to identify them. While prosecuting cybercriminals for the Department of Justice, Elliot Turrini learned that the best way to identify attackers is through their statements to co-conspirators and others. During these candid moments, attackers often reveal themselves and inadvertently provide evidence of their identity, including job, residence, hobbies, other personal attributes, or a valid and traceable IP address. Unfortunately, however, attackers usually carefully limit these candid moments. The cyberbattlefield does not help the defenders and law enforcement access these candid moments. Attackers can hide their genuine IP address, termed source IP address, through spoofing; employing a compromised proxy; launching attacks from public libraries, universities, and cyber-cafes; or utilizing an anonymizer. Under these circumstances, locating the source IP address of the packet used in an attack yields no helpful evidence. Often, an investigation reveals information about an innocent party. When a different computer, say X, usually at a university or in a public library is attacked and taken over by a perpetrator, the attacker can launch subsequent attacks from X, referred to as the compromised proxy. By their very nature, public libraries, Internet-cafes, and universities usually do not keep user records. Anonymizers are websites that permit Internet users to logon and obtain a source IP address that is assigned and controlled by the anonymizer. When an attack is launched from an anonymizer, the source IP address left at the scene of the cybercrime can be successfully traced back to the anonymizer. However, the anonymizer does not keep records of its users and the trail goes cold. In the United States, presently, there are few laws requiring data retention. Even if there were such laws in effect, anonymizers could be relocated to foreign countries, from where attacks may just as easily be launched. Thus, it may be virtually impossible to eliminate anonymizers completely.

  There is one other problem with IP addresses. Like many other concepts in Computer Science and Engineering, an IP address is a pointer or an indirect reference, which does not always immediately and directly link an IP address to a specific computer or an individual. There are levels of evidentiary hurdles that the investigator must systematically pursue to correctly identify the attacker. To summarize, the current cyberbattlefield appears to provide differential stealth advantage to attackers over defenders.

- *Communications*: Both attackers and defenders are able to share information through websites, mailing lists, chat, and conferences. As to communications, the cyberbattlefield appears to favor both parties equally. In the United States, the First Amendment protects attackers' rights to share information about attack strategies and vulnerabilities.

1.2.2.4 Software Vulnerabilities

While software vulnerabilities play an undeniable role in today's cyberbattlefield and tend to favor attackers, they do not necessarily constitute a fundamental attribute of the cyberbattlefield. The vulnerabilities are a direct result of software vendors' desire to be the first to introduce a product to the market, at the expense of incorporating code that is not fully tested and may include flaws. Market forces have rewarded software manufacturers for being first to market and for offering features and functions. During the early years of software manufacturing, from the 1980s to 2000, security was an afterthought, not an integral part of the manufacturing process. While eliminating software vulnerabilities is a difficult and expensive process, software manufacturers can and must do better. With time, software vulnerabilities are expected to become less and less significant. But, as the "convenience overshoot," elaborated in Sect. 1.4, suggests, some level of software vulnerabilities might actually be endemic in the computing arena. The key is to recognize and compensate for this problem through other means.

1.3 Tools for Fighting the Battle to Control the Computing Process

1.3.1 Defining Tools

In general, a tool is a means to an end. It refers to an object, material or abstract, that is used to achieve a desired goal [9]. Under cybercrimes, a tool refers to the following:

- Anything that attackers use to exercise unauthorized control or avoid being apprehended.
- Anything defenders use to prevent unauthorized control by an attacker or to retaliate against attackers, including reporting to law enforcement, seeking civil penalties, or counterstriking with an attack of his or her own.

Clearly, a tool may be used by both attackers and defenders, either in offensive or defensive model.

1.3.2 The Attacker's Technical Tools

The attacker's arsenal includes technical and social tools. The technical weapons include inexpensive and powerful computers, the Internet, software, and anonymity. The social tools are described in Sect. 1.3.3.

- *Inexpensive, powerful computers*: Today's inexpensive yet powerful computers render the conception and execution of any cybercrime relatively easy. The attackers can create malicious code, communicate with each other, acquire information about targets, and launch attacks. Although a distributed denial of service attack may benefit from substantially more computing power than provided by a normal desktop, this is not necessary.
- *The Internet*: As early as August 2001, a respected malicious code expert, Nicholas Weaver, claimed that a cybercriminal may use a computer worm to infect virtually every vulnerable computer connected to the Internet between 15 min and an hour. He termed this hypothetical entity the Warhol Worm. Mr. Weaver indicated, "It is well known that active worms such as Code Red and the Morris Internet worm have the potential to spread very quickly, on the order of hours to days. But it is possible to construct hyper-virulent active worms, capable of infecting all vulnerable hosts in approximately 15 minutes to an hour. Such 'Warhol Worms,' by using optimized scanning routines, hitlist scanning for initial propagation, and permutation scanning for complete, self coordinated coverage, could cause maximum damage before people could respond. The potential mayhem is staggering" [11, 12]. The Internet's overall speed is increasing with each additional broadband subscriber and every new foot of fiber optic cable installed in the system. Market forces are strongly encouraging increased speed.

The Internet's reach into all corners of the world is also growing rapidly. With each new computer connected to the Internet, the potential scope of cybercrime increases. The expansion of embedded computing and the trend toward Internet access for these devices is driving the speed of the Internet and expanding the reach. The sheer number of potential targets, by itself, constitutes a powerful motivation for cybercriminals; and the cost of committing specific cybercrimes, per unit device, is drastically reduced.

- Software constitutes the attacker's weapon of choice. Many cybercrimes involves specific software, i.e., a computer program, written to assist the attacker in gaining unauthorized control. Attack software may be organized into two general forms – (1) self-contained programs such as worms, viruses, spyware, and Trojan horses, that, once installed on a target computer will begin to function on its own and extend unauthorized control, and (2) programs such as intrusion attacks, which assist attackers in acquiring direct control over the target computer and they assume complete supervisory control of every aspect of the computing process. These weapons can assume an indeterminate number of forms; can be easily replicated an indefinite number of times, subject to resource availability; and may be freely shared throughout the world. Under United States law, in particular the First Amendment of the US Constitution, attackers can lawfully share software weapons in the cyberspace. Thus, unlike the military weapons that cannot be lawfully traded and require vast sums of money to replicate, software weapons can be inexpensively duplicated and widely distributed, with full impunity from law.
- *Anonymity*: The combination of the design of the Internet and the current configuration of most computers offers most cybercriminal perfect anonymity when launching an attack. Anonymity reduces the ability to identify and apprehend the perpetrator and cause him or her suffer negative consequences, including civil, criminal, and social punishment. The issue of anonymity runs deep into the operational design of the computer. The computer, by design, is neither able to record nor identify the person or entity that controls it by feeding instructions. The reasoning is complex and involves the different resolutions of time [13]. When an individual types on the keyboard or clicks a mouse button, instructions are sent to the computing process. The same is true whenever the computer opens a document, browses a webpage, or uses an application, with each action feeding instructions into the computing process. Thus, control may be asserted either directly by the individual through his actions involving the keyboard and mouse or derived indirectly from the program being executed, a webpage being browsed or a file being opened. There is no way for the computing process to distinguish with certainty the direct control from the indirect control. To understand this better, consider an experiment involving functional magnetic resonance imaging (fMRI) of a human brain under two distinct scenarios. In the first scenario, the person is struck on the head, lightly, with a sharp object. The individual perceives and reports a concussion. In the second scenario, a deliberate electrical signal is merely sent to an appropriate section of the brain. The individual reports an identical perception of concussion. The fMRI images, obtained for these two scenarios, are indistinguishable, implying that our brain cannot tell whether the

concussion is induced or real. The fundamental limitation of computers relative to anonymity raises two very difficult issues. First, how can we determine with certainty who used the keyboard or mouse to commit a cybercrime? Second, how do we infer with certainty that no outsider committed the cybercrime by gaining control over the computing process of the accused's computer? Consider a scenario where law enforcement authorities trace a cyberattack back to a source IP address that had been assigned to a residential cable Internet access account with a static source IP address. Assume that when authorities seized and searched the computers located at the residence, they confirm the presence of multiple computer intrusion and malicious code programs installed on one of the computers. How does the prosecution prove with certainty that the resident-owner of the residence placed those programs on the computer? What is the probability that an outsider had gained remote control over the computer, loaded those programs, and launched the attack? Experience reveals that in most distributed denial of service attacks, unbeknownst to them, innocent users' computers are hijacked and then used to launch attacks remotely.

1.3.3 The Attacker's Social Tools

An attacker's arsenal of social manipulation tools, labeled social engineering, is a catch-all term, encapsulating different techniques, both oral and written communications, that an attacker may deploy to deceive other individuals and obtain information from them that will help him or her construe and execute technical attacks. Generally, these types of information are present in the target computers; however, they may not be easily accessible since their organization and semantics do not follow a systematic trend or logic. Though the use of social engineering among spies dates back thousands of years, in modern communication networks, social engineering techniques were used as early as the late 1960s and early 1970s to attack telephone networks under phone phreaking [14]. In his book, infamous hacker Kevin Mitnick states, "Social engineering uses influence and persuasion to deceive people by convincing them that the social engineer is someone he isn't, or by manipulation. As a result, the social engineer is able to take advantage of people to obtain information with or without the use of technology." Common examples of social engineering include attackers masquerading as any one of the following:

- An minor employee or contractor who blandly asks a non-technical employee to implement a password change.
- An hurried, powerful executive who cannot remember his or her password and demands immediate assistance in gaining access to the company's computer network.
- A passerby at an airport who acquires telephone numbers, credit card numbers, or automated teller machine (ATM) PINs by observing someone else using a telephone or ATM machine, often referred to as shoulder surfing.
- A visitor at a company who shoulder surfs an unsuspecting worker's username and password.

A common non-technical tool to gather sensitive information is "dumpster diving," which involves an attacker sifting or fishing through trash to find information such as bank statements, usernames, and passwords. In a trick reportedly used in Asia to identify and lure the best IT workers away from a competitor, say X, a human resource department employee from a rival company, say Y, would frequent the restaurants where employees of X eat lunch and befriend many of them. The impersonator would find out about the key projects and key employees associated with them. As a countermeasure, companies often feed their employees lunch in the company premises and at the company's cost. The power of social engineering should never be underestimated; it is often very effective at breaking down and defeating the best technical defenses.

Clever attackers often integrate social engineering and technical attacks. The combination can be deadly. The Melissa Virus effectively incorporated social engineering when it caused infected computers to subsequently send e-mails with infected attachments with the subject heading, "Here is that document you asked for ... don't show anyone else ;-)" [15]. Given the deceptive nature of the subject heading and as the e-mail source address reflected a trusted friend, recipients were more likely than not to click and open the infected attachment. The infection occurred immediately. Often the subject heading serves to lure or trigger intrigue, enough to cause the recipient to click open the attachment. In the Love Letter Worm, the deceptive subject heading associated with the message was, "kindly check the attached LOVELETTER coming from me" [16].

1.3.4 The Defender's Tools

The defenders can be organized into two classes, public, including the government; and private, which would encompass individuals, groups, and companies. Private defenders' efforts include information security policies, password systems, firewalls, anti-virus programs, intrusion detection systems, anti-spyware programs, and anti-social engineering training and policies. The common theme among these tools is that they all help defenders maintain exclusive control over the computing process at all times. Today, most governments have no choice but to join the fight. For, they too are under attack. The US government's efforts include the justice system through criminal sanctions, known as direct regulation; and passing new legislations to assist private defenders, known as indirect regulation. The governments and military are also involved in massive efforts to protect their respective critical infrastructures. These are elaborated subsequently in the book.

Clearly, the most successful approach to controlling cybercrimes is an efficient combination of public and private efforts. However, a crime control system that compels each and every home owner to build concrete walls, surround their homes with moats, and hire armed guards to protect their residences is likely to be a dysfunctional system – wasting valuable societal resources. A progressive modern society would benefit more from home owners using their time to achieve economic, educational, technological, and other advancements.

1.4 The Convenience Overshoot Warning

To understand the gravity of the cybercrime problem and its impact on society, consider the analogy of a driver speeding down a road that appears straight and safe and then suddenly encounters a treacherous curve. By relying blindly on the computer technology, we resemble the unsuspecting, care-free driver unwittingly racing toward the treacherous curve. Had there been a road sign, clearly warning the driver about the upcoming curve, in a timely manner, disaster could have been averted. We hope this book serves as the warning road sign. Possibly, our faith in our computer technology has placed us precariously close to the beginning of this treacherous curve. If this fear is true, we have three choices. First, we can slow down enough to safely navigate the curve. This might be impractical, given that the forces pushing us forward toward greater proliferation of the computer are overwhelming. However, we can temper the expansion through thought and care. Second, we can appropriately modify the environment by straightening the looming curve, redesigning the car, or incorporating strong restraints so that the crash will not fatally injure the driver. In cyberspace, this would involve substantially influencing our ethics and conduct. Third, we can construct amazing technology, in the form of being able to navigate a treacherous curve at any speed, derived from an extraordinarily deep understanding of the scientific principles.

Underlying this analogy is a prescient observation about technological development by Jerold Prothero, titled the "convenience overshoot." According to Prothero, "[t]here is a natural (if unfortunate) tendency for new technologies to favor convenience over safety: that is, to focus on the benefits of the technology more than on mitigating its potential adverse effects. There is frequently a considerable time gap between the introduction of a new technology and the beginning of serious steps to counteract its deleterious consequences." The "convenience overshoot" often manifests in a "time gap," as illustrated by the following three real examples:

- The 47-year gap between the introduction of the Ford Model-T in 1909 [17] and the introduction of seat belts [18] as an optional feature in some Ford cars in 1956.
- The roughly 70-year gap between the introduction of the first steam-powered locomotive in 1804, and of a safe braking system, invented by George Westinghouse in the 1870s [19].
- Similar lengthy time gaps between the introduction of coal power, the pesticide DDT, and CFC coolants and that of legislation to limit their unwanted side-effects.

Prothero correctly observed, "[o]nly over time do we remember that every tool is also a tool that can be used against us." He recognized that the current crisis in computing security "is a case of a traditional convenience overshoot, magnified to alarming proportions by the power of our computer tools." He noted that while "[t]he benefits of a powerful new technology are readily apparent, and tend to give the technology a ready market and vocal supporters on both the industry and consumer side ... [t]he harmful effects of the technology take longer to be discovered, and tend to produce isolated victims without a full understanding of their situation, or of the possible remedies." Prothero's observation of the impediments to measuring the harmful effects of technology is very important and relevant in this discussion. As we have already noted, it is difficult to measure the degree of a specific cybercrime, its economic impact, and the crime prevention value of a specific anti-cybercrime effort. This inability to measure translates directly into the inability to systematically mitigate it.

References

[1] Thompson, K. (1984) On trusting trust. *Unix Review*, *7*(11), 71–74.

[2] Ghosh, S. (2002, February/March). Computer virus attacks on the rise: Causes, mitigation, and the future. *Financial IT Decisions 2002, Vol. 1, a Bi-Annual Technology Publication of the Wall Street Technology Association, Red Bank, New Jersey*. Retrieved from http://www.wsta.org; ISBN 1-85938-369-6, 1:16–17.

[3] GAO, Report to the Chairman, Subcommittee on Telecommunications and Finance, Committee on Energy and Commerce, House of Representatives. (1989, June). *Computer security: Virus highlights need for improved Internet management*. Technical report.

[4] Reitinger, P. (2003, July 15) 'Industry speaks' hearing (without a multidisciplinary effort by both government and industry, we will not succeed). *Testimony at House Select Committee on Homeland Security, Subcommittee on Cybersecurity, Science, Research & Development.*

[5] Conly, C. H. (1989, July 6). *Organizing for computer crime investigation and prosecution.* National Institute of Justice.

[6] Goodman, M. (2001, August). Making computer crime count. *The FBI Law Enforcement Bulletin.*

[7] Computer Crime & Intellectual Property Section (CCIPS), US DoJ. (2007, March). *CCIPS prosecuting computer crimes manual* (p. 5). Retrieved from http://www.justice.gov/criminal/cybercrime/ccmanual/00ccma.html

[8] Lessig, L. (1999). *Code and other laws of cyberspace.* New York, NY: Basic Books.

[9] Microsoft. (2004). *Encarta reference library.* Microsoft Corporation.

[10] Olson, M. (1965). *The logic of collective action.* Cambridge, MA: Harvard University Press.

[11] Weaver, N. C. (2001, August 15). Warhol worms: The potential for very fast Internet plagues.

[12] Staniford, S., Paxson, V., & Weaver, N. (2002). How to own the Internet in your spare time. *Proceedings of the 11th USENIX Security Symposium.*

[13] Ghosh, S., & Lee, T. (2000). *Modeling and asynchronous distributed simulation: Analyzing complex systems.* Piscataway, NJ: IEEE Press.

[14] The Learning Channel. (2001, July 25). *Hackers: Computer outlaws.* Cable Television.

[15] CERT. (1999). *CERT Advisory CA-1999-04 Melissa Macro Virus.* Retrieved from http://www.cert.org/advisories/CA-1999-04.html

[16] CERT. (2000). *CERT Advisory CA-2000-04 Love Letter Worm.* Retrieved from http://www.cert.org/advisories/CA-2000-04.html

[17] Frontenac Motor Company. (2001). *The Ford Model T: A short history of Ford's innovation.* Retrieved from http://www.modelt.ca/background-fs.html

[18] Seat belt history. *School Transportation News Online.* Retrieved from http://www.stnonline.com/stn/occupantrestraint/seatbelthistory/

[19] Railroad history. *The National Railroad Museum.* Retrieved from http://www.nationalrrmuseum.org/EdPacket/html/Tguide1.htm

Part II
Computing and Networking Technology and Cybercrimes

Chapter 2
Unauthorized Intrusions and Denial of Service

Alan Boulanger

2.1 Unauthorized Intrusions

According to Carnegie Mellon University's Computer Emergency Response Team (CERT), the number of computer intrusion incidents reported have increased significantly every year. In 2001, for example, CERT reported over 52,000 computer security incidents; a 140% increase in the number of reported in the previous year. In 2009, F-Secure reported that over 9,000,000 computers worldwide had been compromised and infected with a single type of malicious software.

In collaboration with the Federal Bureau of Investigation's (FBI) Computer Crime Squad in San Francisco, the Computer Security Institute has conducted annual surveys of the computer security practitioners working for US corporations, medical institutions, universities and financial institutions. The results of the 2002–2005 surveys are compelling. Of the respondents, 90% reported a computer security incident within the last 12 months, while 80% reported financial losses related to the security breaches. Of the entities reporting losses, the respondents were able to quantify the amount of damages and they reported combined losses exceeding $450 million annually in 2002. Since 2005, the rate of direct monetary losses through security incidents appears to have stabilized in the $130 million to $200 million range of those reporting organizations. In 2006 the FBI conducted an extensive computer crime survey. After analyzing the results of over 2,000 participants, the FBI reported the total cost of all computer crime to U.S business exceeds $67 billion per year.

Individual information security incidents are too commonplace to be cataloged and reported effectively. This is the result of a major shift in the tools, techniques and targets of the hackers. Historically hackers would target the core systems of public and private sectors. This activity is ongoing and these organizations responded with significant investment in building electronic walls protecting their critical infrastructure. The hacker community has adapted to these defenses and are now focusing their attacks on endpoint computer systems using trojans, viruses, and other assorted malicious software.

Information security is a very serious issue. The media have reported a substantial number of recent attacks on high profile sites, and the number of reported

S. Ghosh and E. Turrini (eds.), *Cybercrimes: A Multidisciplinary Analysis*,
DOI 10.1007/978-3-642-13547-7_2, © Springer-Verlag Berlin Heidelberg 2010

security-related incidents continues to rise. In 1996 the United States Department of Defense (DoD) reported an estimate of 250,000 attacks per year on its computer systems and stated that the rate of attacks is increasing exponentially. The trend has continued to this day.

A key contributing factor for this increase in attacks is the widespread availability of automated, malicious, software packages, or toolkits. Many of these packages are easy to acquire and easy to deploy. No longer are perpetrators required to possess an in-depth knowledge of the Internet or operating systems to successfully carry out attacks. These "point and click" attack tools provide a novice computer user the ability to attack and inflict damages on the victim computer's operations. Both hackers and computer security professionals have developed sophisticated software tools to either break into foreign computer systems or identify potential security breaches in computer networks. These tools are often found left behind in compromised systems and they are also present in the toolkits of legitimate "tiger" teams, authorized to attempt to break into computer systems with the full consent of the network owners.

Data recovered from post mortem analysis of compromised systems as well as from the computers exploited by perpetrators to launch attacks reveal strong similarities in how intruders seek out their targets and launch attacks on their victims. Many of the elements of the attack plan are observed to be automated and based on sophisticated software toolkits.

2.1.1 Tools to Exploit Unauthorized Intrusions

Available toolkits may be organized into six distinct categories, each of which comes with a set of tools and techniques [1] that had been developed to exploit a specific type of system vulnerability [2–4]. These include (1) scanners, (2) remote exploits, (3) local exploits, (4) monitoring tools, also known as sniffers, (5) stealth and backdoor tools, and (6) a new class of tool called the auto-rooter.

2.1.1.1 Scanners

A scanner extracts information about a host or network and comes in two basic categories. The first type of scanner, termed network auditing tools, are utilized to scan a remote host or a series of hosts on a network and report back security-related vulnerabilities. The second type of scanner, known as host-based static auditing tools, is used to report back the security vulnerabilities of a local host.

In 1992, Christopher Klaus developed and released in the public domain the Internet Security Scanner (ISS), which was one of one of the first network auditing tool set and included many of the common security tests. In 1994 and 1995, Dan Farmer of Sun Microsystems and Wietse Venema of Eindhoven University of Technology developed and released the Security Analysis Tool for Auditing Networks

(SATAN). SATAN expanded the functionality of ISS by including additional security tests and was designed to be portable, permitting it to be run on a larger variety of platforms. The popularity and ease of use of SATAN resulted in a large number of unauthorized scans of computer systems by hackers and merely inquisitive users. Today, the number of industrial-grade network security auditing packages available on the Internet has exploded. They are widely available on the World Wide Web (WWW), at anonymous FTP sites, and on underground bulletin boards. Many of the tools that have been used to successfully breach network security are easily found through searching the WWW. A few of the popular, freely available network scanners include:

- SATAN: Available from http://www.porcupine.org
- NESSUS: Available from http://www.tenablesecurity.com
- NMAP: Available from http://www.insecure.org

A NESSUS user can access the following information for specified hosts:

- Host machines on the network that respond and, therefore, will permit subsequent communication
- Servers available on the responding hosts
- Shared disks available through Network File System (NFS) support
- File access through Network Information Service (NIS), a distributed database for shared information
- Remote execution capability
- Sendmail vulnerabilities, namely, versions that may be tricked into running bad commands
- Trivial File Transfer Protocol (TFTP) access and configuration, which can be used to download password files
- Remote shell access, which provides the ability to execute commands on a different system without explicitly logging in with a password
- Unrestricted X Window System server, which allows the hacker to connect to the server, spy on the users on the server, obtain passwords, and "freak out" users through painting "roaches" or "smiley faces" on their screens
- Readable or writeable File Transfer Protocol (FTP) directory, which allows the hacker to upload commercial software or pornographic material onto corporate computing systems

A specialized scanner, called host-based static auditing tools, is deployed to acquire unauthorized privileged access. It was originally developed to enable system administrators uncover common security weaknesses in a local system and thereafter "harden" it before hackers could intrude. In the hands of a clever hacker, the tool allows a perpetrator with an unprivileged account on the system to decipher the vulnerabilities and gain unauthorized privileged access. In 1989, Dan Farmer released one of the first static auditing tools, labeled the COPS package. COPS was a collection of scripts that scanned the local system, seeking out and reporting security vulnerabilities. In 1992, researchers at Texas A&M University developed and released the TIGER toolkit, which greatly expanded on the original ideas in

COPS. Both COPS and TIGER carry out extensive system checks and report on the following vulnerabilities:

- Permission problems in files, directories, and devices, which subsequently allows intruder access.
- Poor, easy-to-guess passwords.
- Poor security for password and group-definition files.
- Known vulnerable services, including anonymous FTP configuration and improperly configured services.
- Signs of past intrusions, particularly in key binary files.

2.1.1.2 Remote Exploits

Remote exploits include all software programs, methods, and techniques through which a foreign user, i.e., with no prior account on a given computer system, can penetrate into the system. The vulnerabilities associated with remote exploits stem from the services provided by computer systems in the network. In general, most services initiate or "open" a communication channel and monitor, i.e., "listen" for any incoming connection requests. For example, under sendmail, which processes electronic mail, the corresponding program will open a port and listen for incoming requests from other sendmail servers. When it detects a request, a sendmail server will "accept" the connection and communicate with the transmitting system or "client" on the network through a Simple Mail Transfer Protocol (SMTP). Where the sendmail server is vulnerable and the weakness may be exploited through data sent over by the client, the sendmail server's host is vulnerable to attack from unprivileged users on any connected system. Remote exploits represent one of the most feared and dangerous vulnerabilities and are, therefore, most closely guarded.

A subcategory of remote exploits is the protocol-based attack. In it, a software program is deployed to acquire unauthorized access by manipulating the Transmission Control Protocol/Internet Protocol network protocol suite, commonly referred to as TCP/IP. Vulnerabilities in TCP/IP have been well known for many years. As far back as 1985, R.T. Morris demonstrated a vulnerability through which a hostile system may hide its true identity and impersonate a different host's IP address. Where the victim computer system relies on address-based authentication, i.e., distinguishing between friend and foe through the IP address, a hostile attacker has a clear advantage in that it can completely circumvent the authentication process and gain access into the target system as a trusted peer. A generalization of this devastating attack coupled with other security-related vulnerabilities in TCP/IP were reported by Steve Bellovin in 1989. Additional vulnerabilities reported included session hijacking and IP spoofing, both at the level of User Datagram Protocol (UDP) and that of TCP; Routing Information Protocol (RIP) attacks; Internet Common Message Protocol (ICMP) attacks; and Border Gateway Protocol (BGP) attacks. The last reported, high-profile incident involving a protocol-based attack was Kevin Mitnick's TCP/IP-spoofing attack reportedly launched in December 1994 and the subject matter of the book, "Takedown," by John Markoff and Tsutomu Shimomura.

The vulnerabilities exposed by remote exploits served to motivate the development and deployment of firewalls and network auditing tools. As in an automobile, where the firewall separates the engine from the passenger compartment, a firewall in a networked computer system, say N, controls access to the services of N from the outside. In essence, the firewall hides information relative to the internal structure of the services and, often, strategically removes key sub-services, thereby minimizing the undue exposure of N.

2.1.1.3 Local Exploits

A local exploit resembles as insider attack in that a user with an existing account on a computer system exploits tools and services to acquire unauthorized privileges. This attack is commonly referred to as unauthorized user-to-root transition. The existing account may either be a prior legitimate one; acquired through a remote exploit; or obtained through trading information with other hackers, intercepting logon information from network traffic, or social engineering. Most local exploits stem from errors in a privileged program's software design and implementation that inadvertently allow an unprivileged user to execute hostile commands at a privileged level or access and modify privileged data. The instant privileged access is acquired, the hacker, in essence, is in complete control of the system. Exceptions notwithstanding, on most operating systems, the intruder is able to successfully modify the system logs to hide illicit activities, install a "backdoor" entrance that allows continuing privileged and unregistered access to the system. On average, new local exploits are reported at over three times the rate of new remote vulnerabilities and are widely available to anyone through security-related newsgroups, mailing lists, and sites on the WWW. It is considered good practice for system administrators to periodically utilize host based auditing tool and help ensure that their systems can withstand such attacks.

2.1.1.4 Monitoring Tools

On the surface, a monitoring tool is a program that simply captures or logs information available to itself. In expert hands, it is analyzed later to uncover weaknesses and vulnerabilities in the system. A monitoring tool resembles the technical readout information that was stored in R2D2 robot in the well-known movie, Star Wars: Part I, analyzing which scientists considered rebels by the Empire were able to uncover a weakness in the Death Star superweapon and successfully destroy it. Monitoring tools come in two forms, sniffers and snoopers.

- A "sniffer" program focuses on the information flowing back and forth between computer systems on a network, local or otherwise. Commonly referred to as network traffic, the information contains user name-password pairs, authentication related data, and other system details that may be exploited by an intruder. For performance reasons, most local systems choose not to encrypt the data flowing on a local computer network. A hacker with physical access to a network can "plug in" a sniffer and log any length of the network traffic. To counteract the deployment and abuse of sniffers, all transmissible data are first encrypted at the host-network interface and then launched on the network. The most commonly utilized technique is the Secure Socket Layer (SSL), designed and developed by Netscape in 1994 to achieve secure transactions through mutual authentication and data encryption. SSL may be deployed within a local network as well as the Internet. Of course, there is no guarantee that SSL will forever prevent the intruder from accessing the information, given that any encryption, in theory, can be broken. When making commercial purchases on the Internet on a web browser, the lock icon on the bottom of the browser frame generally indicates the use of SSL. Any Internet transaction that is transmitted in clear text and not protected through SSL may be immediately vulnerable.

- Unlike a sniffer, a "snooper" focuses on the information confined within a given computer system, namely a user's activities including terminal or terminal emulator sessions, process memory usage, and keystrokes. By installing a trojan or keylogger snooper on a given computer system, a victim's keystrokes and mouse clicks are captured in their native form and stored within the snooper. Normally, the information is retrieved by the attacker over the communications channel and analyzed to uncover vulnerabilities. Even where the communications channel is encrypted, the snooper-logged information is merely encrypted at the host-network interface, i.e., at the boundary of the computer system and the outgoing network link. The encrypted packet is then transmitted to the attacker's computer system via the network link, where the corresponding host-network interface automatically decrypts the encrypted packet and presents it to the intruder.

2.1.1.5 Stealth and Backdoor Tools

Stealth tools comprise a collection of programs and techniques that permit an unauthorized user to alter system logs and eliminate all records of unauthorized entry and activities prior to exiting the system. A stealth tool can also deliberately preempt the system from recording any of the user's activities, while in operation, thus rendering the attacker invisible. Stealth toolkits often include "backdoor" programs, which consist of modified, drop-in, binary code replacements of critical sections of the system that provide authentication and system reporting services. Backdoor programs offer the following capabilities:

- Provide continued, unlogged use of the system when activated; the activation mechanism is often an encrypted password compiled into the program.
- Hide suspicious processes and files from users and system administrators.
- Report false system status to users and system administrators.
- Report false checksums for the modified programs, thereby defeating any alarms and watchdog devices.

A few of the well known backdoor/trojan packages include the following:

- The Back Orifice (BO/BO2K) server package was designed and developed as a remote administration tool by the hacker group, known as the cult of the Dead cow (cDc). When installed on a compromised Microsoft Windows NT/2000 machine, the BO/BO2K software package provides complete control over the host, including the ability to monitor and record keystrokes and mouse clicks and the exclusion and removal of installed application programs. While unauthorized application programs may be installed, new data files may be created and prior files modified or deleted, and hard drives can be reconfigured and reformatted. The presence of a BO/BO2K package on a machine must be viewed as a certain sign of compromise and warrants investigation. The software package is available at the hacker group's website: http://www.cultdeadcow.com. Available anti-virus software products may be utilized to detect and remove BO/BO2K packages. For further details, the reader is referred to CERT Vulnerability Note VN–98.07.
- Freely available on the WWW, the Netbus software package was developed by Carl-Frederik Neikter. It is a trojan, similar to BO/BO2K. Current versions of anti-virus software packages are able to detect NetBus installations.
- SubSeven: The SubSeven software package was designed as an improvement over NetBus. It is designed to serve as a slave to the remote master-attacker. When the software package is installed on a system, it quietly listens for connection requests from the remote master-attacker. Analysis of firewall logs generally reveal numerous attempts of automated scans to locate the presence of SubSeven software packages with default configurations in the target computer system. Most versions of anti-viral packages can detect SubSeven installations.
- As a key operating system of choice of the Computer Science community and given that its design reflects systematic protection mechanisms, Unix has been the focus of the hacker community for a long time. As a response to the challenge offered by Unix, the hacker community has develop a custom rootkit for every flavor of Unix. The term rootkit is derived from the ultimate user account on a Unix system, called the root, with the highest privileges, also referred to as root privileges. The rootkit is a set of tools and trojan devices that are configured and installed on compromised Unix systems. While the tools are designed to sanitize the audit logs, i.e., remove all evidence of intrusion, the trojan devices are altered systems utility programs, which permit the intruder a backdoor entry into the system through a special password. All conventional logging and authentication checks are relaxed and the intruder acquires the highest level system administrator privileges. Many freely available software packages can detect and report the presence of rootkits.

2.1.1.6 Auto-Rooters

Auto-Rooters are attack toolkits with extremely high levels of automation and significant attack ferocity against specific weaknesses of computer systems.

Auto-Rooters are designed by expert hackers for the current generation of point-and-click computer users so that maximal damage is caused, worldwide. Auto-Rooters are an emerging class of attack toolkits and proliferating rapidly. When a vulnerability is first discovered and reported, even in a mainstream scientific forum, a window of opportunity arises for the hacker community to attack a very large number of computer systems that have been just rendered vulnerable. Fully aware that the defenders will soon create a program fragment to temporarily patch the defect, the hacker community races to create and disseminate packages, called Auto-Rooters that represent the ultimate in point-and-click hacking. By design, Auto-Rooters can be utilized by the most unsophisticated users, with little to no knowledge of systems and networks, to attack both local and remote computer systems across the world. Thus, these toolkits are potentially very dangerous. When a basic Auto-Rooter attack is launched against a network, every address within the specified network range is attacked with a specific remote exploit and the results of the attacks are logged. After the package completes phase I execution, the attacker has a report of the machines that are vulnerable. In phase II, automated attacks are launched on the machines identified as vulnerable, thereby enabling the perpetrator to compromise the largest number of machines with the least effort. Each of the compromised machines can then be altered and converted into elements of a distributed denial of service flood-net attack, patched with backdoors, or used as platforms to launch attacks against other internal or external computer systems. Auto-rooter activity is detectable and betrays a behavior profile similar to that of a network worm. Many hosts are scanned and each of the hosts will have the same service accessed with the same data parameters, usually consisting of the remote-exploit payload that will attempt to breach the security of the host. Properly configured firewalls, both internal and external, and intrusion detection systems can detect and mitigate the impact of an Auto-Rooter attack.

2.1.2 Deployment of Toolkits for Unauthorized Intrusions

Armed with a collection of "exploit scripts" that they may have developed, hackers generally attack computer systems on the network, driven primarily by intellectual challenge. At first, the attacks are tested on easy targets but then expert hackers move onto other computer systems that are difficult to break into and therefore offer greater challenge. There is mounting evidence, however, of increasingly focused attacks on the networks of specific organizations for the purpose of fraud, espionage, and monetary gain. As in many scenarios, the initial attacks stem from intellectual challenge and are refreshingly clever; however, they are quickly followed by mundane attacks launched by mediocre individuals whose goals are wanton damage and self-serving exploitation.

A detailed study of attacks launched against thousands of machines reveal two important insights. First, attacks seem to be launched at three levels, namely, (A) blind remote attack, (B) user-level attack, and (C) physical attack. Second, unbeknownst to the community at large, hackers appear to follow a systematic methodology in conceiving and planning their attacks. The methodology is presented in Sect. 2.1.2.1.

(A) Under a blind remote attack, the perpetrator initiates an attempt to remotely penetrate into a computer system or network, armed solely with the network address in either numeric or text form. The attacker is blind in that he neither possesses valid account information nor access to the target. Blind remote attack represents the "classic" attack scenario, where an unknown attacker attempts to access a computer network illegally. Most penetration tests carried out by security consultants include, at the very least, a blind remote attack. The intruder will first deploy scanners and other methods to acquire security-related information on the target system. Following analysis of the data returned by the scanners, the intruder will choose the most appropriate remote exploit from the toolkit arsenal and launch it at the target to gain access to the system.

(B) A user-level attack represents a penetration attempt into a computer system on which the intruder already has a user-level account with unprivileged access, for the purpose of acquiring privileged access. The account exploited may have been legitimately acquired as a customer or employee of the organization; or otherwise acquired through "sniffed" passwords, traded accounts, "shoulder surfing," blind remote attack, cracked passwords, social engineering, or default user accounts. A majority of the losses in the financial industry attributed to breaches in network security stem from insider attacks, where a legitimate user attacks the network from within. In phase I of the attack, the perpetrator launches a COPS or TIGER scanner locally to detect and report common security vulnerabilities in the computer system and users. In phase II, the intruder will analyze the scanner data, identify the most effective local exploit from the toolkit, and launch the attack. If and where successful, the intruder will have gained privileged access to the computer system. In phase III, the intruder will intercept sensitive system data and network traffic to acquire unauthorized access into other machines on the network.

(C) Under physical attack, the individual with physical access to computers and the network equipment circumvents the traditional authentication, namely, login username and password, and plugs in attack computers and hardware scanners directly into the appropriate ports of the computer server and network equipment, thereby intercepting network traffic. As with the other paradigms, analysis of the traffic is likely to yield knowledge of the vulnerabilities which may be subsequently exploited to gain unauthorized access. Physical access greatly facilitates intrusions. It is common practice for most computer users to leave their desks with the computers running and active logged in sessions. An intruder can extract valuable information that will be vital to break into the network. Where the target computer system has no active sessions, the intruder can shut down and reboot the system, thereby gaining administrative privileges on the system for certain system configurations. This renders other systems on the network vulnerable to attack.

2.1.2.1 A Methodology of Attack

A comprehensive analysis of the nature of attacks and evidence from data left behind in compromised machines reveals the following insight. Virtually all intruders' attacks, exceptions notwithstanding, are well considered and systematically organized along seven stages. These include:

1. Reconnaissance: gather information about the target system or network.
2. Probe and attack: probe the system for weaknesses and deploy appropriate tools from the toolkit.
3. Toehold: exploit security weakness and gain entry into the system.
4. Advancement: advance from unprivileged account status to a privileged account.
5. Stealth: hide all tracks of intrusion and install a backdoor.
6. Listening post: establish a listening post to monitor if prior intrusion had been detected.
7. Takeover: expand control from a single host to other hosts on the network.

For the blind remote attack scenario (level A), the intruder would first attempt to gather information about the targeted system, as in stage 1. Utilizing this information, the intruder would apply the remote exploit tools and techniques in an attempt to gain a toehold into the network. This would represent stage 2. Where the penetration attempt is successful and the toehold is that of a privileged account, stage 3 is complete. Should the toehold be limited to an unprivileged account, the intruder would escalate to stage 4 and seek privileged access using an effective local exploit. Next, the intruder can immediately begin covering his or her tracks and establish a listening post, implying completion of stages 5 through 7.

For the user-level attack scenario (level B), the intruder has already achieved a toehold into the target network, implying stage 3. The toehold may have been attained either through username and password guessing or cracking the password file that had been retrieved from the remote system. Generally, once a password file has been stolen there is strong likelihood that the intruder will correctly guess 25% of the passwords. To escalate into stage 4, the intruder obtains information about the local system, as in stage 1, and then applies local exploits, as in stage 2. Eventually, privileged access is acquired, implying stage 4 has been achieved. Next, the intruder hides all visible evidence of intrusion, installs a series of backdoors to ensure future unauthorized access into the target, and begins the takeover process. Stages 5 through 7 are completed.

For the physical attack scenario (level C), the intruder may either reboot the system to gain administrator privileges; identify an active session in the unprotected physical computer and follow up with user-level attack scenario; or physically plug in computers and hardware scanners to download network traffic, analyze sensitive information, and achieve stages 1 through 7 with relative ease. Of great importance is that owners must provide adequate physical protection to their computer systems and network equipment.

2.1.2.2 An Illustrative Example of a Targeted Attack

In this section, we will illustrate the anatomy of an attack on a specific target. Consider a hypothetical company, XYZ Corporation, and that an unknown intruder has decided, for unknown reasons, to attack the computer systems and networks of XYZ. Clearly, the only information available to the intruder at the start of the episode is the public name of the corporation.

Under the reconnaissance step, the intruder begins to search the Internet and WWW for all references to the target corporation, including Internet connections, Web sites, FTP sites, and electronic mail service. Assume that the search yields a domain name, xyzcor.com, registered to XYZ Corporation, without any loss in generality. Armed with the domain name, the intruder then begins to search for more information through a number of different methods. One possibility is to exploit the domain information groper utility program, called "dig," developed by Steve Hotz. To learn more about other machines within the domain, the intruder attempts a "zone transfer" on the domain's name servers. Assuming that the effort is successful, the intruder extracts from the target system a list of host names and their network addresses. In the next step, the intruder begins to compile information about the users on the system. Two excellent sources include the newsgroups and news hierarchy in the domain and the WWW. Gradually, a list of users on the system is compiled. This list is very important to the intruder for it has the potential to reveal many username and password combinations and possibly the domain's policy of determining usernames. For example, if a search yields the line, "From: bobr@host.xyzcorp.com (Bob Reilly)," from a news posting, the intruder can now attempt to break into the account for username, bobr, by repeatedly guessing passwords. If a subsequent search yields the line, "From: sarahg@hostb.xyzcorp.com (Sarah Gregory)," there is a very good chance that the usernames for the entire system have been determined based on a uniform policy of concatenating the individual's first name and the first letter of his or her last name. Next, the intruder can either begin to guess additional usernames and passwords, or search for a given username on chat channels [Internet Relay Chat (IRC) Web Chat] seeking the user's personal information, including full name, address, phone number, etc. Armed with adequate personal information, the intruder might then contact the user either by phone, electronic mail, or chat and acquire account information through persuasion or social engineering. The intruder may even lure the user into inadvertently running a hostile or "Trojan horse" program, the intent being to capture account information and return it to the intruder. At the conclusion of the reconnaissance phase, the intruder may have acquired the following:

- Host name(s)
- Host address(es)
- Host owner
- Host machine type
- Host operating system
- Network owner
- Other hosts in the network

- Network configuration
- Other hosts trusted by the network
- Hosts outside the network
- List of users
- Username assignment policy

In the probe and attack step, the intruder begins to examine the perimeter of the system's security for potential weaknesses. This step is the most heavily automated portion of the penetration cycle. Toolkits left behind and recovered from compromised sites always reveal the presence of some type of scanner that enables the intruder to conduct security surveys on the entire network. Well known scanners include SATAN in the public domain, discussed earlier in this chapter, and commercial scanners such as ISS. This step also represents the most risk for the intruder in that scans and probes are most likely to be detected and logged by intrusion detection systems, where installed, which will promptly alert security-conscious system administrators and users. To uncover vulnerabilities, probe programs determine the remote services provided by the hosts. A freely available, public domain tool, "strobe," allows an intruder to scan a host or range of hosts to generate a list of services offered by each one. Thus, by letting loose strobe on the "host.xyzcorp.com," a list of services is compiled. Assume that the services of interest include FTP, SMTP (for e-mail), finger, WWW, printer, and xterm, the X-Window System server. These generally come with well known vulnerabilities. The intruder selects from the toolkit the most effective remote exploits against these services, one by one, and launches them, until the vulnerabilities are discovered. The FTP server is first checked for known vulnerabilities and configuration errors. Second, the sendmail server, SMTP, is probed to yield the software name and version number, thereby assisting the intruder to select the most effective exploit. Should bogus or no information be retrieved from the server's banner, the intruder's task is complicated and, worse, the likelihood that the intruder may be discovered is increased. Assume that all of the services, except the WWW server, successfully resist the probe. The WWW server on host.xyzcorp.com offers the "phf" service, which has a known vulnerability, and the intruder possesses an effective remote exploit. A hostile command is executed on the server, yielding an X Window System terminal emulation on the intruder's display. A toehold into the target network has just been achieved.

In the toehold step, the intruder has already gained unauthorized entry into the system. Should the user identification (UID) of the X Window System terminal indicate "root," the intruder jumps directly onto the stealth step, skipping the advancement step. Where the UID is that for an unprivileged user, the intruder will attempt to migrate to a privileged or administrative account.

In the advancement step, the intruder uses the information about the host, the operating system, and the services provided to search the toolkit for the most effective local exploit. Assume that the intruder has obtained a local display running a shell on the remote server with the UID, "www." The intruder will deploy the local scanning tools – COPS or TIGER, to search and report configuration errors and other known vulnerabilities, and then apply local exploits from the toolkit. If the local scan using COPS reveals the host to be an AIX* 3.2 (Advanced Interactive

Executive) machine, vulnerable to the "tprof" exploit, the intruder can successfully advance from UID "www" to UID "root," the privileged account. At the highest privileged level, the intruder is in full control of the target computer system. On most systems, any local file may be accessed, modified, and deleted. A malicious intruder may look around for any interesting data and delete the entire file system. Most intruders, however, retain their access to the compromised system, and move to the subsequent step.

In the stealth step, the intruder is the root, with complete access to all of the files on the local system. To erase all evidence of unauthorized entry and preempt detection, the intruder will edit the files containing the log entries. Given that intrusion had been gained through an exploit on the WWW, the intruder will check the WWW server access log for records of previous intrusions and delete all traces of illicit activity. By replacing the system's not-so-easy-to-read binary code with modified versions that hide process, file, and network connection information, effectively, all incriminating traces are removed.

In the listening post step, the intruder ensures continued, unlogged, and undetected access to the compromised system at anytime. Using an appropriate "rootkit" package, the intruder "patches" the system's binary files to serve three key objectives. The first is to ensure that any future activity will be never logged. The patched binary files have been deliberately designed to report false information on files, processes, and network interface status in response to the administrator's queries. The second objective is to facilitate continued and unlogged access to the system through a number of backdoors. The third objective is to establish a listening post for the network, for which a sniffer program is installed in the target. In the event the target computer system's network interface supports "promiscuous mode," the sniffer program allows the intruder's privileged account to intercept and record all network traffic. Where the "promiscuous mode" is unsupported, the intruder is limited to intercepting traffic for users on the local system, one at a time. Network traffic carries sensitive information, including e-mails and username-password combinations for other systems and networks. By recording and subsequently analyzing them, the intruder can easily widen the scope of control.

In the final takeover step, utilizing sniffed username-password combinations and a toolkit of local and remote exploits, the intruder can successfully extend attacks onto other hosts of the increasingly encompassing network. Starting with a single weakness in a single machine within an ever increasing hierarchy of interconnected computer networks, the intruder exercises control over a vast array of computer systems and networks. As more and more hosts fall victim, the intruder's base of platforms from which to launch new attacks keeps growing unabated. For each new compromised host, the installed backdoor programs ensure detection preemption and continued, unlogged, privileged access to the hosts. The username-password combinations obtained from the listening posts provide ammunition to continue acquiring future toeholds and root compromises. In theory, takeover step may continue indefinitely, ad infinitum, across any and every computer system that is linked to any portion of the compromised network.

The most important lesson in securing computer systems and networks is the following. While no system is totally secure [5], the application of basic precautions, described in this chapter, can go a long way to substantially reduce the possibility of a successful and damaging attack on an organization's vital assets. It has been common practice for a long time to first develop a system and, if and when it begins to function successfully, incorporate security precautions. Thus, security has been an afterthought, a reactionary measure, which is never strong and robust. Security concerns need to be addressed throughout the development and maintenance phases of every project. Organizations, worldwide, have begun to address the security issue seriously.

2.2 Denial of Service

Denial of service (DoS) attacks are characterized by deliberate and carefully considered efforts to limit or prevent legitimate users from accessing network resources. Most practical DoS attacks involve multiple target machines and multiple machines from which attacks are launched, implying distributed denial of service attacks, labeled DDoS attacks. Given the ubiquity of computers and their role in critical areas including control of the power grid, e-commerce, etc., DDoS attacks are quickly becoming the most serious problem on the Internet. Sustained DDoS attacks on a corporation's computer systems and network can cause significant financial loss and other damages to the target. As an analogy, a DoS attack on a telephone unit may work as follows. Assume that a subscriber, X, wishes to deny another subscriber, say Y, the ability to receive calls from the outside. Assume also that Y does not have call waiting or other sophisticated services. X would dial the number for Y on his or her own telephone and hang-up just as Y's telephone is about to start ringing. X would repeat this action immediately and continue the process indefinitely. The local telephone switching station that is directly connected to Y would be busy oscillating between ringing Y's telephone and cutting it off, implying that it would be difficult for some other subscriber to get connected to Y.

Although DDoS attacks have been known for a while, in February 2000, the first of a series of large-scale, coordinated DoS attacks were launched against key popular websites on the Internet, including Buy.com, CNN, Datek online trader, E*trade trader, and eBay. Even the DOJ and FBI websites were attacked and rendered unreachable by users, worldwide. Hundreds, possibly thousands of compromised machines were directed to attack target systems in a well-coordinated manner. The massive and precise coordination rendered the attacks exceptionally successful in that legitimate users were precluded from accessing the systems within a wide geographical area. For the duration of the attacks, subscribers were unable to access new information; customers were unable to places orders or execute bids at auctions; and financial traders were unable to access their accounts and place securities orders. The attacks lasted several hours and the technical staff of the target organizations could not track the sources of the attacks for the simple reason that an isolated

IP packet cannot be traced effectively. The attackers had utilized a packet spoofing technique to obscure the true source(s) of the attack. With source addresses of the attacking IP packets spoofed, attempts to identify abusive packets and filter them out fails. The attacks were a major media event and most of the mainstream television and media covered the attacks and the impact on the victims, namely, the Internet users. Conceptually, under DDoS attacks, a single attack computer can target multiple hosts simultaneously or in accordance to a specific schedule; multiple attack computers may be directed to attack a single host; or multiple attack computers can attack multiple hosts in a coordinated manner, where the coordination may be based either on timing or causality. This provides perpetrators the ability to control the granularity of attack over a wide dynamic range, i.e., they can attack a single host with surgical precision or large group of hosts and cut off from the rest of the world.

Historically, DoS attacks were originally developed for use on Internet Relay Chat (IRC). They were the result of on-line squabbles within the chatrooms. Rival IRC users would launch DoS attacks against each other in attempts to knock other users out of the chatroom. A rival would attempt to either overload the network connection or the computer system of the target with bogus packets. The sheer volume of the packets would consume all of the available bandwidth and clog the network connection. No data would either come in or get out of the target system, effectively knocking the opponent offline. The IRC user with the most network bandwidth at his or her disposal would emerge as the winner of these online virtual skirmishes.

Another form of DDoS attack targets vulnerabilities in the client and server software. Server software is the program that provides service to clients on the network. On the WWW for example, a user will use a local web browser program, or http client, to connect to computers running the web server software. The user will access and download HTML formatted code and resources. The web browser will the interpret the downloaded code and resources and display the results to user's computer screen. Under attack, the perpetrator sends deliberately malformed data to the server software program, which exploits a vulnerability in the application, causing the server software program to lockup, consume large amounts of CPU, memory, or disk space, or simply fail and exit. In the IRC community, such DoS attacks on IRC servers would enable the attacker to acquire special operator privileges or 'ops' in the chatrooms, granting complete control over the channel.

2.2.1 Different Manifestations of DDoS Attacks

- A mail bomb DoS attack is a technique wherein an user attempts to overload the e-mail processing capabilities of a specific user or network. It is the oldest and most crude of all DoS attacks. The attacker constructs a specific e-mail and sends it repeatedly to the same user or multiple users at a particular site. A variation of the attack may involve attaching with the e-mail a large file containing image, audio, video, or random garbage data. Under normal operation, an e-mail consumes a limited amount of available resources, including bandwidth, memory, and disk space. Under attack, all of the available resources are virtually depleted by the sheer number of bogus e-mails, thereby crashing the target system or impacting it severely.

- In 1995, the popular underground magazine, Phrack, documented the SYN flood vulnerability and even provided the source code for launching an attack. A SYN attack focuses on the TCP protocol, which governs the establishment of reliable and full-duplex connections between clients and servers across IP networks through a 3-way handshake. First, the client's computer initiating the connection sends a connection request message, SYN, to the server computer. The server responds by sending back to the client a SYN/ACK acknowledgment message. This signifies that the server is ready to communicate with the client. Upon receipt of the SYN/ACK, the client knows with certainty that it has gotten the server's attention. Of course, the server needs to know with certainty that the client has received its SYN/ACK, which is where the third and final step of the 3-way handshake becomes necessary. The client transmits a message to the server acknowledging the SYN/ACK it has received. Upon receipt, the server and the client are now both certain that they are in communication with each other. The connection is deemed to have been established. The SYN attack is conceived based on a known fact that the server has already allocated a part of its resources when it sends the SYN/ACK to the client and is waiting for the final acknowledgment from the client in step 3. The expectation is that the acknowledgment will arrive soon, after which the connection will be established and communication will ensue. Initial implementations of the server allowed for a limited number, namely 5, of outstanding, half-open connections, implying that further requests for connections from other clients would be ignored. Clearly, in attack mode, the perpetrator would strategically send five bogus requests to the server, intercept the SYN/ACK responses from the server, and deliberately refrain from sending the final acknowledgments to the server. As a result, the server is inhibited from accepting additional requests from clients and denying service. Where revised implementations of the server program attempt to time out and retire the half-open connections, the attacker would continuously send connection request messages, under flood mode, from the clients to the server, eventually locking it out. To render it robust, the server program was revised to detect flooding activity by uncovering the source address(es) of the connection requests and applying appropriate filters to block them. The Octopus toolkit provided the resources for launching the SYN flood attack.
- Under a smurf DoS attack, an attack host computer sends out a ICMP request targeted at the network's broadcast address but deliberately inserts the victim's IP address in the return address field. The machines on the network, possibly numbering in the hundreds, will respond with a ICMP message directed at the victim, who is quickly inundated. Smurf toolkits can even amplify the aggravation of the attack by sending the ICMP request to multiple broadcast addresses, triggering thousands of ICMP responses to the victim. For obvious reasons, smurf DoS attack is also known as traffic amplifier attack. Mitigation techniques focus on proper configuration of the border routers.

- The Teardrop or Bonk DoS attack was first introduced in 1997 and it targets the TCP/IP protocol. Some implementations of the TCP/IP driver lack the ability to properly handle overlapping IP datagram fragments, thereby causing the system to crash. The attack consists in transmitting malformed sequence of IP datagrams to the target host. Patches for the weaknesses are available from appropriate vendors.
- Under the Land DoS attack, a malformed TCP SYN packet is synthesized, where the source address and port are deliberately set identical to that of the victim machine. Upon receipt of this malformed packet, the target will fault and hang since it had not sent a connection request message.
- In the ping of death (POD) DoS attack, first reported in 1997, the attacker causes an oversized ICMP packet to be transmitted to the target machine. Unable to process the oversized packet, the victim locks up. The weakness has since been eliminated but older versions remain vulnerable.
- The Trin00/TFN/Shaft/Stacheldraht attack was one of the earliest DDoS attack toolkit introduced in 1999. The toolkit contains both server and client components. In the pre-attack phase, the client component is installed on the attacker's computer or a specific compromised client machine, while the server components are configured and installed on all compromised server systems. In the attack phase, the single compromised client machine compels all of the compromised servers in the flood-net to launch DoS attack at a single host or the network.

2.2.2 Toolkits for DDoS

A typical DDoS attack toolkit consists of two basic software packages, namely, master and slave component packages. The slave package is installed on each of the computers that have already been compromised, while the master package is installed on the attacking computer. Perpetrators are known to have employed different techniques to install the slave packages. Under approach 1, the attacker first scans and locates a vulnerable host, then compromises it, and subsequently installs the slave package. Hackers will often utilize auto-rooter toolkits to seek out and attack large numbers of networked computer systems, the goal being to create a large network of subverted computers, collectively known as a "bot-net". The larger the bot-net, the greater the resource base upon which the attack is launched. Under approach 2, the slave package is distributed as a payload of computer viruses and network worms. The compromised machines are termed "zombies." There have been reported instances where a large bot-net had generated over 500 Mb/s of network traffic, which is capable of saturating over 300 T-1 links, where a T-1 link is rated at 1.5 Mb/s. A typical countermeasure against a DDoS attack consists in first identifying, where possible, the source address of the computers that are launching and directing the bogus messages, and then filtering them out of the network. A limitation of this technique stems from the fact that the bogus network traffic being generated by the zombies contain false, spoofed source addresses which are created through pseudo-random number sequence generators. If an attack involves UDP packets, the network administrator can reconfigure the border routers to drop all UDP traffic. If this fails, the network administrator may then contact the organization's Internet Service Provider (ISP), who can then attempt to locate the source of the attack and install appropriate filters. Where the ISP is unable to mitigate the attack, it may then contact the service provider at the next higher level, and so on until the source of the attack is located and blocked. Given that the process is manual, clearly, the effects of a DDoS attack can cripple a network for a very long duration, relative to the network speed.

References

[1] Boulanger, A. (1998). Catapults and grappling hooks: the tools and techniques of information warfare. *IBM Systems Journal, 37*(1), 106–114.
[2] Boulanger, A. (1997, Summer). Cyber-crackers: computer fraud and vulnerabilities, invited article. *The Journal of Public Inquiry: President's Council on Integrity and Efficiency.*
[3] Weaver, R., & Stroz, E. (1998). *Counterfeit chip detection.* Internal Report for US FBI/US Secret Service.
[4] Boulanger, A. (2006). *Electronic identification as economic commodities in the black market.* IBM Technical Report.
[5] Boulanger, A. (2005). Open-source versus proprietary software: Is one more reliable and secure than the other? *IBM Systems Journal, 44*(2), 239–248.

Chapter 3
Malicious Code

Alan Boulanger and Sumit Ghosh

3.1 Introduction

In a mere 16 months, from March 1918 to June 1919, the Influenza Pandemic infected and killed between 20 and 70 million people, worldwide [1]. While the virus infected nearly one-fifth of the world's population, the fatality rate was a startling 2.5% of the infected victims, implying one new death every 2 s [2]. One might ask, why this digression into epidemiological history? The answer is simply, this is the closest analogy to what we are up against. Our modern computing infrastructure, comprised of personal computers, servers, Internet routers, cell phones, personal digital assistants (PDAs) and a myriad of other devices, are all viable "hosts" for an equivalent "digital" pandemic. Given our growing reliance on these computers for virtually every aspect of our modern lives, although much of it is invisible to the layperson, an intelligently designed and strategically deployed computer virus, an uber Code Red for instance, can easily decimate entire economic sectors and even severely cripple our "physical infrastructure."

Clearly, isolated cybercrime incidents, including hacking and directed denial of service attacks at individual computers, have the potential to severely damage businesses and targeted "physical infrastructure." In contrast, however, self-spreading malicious software is unique in its ability to compromise and leverage literally millions to tens of millions of machines in a matter of seconds to launch massive attacks. Recent research projects that properly designed malicious code can infect and potentially obliterate a substantial fraction of the Internet's devices in less than 30 s [3]. By the time security analysts' pagers go off in major corporations around the world, assuming the paging system still functions, the damage would be done.

Over the past several years, malicious code threats including Code Red, Nimda and Slammer have started to demonstrate their potential destructive power. In 2001, the Code Red worm spread to 359,000 server computers in a short 14 h [4], infecting, at its peak, 2,000 new servers every second. In the same year, the Nimda worm upped the ante by using no less than six different mechanisms to spread itself across the Internet, compromising an estimated 2.2 million machines within a 24-h period [5]. The Slammer worm of 2002, also known as Sapphire, exceeded the combined

S. Ghosh and E. Turrini (eds.), *Cybercrimes: A Multidisciplinary Analysis*,
DOI 10.1007/978-3-642-13547-7_3, © Springer-Verlag Berlin Heidelberg 2010

damage of Code Red and Nimda, compromising 90% of the vulnerable population of 75,000 servers in its first 10 min of proliferation. As Slammer continued to spread autonomously through the Internet, the number of infected computers doubled every 8.5 s [6]. Although Slammer was programmed merely to reproduce itself and refrain from causing any secondary damage, it inadvertently disrupted automated teller machines (ATMs), credit card networks, emergency telephone services, and airline reservation systems [7], causing an estimated loss of billions of dollars. If the Slammer virus was designed with a destructive payload, one can only shudder at the unimaginable damage.

In January 2010, Intel [8], Google, Microsoft, IBM, and dozens of other high profile companies were attacked by a sophisticated example of malware that utilized encryption, code obfuscation, and other stealth techniques to avoid detection. When a user, inside of an corporate network, visited an infected website or received the malicious code through an advertisement, a piece of malicious code would be automatically downloaded and then executed. This hostile code would break out of the browser and download a trojan horse into a folder named "Aurora" on the local system. This high profile attack exploited a previously unknown software defect in a popular web browser that bypassed the browser security settings and allowed the installation of the trojan horse. Once installed, the trojan horse enabled the attackers to bypass the security controls of the organization and access the infected system.

While such high-profile, mass-spreading malware was a staple of the first decade of the twenty-first century, the majority of today's malware (circa 2010) is designed not to rapidly spread, per se, but to silently infiltrate a victim's computer and then steal information or trick the user for monetary gain. Research suggests that the majority of today's malware authors and distributors are organized criminals who are seeking to leverage their malicious code to make a profit rather than to obtain notoriety by making cable news headlines. While much of the malware of the 2000s was aimed at mass-propagation, today's malware is designed to be stealthy and to avoid detection by security software. Attackers have shifted to using both compromised legitimate and malicious websites, and (often illicit) file sharing networks as a distribution medium to infect unwitting home and corporate computer users. Unlike the mass-spreading strains of Nimda, Code Red and Slammer, where a single, identical infection targeted thousands or millions of users, today's malware is generated on-the-fly at the time of infection, often infecting each victim with a new distinct strain. The result is often that no two infections are the same – two visitors to a malicious website over a 10 min period may both be infected, but by entirely different malware variants, each with a different digital fingerprint. This approach of micro-distribution, rather than the prior approach of mass-propagation, has enabled attackers to avoid detection by traditional security programs, while staying under the radar of both home users and corporate administrators alike.

3.1.1 Trends that Facilitate Malicious Code to Thrive

Three factors that have unwittingly permitted malicious code to thrive and facilitated their growing menace include (1) infrastructural susceptibility, (2) increased societal dependence on the Internet, and (3) the increasing availability of information.

First, today's highly interconnected computing infrastructure represents a vast population of machines that is highly susceptible to a digital pathogen, exceeding the threat of a biological virus relative to human beings. The key reason is that the human population is genetically heterogeneous, i.e., different races and groups of people across the world possess different genes, implying a range of susceptibilities among people to diseases. In contrast, the computing infrastructure is essentially a collection of homogeneous machines; in essence, a monoculture. Hundreds of millions of computers run identical operating systems and applications, implying uniformly similar vulnerabilities. While the homogeneity in the computing infrastructure has brought great benefits to modern society and has been extremely important to the growth of the computing industry, it has also introduced a serious vulnerability. If a single machine falls prey to a digital pathogen, hundred million other computers may follow suit. Computer systems' vulnerabilities originate from the fact that people write software and to err is human. It is generally believed within the software engineering community that an average software product inherits between 2 and 8 software flaws per thousand lines of code [9]. Many of the flaws are minor nuisances. However, a few of the flaws are serious in that they expose the computer to attacks. They are analogous to a faulty lock on the patio door. While hackers have traditionally exploited these weaknesses in the past, the present-generation malicious code goes one step further. They exploit the vulnerabilities to increasingly compromise and recruit new systems. The large collection of compromised machines constitutes a formidable attack force and results in unparalleled spread rates. In addition to the unintentional software flaws, operating systems offer attractive features, many of which are inadvertently vulnerable. A noteworthy feature found in modern operating systems is "software automation," which permits a software application on a computer system to leverage the functionalities of other application programs on the same system. An accounting software application, for example, can leverage the e-mail program, via automation facility, to transmit e-mail messages to all delinquent customers who are behind in their payments. Thus, despite the lack of knowledge of the e-mail program, the author of the accounting program can provide a valuable service, namely timely notification. While the ability to integrate different system applications represents unquestionable improvement, it also introduces a weakness. Where the operating system allows legitimate application programs to perform such activities, it unwittingly opens up the same opportunities for malicious software. Thus, a hacker can easily synthesize a virus that spreads itself via e-mail, without being aware of the details of the e-mail protocol. In fact, the Nimda virus, which we will describe later in this chapter, exploits this very mechanism to spread itself via e-mail.

Second, in addition to the infrastructural factors, society's increased dependence on the Internet has invited significant losses from malicious code attacks and spurred tremendous apprehension. Today, a number of critical business operations and government functions are controlled through the Internet, including transportation, business supply chain management, government services, business-to-consumer sales, physical infrastructure control, and healthcare. Widespread Internet adoption has revolutionized the business world, however, at a significant price. Virtually each and every one of the business systems have become potential targets for a malicious program attack. Worse, even undirected attacks on the geographically distributed and diffused Internet infrastructure may sever the underlying lines of communication, critically required by so many business applications.

Third, the increasing and ubiquitous availability of information has greatly facilitated non-experts to synthesize malicious computer software. Today, novice programmers can easily locate and download virus construction "toolkits" and pre-instilled self-mutation logic, enabling them to create computer viruses with polymorphic (self-mutating) capabilities. In fact, documents reveal that an unnamed individual utilized a point-and-click construction kit in the late 1990s to synthesize 15,000 new and distinct viruses over the course of a single weekend.

3.2 The Nature of Malicious Code

Malicious code, by definition, is a piece of software program that is designed by deliberately carry out unauthorized actions on a computer system or network. Examples of unauthorized actions may include the deletion or modification of data, attacks on other computers via the network, changes to the target computer's parameter settings, theft of data from a compromised system, or attempts by the code to spread copies of itself to other computers on the network. The literature notes the presence of over 3.5 million known distinct strains of malicious code and growing. The bulk of the malicious code, virtually 99.99%, is created by automated computer systems. The three major categories of malicious code, namely, viruses, worms, and Trojan horses, are comprised of computer instructions, no different from any legitimate application software on the computer. Today, computer viruses and worms represent a minority of all actively deployed malicious software; Trojan horses, of which data-stealing Spyware is a noteworthy subcategory, currently predominates.

Through the 1990s and early 2000s, most malicious programs were manually synthesized by human programmers from scratch and then released to victims. In contrast, the majority of today's infections (circa 2010) are automatically generated and mutated by purpose-built malware generation computer systems hosted by attackers. The malicious programmer first designs the core functionality of their threat (e.g., they build a malicious program that steals passwords or credit card information) and then provides this core malicious logic as input to a malware generation system. As new victims visit a compromised website, the malware generation system generates new variants of the core logic (using encryption and other obfuscation techniques) with the result that each victim gets a functionally similar, yet entirely unknown malware variant. Such micro-customization has made detection of new malware strains extremely difficult.

In addition, there exist a number of "point-and-click" kits that enable anyone with basic computer skills to create entirely new instances of malicious software. In a fascinating development, a small portion of new malicious code is the result of random mutation and the automatic mating of pre-existing malicious code programs. As an example, while a string of binary 0s and 1s, representing a malicious program, travels down the Internet, stray disturbances may garble the sequence, thereby giving rise to a new and heretofore unknown strain. As a second example, earlier viruses have been known to inadvertently "mate" within other viruses in infected files, i.e., the programming logic in the viruses intermix and give rise to a hybrid strain which then spreads on its own.

Nearly all malicious code comes in the form of computer files, including application program files, documents, and spreadsheet files. When an unsuspecting user runs an application program file that either contains malicious code or utilizes an infected data file, unbeknownst to the user, he or she is invoking and executing the malicious logic. The subverted logic can then take over control of the user's computer, attempt to spread itself, steal data, or cause other form of mischief. Files represent a natural choice for infectious malicious code, given that users routinely work with them and share them over drive shares, thumb drives, and via e-mail. While the majority of malware attacks come in the form of application (EXE) files, these programs need to be introduced into a victim computer before they can cause damage. Such introduction is generally accomplished in one of two ways: First, a computer user can be tricked into downloading and installing such a malicious program (e.g., "Your computer is infected and you need to download this security program to clean up your computer." Or "Download and run this file to see an Oscar-winning movie"). Second, attackers have learned how to exploit flaws in users' web browsers (such as Internet Explorer, Firefox or Safari) and file viewers (e.g., Adobe Acrobat Reader or Macromedia Flash Player) to automatically and silently install the malicious software on the user's computer. Essentially, the attackers embed malicious instructions into the web page or data file that tricks the computer into silently downloading and running the malicious program.

In contrast to the norm, a small but significant number of threats like Slammer and Code Red are not delivered to the victim in the form of a file. Instead, threats like Slammer and Code Red exist in the form of a string of 1s and 0s as they travel through the Internet, via cable or wireless, from one computer to another. Once running on a victim computer system, these worms identify other vulnerable computer systems, connect to them, and send intentionally malformed messages to these victim machines. Assuming the victim computers are running the targeted vulnerable software, the malformed messages sent by the worm will exploit the vulnerabilities in that software and introduce the malicious logic into the target computer system. Once running on the new system, the malicious software repeats this process and infects further machines.

3.2.1 Operational Phases of Malicious Code

The operation of malicious code may be classified into three key phases, namely, infiltration, propagation, and payload delivery.

For a malicious program to run on a computer, logically, it must first gain access to that computer; this constitutes the infiltration phase. In some cases, malicious code can and does little to infiltrate a new system. Unwitting users come into contact with malicious code files on the World Wide Web and in incoming e-mail messages on a daily basis. Once the user double-clicks their mouse cursor on the file, the threat is downloaded onto their computer where it is subsequently run. The second method of infiltration involves an attack by a compromised website on the victim's web browser or file viewer program (e.g., Adobe Acrobat Reader). The malicious (or compromised legitimate) website sends down malformed data (e.g., a malicious HTML web-page) to the victim computer system. When the browser or file viewer attempts to display this webpage on the screen, it gets tricked by the malformed data embedded in the web page into running malicious computer instructions on behalf of the attacker. These malicious computer instructions often silently download and install a malicious program on the victim's machine.

Finally, a number of self-propagating malicious programs, such as viruses and worms, can automatically infiltrate target computers without requiring any human interaction. These "pathogens" attempt to break into a target computer system by connecting to the target and sending malicious data, exploiting pre-existing vulnerabilities in the computer's operating system or applications, similar to a burglar physically entering a house by breaking in through a vulnerable window. Once the malicious code correctly identifies a vulnerable entry into a target machine, it can then successfully inject itself and take control.

Immediately upon infiltration into a target, a malicious program's self-propagating threat will attempt to spread itself either throughout the compromised machine or to other computers over the network. Under a popular form of propagation, the malicious code first seeks out in the target computer a list of e-mail addresses and then e-mails a copy of itself to each of the recipients via standard Internet e-mail. As an alternate strategy, some malicious code randomly seek out new victim computers on the Internet and then attempt to infiltrate them, similar to a burglar that randomly picks street addresses and house numbers and attempts to break in. Today, the majority of malicious programs do not attempt this propagation step, post-infection of a victim computer system; instead, they simply deliver a payload.

Under payload delivery, a malicious program that contains a destructive "payload" will launch activities that transcend the infiltration and propagation phases. These actions may include modifying the security settings, thereby lowering the machine's guard; capturing the audio stream from the machine's microphone and broadcasting it to a different computer; and stealing user passwords and financial credentials such as credit card numbers. Malicious code threats may contain a set of "trigger" criteria and will lie patiently dormant. When the criteria are satisfied, the payload is delivered, i.e., executed, an example being deleting all the files on an infected system starting at 5 PM on a Friday.

3.3 Categories of Malicious Code

Although a malicious program can launch any attack that could manually be performed by a human hacker, it features two major advantages. First, as fully automated, i.e., not requiring human intervention, it can execute attacks extremely fast. Second, given its ability to rapidly clone and spread, a malicious program can leverage massive parallelism in its attack. A single worm can coerce millions of machines to simultaneous launch an attack on a network, far surpassing a individual who can, at best, control a few dozen computers. Based on analysis of their operational phases over the past two decades, security researchers have organized malicious code into five broad categories, namely (1) viruses, (2) worms, (3) Trojan horse programs, which include botnets or zombies and spyware, and (4) Adware.

3.3.1 Viruses

A virus is a series of malicious instructions that inject itself into an existing, legitimate, program file. Whenever an infected file is utilized, the virus' logic takes over control, locates other victim files on the computer, and then inserts its logic into each of the target files. To understand how a virus works, consider an obedient employee who reads all of his or her instructions off of a simple chore-notepad and faithfully follows them as directed. There may be many types of chore-notepads, one for faxing, another for making coffee, a third for shipping a package, etc. Assume, for example, that a chore-notepad for faxing contains the following instructions to fax any document:

```
1. Turn the fax machine on
2. Insert the documents face down into the fax feeder
3. Enter the phone number on the keypad and hit the
   send/enter button
```

Under operation, personal computers obediently follow similar lists of instructions that constitute computer programs. Exceptions notwithstanding, computers never attempt to determine whether or not a list of instructions is meaningful or sensible; they blindly execute the instructions. Under these circumstances, assume that a perpetrator surreptitiously replaces the previous instructions on the employee's chore-notepad for faxing with the following, a slightly modified version:

```
1. Turn the fax machine on
2. Insert the documents, face down, in the feeder
3. Enter the phone number on the keypad and hit the
   send/enter button
4. Find a new chore-notepad, for making coffee,
   shipping a package, etc
5. Append the last two instructions, namely 4 and 5,
   from this chore-notepad onto the new chore-notepad
```

Note that the last two instructions are not present in the original set of instructions; these represent the viral infection, and work as follows: When the obedient employee follows the modified instructions, each and every time he or she faxes a document, the employee would also attempt to find a new chore-notepad and append the last two instructions, namely 4 and 5, at the end of its checklist. The modified chore-notepad may now be used to further spread the infection by another employee or the same employee at a later time. Assume that the employee locates a chore-notepad for making coffee and appends the last two instructions onto the notepad. A subsequent employee or the same individual, when undertaking the task of making coffee will locate another chore-notepad, say for shipping a package, and append the last two instructions onto the notepad. Clearly, the virus will spread, infecting virtually all chore-notepads very quickly. A typical virus works in the exact same manner, infecting dozens, even hundreds of susceptible files on a single personal computer. Often, viruses infiltrate systems through malicious web pages or via downloads from illicit file sharing networks. Depending on the intent of the virus' author, a virus may or may not come with a payload. While some viruses merely spread themselves, consuming memory but, otherwise, not causing any secondary damage, others may utilize any of the payload techniques described earlier in this chapter. Viruses may be organized based on the types of files they infect. The most common virus types include:

- *Executable file viruses*: These are viruses that attack application programs including games, finance programs, etc., and spread when a user executes an infected application program.
- *Macro viruses*: These viruses infect document and spreadsheet files when the user opens or views the infected documents. Due to security advancements, these viruses are extremely rare (circa 2010).
- *"Boot record" viruses*: Viruses of this class tend to localize themselves in specially reserved areas, namely, memory locations, of floppy diskettes and hard drives, spreading from one computer to another when users share infected diskettes. Due to enhancements in modern operating systems, such boot record threats are also extremely rare.

3.3.2 Worms

A malicious program of type worm differs from that of a virus in term of its key objective. Unlike a virus, which attempts to infect many files on a single compromised computer system, the prototypical worm propagates by spreading itself to other computers over the network. Thus, a typical worm executes only once on a target computer system during which it infects it and then focuses on spreading through to other machines over the network. With respect to the chore-notepad analogy, utilized earlier, a chore-notepad worm might look as follows:

```
11. Make a XEROX copy of this notepad
12. Insert the copy into an envelope
```

```
13. Find a street address from the Rolodex, and write
    this address on the envelope
14. Affix a stamp onto the envelope and seal the
    envelope
15. Drop the envelope into the mailbox
16. Repeat steps 11 through 15 for ten or more times,
    each for a different address
```

When an obedient employee receives such a chore-notepad in the regular mail and follows the instructions, he or she would send out ten or more new chore-notepads to unsuspecting recipients. Upon receiving and opening their regular mail, the recipients, in turn, would follow instructions and send out ten more copies, and the process would continue. Unlike the virus, this chore-notepad worm does not infect different chore-notepads within the company; instead, it transmits copies of itself to more and more companies. Earlier, computer worms spread and infiltrated new machines via standard Internet e-mail. Once an unsuspecting user opened and ran a malicious attachment, the worm took control of the victim computer, searched for the user's e-mail address book, and then sent a copy of itself to as many of the new e-mail addresses in the address book. The process continues, unless security vendors produce a cure, infecting many machines on the network.

A growing number of computer worms, including Code Red, Nimda and Slammer, attempt to infiltrate new machines by first directly connecting to them via the Internet and then probing for known vulnerabilities. Sophisticated computer systems provide a remote login feature, where a legitimate user may logon through a username and password combination, and then accesses the remote machine. The convenience allows employees to easily share files across corporations or from home networks. Some worms attempt to exploit such features by guessing usernames and passwords. For convenience, many users choose to use easy-to-remember passwords, including the phrase, "password." Worms are designed to exploit this weakness by repeatedly trying commonly used passwords from its repository. Other computer worms attempt to locate and exploit vulnerabilities in software running on a target system. For example, legitimate web server software (e.g., Apache) running on a typical Internet server may have a software flaw that allows an attacker to send the web server malicious instructions. If the worm has been programmed to identify such a vulnerable web server and send the right series of instructions to the web server, it can inject itself into the vulnerable web server and then begin running on the victim computer.

Often, as in the case of the infamous Morris Internet worm of 1988, worms are highly successful in breaking into unsuspecting systems. Once it identifies a known vulnerability that it knows it can defeat, a worm injects itself into the target machine, completes the infiltration, and then initiates the propagation process anew. Since worms can spread without any human intervention, they have been observed to replicate orders of magnitude faster than worms that exploit e-mail as well as viruses. Similar to computer viruses, worms may or may not come with a destructive payload. Depending on the ferocity of the payload, worms may cause unimaginable damage. Even without any payload, many worms can spread so rapidly and widely that they are likely to congest the Internet, thereby considerably slowing down WWW traffic, e-mail delivery, etc. Thus, as with viruses, even a worm with no explicit payload can cause extensive damage.

3.3.2.1 Categories of Worms

While there is no universal agreement in the literature on a taxonomy for worms, they may be broadly categorized, based on four key attributes, namely, (1) manifestation of the worm, (2) target selection strategy, i.e. how they select new victim computers, (3) propagation vector, i.e., how they transmit copies of themselves over the network, and (4) infiltration approach, i.e., how they infiltrate new computers.

Though not their preferred style, worms can assume, similar to viruses, the form of standard computer files, including application files, document files, or spreadsheet files. In addition, a large number of worms are also delivered in the form of "script files," which represent a special type of application files that include programming logic. Script files are generally used by experts to automate routine tasks on the computer. Since they are allowed to contain any arbitrary programming logic, script files may be composed to effect self-propagation in a worm-like fashion. As indicated earlier, many worms never take the form of a file, existing only as a series of 0s and 1s traveling over network cables and found within the computer's memory. They may not be accessed by the typical user and are able to spread without any human intervention.

Virtually all worms employ the following strategy. First, they select new target computers to infect; second, they connect to the target computers through remote login mechanisms; and, third, they successfully infiltrate the selected targets. The process is often repeated many, many times. The following is a partial list of target selection strategies. Often, worms are observed to employ one or more of these schemes:

- *Random targeting strategy*: The worm randomly selects new target computers to infect. This is analogous to a malicious person sending out nasty chain letters to homes on randomly chosen street addresses.
- *A scanning approach*: The worm scans the network, carefully examining and non-invasively probing for new target computers to attack. This would be analogous to a malicious person sending out letters, under phase 1, to a large number of home addresses. Under phase 2, the perpetrator would wait for return-to-sender notifications back from the post office. Each time a letter is returned to the attacker as undeliverable, the perpetrator would eliminate the corresponding address. Finally, under phase 3, the attacker will compile a list of homes with potential victims, to whom he can direct his nasty chain letter.
- *"Topological" strategy*: When a worm infects a computer, it can explore and analyze the computer's contents to identify new victims for the next round of infection. The e-mail worm constitutes a classic example in that once a a new computer is infected, its mail file or addressbook are probed to yield new victims.

- *A "hit-list" strategy*: A worm can carry its own hit-list of target computers as it spreads. Such a worm can potentially coordinate the infection activity in that successively infiltrated computer system may be granted responsibility to infect exclusive sets of computer systems from the hit-list.

Once a worm has successfully located one or more new target computers to attack, it must then propagate a copy of itself over the network to the target. The most common approaches include:

- The worm can open a direct connection from the infected machine to the target computer via the Internet, and then launch the attack. Code Red and Slammer employed this approach.
- The worm can leverage one or more of the existing communications protocols, supported by Internet, to propagate itself. Worms that spread via e-mail exploit this technique. The worm launches an e-mail, attaching a copy of itself to the e-mail, and relies on the Internet infrastructure to carry out its mission. Although the worm lacks the exact knowledge of how to reach the target computer, it relies on the Internet to carry out its objective. Additional infrastructural protocols exploited by worms include:
  - *Instant messaging*: Often, worms have been observed to leverage existing instant messaging infrastructure, including Microsoft's Messenger and AOL Instant Messenger, to identify new targets and propagate a copy of themselves via the Internet.
  - *Peer-to-peer file sharing*: Worms have also been observed to spread through popular file-sharing services, including Kazaa. When users exchange music files, they may inadvertently download a worm instead of a popular song they had intended to transfer.
- Clever worms can employ a hybrid approach by combining remote login and leveraging existing protocols.

After the worm has successfully identified and connected to a new victim computer, it must find a way to infiltrate, i.e., gain control of the target. Current worms are known to employ one of the following infiltration approaches:

- *"Invited infiltration"*: When a user has received a worm through an e-mail attachment, the worm can only gain control of the computer if and when the user clicks on the infected attachment. Clearly, the user must invite the worm onto the system; for, without the user's interaction, the worm cannot complete the infiltration.
- *Vulnerability exploitation*: Armed with the knowledge of defeating a known vulnerability, a worm can successfully infiltrate a new target computer.
- *Exploiting a user-induced vulnerability*: When a user chooses to employ a simple, easy-to-guess password for the sake of convenience, a worm may easily crack it by repeatedly trying up to 100 most likely passwords. This is analogous to a burglar trying the popular combination 1-2-3 to crack open a safe, which

is often the choice of many safe owners who are either unable or unwilling to formulate and remember more complex combinations.
- Hybrid worms may employ one or more of the above approaches.

In the remainder of the chapter, we will examine how Code Red, Nimda, and Slammer fit into these categories.

3.3.3 Trojan Horse Programs

A malicious program of type Trojan Horse attempts to perform malicious activities but does not attempt to spread itself like a virus or worm. In some instances, a Trojan Horse program will impersonates a healthy legitimate computer application program, and will be deliberately downloaded by the duped user. In other cases, the Trojan horse will be delivered onto the victim's computer through exploitation of a vulnerability in the user's web browser or file viewing applications. Once on the computer, the Trojan Horse program can cause wanton destruction to the computer system. Unlike computer viruses and worms, Trojan Horse programs generally do not attempt to self-propagate to other files and across the network. In essence, a Trojan Horse acts as a proxy for the real attacker and, once it has gained access, it can launch malicious actions. Trojan Horse programs have been observed to steal passwords and information from files and relay them back to the attacker via the network; damage select contents of the computer, including deleting and corrupting files; and subvert the computer's security settings, thereby enabling subsequent attackers to compromise the machine more easily. A special type of Trojan Horse programs, called "remote-control," can first assume control of a machine and then accept commands from the external attacker via the network. The Trojan Horse faithfully executes the commands on behalf of the attacker, enabling repeated access the machine's files over time, record the user's activities, modify the machine's data, etc. To an unsuspecting user, it would seem that a poltergeist had taken up residence in the machine.

3.3.4 Zombies

Zombies or Bot Nets constitute a sub-class of Trojan Horse programs. These programs can be controlled en-masse using a centralized control protocol and then used to launch attacks. Zombie attacks include inundating a legitimate website with fake requests to cause it drop legitimate requests, sending mass volumes of spam email, or stealing large numbers of credit cards. Zombies may be delivered to the victim computer in the form of application files, through e-mail attachments, while visiting a questionable website on the Internet, via instant messaging chat software, or through song-swapping software. Immediately upon gaining control of the machine, the zombie lies dormant to elude detection, while it awaits commands from the hacker on the Internet. Typically, a perpetrator will attempt to infect hundreds or even thousands of computers with these zombie programs. Employing especially designed zombie control programs, the hacker, at a time of his or her own choosing, can transmit a "kill signal" to all zombie-infected computers, causing them to direct huge volumes of bogus data at a target website, or to send spam e-mails to unsuspecting victims. In the case of a denial of service attack, the overloaded website fails to respond in a timely fashion to requests from legitimate users. Clearly, the hacker can transmit a single potent command over to the zombies from anywhere in the world, remaining elusive and virtually impossible to track. In February of 2000, zombie malicious code was utilized to attack a number of high-profile websites, including Yahoo!, Amazon.com, and CNN.com [10].

3.3.5 Adware

Adware is a controversial class of software that resides in a gray area, between legitimate and malicious code. Adware is a mechanism to monetize free software and services which are supported financially through the use of advertising sponsors. Sponsors will pay a fee to have their advertisements delivered to the end user. One can think of adware as a software incarnation of off-the-air broadcast television. With broadcast television, viewers essentially get free service. Unlike viewing a movie at a theater, viewers do not pay to watch a television show. Television programs are funded by selling time slots to commercial vendors and displaying their advertisements in the allocated time slots during the airing of the show.

What renders adware controversial is that while many are legitimate, some are malicious in nature. With adware, a user may wish to play a computer game or use an application, which are supported by adware. The user will download the software package and launch the installation sequence. During the installation, the software will present a Terms of Use (TOU) or End Users License Agreement (EULA) and prompt the user to agree to continue with the process. Most users will click on the "Accept" button without fully reading the agreement. Thereafter, the user has no way of knowing for sure exactly how the installation sequence modified their computer system.

In the case of legitimate adware, the installed software contacts a remote computer system. The adware process then downloads and periodically presents advertisements when the sponsored software is in use. These advertisements can be in the form of pop-up windows or as a subtle scrolling banner advertisement in the application window. When the user performs an Internet search, the browser may be redirected to a sponsor's search site.

Malicious variants of adware are essentially indistinguishable from Trojan horses. Once activated, the malware will deliberately embed ad-serving processes throughout the system, including spyware and other malicious programs. Once installed, the spyware can intercept keystrokes and spy on the activities of the user without their consent or knowledge. The acquired information is then transmitted remotely to other systems where it is archived, analyzed, and redistributed. A unique feature of malicious adware is that it is designed to pose great difficulty in detecting and removing it from the infected computer system. Only through the use of widely-available, specialized tools can the compromised system be fully cleansed and restored.

3.3.6 *Malicious Mobile Code*

The term, "Malicious Mobile Code," characterizes malicious code that are surreptitiously injected into a target computer, while it is engaged in visiting websites on the Internet. When an unscrupulous website operator embeds a Trojan Horse program into a specific tainted web page, upon viewing the page, the user's web browser, such as the popular Internet Explorer, will have automatically downloaded the web page as well as the Trojan Horse program. The malicious code will execute on the user's program without explicit permission, infect it, and begin to cause harm. Malicious Mobile Code attacks are relatively rare, stemming from two reasons. First, aware of these attacks, website browser developers have incorporated special code to discourage and outright block such attacks. Second, fearful of potential legal liabilities, website owners and operators refrain from embedding Trojan Horse programs into their own websites and take extra precaution not to allow such attacks.

3.4 A Closer Look into the Inner Workings of Malicious Code

In this section, we will examine the inner workings of three of the well-known high-profile malicious code threats, namely, Code Red, Nimda, and Slammer. We will focus on the mechanisms employed to select new targets, transmit copies of itself over to the victims, infiltrate the victim computers, the range of secondary damage that may be inflicted, either intentionally or unintentionally.

3.4.1 *Code Red*

On Friday, July 12, 2001, an unnamed attacker unleashed the Code Red worm on the Internet. Unbeknownst to security experts at the time, this new infection was the first of three increasingly virulent strains to arrive on the world scene [11]. The first version, "Code Red version 1" or CRv1, did not spread through an application file or e-mail attachment nor did it require any user invitation. It was unlike most worms, known at that time. The CRv1 would select its targets at random and once one computer was successfully infected, the worm would launch 100 replicas of itself on the infected machine. Each of these clones would then independently and simultaneously seek out and target new computers in an attempt to dramatically speed up the worm's time rate of infection. For reasons known only to the worm's author, the worm was designed to spread only between the first and the 19th day of every month, hibernating on the infected machine the remainder of the time.

When they begin to execute on an infected computer, each clone would randomly attack new computers as quickly as possible. Upon identifying a target, a clone would first connect to the target computer remotely and then attempt to break into the system by exploiting a well-known vulnerability in Microsoft's "Internet Information Service" (IIS) web server software. IIS is a popular software, executed by millions of computers to operate web sites. In general, web-server programs wait for requests to arrive from clients all over the Internet and then service them as they arrive. Thus, when a user types the address of a website on his or her machine, such as www.anywebsite.com, the local web browser on the user's machine will reach out to the server computer corresponding to www.anywebsite.com and request the appropriate web page(s). Upon receipt of the web page from the server, the local web browser will display the contents on the user's screen. Earlier versions of Microsoft's IIS featured a fatal flaw, no different than a dead-bolt lock on a supposedly secure home that could be easily picked with a paperclip. When successfully exploited, this flaw would enable an attacker, individual or worm, to gain total control over the computer, running the web-server software. The flaw was well-known and apparently Microsoft had even posted a free "patch," a fix for the flawed logic, on their official website a month before CRv1 was released. If the owners of IIS had downloaded the patch and installed it correctly, they would have been immune from CRv1. A majority of the deployed IIS servers on the Internet had not installed the patch, enabling the worm to attack a large population of computers. Since CRv1 chose its victims at random, its attempt to break into many computers that did not run ISS effectively reduced its rate of spread.

In addition to spreading, CRv1 featured two destructive payloads. The first payload was designed to launch a massive distributed denial of service attack against the White House's official website, www.whitehouse.gov, between the 20th and the 28th day of each month. Fortunately for the White House, the worm had a flaw and software engineers were able to prevent extensive damage. The second payload "defaced" webpages on every web-server that had been compromised by overlaying the phrase, "Hacked by Chinese." Thus, once CRv1 had successfully infiltrated a server computer, a user requesting the web page from the server would receive the phrase "Hacked by Chinese," instead of the actual webpage.

The CRv1 logic incurred a severe flaw in that every clone of CRv1 was instructed to infect the exact same set of victim computers. As a result, CRv1 began to spin around the same set of victim computers that it had infected earlier and its spread was contained. While the vulnerable computers were attacked over and over again, those that did not contain IIS continued to deflect the attack repeatedly. As an analogy, consider that a group of ten traveling salesmen, each of whom is provided by the manager the exact same set of random street addresses for solicitation. As a result, each salesman goes to the exact same series of houses, encountering the same frustrated homeowners. While a handful of these homeowners will purchase goods once, the rest will simply turn away the onslaught of salesmen. Had the manager selected an exclusive and distinct set of random street addresses for each salesman, the company would have made far more sales to more homeowners. The flaw was quickly discovered, patched, and a new variant of the original worm, Code Red version 2 (CRv2), was released at 10:00 UTC on the morning of July 19th, 2001. CRv2 was identical to CRv1 in every respect, except that each copy of the worm would randomly select an entirely different set of machines for its target and launch attacks. As a result of this subtle logic modification, CRv2 successfully compromised an estimated 359,000 susceptible computers in 14 h [11]. It was this updated version of Code Red that made the headlines. At least six different variants of the original Code Red worm are known to exist and copycat versions abound in plenty. Some of these variants will open up back-doors on infected systems, facilitating other attackers to break into the system at a later time. Majority of IIS systems have been properly "patched," effectively neutralizing the threat of the Code Red worm.

3.4.2 Nimda

On 18 September 2001, computer administrators began to notice an abrupt and significant increase in the number of connections to web-servers. There was no commensurate increase in web-surfing by home users. It became quickly apparent that a new fast spreading computer worm was the culprit, now known as Nimda. Unlike the Code Red worm, which targeted a specific type of computer server running Microsoft IIS, Nimda targeted all types of desktop computers running Microsoft Windows operating system. Nimda began to infect corporate desktops, home computers, and large servers with equal ferocity and it has been estimated to have infected at least 2.2 million computers, worldwide, in the first 24 h [12, 13].

Nimda assumes the form of an application file and is the legendary "Swiss Army Knife" of malicious code. Unlike Code Red, which exploited a single vulnerability, Nimda used a combination of six different mechanisms to spread itself [14]. For each new target, Nimda would attempt all six mechanisms, one by one, until either the machine succumbed or the Nimda worm moved onto other machines. Nimda's first mechanism was identical to CRv2. Although its predecessor, CRv2's, exploits have been well publicized, many computers running IIS web-server software had still not been properly patched by the administrators. Nimda's goal was to infect these left over computer systems. Nimda's second mechanism centered around backdoors that had been left open by later variants of the Code Red worm and the Sadmind worm. While administering the Microsoft patch for the IIS vulnerability, many computer administrators were either unaware or unable to close these backdoors. Under the third mechanism, if Nimda successfully infiltrated a new computer running IIS, it would tamper the web-related files stored on the computer. These files contain the website's webpage data, which is typically downloaded by an individual user visiting the webpage. Nimda would modify these files and place copies of itself at strategic locations on the computer, such that worm would be downloaded onto the individual's computer, which would be subsequently infected. This mechanism resembles a Malicious Mobile Code, described in Sect. 3.3.5 earlier. Nimda's fourth mechanism was extremely surreptitious. It would transmit a copy of itself through an e-mail with an attachment. Upon arrival at a new computer, the worm would seek out new e-mail addresses and transmit e-mails to these addresses, disguising copies of itself in the attachments. The nature of the attachment was so clever that the worm would get executed as soon as the user viewed the message, even if the attachment is never opened with the click of the mouse. This mechanism permitted the worm to spread through e-mail at great speed to corporate machines and home computers. Under the fifth mechanism, Nimda targets corporate intra-networks, where security parameters are deliberately kept low in order to facilitate free and quick sharing of files between users and across computers. Once Nimda has successfully infected a single computer on a corporate intranet, it methodically targets each and every computer in which file sharing features are enabled, and propagates a copy of itself over. As a result, Nimda has been observed to spread like wildfire through corporations' network, even without human intervention. Nimda's sixth mechanism consists of infecting files on a compromised computer using viral techniques, i.e., it injects its logic onto as many application files, including game files, word processor files, accounting applications, etc. In essence, Nimda is a hybrid malicious code, inheriting the worst of worms and viruses. Nimda opens and leaves behind backdoors in compromised machines. As a result, even where the worm is removed, the machines remain vulnerable to expert hackers.

Nimda has also been observed to lower security settings in infected computers, thereby enabling remote users to read and modify the computer's files remotely, bypassing the need of passwords and user authentication. More than 20 variants of Nimda are known, each with its own set of peculiarities.

3.4.3 Slammer

The Slammer worm [15] is undeniably one of the fastest spreading computer worm, two orders of magnitude faster than Code Red. In the first minute of its infection, Slammer doubled the population of infected computers every 8.5 s and scanned over 55 million computers per second with the intent to infect them. Within the first 10 min of propagation, Slammer had infected 90% of all susceptible computers, eventually infecting 75,000 server computers. Similar to Code Red, Slammer employed a random selection technique to identify new computers to attack. As soon as it compromised a computer, Slammer began to send copies of itself out rapidly to other randomly selected computers.

Unlike Code Red and Nimda that exploited vulnerabilities in Microsoft's IIS Slammer exploited a vulnerability in Microsoft's SQL Server Database product to gain control over new computer systems. The SQL Server Database software enables corporations to store, index, and retrieve large volumes of information, including customer data, product information, sales records, etc. The typical database waits idly until it receives a request from another computer, and then jumps into action. It processes the request, retrieves the appropriate data, and then transmits it back to the requesting computer. A typical request may assume the form, "give me a list of all the customers in the 408 area code." After the vulnerability was discovered, Microsoft published a patch to fix the problem in SQL Server Database but many computer administrators had either failed or neglected to install it. Slammer took advantage of this inefficiency by transmitting to the database a single, malformed 404-character long "packet" of information over the Internet. In the process of attempting to process it, the database became confused and was misled to execute the malicious instructions contained within the packet. The underlying computer inadvertently launched the replication process.

Slammer is an extremely simple worm, comprised of only 376 bytes of data, and did nothing but propagate clones of itself. It contained no destructive payload. However, its simple design and single-minded focus imparted to it the ability to spread extremely rapidly. Infected computers sent out so many attack packets and so rapidly that they overwhelmed the Internet. The congestion caused other legitimate packets to be dropped, resulting in outages in ATM Cash Machines, Airline Ticketing systems, and even emergency 911 systems.

3.5 Malicious Code Creation Process

Viruses, worms, Trojan horses and other types of malicious code are similar to normal code, except that their goal is destructive. Logically, their authors utilize the same programming tools that legitimate software engineers use to develop constructive software applications. The first and most common tool is a compiler. Individuals prefer to write software in high-level computer programming languages that are easy to comprehend. Since computers work in the world of binary logic, expressed through 0s and 1s, a compiler is invoked to translate the composition in the high-level language into the binary language of the computer. For example, the author of a worm might composes a program that is described as:

```
1.  Pick a random internet address to attack
2.  Connect to the computer at the specified address
3.  Send a packet of data to the computer
4.  etc...
```

The compiler generates the following binary sequence, which the computer can understand and execute.

```
1011110100101010111010000101010101010011110100111
```

Malicious computer code may be written in any of the available computer programming languages, provided compilers are available. The most common languages employed include, Visual Basic, used by the author of Love Letter; C or

C++, used by numerous malcode threats; and Assembly language, the most common language used to write viruses. Almost all programmers inadvertently leave one or more logic flaws, termed "bugs" in their programs. Bugs may originate from simple typos to basic flaws with the logic of the software. Thus, when a programmer accidentally types "b = a + 5" instead of "b = a + 4", on the keyboard, a flaw arises. Fundamental design flaws are more complex. To detect and locate bugs, programmers often employ a tool called debugger. The debugger, in general, artificially slows down the extremely fast execution of the computer so that the programmer can literally perceive the results as the program executes, one instruction at a time. This allows the programmer to identify the instruction, where the program fails to work as expected and then remedy the problem.

In contrast to compiler and debuggers, the choice of expert programmers to write normal or malicious code, a number of simplified toolkits are widely available that permit computer users with little or no formal programming abilities to compose viruses and worms. They are literally point-and-click with the mouse type tools. Toolkits offer limited choices to the malware code author, including what types of files the new virus should infect and whether the virus should delete files, format the hard drive, or simply print nasty messages on the screen. Once the author has made his or her selections, a simple click on "Go" will cause the toolkit program to spit out a brand-new, never-before-seen computer virus. The author can then send the virus to an unsuspecting user or run it on a computer within a poorly monitored university laboratory and the virus will acquire a life of its own. As had been noted earlier in this chapter, in late 1999, an unnamed individual generated over 15,000 new viruses in a single weekend.

Malicious code authors also use the "packer" tool, which essentially compresses application programs to yield a smaller size or footprint. Legitimate software engineers generally use compression tools to minimize the storage requirement of any software when not in use, for archiving, and during transmission over the Internet to minimize transit times, when messages are generally subject to external interference and disturbances. Increasingly, malicious code authors are observed to pack select sections of their toolkit to obscure the logic of their original program, thereby preventing subsequent hackers from reverse engineering the software and stealing the trade secrets. The packing process also alters the signature, namely, the pattern of 0s and 1s, a common technique to defeat antivirus software techniques.

Often, authors of malicious code will release their entire high-level composition or specific components of the composition, referred to as source code, which permits others to construct creative variants of the original virus or worm. Observations reveal that expert authors have released source codes for mutation logic, i.e., how a specific worm may mutate its subsequent forms so to defeat detection and removal by anti-virus software. Virus authors may download self-mutation logic pre-packages from hundreds of choices, available at "VX" sites or Viral eXchange Internet websites, and integrate into their virus codes to create even more destructive malicious software.

3.6 Techniques to Defeat Malicious Code

The onslaught of worms, viruses, and other forms of malicious code has helped fuel the growth of a whole new, antivirus industry that has devised new technologies to protect against malicious code. These techniques may be organized into two groups, namely, host-based protection and network-based protection. While the host-based protection approach attempts to protect the computer systems and the software programs they contain, the goal of the network-based protection techniques is to protect the network.

3.6.1 Host-Based Protection

The host-based protection techniques may be further organized into: Bulletproofing, Scanning, and Behavioral Monitoring.

3.6.1.1 Bulletproofing

The term bulletproofing implies that the legitimate programmer has made conscientious attempts to render the program less susceptible to attacks. The three key approaches to bulletproofing include manual bulletproofing, automated bulletproofing, and digital signature verification. Under manual bulletproofing, the programmer deliberately adds extra safety checks, i.e., more code than is needed for the correct operation of the software under normal conditions, to the program's logic. The additional code monitors and remedies, where possible, anomalous conditions that tend to arise when the software is being attacked. Under automated bulletproofing, automated tools such as compilers may be redesigned to check for common vulnerabilities in programming logic. If and where successful, compilers can either flag potential problems and draw the attention of the programmer or proceed to automatically insert appropriate extra code to patch up the vulnerability. Of course, this is easier said than done.

The digital signature verification technique is commonly used to discourage and detect efforts to tamper or infect application program files. As an analogy, consider how we ensure that the contents of an envelope have not be tampered during transit. The sender will often sign his or her name over the fold on the back of the envelope. Upon receipt, the recipient will verify the integrity of the signature. If the fold had been opened, the integrity of the signature will have been destroyed, implying a clear case of tampering. Software vendors protect each program by enclosing it in a virtual envelope and imprinting a digital signature on the seal. To alter the program, the attacker or malicious code must reach into the envelope, which will inevitably break the seal and destroy the integrity of the signature. Computer operating systems will verify that an application has a valid digital signature before it is permitted to execute on the computer.

The digital signature verification approach offers three benefits. First, the digital signature identifies the author of the program, which implies their liability and arguably prevents them from adding malicious code to their own application. Second, it prevents perpetrators from impersonating genuine software vendors and shipping malicious software attributed to the vendor. Only the original vendor has the ability to sign the software product with the vendor's signature. Third, it discourages viruses and hackers from tampering with signed programs, since such alterations will inevitably void the signature.

3.6.1.2 Scanning

In this approach, before an application program may be executed on the computer, a special security software scans the application. If the scanner suspects the application is malicious, execution is blocked, in accordance with computer's security policy. For, once a malicious application is allowed to execute, it is too late to contain the damage. The prevalent scanning techniques include signature and heuristic scanning.

Under signature scanning, when malicious program is captured, perhaps by a savvy user who observes suspicious behavior on a computer, it is analyzed under laboratory settings. A security researcher then identifies a sequence of 1s and 0s in the code that can be used to uniquely identify the malicious code. This binary sequence is placed into a zero-one-pattern database, similar to the fingerprint database for criminals, and shipped to customers on a regular basis. The scanning software on the computer then scans each application file on the system against every sequence in the zero-one-pattern database. If a match is observed, the application program is quarantined or repaired. Clearly, signature scanning is only capable of detecting already known malicious code and may fail to detect entirely new infections, given that the database may lack the corresponding zero-one-pattern.

Heuristic scanning is designed as a proactive technique to protect against new and heretofore unknown threats. It performs a detailed analysis of a program's logic and structure, searching for the presence of instructions involved in deleting files, formatting hard drives, and displaying nasty messages on the screen. If the result of the search is affirmative, the application program is confidently classified as malicious.

3.6.1.3 Behavioral Monitoring

Under behavioral monitoring, a special security software closely monitors an application program's actual behavior while executing on a computer system. The behavior monitor will track an application program's operation and intercept any critical activity including accessing or deleting files or changing important computer settings. If the monitor determines that the activity will harm the computer, it can alert the user or block the activity from moving forward. Behavior monitoring systems can detect attacks that are otherwise elusive to signature and heuristic scanners. Scanners can only make guesses about the ultimate operational behavior of a suspect program. In contrast, behavior monitors actually observe the program during operation. As an analogy, consider a real world scenario. A police officer may notice an old lady and might not care to give the woman a second glance, thinking she is innocuous. A mere "scan" of the woman would probably reveal no threat. In contrast, if the same officer were to observe the old lady attempting to shoplift, he can intercept the errant behavior and block it from occurring.

3.6.2 Network-Based Protection

The two major techniques under network-based protection include network intrusion detection systems; and firewalls and honey-pots.

3.6.2.1 Network Intrusion Detection Systems

Network intrusion detection systems (NIDS) can detect fast-spreading malicious code threats by scrutinizing the flow of packets between computers on the network. In many large organizations, NIDS are deployed at key choke-points on the network, including the gateway between the corporation's network and the Internet. While NIDS have proven effective at detecting hackers, they have successfully detected unusual traffic patterns generated by fast-spreading worms. NIDS are often augmented with blocking capabilities to filter out suspect network packets and defeating the attack. A few of the available NIDS products use signatures to detect attacks, similar to signature-based antivirus software. They can detect and block known worms as they migrate over the network. A second type of NIDS products attempt to develop a baseline statistical profile of the normal traffic flowing through a network and then alert the security administrator whenever it detects statistically significant deviations from the baseline profile, a common occurrence when a new worm begins to spread. A third type of NIDS products is designed to detect the specific dialects of different business systems' network traffic. Many computer systems are susceptible to attack when they intercept malformed network data. These products can alert the administrator whenever they detect grammatically incorrect messages between the monitored business systems. Slammer and Code Red worms employ grammatically invalid network transmissions to break into new systems and will be readily detected by these products.

3.6.2.2 Firewalls and Honey-Pots

Firewalls are software programs that are deployed between a company's intranet and the Internet ingress. They inspect all traffic flowing between the Internet and the intranet and block any inappropriate packets. While effective in blocking hackers, they are increasingly becoming important in preventing computer worms from infecting computers. Corporations that had deployed properly-configured firewalls during the Code Red and Slammer outbreaks were protected. A special kind of firewalls, termed proxy firewalls, can inspect and block potentially harmful e-mail attachments and other files transmitted over other Internet protocols.

"Honey-pots" are otherwise idle computers with no legitimate users, whose sole purpose is to detect and possibly entrap attackers. They are placed on the network and are specially instrumented to detect anomalies that typically accompany attacks. Worms would attack a honey-pot computer, just as it would target any other machine, and their ill behaviors would be noticed without risking any of the sensitive application programs. In fact, any activity on a honey-pot computer must arise from an attack and it can quickly alert a security administrator, providing visibility as well as forensic logs during the early stages of a worm attack. Research suggests that by deploying a minimum number of honey-pots and placing them at strategic locations on the Internet, fast spreading worms may be detected before causing damage to a substantial number of computers, worldwide [16].

3.7 Vulnerability Management and Patching

In addition to deploying available security measures including antivirus software, firewalls, etc., security experts often recommend the practice of vulnerability management, where a corporate computer system is periodically assessed to discover new susceptibilities. The management process consists of three phases, namely, assessing vulnerabilities, prioritizing newly discovered vulnerabilities, and eliminating them systematically. The purpose of prioritizing is to address those threats, if any, that are most severe and promise the biggest return on investment. Vulnerability assessment tools analyze the individual security posture of each machine as well as the overall configuration of the network and can identify insecure system settings, older software products with known exploitable flaws, etc. The prioritization process uses mathematical techniques to rank each vulnerability based on the cost to remedy it as well as the benefits that it may yield. It is then presented to the administrator with a recommended plan of action.

Patches are small code fragments designed to be placed at strategic locations in the original software application in order to remedy a specific vulnerability. Patches are frequently referred to as updates, which a software vendor will develop and make available to the customers once a flaw has been discovered. The computer administrator will install the patch, per the vendor's instructions, and the flaw is expected to be eliminated. Since patches reflect an afterthought, often they introduce several new problems while eliminating one flaw. Observations indicate that a new patch will often cause the computer to misbehave, render former functionalities unavailable, and sometimes crash the system. As a result, administrators have become weary of deploying new patches, especially on mission critical systems, and often choose to leave systems as is rather than crashed and unavailable.

While may be relatively easy to patch a single computer, efforts to patch literally hundreds of thousands of computers, especially remotely, is extremely costly and risky. Even where only 0.5% of machines experience problems with the patch and are subject to crash, a system administrator might have a crippled network with thousands of users unable to get their work done. These two difficulties have resulted in a unique corporate culture of "don't ask, don't tell," when it comes to vulnerability management. It explains why Code Red, Nimda, and Slammer were so successful in exploiting well-known vulnerabilities months after these vulnerabilities became public knowledge and had already been addressed by the corresponding vendors.

3.8 The Future of Malicious Code and New Mitigation Approaches

3.8.1 The Future of Malicious Code

Back in the early 1990s, computer viruses were viewed as no more than an urban myth. That is, a virus could, at best, infect two dozen machines within a corporation over the course of a month, causing a support engineer to waste a few days to clean up the mess. Times have changed and the problem has deteriorated into orders of magnitude more serious. Experts predict that, in the future, the situation will become so dire that, in contrast, the Slammer virus may appear as benign as common cold. As noted earlier in this book [17, 18], new virulent worm propagation strategies will enable new worms to spread to a large fraction of susceptible computers on the worldwide network with extreme speed.

In the future, hackers may adopt a more elaborate strategy. First, a worm would utilize a hacker-provided hit-list of vulnerable machines to target. These would have been obtained through reconnaissance. The worm would be transmitted to the target to germinate the infection. In the second stage, the compromised machines would partake in "permutation" scanning of the network to seek other targets. In this approach, each worm runs on a separate compromised machine and methodically scans a different section of the Internet. Every computer on the Internet has a unique Internet address, no different from the house numbers on any street. While one burglar may target homes with numbers 1–10, another member of his team can target 11 through 20 simultaneously, and so on, thereby increasing the chance of systematically attacking each and every vulnerable machine without mercy. The hypothetical "Flash worm," according to its unnamed inventors, can infect a large fraction of susceptible machines, worldwide, in less than tens of seconds. Clearly, reconnaissance would need to be carried out over long periods of time and surreptitiously. When the structure of the worm is finalized, it would attack with deadly accuracy. Future malicious code will also incorporate stealth techniques to avoid detection and hide the original source-worm. A technique in use today is self-mutation, also known as polymorphism or metamorphism, where the attack logic changes with each new mutation. Thus, the instructions for each new mutation is different, implying totally different signatures and very hard to detect with conventional tools. While this technique is yet to be deployed, we believe it is only a matter of time before one such worm is launched. If and when this hypothetical worm is launched, it will likely require several weeks to collect copies of different mutations to produce a sufficient antivirus signature before a patch may be developed. By then, most of the computers and networks will have come to a halt. The same effect may be realized by several thousand virus authors all launching a coordinated attack, each deploying a completely different strategy and, together, flooding the Internet with hundreds of thousands of new worms. As a final thought, unthinkable damage may be caused by increasingly devastating payloads, which until now, had been largely absent. One can only imagine the repercussions if 100,000 databases, owned by businesses and government worldwide, are corrupted and the data scrambled beyond recognition. Millions of brokerage balances could be randomized in the blink of an eye and customers would log into their broker's website, only to find their life savings turned into a few pennies. In a new wave of crime, attackers may hold the "data" hostage until a ransom of some kind is paid. Worms payload may attempt to launch a massive denial of service attack on entire sectors of our physical and business-to-business infrastructures including the critical power grid. These attacks represent only the tip of the iceberg. Given a determined and intelligent attacker, far worse is possible. As nation states and terrorist organizations accelerate their malicious code writing skills, we will see a paradigm shift from proof-of-concept attacks to those that seek to cause irreparable harm.

3.8.2 The Future of Mitigation Approaches

Most security technologies today, including firewalls, intrusion detection systems, and antivirus software are ill equipped to deal with the next generation of ultra-fast spreading malicious code. Most of today's security technologies require manual operation by security personnel, where even the current generation of worms can spread faster than humans can respond. It is therefore imperative that we explore new security approaches if we expect the Internet to continue its immense role in society.

Arguably, the most promising approach is to bulletproof software. Malicious code infiltrates computers by exploiting vulnerabilities in software. If we can reduce or completely eliminate the flaws in future software products, we can get a handle on the malicious code problem. Already, major software vendors, university research labs, and startup companies are investigating software development tools that can automatically identify potential red flags in the programmer's logic and schedule them for correction. These tools, similar to spell-checker in word processing software, will track down and identify security-related flaws in the program logic as opposed to typos. Other approaches include automatically insert error-checking instructions into the programmer's logic to defeat exploitation by malicious code; and new behavior monitoring and blocking techniques that are analogous to retrofitting existing cars with roll-bars to increase safety. Monitoring software can also detect and block exploitation of common software vulnerabilities, such as "buffer overflow" attacks. In addition to software-based approaches, corporations that build CPUs and microprocessors, the brains inside the computer, are also looking at ways to shield them from attack. Current processors are designed to obediently follow whatever instructions they are provided, regardless of whether they are from legitimate programs or worms. The next-generation processors may be designed to be much more picky, carefully scrutinizing each instruction before executing it. If an instruction looks suspicious, as if it had been injected by a worm and illegitimate, the microprocessor may raise a red flag and block it from causing harm.

The migration to "trusted computing platforms," such as Microsoft's Palladium, can also help counter the damage caused by computer worms. A trusted computing platform is a computer that has security-enabled hardware and software components that work together to help protect data on the computer. These platforms are being developed primarily to provide secure content distribution. Thus, when a consumer purchases over the Internet and downloads a music album from a recording company, the latter would resort to trusted computing platform techniques to ensure that it is not shared with 500 friends, thereby enforcing anti-piracy objectives. Trusted computing platforms can also enable users to encrypt their own critical data, protecting it from the prying eyes of a malicious virus or worm. Even if the worm sends private files or data off the computer, the data will be rendered useless on another computer. The idea is that while computers might still be infected by malicious code, the malicious program will have reduced ability to steal or tamper with data on the computer.

In addition to focusing on individual computers, researchers are also investigating into network-wide quarantine strategies. These approaches are immense in scope and, for effectiveness, they may require participation by governments, Internet service providers, Internet backbone providers, corporations, and home users. They may require the deployment of numerous security sensors throughout the Internet infrastructure, including honey-pots, intrusion detection systems, behavior monitors, etc. The sensors can attempt to detect events, indicative of an imminent attack, and quickly forward the information onto special correlation computers. The correlation system is expected to accurately identify an attack in-progress and necessarily requires Internet-wide visibility. Thus, when an alert is received from Delaware and a similar alert arrives from California, the correlation system can verify if the two events are associated with an attack in progress and the deploy virtual "roadblocks" to defeat the malicious network transmissions. Such large-scale systems are in very early stages of research and are, at best, speculative. However, they offer the promise to automatically detect and respond to worldwide attacks, which is beyond our current capabilities.

An integrity checker is a program that takes a "snapshot" of each application program on a computer when the computer is known to be in an uninfected state. At subsequent points in time, the integrity checker then rechecks each application file to make sure it hasn't been altered. Since application files should only change when the user installs a new update (which can be detected), any other changes to application files indicate an intrusion or viral infection and is reported to the user. As an analogy, consider the paranoid parent that measures how much alcohol is in each bottle under bar. The parent can tell if the child has been sneaking a drink by measuring for changes to the amount of liquid in any of the bottles.

The proof-carrying-code approach enables a computer system to determine, with certainty, whether or not it is safe to run a program supplied by an untrusted source. To accomplish this, all programs must be accompanied by a "safety proof" (the proof data would be embedded within the application file for convenience) that proves, mathematically, that the program does what it says it does, and nothing else. Before the computer runs any program, it must first verify that the application program corroborates the accompanying proof to ensure that the program works as claimed. Such proof-carrying code systems work well for extremely simple programs, but are largely ineffective for larger programs like those used on most modern computers. Consequently, proof-carrying code has largely been relegated to laboratory use.

One area of potential improvement is that of program-based access control. Today, most operating systems are designed to enforce security through a user-based model. Thus, when a user, say "John," logs in to the computer, the operating system permits him to read and modify files in the Documents folder, but disallows him from deleting files in the operating system folder. In contrast, when the "Administrator" logs in, the operating system grants him or her the ability to read and modify all files in the system. While the access control policy generally helps secure the computer from malicious users, it suffers from a vulnerability. Often, a non-malicious user is tricked into unknowingly executing malicious software, at which point the malicious code immediately acquires all the user's access rights and privileges and can cause wanton damage.

References

[1] Retrieved from http://www.cdc.gov/od/nvpo/intro8.htm
[2] Retrieved from http://www.fsbassociates.com/fsg/flu.htm
[3] Retrieved from http://www.icir.org/vern/papers/cdc-usenix-sec02/
[4] Retrieved from http://www.caida.org/outreach/papers/2002/codered/codered.pdf
[5] Retrieved from http://enterprisesecurity.symantec.com/article.cfm?articleid=967&EID=0
[6] Retrieved from http://www.cs.berkeley.edu/nweaver/sapphire/
[7] Retrieved from http://itmanagement.earthweb.com/secu/article.php/1577611
[8] Keizer, G. (2010, February 23). Intel confirms 'sophisticated' attacks in January: Denies link to Google-China hacks, which used IE6 zero-day to breach networks and steal information. *Computerworld*
[9] Retrieved from http://home.apu.edu/jcox/projects/individual/Testing/
[10] Retrieved from http://www.cnn.com/2000/TECH/computing/05/02/new.ddos.tool/
[11] Retrieved from http://www.caida.org/analysis/security/code-red/#crv1
[12] Retrieved from http://www.sans.org/rr/paper.php?id=96
[13] Retrieved from http://www.itsecurity.com/papers/iss4.htm
[14] Retrieved from http://www.cert.org/advisories/CA-2001-26.html

[15] Retrieved from http://www.caida.org/outreach/papers/2003/sapphire/sapphire.html
[16] Retrieved from http://project.honeynet.org/papers/honeynet/
[17] Weaver, N. C. (2001, August 15). Warhol worms: The potential for very fast Internet plagues.
[18] Staniford, S., Paxson, V., & Weaver, N. (2002). How to own the Internet in your spare time. *Proceedings of the 11th USENIX Security Symposium*

Chapter 4
Restricting Anti-Circumvention Devices

Paul Schneck

4.1 Background: The Difference Between Digital and Analog

Until recently, information was recorded in analog form. Early cave paintings may be the oldest known examples of information recording in analog form. The only way to copy a cave painting was to create another painting, close to the original. This situation continued for a long time until the development of the pantograph, an instrument that allows fairly accurate copying of planar line drawings. The subsequent invention of black and white photography provided the ability to faithfully copy images, beyond those of lines on a planar surface. The ability to produce color photographs extended the domain of images to color. Exceptions notwithstanding, in each of these cases, it was unlikely that a copy would have be mistaken for the original. This was due to the fact that it was virtually impossible to capture the precise value of any element in the original analog image. Further, the original and its copy would generally employ different materials.

Marshall McLuhan [1] had written, "The message is the medium." In the context of this chapter, this phrase recognizes the fact that with respect to the analog information, namely, the message, the medium is an essential part of the message recipient's experience. That is, the medium in which the message is expressed conveys a great deal of (meta) information, beyond the content of the message. For example, although today we can photocopy individual pages of a book with great fidelity, we are far away from being able to "photocopy" the entire book including the binding, covers, etc. Thus, along with the contents of the book, the binding, covers, etc., comprise the total message of the book. A "coffee table book" exemplifies the impact of the medium as distinct from the message.

Diffie and Landau [2] point out:

> "Scarcely a generation ago, phone calls traveled through wires between fixed locations, encoded as fluctuating electric signals. Now phones are mobile, and, through most of their journeys, phone calls are encoded in bits. Voices are digitized shortly after they leave the speaker's lips, carried over an IP network as packets, and returned to analog for presentation to the listener's ears."

S. Ghosh and E. Turrini (eds.), *Cybercrimes: A Multidisciplinary Analysis*,
DOI 10.1007/978-3-642-13547-7_4,

Digital representation of information is fundamentally different.[1] The reason is twofold. First, digital data must be transformed before presenting it to an individual, where the transformation is independent of the medium that delivered the data. That is, regardless of how a stream of digital data is delivered, the ultimate results are identical. For example, regardless of whether a digital movie is delivered through broadcast digital TV (DTV), a digital satellite or cable system, via a DVD, or downloaded via the Internet, the result is precisely the same set of images flashed on the television screen and identical sounds from the speakers. Second, digital data may be copied exactly, with no changes from the original data. No viewer may perceive any difference between the original and the copy, because there is no difference. Indeed, the notion of copy becomes meaningless, in the sense that the copy and the original are indistinguishable. Given that an original may be on a DVD and the copy resides on a hard drive, one can label them as different, but there is distinction without a difference.

Early on in the history of television, movie producers, primarily Hollywood studios, believed that the intangible and highly technical nature of analog TV signals would render it impractical for pirates to capture and distribute programs in an economically threatening manner, if not impossible. The development of the consumer videocassette recorder (VCR) proved them wrong. They sued the VCR manufacturers to prevent the introduction of VCRs and failed [3]. Ironically, the movie studios were able to generate a new revenue source through the sale and rental of recorded copies of their shows, a capability not previously available. Once this new market for recorded video had developed, the studios' subsequent concern was the sale of pirated copies of the videocassettes. They sought and obtained relief from the US Congress in the form of legislation that prohibited consumers from circumventing the technology used to prevent copying protected content [4]. Today, inexpensive devices abound that can capture unprotected analog TV signals, whether created by a broadcaster, playback of an analog videocassette, or playback of a digital disk; transform them into a digital representation; and then copy and distribute without authorization.

Early in the nineteenth century, Jefferson [5] stated, "he who lights his taper at mine, receives light without darkening me." Although literally true, the "keeper of the flame" would soon learn that the market value for his services is considerably reduced once a second or third flame becomes available. In the same vein, the uncontrolled spread of a specific information lowers the return to the originator.

In the analog world, where property is based on constituent atoms, the practical difficulties of making and distributing high-quality copies tend to constrain the economic benefits of copying. Thus, even though the modern photocopier can reproduce a textbook, one does not see unauthorized copies of textbooks advertised for sale. A number of such copies are sold in the vicinity of college campuses, often by students with a different "business model" than that of a mass-market pirate. In contrast, in the digital world, property is based on bits; the personal computer plays

[1] The preceding overview excludes consideration of text, which is digital.

the role of a universal copying machine; and the Internet is a ubiquitous distribution mechanism. Thus, while unauthorized copies can be sent around the world at virtually no cost and without significant fear of interception by the authorities, the widespread availability of unauthorized copies threatens the economic foundation of a number of industries. In the remainder of this chapter, we will examine key issues associated with these two very different worlds.

4.2 Law is Inadequate and Technology is Necessitated

When it comes to tangible copies of tangible products, a property owner can protect his or her interests against unauthorized copying in one of three ways. First, he or she can keep hidden knowledge of the key ingredients of the product or the entire manufacturing process. For a 1,000 years, the Chinese protected the precise ingredients and formula for preparing gunpowder and also protected the process of producing silk from silk moth cocoons, under the threat of execution. Today, soft drinks and perfumes are examples of products whose compositions are maintained secret. Similarly, semiconductor chips are manufactured through proprietary processes, with manufacturers claiming unique advantages for their own approach. Second, some products are protected by legal means. Trademarks and patents are used to limit those who may manufacture or import products into a country. Proprietary licenses are made available only to those who are willing to accept the terms and conditions of the licensors. Third, through high-cost capital equipment, some industries may indirectly establish a significant barrier, limiting potential copiers to those able and willing to make a similar investment. National currencies are typically protected in this manner. Certificates bearing holographic images are used to attest to authenticity and are an example of copy protection based on the requirement for high-cost and difficult-to-obtain equipment.

Even where technological and financial barriers fail to deter a copier or digital pirate, the products must be delivered to the consumers to generate profit. In an open, mass market situation, this provides the opportunity for law enforcement officials to track and locate the site of operation, forcibly shut it down, and apprehend the perpetrators. The equipment is impounded and destroyed, removing one unauthorized supplier from the market. This achieves a state of equilibrium where the volume of unauthorized copies, while not zero, is significantly reduced and it is no longer economically wise to expend further resources to recover additional market share. Thus, the role of the legal system is essentially to maintain a balance.

In the digital world, information products and other intellectual property are but bit streams. Regardless of the protections employed, the bit stream must be ultimately delivered to the customer. A number of schemes are deployed which limit the customer's direct access to the bit stream, while allowing him or her to use the bit stream for a specific purpose, including viewing a movie, listening to music, running a program, playing a game, or running a business. If the customer happens to be an information pirate and is somehow able to copy the bit stream, unauthorized copies may be generated and delivered to others. In contrast to the situation with tangible copies where shutting down an unauthorized manufacturer eliminated further copying of the goods, shutting down an information pirate does not completely eliminate the threat. At least one unauthorized copy of the bit stream continues to exist in cyberspace, unprotected and ready to be sold again. Once a bit stream is available without protection it is virtually impossible to return to the state where the owner had sole control over copying and sale of the item. Consequently, although the legal system may be successful in limiting the activities of individual pirates, it cannot secure the same degree of balance as with tangible products.

4.3 Content Protection Efforts

4.3.1 Copy Prevention

Relying on their experience in the "tangible domain," creators of information products attempted to develop systems to prevent users from copying bit streams and files.

4.3.1.1 "Uncopyable" Computer Files

Early in the history of personal computers, manufacturers developed an uncopyable disk program to prevent consumer from copying files. This was accomplished by using a proprietary "driver" program to write onto disks in a way that made them unreadable by the user's operating system. Authorized users were provided special driver programs to successfully read the disks. Hackers quickly developed their own driver programs to read and copy the supposedly uncopyable disks.

4.3.1.2 Dongles

Given that the software protection incorporated in the form of driver programs in uncopyable disks was defeated by hackers, vendors of high-value software, including computer-aided design systems, replaced the disk with a small, external device, called a dongle. The protected application could not be executed with the critical hardware support provided by the dongle. This use of hardware significantly raised the barrier to defeating the protection system. Although technically successful and in small-scale use today, this approach was inconvenient and expensive to achieve mass market penetration.

4.3.2 Licenses and Legal Agreements

It is a general practice to license, rather than sell, software, such that the license places limits on how users can employ the product. Typically, licenses limit copying and multiple uses of a product. Without additional technical means to enforce compliance, however, such provisions are frequently ignored or violated. Licenses have proven reasonably successful for commercial software used by large corporate entities. Business ethics coupled with the threat of prosecution result in reasonable compliance with the terms of the license. It is widely alleged that most consumers do not even bother to read the terms of the shrink wrap licenses or embedded user license agreements (EULAs) which are included within software and must be acknowledged for the software to perform. As a result, license terms are unknown and ignored.

4.3.3 Data Format as Barriers

When compact audio disks (CDs) were first introduced in the early 1980s, compact disk players were the only devices available to consumers that were capable of reading them. Creating a CD, i.e., writing onto a blank CD, required expensive capital equipment, which was available from a limited number of suppliers. The music industry felt secure in the thought that consumers would have no choice but to use the CD players and that only legitimate producers could create new audio CDs. Lured by this false sense of security, they recorded audio files on CDs in plaintext, i.e., without encryption. Within 10 years, it became possible for consumers using inexpensive CD "burners" to copy CDs onto "writeable" CD disks. Such copying, although far greater than mere annoyance, was not a mortal blow to the music industry. The use of a tangible medium (the CD) limited the impact of copying. However, within another few years, the situation changed dramatically. The widespread availability of high bandwidth connectivity ("broadband") to the Internet means that a consumer can make the contents of a CD available to anyone, anywhere in the world, by uploading its digital contents on a website on the Internet. The development of MP3, a system that allows the number of bits representing music to be reduced (compressed) by more than a factor of ten, made the transmission and storage of music fast and inexpensive. The rise of peer-to-peer file-sharing systems enable even technically unsophisticated consumers to obtain copied music free of payment. At the same time, a cultural shift occurred that lessened the stigma of this form of copyright theft.

Aware of the new landscape, movie studios attempted to restrict consumer access to movie files beyond that of music files. It was clear that even if DVDs were initially readable only in the DVD players, manufactured by legitimate manufacturers, DVDs would soon face the same fate as music CDs. DVD burners would become available on PCs, and movies would be read, distributed, and made into DVDs with ease. To thwart large-scale piracy, the movie industry encrypted (Content Scrambling

System, CSS) movie files before recording them on DVDs and attempted to control the sale of DVD stamping equipment. Single-layer DVDs with movies (or CDs with music) imprinted on them are created in ways remarkably similar to letterpress printing, namely, through embossing a pattern of depressions onto metal foil to represent 1s and 0s. This technology is not easily recreated, so control of the manufacturing equipment is a deterrent to piracy. Of course, in order for a movie to be viewed, every DVD player must come with its own decryption mechanism. The encryption algorithms remained secure until the unauthorized release of software and keys on the Internet. Soon, software was developed for PCs that could decrypt and copy movie files (DeCSS). The court trying MPAA's case [6] to remove DeCSS from websites stated, "In September 1999, Jon Johansen, a Norwegian teenager, collaborating with two unidentified individuals he met on the Internet, reverse engineered a licensed DVD player designed to operate on the Microsoft operating system, and culled from it the player keys and other information necessary to decrypt CSS." Quickly, using readily available compression software, consumers began widespread trading of movies on the Internet. As one consumer electronics manufacturer [7] observed, "Any consumer electronics system based on a global, shared secret, although it will last a few years, is doomed to fail. When it is broken (and it will be) Hollywood will insist on replacing it. Everyone wins: Hollywood gets to market their movies now, without waiting for development of a better system, they ultimately get the protection they want, and we get to sell two generations of consumer electronics."

4.3.4 Software-Based Copy-Protection Systems

Although specialized hardware represents the greatest barrier to hackers, computer software can be made sufficiently complex to discourage many hackers and most technologically novice consumers. However, software-based copy protection cannot withstand a determined attacker. Well-known techniques, including screen capture and snooping to obtain unprotected content, and in-circuit emulation and reverse-engineering to uncover the secrets incorporated by manufacturers to protect content. "Screen capture" programs make a copy of the information displayed on the PC screen and save it in a file. Thus, as each page of a copy-protected document is displayed on the screen for legitimate viewing, it may be copied. Manufacturers continually develop new software to defeat screen capture. However, as in any arms race, the latest anti-circumvention effort will inevitably fall victim to the next generation offensive weapon. "Snooping" is similar to screen capture, except that it copies information from within the RAM memory. Ironically, "cache snooping" was developed by advanced computer architects in the 1970s to improve computer performance. While the average user will not know where in memory particular information is stored, hackers develop snooping programs and target specific software copy-protection mechanisms, and then make them available on the WWW where anyone can download a copy and use them. "In-circuit" emulation uses specialized hardware to analyze each instruction of a program as it is running, with the goal of identifying the instructions that locate and utilize encryption keys. Reverse-engineering is a complex process of examining a software product and analytically discerning the underlying architecture as well as the embedded instructions. Using the information obtained, a pirate can then locate the secret key or the instructions that deploy the key to limit access to content.

Easily available through any search engine are many detailed descriptions of how to circumvent the software protection mechanisms of major applications. There are many examples of widely distributed "player software" systems that incorporate the functionality of a DVD player unit in a PC. Generally, end-users do not create their own unauthorized copies of material from originals – they obtain such copies created by others. In this way, a small number of unauthorized copiers provide widespread unauthorized access to content. Because there are no tangible copies, cost barriers of manufacturing and distribution are not relevant and opportunities for authorities to raid the manufacturing and distribution facilities are minimal.

4.3.5 Digital Millennium Copyright Act

The US Congress' Digital Millennium Copyright Act (DMCA) prohibits the development of "circumvention devices" or mechanisms designed to enable users to obtain access to copyrighted material, notwithstanding the manufacturer's use of technology to ensure protection. The interpretation and applicability of the law is, at best, fluid. No matter how those issues are resolved by the courts, to be truly effective similar laws must be in place worldwide. Until worldwide acceptance of such legal principles, pirates will continue to locate their wares and operations in "copy havens," where they can create circumvention devices with full immunity and place purloined contents on the WWW, available to anyone. Even the most optimistic view of legislation recognizes that it takes only a single, successful act of stealing content and making it available to defeat such protection.

4.3.6 Conditional Access

For content whose value to the consumer deteriorates very rapidly with time, for example, televised sporting events, copying does not pose a major economic threat to the producers. Under such circumstances, obtaining payment for *access* is often adequate. Paradoxically, even though long-term protection from copying appears less than significant, the difficulty of achieving protection for the short duration is not diminished. The vulnerabilities and techniques described earlier are exploited to obtain access without payment. Thieves may obtain access to encryption variables, equipment identifiers, or other secrets. Ironically, one of the strongest potential protections against theft of time-sensitive material was the individual circuit from the telephone company to a subscriber's residence. No secrets were needed. Without physical access to the wiring it was virtually impossible to obtain access. The protections afforded by this mechanism are fading as a result of the widespread use of "packet-based" systems (e.g., the Internet) in lieu of "circuit-switched" systems (e.g., land-based telephony).

4.4 The Nature of the Threat

In this section, we briefly explore three levels of threats that typically confront sellers of content.

4.4.1 Casual Copiers

The Copy Protection Technical Working Group (CPTWG) [8] has a working goal of "keeping honest people honest," an expression that describes the first level of threat and the resources available to small-scale, consumer pirates. A consumer pirate is an ordinary person who would occasionally make copies of videocassettes and make them available to relatives and a few friends. The industry considers such consumer piracy unacceptable, but not worth the investment of major resources. The greatest efforts directed against consumer piracy have been advertising and a series of lawsuits by the Recording Industry Association of America (RIAA). With peer-to-peer systems, the consumer does not directly make an illicit copy, but receives a copy, and consumer piracy has become a significant problem.

4.4.2 Peer-to-Peer Pirates

Peer-to-peer pirates have received great attention in the media. College students with easy access to high-speed Internet connections constitute a significant fraction of the population who make available to others copies of music and movies and download them for personal use. Undergraduate and graduate students of computer science and electrical engineering possess a wide set of highly advanced tools at their disposal, which can be utilized to realize piracy. Peer-to-peer pirates are generally not interested in selling content; most of them are driven by the challenge to defeat the protection systems and will expend a disproportionately high level of effort to break into systems. Upon success, they share their exploits with anyone and everyone on the Internet. The widespread dissemination of DeCSS (not an example of peer-to-peer software) and other exploits constitute evidence of their non-economic motivation, which is very hard to deter through established mechanisms.

4.4.3 Professional Pirates Who Profit from Distributing Large Volumes

The greatest threat to the content-based industries is posed by pirates who engage in the business of obtaining and selling content without authorization for their own profit. They are willing to lay out large sums of money to obtain access, distribute content, and cover their tracks. They will locate their operations whatever place offers them the greatest overall advantage, whether legal, technological, or economic.

In summary, content must be secured in all markets, at all points, and at all times. Once unprotected content becomes available to a pirate, the battle is lost. Content protection is an economic battle. A would-be pirate will generally give up if the cost and risk of obtaining content is not worth the potential rewards. The nature of rewards and resources differ for the three major categories of would-be pirates. Software-only solutions are inadequate and likely to be compromised relatively quickly. Some level of hardware involvement is advised, even if only to deter attacks on the underlying software.

4.5 What Can and Cannot be Protected?

Up to this point, the discussions have focused on the characteristics of systems used to protect against piracy. While it may appear that a perfect system to protect any content is elusive, we will explore important details.

As we had indicated earlier, entertainment content must be transformed from its digital representation to a suitable analog form so it may be perceived by a person. This represents an attack point for a pirate to intercept the analog stream and transform it into digital form for subsequent copying. Consider two scenarios. In the first, representing one extreme of size, we intend to protect a simple, 500-character message, "The recipe for a popular soft drink is ..." No matter how secure the transmission, upon receipt, an authorized must copy the message onto a writing pad. Later, the message can be entered into a computer and transmitted to anyone. In the second scenario, representing the other extreme of size, a high-definition movie contains over ten terabits (10^{12} or a million million bits) of data and it is not possible to copy the bit string manually. A large capital investment is required for the specialized automatic equipment needed to capture the bit string, due to its volume. High-definition movies are distributed to theaters and projected by secure equipment that are beyond the reach of everyone except the theater operators. Further, the projected content may be altered in subtle ways not noticeable by viewers ("watermarks") so that identifying information such as theater name, location, and time of projection are placed within the pirated video and render it traceable to the perpetrator [9]. Audio and music recordings fall between these two extremes of size and, using off the shelf equipment and without great expense, can be captured and digitally re-recorded at the point where they are available to listeners. Even if such an approach was precluded, this author believes that, regardless of the technology employed to secure audio and music, a set of high-quality microphones, located in a quiet environment in front of the loudspeakers is adequate to create a nearly identical copy.

We point out that any content must be subject to end-to-end protection. For, if unprotected at any point between creation and use, the content may be captured at the vulnerability point. Clearly, systems comprised of interconnected pieces must ensure that the constituent elements and the interfaces are protected. The situation is slightly better for computer software and other digital content that do not require to be converted into analog form. Unlike audio and movies, software programs typically operate within a PC and are never exposed to the analog world outside the computer.

4.5.1 The Price Point

While the focus of this chapter is technology, we point out that the market for pirated copies would disappear overnight if the price difference between a legitimate product and its copy drops dramatically. This calls for alternative business models that are based on lower consumer prices and new features that render technological protection unnecessary. There are clearly signs that the marketplace is moving in this direction. Both music and video are now available as inexpensive download and streaming options at such retail Internet outlets as Apple's iTunes, TunesPro, NetFlix, and Blockbuster. Beyond economic reasons, prevention of unauthorized copying is important in retaining one's ability to control his or her creations. European intellectual property law recognizes this as droit d'auteur an droit moral. The United States, which does not provide similar protection for artistic creations, witnessed skirmishes over the colorization of the classic black and white movies. There are other issues of individuals creating and distributing, whether or not for economic gain, unauthorized versions or edits of movies, as was the case with Star Wars: Episode 1 [10].

4.5.2 Cheaper to Buy than to Steal

As an additional level of protection, it may be worthwhile to lower the cost of a mass-produced item, where technically feasible, beneath the cost of making an individual copy. Consumers would more likely purchase than resort to illegal copying. The per-copy cost of a mass-produced CD or DVD is far below the cost of making a single copy for personal use. To this cost must be added costs for advertising, distribution, and content creation. Pirates pay none of these additional costs. Nevertheless, content producers are unwilling to lower the price of the mass-produced

CDs and DVDs. As described earlier, "read only" CDs and DVDs are mass produced by a process similar to letterpress printing. In contrast, a "writeable" CD or DVD is recorded by using a relatively high power laser to melt the recording material and create a "pit." The presence or absence of pits represents the stream of 1s and 0s of the audio or video stream. This serial recording process takes significantly more time and is inherently more expensive than merely stamping the metal foil at one time.

Making multiple copies of writeable CDs and DVDs is no different than making many different individual CDs and DVDs. Some have proposed the elimination of writable storage media, leaving only read-only DVDs. However appealing that may be to the content producers, the information technology industry's need for writable storage media negates the proposal outright. The European Union's Directive on the Harmonization of Certain Aspects of Copyright and Related Rights in the Information Society, passed in 2001, requires that member states ensure "fair compensation" to copyright holders for copies made via digital equipment [11]. Greece and Denmark have enacted laws and Germany is poised to enact a tax of $13 per computer with the possibility of an extending the tax to computer peripherals. Consumer electronics equipment, including the tape recorders, photocopiers, and scanners, are already taxed in many European countries. Blank magnetic media, e.g., recordable CDs and DVDs, are taxed in many countries, including the US and Canada.

4.6 Logical Consequences

It may be inferred that for protection, it is necessary either to (1) contain the information completely within a closed system, i.e., throughout its life cycle, or (2) protect the information after it exits the closed system in the form of a final product, including a printed page, image, or sound. These two ideas may lead to two very different manifestations, both from the technical and users' perspectives.

4.6.1 Closed Architecture

Under the closed architecture model, only those devices that are trusted members of the system would be permitted to receive and process secure information. It may be necessary for each device to possess the ability to authenticate itself when it requests connection to a device that is already included in the closed system and not require authentication by a centralized authority. For, then, the cost and delay associated with communication with a centralized authority at any time and from any place would be unacceptable. Thus, each device must contain a secret known only to all other trusted devices in the system. As discussed earlier, the use of a globally distributed secret is a flawed approach that creates a significant target. A determined adversary can mount an incremental attack over multiple devices, gaining access to the secret, little at a time, until the entire secret becomes known.

In many closed architecture systems, every devices must be built, by fiat, as trustworthy devices. As an example, the US Federal Communications Commission (FCC) enacted a requirement that all digital televisions must respond to the presence of a "broadcast flag" [12] associated with a television program by inhibiting that program from being output in digital form except on a trusted display or trusted device. An appeals court later overturned the requirement. The success of such a regulatory approach is inherently doomed for two reasons. First, a domestic pirate can modify an otherwise compliant television receiver to ignore the broadcast flag. Second, FCC's jurisdiction is limited to the US and cannot prevent individuals in other nations from utilizing non-compliant television receivers to intercept the broadcast signal and capture it on a recorder. This is especially true where a standard, such as that used for broadcast of digital television [Advanced Television Systems Committee (ATSC) A-53] is used both domestically and in other countries.

4.6.2 Open Architecture

In contrast to the closed architecture, under open architecture, while the content is distributed in protected form, only trusted devices can access the content. This approach, termed superdistribution, was first described by Mori [13] in 1980. Under this scenario, the infrastructure, including the Internet and other networks, do not need to be modified. Only trusted devices have the ability to access the protected content. While superdistribution permits end-users to copy the encrypted content, decrypt, and process it, and even (after re-encryption) redistribute it, the trusted devices must follow the rules established by the owner of the content. In essence, the customer becomes a part of the distribution chain. Each trusted device possesses a unique secret, i.e., known only to itself, that serves as the basis for authenticating the device. (For various reasons, device manufacturers may retain a copy of this secret information. That creates a second point of vulnerability. We ignore that in this chapter.) This poses a barrier to an adversary to acquire knowledge of a trusted device's secret through an incremental attack – especially where such an attack may require the destruction of multiple devices. Even if partial secrets of any number of trusted devices are obtained, it provides little or no advantage into determining the secret of any trusted device.

4.7 A Primer on Encryption

This section provides a non-mathematical overview of hiding information by encryption.

4.7.1 Nomenclature

The term "encryption" originates from the Latin root "crypt" meaning hidden, and represents the process of transforming an original (plaintext) message into a hidden (ciphertext) form. The reverse process, namely converting an encrypted, or ciphertext, message into its original plaintext form, is termed "decryption." A system based on encryption and decryption is called a cipher. A cipher works at the level of every letter or bit and, does not repeat the same substitution each time an identical string of letters or bits recurs. Given this property, known to mathematicians as a non-stationary process, ciphers can be extraordinarily difficult to analyze and "break." A cipher is a sequence of operations that replaces the plaintext with ciphertext depending on an initial secret "key." The length of the key determines the complexity of the cipher. A key length of n bits means there are 2^n possible keys. In the absence of a solution method for a cipher (ideally there is none), an attacker must try all possible keys, an approach known as "brute force." The complexity of the Advanced Encryption Standard (AES) [14, 15] is so great that it is estimated that to "break" it, i.e., to recover the plaintext of a message encrypted by AES, would require more time than the age of the universe.

4.7.2 Ciphers, Keys, and Security

To gain an insight into some of the characteristics of ciphers and their use, a re-examination of the common door lock may prove useful. For example, to allow a community of users to open or secure a door with a lock, one might choose among the following three approaches. First, one might design, build, and install a unique lock on one's own, providing a copy of the key to each user. In this case, the design of the lock is known only to the designer/builder and the lock's security is only as strong as the individual's personal skills and knowledge. Further, if any of the keys become available to an outsider, security is compromised and the lock must be re-keyed. Second, the community of users might jointly design, build, and install the lock. In this case, both the design of the lock and the key are available to each of the users. The security of the lock is improved as a result of the input and critical analysis from each user. However, the shared design secrets must be kept secure by each of the users. If any of the design secrets are compromised, the lock must be re-keyed. In the third approach, one might purchase a lock designed and built by acknowledged experts, where each individual who requires access is provided a unique "key" that will leave behind a distinct record of entry. In this case, the security of the lock does not depend on maintaining the secrecy of the design. This approach has two important advantages. As the design is not secret, the security analysis of the lock takes into account that attackers will have complete knowledge. Indeed, such open designs evolve and improve over time, as sources of vulnerabilities are discovered and removed. The security of the lock is only in the keys – the difficulty of determining one of the correct profiles from among, e.g., tens of millions of possibilities. Also, each user possesses an individual entry key and is motivated to safeguard it so that no one else can gain entry by using the key or a copy and implicate him or her. The commonly available door lock provides security through its design and construction. It was produced by experts and is the result of years of improvement and elimination of known vulnerabilities. The methodology to build a lock is well known, i.e., the use of pins and tumblers is known to lock makers as well as lock pickers. Yet, a high quality lock can be successfully operated only by an individual with the appropriately shaped key that embodies the precise length of the pins.

4.7.3 Secret-Key Encryption

Consider a combination lock, of the type found on the in-room safes used by many high-end hotels. Each time the lock is opened, the key is erased and the user must re-enter a new key to close the lock. This new key will be required to subsequently re-open the safe. Thus, anyone possessing knowledge of the new key is able to successfully open the lock. Symmetric-key encryption systems, where a single key is used both to encrypt and decrypt messages, is derived from the context of the mechanical lock and key. Locking and unlocking the system uses the same key. As long as all users transmit the key securely among themselves, the system remains uncompromised. In the event a user shares the key with an unauthorized party, the entire system is compromised. Symmetric-key systems are widely used by the military. Even if the encryption equipment is obtained by the enemy, the integrity of secret messages is not compromised. Normally, communications is generally limited to a pair of individuals, so the system's security depends on the integrity of only two individuals. When the key is shared among a group of users, each user represents a weak point, and the likelihood of compromise increases. A secret-key system requires a key-management authority, distribution infrastructure, and the discipline to coordinate the use of keys. Although not an absolute requirement, establishment of a key management authority provides the opportunity to concentrate resources toward the secure generation and distribution of keys. Unless the keys are synthesized with great care so that they lack any predictable order, a clever adversary may be able independently to construct them. For example, an early release of the Netscape browser used the value of the clock to create keys for a secure web session [16]. Hackers quickly were able to determine the keys. Following their generation, keys must be delivered securely and timely to legitimate users. Any attempt to use secret-key encryption for this phase would be circular effort, requiring the establishment of keys for the encryption of other keys. Last, users must be trained not to misuse keys, even inadvertently. While beyond the scope of this chapter, in a crisis, users are advised to refrain from re-using the keys as this would enable hackers to break into the system.

4.7.4 Public-Key Encryption

As a rough analogy, public-key encryption may be compared with a Post Office Box. For our example, we assume that the post office openly publishes the names of owners of post office boxes, allowing anyone to send a letter to the owner. However, only the owner of a post office box can unlock and obtain the letter. Public-key cryptography systems utilize mathematical techniques to generate a pair of non-interchangeable keys, one of which is the public key and the other is the private key. Neither key may be derived from knowledge of the other. The public key is analogous to the name of the owner of a specific PO box. It is openly shared with potential correspondents and is used to encrypt a message from a correspondent to the owner of the private key. The private key, known only to its owner, is the only key that can decrypt a sender's message that has been encrypted with associated public key. In addition to maintaining secrecy one characteristic of the use of public keys is that the owner of a private key cannot repudiate, i.e., deny responsibility, in the event the content of an encrypted message sent to him is found in plaintext. No one else could have decrypted the message that had been sent to him encrypted with his or her public key.

Public-key cryptography offers another, interesting attribute. If an individual encrypts a message with his private-key and releases the encrypted message to the world, anyone can decrypt it using the sender's openly available public-key. Although this does not provide security for the message, it provides authentication capability. The decrypted message must have come from the sender associated with the public key used for decryption. Only that sender, with unique access to his private key, can encrypt a message to be accessed by the public key. This creates an additional incentive for an individual to protect the integrity of his or her private key.

Public-key cryptography eliminates the need for centralized key management and avoids those vulnerabilities associated with the widespread distribution of secret keys. Members of a community may each place their individual public keys with a trusted third-party directory service and, as a result, they will be able securely to communicate among themselves. Should a new member wish to join the community, it must first establish its identity with the trusted third party and deposit a copy of its public key. The third-party directory service ensures the correct binding of each owner with its own public key, protecting against outsiders gaining access to the community by somehow inserting their public keys. Most importantly, at no time is any private key ever divulged.

4.8 Content-Protection Approaches

In an ideal world, there would be a universal content protection architecture encompassing personal computers as well as consumer electronics equipment, offering complete protection for any content. In the real world, however, products offered by vendors offer partial solutions limited to specific equipment and configurations.

Content protection is found in the form of standalone devices or of software modules for use on a PC. In the remainder of this section, we will first review the key components that require protection and corresponding products available in the market. Next, we will present the types of content protection available at different levels of implementation, including (1) system-level, (2) operating system-based, and (3) firmware-based.

4.8.1 Systems Providing Read Access to Content

A "reader" denotes a system or device that allows a user read-only access to content, and does not allow the user to modify content.

4.8.1.1 Software Devices Providing Read Access to Content

Among the best known PC-software products for providing read-only access are Adobe Corporation's Acrobat Reader and Microsoft's Media Player.

- Acrobat Reader, available without charge, permits the user to read documents prepared in the "portable document format" ("pdf") by the companion Acrobat software sold by Adobe. The author of a pdf file can specify the accesses available to a user, namely, print, modify, add annotations, etc. Thus, all information necessary to read a pdf document is contained in the reader and the document. Where a document is available to all users and symmetric-key encryption is used to protect content, a shared key must be used for all. The key must be securely hidden within the standard reader software or must be part of the document file with the intention of being visible only to the reader software. Either alternative presents a focused opportunity to obtain the key. "Advanced PDF Password Recovery," a tool available from software company, Elcomsoft, enables users to defeat the author restrictions placed on pdf files. A court found Elcomsoft not guilty of violating the DMCA [17] for selling a tool that allowed users to access the content of Adobe's e-book reader. The jury agreed that the software's stated purpose of allowing purchasers to make backup copies or to transfer copies to other systems for their personal use is permitted within the law.
- Media Player is distributed by Microsoft as a Windows component and works with the operating system to play audio and video files. The security underlying Media Player content protection was broken and the technique [18] described on the WWW. A determined hacker can successfully re-trace the steps of the "protection program," learn the location of the key or the steps necessary to re-create the key, and then use the duplicate key to extract the content. The bottom line: A software-only solution is not adequate to protect content.

4.8.1.2 Hardware Devices Providing Read Access to Content

In contrast to software, content protection that is built on a hardware and software platform offers significantly higher resistance to compromise. The hardware may be thought of as providing additional fortification that must be breached by an attacker. The simplest hardware approach erases the key(s) and programming when an attack (e.g., opening the hardware enclosure) is detected. As compared with software protection, hardware significantly increases the cost of attack both in time and in resources, so as to discourage the attacker. The hardware implementation must remain resistant to advances in technology for a reasonably long time to justify the increased cost of protection. Additionally, there must be avenues to update the hardware protection in the face of later developments. In the remainder of this section, we will analyze several devices that are available in the market.

- The "DVD player" represents an archetype of a system whose vulnerability stems from shared secrets. When the movie studios oversaw the development of security for DVD technology, few foresaw the widespread availability of broadband connections that would lead to the distribution of movies via the Internet. The industry chose an approach called "Content Scrambling System" or CSS in which a standard encryption system was used to encipher all movie content. The keys used would be available only within the confines of a DVD player. A closed system by design, only licensed DVD players have access to the industry's shared secrets as maintained by the DVD Copy Control Association [19]. A DVD player cannot output a digital signal and the analog output must comply with the movie industry's copy protection requirements. All DVD players incorporate Macrovision's copy protection technology [20] to protect against unauthorized recording of DVD programming and the protection is turned on under control of a signal on a DVD. As indicated earlier, after the DVD player's shared secrets were discovered and released on the WWW, anyone could download the program to retrieve the content encrypted on a DVD. No mechanism was provided to renew the secrets in DVD players, thus newly released DVDs are subject to immediate decryption. The movie industry did not discontinue releasing DVDs. The DVD Copy Control Association that licenses CSS has turned to the courts for protection. The World Airline Entertainment Association (WAEA) has released a security specification [21] for DVDs and players for in-flight entertainment systems. Each player will possess a unique private key that is erased when the player is removed from the aircraft. Each DVD will contain a set of "tickets", i.e., access conditions and keys for the encrypted movie on the DVD, valid for all players. Each ticket will be encrypted with the public key of one of the DVD players, so that a single pressing can be used to create DVDs for distribution to all airlines. If a DVD were to be stolen, it could not be played elsewhere, as the private keys capable of decrypting the tickets reside only in the DVD players in aircraft. If a DVD player is stolen, the private key would be automatically erased, rendering the player unable to decrypt the ticket on a DVD and unable to play the movie. This author expects that future DVD technology standards will refrain from relying on globally shared secrets.

- Current cable or satellite "set top boxes" provide owners with signals to their television sets for viewing. Previous generations of set top boxes relied on shared secrets and were soon hacked, allowing viewers to obtain unauthorized access to pay-per-view programming (i.e., without payment). Despite repeated refresh of the secrets by the cable and satellite companies, hackers resorted to reverse engineering and defeated the security every time. Current set top boxes employ an inexpensive, renewable, and removable security module, termed point of deployment (POD). Similar to DVD players, set top boxes incorporate licensed Macrovision copy protection for their analog outputs, which is controlled by a signal (the Broadcast Flag) accompanying the television program. Because of the transition to digital television in June of 2009, set top boxes output either a standard definition analog signal or a protected digital signal. (Many DVD players and BluRay players output a protected digital signal.) The protected digital signal uses the "High bandwidth Digital Copy Protection" (HDCP) to protect the content between set top box and display. The content is output in encrypted form and can be decrypted by an HDCP-compliant display. An important feature of HDCP is that it processes a "key-revocation list", which enables the system to be refreshed to exclude devices that have been hacked. Each newly released program contains an updated key-revocation list that will reset those players whose keys have been compromised.

  HDCP is an example of "Broadcast Encryption," which is similar to the use of a relatively small number of unique keys for a large set of automobiles. Although the number of possible keys for a given car make and model is in the thousands (and could easily be made to exceed the number of cars sold), the number of keys placed in use is limited, giving rise to rare but plausible scenarios where an individual inadvertently drives away someone else's car from the parking lot. With broadcast encryption an attacker might be able to glean a few bits of secret from each system attacked. However, combining the bits together is not likely to be fruitful since the bits would correspond to different keys. The other important characteristic of broadcast encryption is that upon detection of a compromise, all devices using the compromised key may be revoked and withdrawn from future use. This advantage is not unlimited, for when a sufficiently large number of keys have been discovered, keys will be revoked on many devices that are not involved. Only time will tell how well the balance has been drawn between the content owners' need for security and consumers' need for reliability.
- Many current"MP3" players employ proprietary and undisclosed content protection approaches. We believe that some players use a shared secret approach for keys, supplemented by a unique serial number, possibly serving as the basis of a secondary key that is used to prevent content from being shared among MP3 players.
- "E-books" have not yet met with great success in the marketplace, perhaps because readers prefer the look and feel of paper. The second generation "Kindle", by Amazon, has brought new levels of convenience to readers, both in usability and in the ability to wirelessly purchase and download books. For many e-book systems, especially those available as software for PCs, pirates have already

successfully reverse engineered the logic and created PC software that can be used to decrypt and distribute content.

4.8.2 System-Level Content Protection

Content protection is not a "feature" sought after by users. It is a requirement of content providers, to preserve the viability of their business model. If content protection mechanisms were incorporated at a deeper, system level, far below user-level application programs, users would have limited access to them and would be less tempted to attack the system. Such systems would also be less intrusive, perhaps invoking less resentment among users. Of course, it would not necessarily deter determined and technically capable pirates.

System-level content protection may be realized at either of two levels, namely, operating system (OS) or hardware-firmware. While system-level protection may raise the cost of piracy to a point where it is no longer worthwhile for a perpetrator to launch attacks, these techniques require extreme care in design and in implementation and are vulnerable to mistakes. Although the OS is more resistant to attack than application programs, it is by no means invulnerable. The end result is that an OS-level implementation lowers the likelihood of, but by no means eliminates, the possibility of a successful attack. As discussed earlier, a software-only approach cannot ensure complete protection. In a properly implemented hardware-firmware-based system, a pure software attack will not succeed – the system will not allow secrets to be exported by software. A hardware attack on such a system would result in erasure of the secrets, denying success to the attacker but, at the same time, rendering the system unusable. Consumers who do not attack their systems need not worry about this outcome.

4.8.2.1 Operating System-Based Content Protection

Mitsubishi's "ReEncryption" technology augments Microsoft's operating system in that whenever a file is written, it is encrypted with a key supplied by Mitsubishi's key-server. Encrypted files may be shared, but can be accessed only after a user obtains the appropriate key from the key-server. The technology, which is focused on enterprise-level file protection, assumes that an attacker is not able to mount a physical attack. That is, if the computer case is opened, the computer becomes inoperable until the administrator restores the system to operation. Since file decryption and encryption must occur utilizing a Microsoft interface deep within the OS, this software is deemed beyond the reach of the user. Furthermore, Internet connection is disallowed since network connections are neither encrypted nor protected.

Microsoft's "palladium" project, appeared to have been intended to develop a "trusted operating root," which would certify applications programs as trustworthy should data require trusted processing. The Trusted Computing Group created

[6] US Court of Appeals for the Second Circuit. Docket No. 00-9185, Argued: May 1, 2001, Decided: November 28, 2001. Technical report, 2001.
[7] Copy Protection Technical Working Group. Private conversation in the hallway at a meeting.
[8] Retrieved from http://www.cptwg.org/
[9] Cinea. (2002, October 9). Cinea announced it was awarded a $2M grant from national Institute of Science and Technology to develop its anti-piracy technology to prevent digital camera capture of movies.
[10] Kraus, D. (2001, November 5). *The Phantom Edit, Salon.com*. Retrieved from http://dir.salon.com/ent/movies/feature/2001/11/05/phantom_edit/index.html
[11] Official Journal C 180 of 25/06/99. Amended proposal for a European Parliament and Council Directive on the harmonisation of certain aspects of copyright and related rights in the Information Society. COM (1999) 250 final of 21/05/99.
[12] FCC Press Release. FCC EXPLORES DIGITAL BROADCAST COPY, 8 August 2002.
[13] Mori, R. et al. (1990). Superdistribution: The concept and the architecture. *Transactions of the IEICE, Tokyo, E73*(7), 1133–1146.
[14] US Department of Commerce. (2001, December 4). Press Release. http://www.nist.gov/public_affairs/releases/g01-111.htm
[15] AES. AES Homepage on the National Institute of Standards and Technology website. Retrieved from http://csrc.nist.gov/CryptoToolkit/aes/
[16] Goldberger, I, & Wagner, D. (1996, January). Randomness and the Netscape Browser. *Dr. Dobb's Journal*, pp 66–70.
[17] San Jose Division United States District Court for the Northen District of California. United States of America v. Elcom Ltd., a/k/a Elcomsoft Co., Ltd. and Dmitry Sklyarov, Case No.: CR 01-20138 RMW. Technical report.
[18] The pseudonym of the author Screamer. Retrieved from http://cryptome.org/
[19] Retrieved from http://www.dvdcca.org/faq.html
[20] Retrieved from http://www.macrovision.com/solutions/video/copyprotect/index.php3
[21] WAEA Specification 0598. Retrieved from http://www.macrovision.com/solutions/video/copyprotect/index.php3
[22] Attanasio, C. R. (1973). Virtual machines and data security. *Proceedings of the Workshop on Virtual Computer Systems*, Cambridge, MA.
[23] Schneck, P. B. (1999, July). Persistent access control to prevent piracy of digital information. *Proceedings of the IEEE* (pp. 1239–1250).

Chapter 5
Information Security

Richard Stanley

5.1 Introduction

In the field of information security, it is commonly accepted that security belongs at the lowest possible level of the processing stack [1]. If affirmative, one might ask, why is the issue of application security even being considered? Applications, after all, sit at the very top of the stack. The analog of a house built on a firm foundation is well known and easily understood. If he foundation is unsound, no structure will stand on it for too long. What is less well understood is that the converse is equally true. No matter how strong the foundation, where the house erected on the foundation is flimsy, the overall structure is unsound. The same is true with information security. It is essential that the foundation be sturdy, through the constituent ingredients, including secure operating systems. However, if the applications are not also secure, the user is lulled into a false sense of security. Application level security seeks to provide another layer of protection at the layer where most users interact with the system. It inevitably requires the foundation of security at the lower layers, for without these there are no "hooks" to provide the basic security functions so vital to overall system security.

Modern computer applications are extremely complex. The most common microprocessor contains millions of transistors, organized into tens of thousands of circuits. A human being can comprehend it only at a very high level of abstraction. Today's computers are essentially designed by other computers running programs written by large teams of individuals, not a single person. The Windows XP operating system alone contains over 35 million lines of code [2], and the applications that run on it are equally complex. Presently, there are no known ways to test exhaustively software of that level of complexity. Consequently, bugs are inevitable, almost given. In addition, complexity makes it difficult to monitor accurately the machine state in real time and to infer precisely if the current condition represents a security violation, normal operation, or operator error. Bugs and complexity are the entry mechanisms of choice for those who would compromise system security. Surprisingly, it also turns out that the operating signature of the most sophisticated and intensive system users looks a great deal like the operating signature of malevolent actions. This only serves to further complicate the problem.

S. Ghosh and E. Turrini (eds.), *Cybercrimes: A Multidisciplinary Analysis*,
DOI 10.1007/978-3-642-13547-7_5, © Springer-Verlag Berlin Heidelberg 2010

This chapter addresses technological threats and potential solutions. We must constantly bear in mind, however, that technology does not act alone. It responds to human input. To steal a line from the National Rifle Association, computers do not break into computers, people do. There is no "silver bullet" that will put and end to the security problem, nor is there a suite of technology that will make this problem go away. Security is, at its heart, a problem resulting from human behavior, and any effective measure of dealing with it must be multidisciplinary. We will examine in this chapter technical problems and tools that enable people to attack information systems. Their motives are identical to those that have driven criminals since Cain and Abel in the Bible. We ignore this reality of the security landscape only at our peril.

5.2 Current Technological Threats

5.2.1 Trusted Computing

The goal of information security efforts is to provide a trusted computing environment. Trusted computing infers a closely-knit suite of software programs operating on a hardware computing engine and a network base that provides security features from the bottom layer of the protocol stack all the way up to and through the topmost, application layer [3]. The theory is great, but the devil is in realizing the details.

Secure computers have been a goal of information security technologists since at least the 1970s. Working at MITRE Corporation for the US Air Force, research scientists David Bell and Leonard LaPadula developed a basic computer security theorem in the 1970s, based on the model of a computer as a finite state machine [4]. Leaving the technical details aside, the theory essentially states that if we place secure information into a computer, and all the transitions that the computer undergoes from one state to another are secure, then the output information is guaranteed to be secure. A state is a precise description of all of the constituent elements of the machine and the computer typically experiences transitions between billions of states every second. A secure operating system, Multics [5], was actually built and used for many years. It implemented Bell and LaPadula's basic computer security theorem, becoming the only general purpose operating system to be awarded a B2 security rating under the US DoD's Orange Book criteria. Multics was not a commercial success, for multiple reasons. First, it was too costly. Second, the need for security beyond the military environment was unclear. The real problem, however, was much more basic.

In reality, when a provably secure software program, say an operating system, is installed on a real computer, it ceases to be provably secure. The reason is that the underlying computer cannot be easily proven to be absolutely secure. Although hardware appears to be quite stable, the data inside it is fragile and the devices used to build computers are more stochastic, i.e., probabilistic, rather than absolutely deterministic. Thus, while the average numbers of holes and electrons flowing across a P-N junction of a transistor may be computed, the exact number of carriers at any instant of time is subject to Heisenberg's Uncertainty Principle and cannot be known with any precision. Even a passing cosmic ray can flip a bit from 0 to 1 or vice versa, destroying the integrity of the entire system. Put differently, the real machine potentially contains states that cannot be captured in the state model, which is at the heart of the security model.

Around the same point in time as Multics' introduction, computers began to be networked. Securing a single computer is possible, though difficult. Securing a network to the standard of mathematical precision is virtually impossible and unrealistic. These unfortunate but true facts stunted the development of secure software, and launched a trend wherein the dominant paradigm was to brush aside any genuine concern for security in the design of computers and applications that execute on them.

Trusted computing seeks to enforce the stated system security policy [6], a key being the principle of least privilege. That is, users are granted only those privileges that are absolutely necessary for them to perform their legitimate functions, and no more. The trusted computing system keeps users within their defined bounds, and raises an alarm if the users themselves attempt to increase their privilege level, or if their privilege level is increased by any unauthorized means. In practice, this is more easily said than done. Defining the bounds of a user's privilege is difficult, both because people are often pressed into duties exceeding the norm, and also because no one wants to remain on the "outside." Those who define user privileges are constantly beset by demands for increased privileges from all categories of users. Of course, there are those who regard any use of certification by some third party as a threat [7]. Even in the best of worlds, creating and maintaining a set of viable user privileges requires dedicated management support and staffing, two areas increasingly seen as overhead costs to be eliminated in the interest of efficiency.

In many ways, legal arguments and concerns appear to have outrun technology and unwittingly stunted its growth. Where no one has successfully demonstrated a trusted computing solution, two arguments are conceivable. First, trying to develop a genuine solution is too expensive to be practical. Second, even if one were to make an attempt and get it wrong [8], the liability would be immense. The situation is worsened by the acute difficulty of computing the return on investment (ROI) for information security. While costs tend to be well known and computable, the benefits are hard to measure. As an analogy, consider the current model of fire insurance on a dwelling and our current practice. For the most part, prudent people carry fire insurance to replace or repair their homes in the unfortunate event of a fire. Clearly, if the home does not burn down during the time period of the policy, the owner does not demand the premium back, complaining that the money has been wasted. On the contrary, the owner looks back at the past year, expresses a sigh of relief, and pays for the subsequent year's coverage. This model and mindset is acutely lacking in the world of secure computing. Perhaps, it should be more common.

Given that there has been little impetus for the development of secure information systems, it is no surprise that security problems persist. In the remainder of this chapter, we will discuss the technical nature of some of the most common security issues; followed by potential technological solutions; and then the human factors that enable and exacerbate these security problems, with an emphasis on their impact in law enforcement.

5.2.2 Software Weaknesses: A Root Cause

Although a mathematically-provable trusted computing platform is elusive, an environment that provides a reasonable degree of security is realistic and achievable. As we have seen, this has not been the tradition. As a result, the combination of insecure computers and insecure operating systems running insecure applications has become the norm rather than the exception. In general, software developers believe, and until quite recent rightly so, that users are unwilling to pay for security, so they ignore it. If the programmers had only paid attention to the security issues as they were developing the code [9], many of the program features, including buffer overflows, which are regularly exploited to compromise security, would have been eliminated. As a result, users have to live with the consequences of their decisions.

It is obvious that developing secure software to execute on top of insecure operating systems is a waste of time and energy. Most earlier consumer-oriented operating systems, including Windows 95, 98, and ME, as well as most of the pre-OS X Macintosh systems, are simply not capable of providing security. They reveal no security features in their design. Security in the operating system requires moving to some version of Unix, Linux, Windows 2000, XP, or Vista, and installing a secure file system such as NTFS. The FAT16/32 file systems in older Windows products lack the ability to store any security labels or other information and are inherently insecure. Indeed, if one insists on a FAT32 file system with an otherwise secure OS, one has only the illusion of security; the necessary tags and labels are simply not there. The newer operating systems, while capable of providing a very good level of security, frequently require a significant investment in training and maintenance to achieve an acceptable security level [10]. Security is a process, not a single event, and requires significant commitment and investment.

We will subsequently examine how software is exploited to compromise system security. In most countries and under many situations, such exploitations are deemed either intrinsically criminal or that they directly enable behavior that is in and of itself criminal. In Canada, for example, Criminal Code §342.1 (c) would apply. Regardless of criminal intent, poor system security should be a cause for serious concern. The integrity of the data in the information system – its very sine qua non – becomes a constant suspect. If the data that is generated from all this costly information processing machinery cannot be relied upon, what have we achieved?

5.2.3 Malicious Code: Viruses and Worms

Of the many threats to application programs, the most frequently encountered technical threats include viruses, worms, and other forms of malicious code [11]. The ultimate source of the threats is people, which we will discuss later in this chapter. At this point, we will focus on understanding the tools that people deploy to compromise the security of computers and networks. All of these tools exploit faults in the application software, the underlying operating system, or create a situation in which security can be compromised. These programs are composed with the intent that users, who lack a true understanding of the real function of the malicious code, will be lured into executing them on behalf of the perpetrator. Much has been written about these malicious programs, but most of them, especially those "explanations" found in the popular press, are inaccurate. As a result, they unwittingly cause more problems. Malicious code is the overarching term for software that executes on a computer without the consent or frequently without the knowledge of the user and accomplishes objectives contrary to those of the legitimate owner [12]. Some malicious programs are disguised as useful utilities such as file explorers, and usually do a very good job at their stated task. In the background, unseen and unbeknownst to the user, they do their dirty work, such as logging all keystrokes and sending them to the perpetrator for analysis.

Malicious code can comprise everything from viruses to freestanding applications. Viruses, to be a purist, are code segments that attach themselves to other executable code such as elements of the operating system [1] which perform useful tasks. A true virus, similar to its biological analog, cannot harm the host all by itself; it must insert itself into executable code. A biological virus is "... somewhere between being living and non-living"; it is nothing more than a partial strand of DNA or RNA that must attach itself to a cell in order to access a "factory" to replicate itself [13]. In the process, it disrupts the normal functioning of the cell, and the byproducts of this infection can cause illness or discomfort in the host organism. A software virus does the same thing to executable code. Not long ago, true viruses were the primary threat to computer software. Perhaps, the increased sophistication of software or the decreased sophistication of users and cyber criminals have rendered other approaches more attractive, probably because they are easier to implement.

Just like its biological analog, a creature that exists in its own right, a software worm is a program in its own right. A software worm is an actual program that is capable of doing mischief on its own; it does not require a host, as does the virus. This fine distinction is missing in nontechnical reports and many instances of worm-based computer mischief are otherwise attributed to viruses. It is unlikely that this fine distinction will ever be rectified, and we can expect future software exploits to be erroneously described as viruses. Ordinarily, this would be of little concern outside academia. However, many texts and guidelines have been written that fail to recognize the difference and following their advice blindly can lead the unwary user into serious trouble. For example, it has been long believed that simple text files cannot harbor viruses, and were therefore "safe." That is true. But simple text files have largely been replaced by complex word processing files and HTML documents, which can definitely harbor worms and other forms of unsafe active code. Arguably, a Microsoft Word document file or an Excel spreadsheet is a program that is interpreted line by line by the host application to present the document to the user. These files routinely contain macros and Visual Basic code. They are far from being flat files.

A common technique used to attack application software is labeled buffer overflow [1]. A buffer refers to a finite section of the computer's memory that is temporary allocated to hold specific data. When one types on the keyboard, for example, the keystrokes are collected in a buffer until the computer is ready to receive and process them. Since the computer is significantly faster than human programmers, for efficiency reasons, multiple keystrokes are usually collected in the buffer before they are transferred to the main application. Following the successful transfer, the buffer is emptied and it is ready to accept new keystrokes. By the same token, when it is full, the buffer should refuse additional keystrokes. Otherwise, the previously collected keystrokes would be accidentally erased. In reality, buffer management algorithms are often poorly written and, as a result, they keep accepting data until either the data source stops transmitting or the buffer overflows. Just as an overfull garbage can, the data runs out of space allotted for it and it begins to fill other memory segments located above the space originally intended to serve as the buffer memory. Often, those parts of memory are used to hold the operating instructions for the application under execution. A clever attacker can choose what extra data to send to the buffer, with the result that the application's code can be modified in near real time. This provides the attacker control of the application [14], which can then be exploited to modify how the application works. The user is generally completely unaware of the activities.

Good programming practices and standards are necessary to prevent buffer overflows. Programming is unlike drilling holes; there are no standard size inputs. Given the indeterminate number of ways in which a software program may be composed, each programmer develops a unique code and the end result is generally measured by whether or not the program works correctly. Little effort is expended to investigate and eliminate buffer overflow problems, primarily because such efforts would invariably slow down code development and delay the release of the application in the market. Although leading software professionals have been trying to enforce programming standards for at least two decades, common standards are yet to be widely accepted. The reason is that customers are unwilling to pay for security until their machines have been compromised. By then, it is too late. Modern applications are immensely complex and efforts to reverse engineer them to locate and exterminate security problems is inevitably uneconomical and virtually impossible.

The attack strategy for most worms is to overload computers and networks, computationally, thereby forcing them to simply come to a halt. No computer nor network has infinite capacity. If they are forced to generate one megabyte bogus files forever, eventually they will run out of resources and halt. Rebooting the computer or network may not help unless the root cause of the problem has been eliminated. Worms can arrive as free-standing programs, or they may have been implemented as macros or Visual Basic script in word-processing documents or spreadsheets. There are several toolkits available to create worms, and even a marginally capable programmer should be able to author a worm that can have worldwide impact in a matter of few minutes. In February 2001, a Dutch hacker used such a tool to write the infamous "Anna Kournikova" worm [15]. These toolkits often exploit a loophole found in many countries, namely, while creating and disseminating a worm is illegal, creating a toolkit falls on the right side of law. As long as the toolkit author is careful not get caught actually writing worms, no law has been violated. The Internet has facilitated the distribution of malicious code much faster today than just a few years ago. While the preferred method of malicious code propagation in the past involved a floppy disk which needed to be inserted into a computer drive in order to infect that machine, today, it is possible to infect numerous machines all over the world in a very short time.

Worms have also been observed to arrive on unsuspecting users' computers by way of an email attachment that contains mobile code, which we will examine in Sect. 5.2.4 subsequently.

5.2.4 Mobile Code

Mobile code refers to software code that is transmitted from one location to another. Unheard of a decade ago, today, it is necessary for the correct operation of many network-based application features [1]. While surfing the Internet, most users have encountered mobile code, unbeknownst to them. For example, the clever animated advertisements are enabled by mobile code. The ability of shopping sites to track the preferences of shoppers is also enabled by either mobile code or another piece of code termed a cookie, which may contain unauthorized executable code. Mobile code facilitates the ability to play video games with people half the world away and it has become a major business. As a visually stimulated species, we are much more viscerally attracted to activities that are dynamic relative to stationary activities. As a result, often, our actions are illogical. For example, consider that during a computer session, users are presented with a warning screen that states, "WARNING! By pressing the OK button, you will see a video of dancing pigs. In addition, your bank account will be debited $10,000, your home will be foreclosed, and your firstborn child will be sold into slavery." In the author's experiences [16], nearly everyone will press the OK button! Researchers in psychology have illustrated this human trait time after time and law enforcement officers are all too familiar with it.

Mobile code is not necessarily malevolent but there is no certainty about its nature. The challenge is that computer applications almost never seek the users' permission before accepting mobile code. Ironically, if the user were to be asked, it is more likely than not that the user will choose the dancing pigs. In addition, most dialog boxes are not as specific as the notional one about the pigs. Users have been conditioned to click on "OK" even where the act signifies acceptance of a major processing fault. Even veteran computer professionals have a hard time figuring out the function and intent of some specific mobile code. The mobile code arrives, unannounced, unheralded, and without the user's knowledge and permission. While the intent may be good or to compromise the machine, one can be certain that where a mobile code originates from a cybercriminal, the result is always grief.

Mobile code usually consists of programs written in languages including Java, JavaScript, Visual Basic Scripting language, or ActiveX controls; however, code written in any computer language may be cast to run as mobile code. The aforementioned languages merely facilitate that objective. Each of the different kinds of mobile code has its own set of advantages and disadvantages from the security and functional points of view. Entire books have been written about each of them and a detailed discussion is beyond the scope of this chapter. A critical property of mobile code is that, when correctly written, it is capable of matching any authorized user's actions and operations on an information system. Therein lie its power and its potential threat. It can completely take over control of an information system, carry out the programmed tasks, cover its tracks, and delete itself when its objective has been accomplished. It can steal all that is of value on the system and then destroy the evidence. Many tools exist to help control the actions of mobile code. In the past, the simple solution was to disable mobile code completely, which does not appear to be a feasible alternative, as many desirable functions (such as calculating mortgage payments) may depend upon it. Instead, each system must be analyzed to determine its exact mobile code needs and all other mobile code activities should be disallowed. This is a nontrivial task, requiring detailed analysis of the system operations and a lengthy, iterative approach to implementation. It is imperative that information security and law enforcement professionals should be cognizant of mobile code and that, to enforce security, mobile code cannot be given free rein on information systems.

In 1997, a group of German cybercriminals known as the Chaos Computing Club developed mobile code using Microsoft's ActiveX controls, which permitted them to exploit the Quicken home finance program [17]. Unbeknownst to the user, this piece of mobile code could enter the user's computer and transfer funds from one or more of the user's accounts to a different account, belonging to the author of the mobile code. This exploit was even demonstrated on German television, with the Chaos Computing Club assuring viewers that they had never actually conducted such an attack. First, no one can be certain of the claim. Even if the statement were true at the time it was first stated, there is nothing to prevent an exploit in the future. Intuit, the manufacturer of Quicken, quickly rushed a new version of their software into the market, claiming that the new version was immune to the attack. Intuit also assured their North American customers that such an attack would fail to penetrate the North American versions of Quicken, citing that the versions required preauthorization for accessing online accounts, which had been disabled in the German version. Of course, Intuit's assurance means little since mobile code may be easily written to establish just such a preauthorization dialog box on selected accounts found in a user's database. The author is not suggesting that current versions of Quicken are vulnerable to this attack; we just don't know. However, it is prudent to suggest that every software product needs to be thoroughly investigated for to ensure security be assured. The workload may be enormous.

One might think that these problems are behind us, given the date of the Quicken exploit. That would be a grave mistake. Mobile code attacks occur with painful frequency. Attacks based on e-mail, including the "I Love You" and "Anna Kournikova" worms are so frequent and so costly that they are often reported in the pages of the popular press. While technologically unsophisticated, these attacks are responsible for considerable losses to the victims. The losses fall into the categories of the cost to remove the worm; costs of surveillance to attempt to avoid such attacks in the first place; opportunity costs, i.e., business lost while systems were out of service due to the worm; and liabilities resulting from being a witting or unwitting site used to distribute the worm. The "Love Bug" worm, a relatively simple exploit written by a Filipino student, is estimated to have cost between US$8.7 B and US$15 B to exterminate [18].

A challenging problem is to document the economic and other damages caused by a mobile code for the purpose of prosecution. The "Anna Kournikova" worm was written using a virus-writing toolkit [19]. It started to function at the beginning of the business day in the Pacific Rim, resulting in widespread damage to businesses in Australia, New Zealand, and Japan. By the time business opened in India and points west, the word was out, and most networks had put in place crude but effective barriers to the worm. The perpetrator, a young Dutch male, had failed to mask the IP address of his computer and was arrested by the Dutch police within a day or so of his exploit. Powerful toolkits had placed a serious level of illegal conduct within the reach of anyone capable of maneuvering a computer mouse. Although some estimates of loss ranged into the tens of billions of dollars, the US FBI was able to document only US$166,827 in total damages to 55 victims, which was used in the prosecution [20].

Perhaps, the most pernicious aspect of mobile code is that it can be used to open a door into the unsuspecting user's computer and network for a wide variety of malicious actions over time. Worms are nuisances, but mobile code is capable of providing a "back door" into the computer that can stay in place for a long time [21]. We note that a network is only as secure as the least secure computer connected to it. Where all computers on a specific network are allowed specific access privileges since they belong to the network, malefactors need only to gain access to one of the networked machines in order to gain a "place at the table." One of the most common ways to do this is to modify applications so that the criminal is able to access the computer and network at will.

5.2.5 Illicit Connections

The easiest way to gain access to the data on a computer or network is to connect to the target system when desired and acquire the maximum level of privileges. This is the common goal of sophisticated cyber criminals, and many tools exist to help achieve the objective. These tools are freely available through the WWW and the Internet, generally, free of cost [22]. Unlike in the past, most computers today are networked. Even the home laptop or the office desktop that facilitates Internet surfing and access to the workgroup network is vulnerable to attack, 24 h a day from virtually anywhere on earth, with a fast-growing variety of technologically sophisticated attacks. Cybercriminals are very good at using many intermediary computers to cover their tracks, so tracing the source of the attack is a nontrivial problem. Although tools exist to help determine whether an attack is underway, they are not free. It costs time and money to install, configure, and monitor such applications. Furthermore, none of the attack detectors are foolproof. Cybercriminals often target theft of the data on targeted information systems. For example, credit card numbers are valuable and readily marketable worldwide. There have been many examples of thieves stealing data from databases and either holding them for ransom or selling it to the highest bidder. Such events create adverse publicity for the victimized organizations, often leading to reluctance in reporting the incident to law enforcement and to collect and provide requisite evidentiary material [23]. Although understandable, this human reaction only serves to increase the impact of the current and future crime.

Theft of service is also a frequent goal of cybercriminals and has been a popular target since the early days of computing when service was available only through the computing service bureaus. Theft of service continues to be popular since it provides the promise of anonymity. By stealing any magnitude of service, cybercriminals are able to route their cybercrimes through trusted information systems, including hospitals and government agencies. Although there is a cost to the victimized information system, the real problem is the risk of liability as an accomplice to the crime. Tort law generally requires service providers of every kind to exercise due diligence in the conduct of their duties and to observe the standard of care expected of a "prudent man [24]." Increasingly, the ultimate victims of cybercrime have adopted the philosophy of filing suit against all those whose information systems have been participants, wittingly or not, in the commission of the ultimate crime. In an environment where liability insurance covering such eventualities is scarce, one would think that this overhanging liability would have caused corporate information system operators to demonstrate more prudence and attention to security. On the whole, this does not appear to be the case.

In addition to outright theft of service and data, there are other incentives for cybercriminals to gain unauthorized entry to information systems. One in particular is to gain the ability to modify critical data, unbeknownst to the user. As a result, a criminal can completely distort or destroy the operations of the victims. Selective modification of data, for instance, could cause a victim organization to order much more equipment than it actually requires, tying up excessive current assets and even facing bankruptcy. As a true anecdote, which occurred inadvertently in the 1960s during a conversion from manual to punched card systems, Britain's Royal Air Force, which normally kept ten sets of family housing furniture for troops posted to the Middle East in storage in Bahrain, sent instead one thousand such furniture sets to the storage facility. The data entry clerk had inadvertently placed the decimal point in the wrong place. As reshipping the goods back to the United Kingdom was deemed too costly, they were placed in storage and may be there to this day. It's a humorous story when it relates to the infamous "government incompetence" syndrome but it is grim when a company's credit line is maxed out because someone is fiddling the accounting books from the outside.

5.2.6 Eavesdropping

Nowhere is information more vulnerable to inadvertent disclosure than when it is being handled by the end application. Here the data is created, modified, formatted, and processed. In general, before data is archived or transmitted, it is encrypted. To an application, however, encrypted data is gibberish and it must be decrypted before it may be processed. Thus, at the end application, data is in its raw form i.e., without any protection of encryption, and poses a lucrative target to the cybercriminal, given its value to the legitimate owner. Even the best encryption tools are impotent to protect data when it is being processed by an application. It is not difficult for an attacker to get control of an application and intercept the raw data.

Eavesdropping in the computing world is similar to classic wiretapping, but with an important difference. Where one employs encrypted transmission, an eavesdropper listening on the network must engage in cryptanalysis to learn the contents of the underlying data. While this is technically possible, given the strengths of today's ciphers, it may require significant time. Where the code is finally broken, it is unlikely that the underlying data would be of great value. For example, it would do little good to learn today that the Japanese had planned to attack Pearl Harbor on December 7, 1941. If the US had known about it prior to December 6, 1941, it could have been useful.

Imagine, however, that instead of encountering encrypted data, the attacker had gained access to the keystrokes and mouseclicks that created or edited the data or a shot of the user's computer screen. Today, these are no longer in the realm of science fiction; they are not only feasible, they are readily available and inexpensive. Under the pretext of monitoring employee web-surfing, small devices have been developed to capture all keystrokes on a target computer and which are installed between the keyboard plug and the socket on the computer. A few of these hardware devices come with internal memory to store keystrokes, while others transmit them to a file or to a different computer on the network. The information can be viewed using a password-protected option in a standard word processing program. The keyboard connection supplies the small amount of power required to operate the hardware key logger and they cost less than US$80 in small quantities [25]. In addition to hardware key loggers, software versions are available at less cost, around US$30 [26]. One may argue that under an aggressive physical security policy, these devices could not be installed. However, these devices would require only a moment to connect and are small enough as to be physically unobtrusive. Besides, when was the last time a user thoroughly checked out what was plugged into the back of the computer?

Even where a hardware or software logger is installed deliberately for the purpose of monitoring employee web-surfing, it is difficult to guarantee its operational integrity. One cannot be certain that the device only monitors the keystrokes for the employer, as opposed to capturing and transmitting them to a competitor. Verifying the operation of such a device is not straightforward; at the least, inputs and outputs must be monitored for a long period to determine if anything unexpected is being transmitted. One must also consider the possibility that malicious code on the host computer may corrupt or co-opt the software underlying the device. In the same vein, there is no technical barrier to developing similar devices for insertion between the computer and the video monitor. Although the signals are more complex, they are of known format and data captured can be readily saved and reinterpreted somewhere else at a later time. The argument that such devices are too difficult or too costly to develop is simply without merit.

An age-old form of eavesdropping is simply looking over the shoulder of the computer operator while he or she types on the keyboard or reads a document of interest. This technique, termed shoulder-surfing, is a popular sport, and many screen-savers offer "instant-on" keys to enable a user to quickly activate the screen saver when someone else walks into the office. While someone standing and looking over the user's shoulder for a long period is likely to attract attention, such activity happens all the time on long airplane trips, and valuable information has been given up by having it read by competitors from a laptop computer enroute across an ocean.

Even more disturbing, technological developments have made it possible to read and recreate images of a computer screen through a glass window at a distance of several tens of feet. It had long been believed that computer screens could not be read at a distance, especially from a significant angle off the perpendicular to the screen. This turns out to be incorrect. Not only can the screen be read, it can be captured in real-time. The clever eavesdropper can now gain access to the keystrokes as well see what is being displayed on the computer screen. This is clearly not good news for application security, and requires the application of active countermeasures. For one, computer screens that routinely display sensitive information should be moved away from windows. Conceivably, while a user is working on a computer system, an eavesdropper can "listen" to the electromagnetic signals that are generated and radiated into space or carried through the wires and cables that connect to the system. Modern desktop and laptop computers employ bus speeds, the rate at which information moves between the internal components, on the order of 667 MHz or higher, a frequency close to those used for communications. These signals can be picked up by modern scanners up to a reasonable distance away from the source. The entire area of compromising emanations from information systems is labeled TEMPEST by the US Government, and is the subject of much debate. A great deal of TEMPEST literature is classified. Much of the available literature about this topic on the WWW is hopelessly inaccurate. However, unclassified work confirms that under certain conditions it is possible to recreate a real time image of a computer screen significantly far away from the source computer. While exploiting this technology is not inexpensive, the cost is relative to the value of the information the attacker hopes to gain. Forewarned is forearmed. Where one is processing highly sensitive information, such as order books in a securities market, this threat should be seriously considered.

When an organization is engaged in using a wireless local area network (WLAN) to extend the wired network, there is no need to worry about TEMPEST; the information is being broadcast to the entire world anyway. The state of wireless local area network security is troubling. Although there are built-in cryptographic protections, few administrators turn them on or configure them effectively. For those who do use the built-in WEP cryptography, it turns out to be ineffective, for the code can be broken in a few seconds. Even the crypto system author [27] advises users to avoid it! WPA and WPA2 are better, but are rarely the system default. WLANs suffer from an even more serious problem. To work properly, they must advertise their presence to all potential users. Absent some form of strong authentication, which according to our experience is rarely used, anyone who can detect the beacon signal can logon into the network with more or less inconvenience and appear as an authorized user. Clearly, this is a security black hole. Free software exists on the WWW that can reconfigure a laptop computer equipped with a wireless network card to become a network sniffer, i.e., a system that can intercept all of the packets passing through the ether. Given this tool, a cybercriminal can simply drive by and become aware of all the available WLANs in the neighborhood in real time. One writer armed with such a tool stated that he drove from downtown San Francisco, California, down Highway 101 to Santa Clara, California, a distance of roughly 45 miles, and was never out of touch [28] with one or more wireless networks! Analysis of his data shows that he could potentially have logged into more than 75% of them. He claims not to have attempted unauthorized logons. This activity is termed wardriving and an example of a data collection run is described below.

5.2.6.1 Netstumbler Screenshot

A few decades earlier, when data communications predominantly employed dial-up telephone lines, cybercriminals would use automated tools to dial every possible telephone number and listen for a response from a modem. Where affirmative, the information was later used to mount an attack against the network through the modem. The attack was termed, wardialing. Today, warchalking [29] involves creating and making available on the WWW a database of all known WLANs that may be accessed from their corresponding physical locations. The database saves other cybercriminals from having to scan for available networks themselves; they can survey the vulnerable territory without ever leaving home. The term, warchalking, comes from the old hobo trick of chalk marking homes to identify for their peers home owners who were good for handouts. Figure 5.1 shows a screenshot [30].

In most office networks, wired or wireless, encryption is provided at the network edge, if at all. Traffic entering and leaving the premises is decrypted and encrypted, respectively, providing good security against data interception during transit. Within the office network, the data is completely unencrypted and vulnerable to interception. Many programs have been developed that can transform any computer into

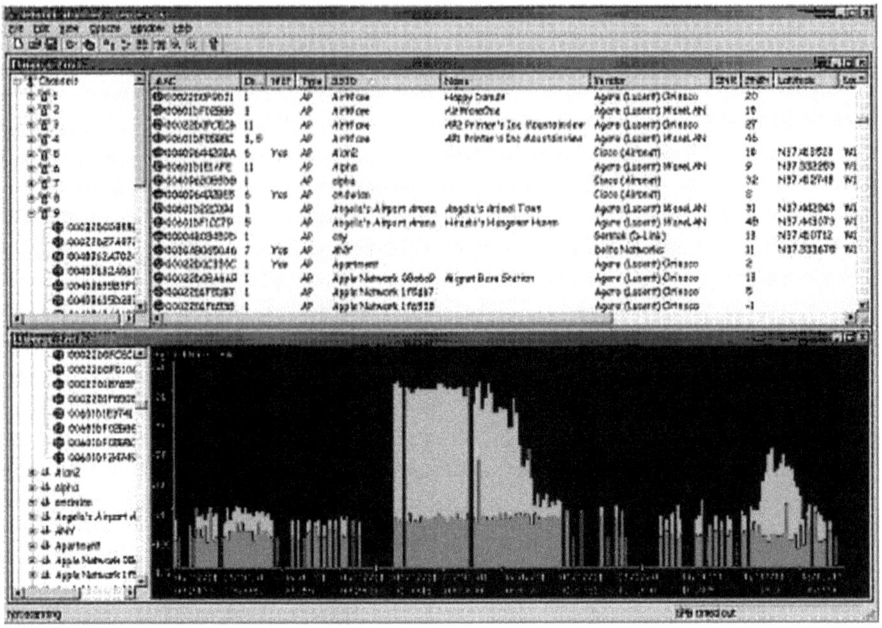

Fig. 5.1 Netstumbler screenshot

an unwitting packet sniffer that will detect and decode, where necessary, all the packets on the network to which it is connected [31]. Most office networks are provisioned over cables which terminate in crowded wiring closets that house routers and switches. The equipment nearly always maintains unused ports, and by inserting another ordinary cable into the router or switch, an eavesdropper can gain nearly complete access to the office network backbone. The attacker can intercept and read everything! Given the crowded nature of wiring closets, unless the eavesdropper uses a bright red cable where all the others are dull gray, one more cable in a nest of hundreds of cables is unlikely to attract attention. Where the attacker is unable to gain access to the network-wiring closet, there is always the network-based attack, described subsequently.

5.2.7 Network-Based Attacks

Given that the primary reason for computer networking is to provide access to any computer, from anywhere in the world, even a direct connection rarely requires access to the wiring closet. Similar to legitimate users, cybercriminals can establish remote connections to any network that is reachable.

The common thinking that computer criminals are talented thieves needs to be revised. Although there are true information system experts who are capable of launching unprecedented attacks, a majority of the attacks against information systems come from computer hackers who are merely adept at using the toolkits available free of charge on the WWW. These toolkit users, termed script kiddies, may be the objects of technical experts' scorn, but they can cause as much damage to a system as a technical expert [32]. Exceptions notwithstanding, while the technical expert is driven by the challenge to demonstrate his or her prowess at breaking into a well-guarded system than in stealing data, the tool user is driven by the desire to steal.

Defense against attacks is prudent and typical defenses resemble the concentric walls of a medieval fortress. There is an outer perimeter that contains an inner perimeter, which contains yet another perimeter further inside, and so on. This design is ideally suited for attacks originating from outside the perimeter. In contrast, in the computing world, a significant proportion of all attempts to compromise the security of organizational networks originate from within the network perimeter [33]. Stated differently, a major threat comes from the employees. The employees have the greatest access or knowledge of what is valuable, where to find it, and how to exploit it. Thus, instead of viewing the external Internet as a threat, defenses must focus on internal attacks. Technical solutions to insider attacks will be discussed subsequently in this chapter.

5.2.8 Denial of Service (DoS)

One specific type of network-based attack that has become prevalent is the denial of service (DoS) attack [34–36]. The technical nature of DoS attacks has been detailed in Chap. 2. DoS attacks aim at disabling competitors, thereby gaining sales while they are immobilized, and preventing the target from "seeing" what is going on elsewhere while they are busy dealing with the attack. DoS attacks are easy to launch, difficult to defend, hard to forensically analyze, and frighteningly effective if superbly executed. At the root, every information system possesses finite resources and will come to a halt when compelled to exceed its capability. Depending on the design, the system may degrade gracefully or incur catastrophic failure. Of significant concern are the unwitting accomplices, usually computers at universities, hospitals, and even in trusted organizations. Demonstrably, they may be said to have aided and abetted the attack, with or without prior knowledge. Thus, prima facie, the claim that due diligence was not exercised appears sound. However, given that modern information systems are highly complex, the exact definition and scope of due diligence is missing. Of great concern is how should the definition differ for a non-for-profit university, versus an investment banking firm, manufacturing business, or a public corporation. From the victim's viewpoint, a DoS attack is a miserable experience. Without any warning, systems cease to respond to commands and critical processing activities halt. When systems are restarted in an effort to restore operations, often with concomitant loss of data and auditing capabilities, frequently, the attack resumes where it left off, and the process repeats. The security staff tries diligently to locate the source of the offending load, so that it may be blocked. If the attacker is so unsophisticated as to launch a DoS attack from a single, unmasked computer, then tracing and blocking the source of the attack is relatively straightforward and quick. Unfortunately, attackers know this, too and the distributed DoS (DDoS) attack is their more common choice, as it spreads the attack source across many computers.

5.2.9 Patchwork Quilt

For many of the problems that surface, program patches appear to solve them temporarily. A software patch is a segment of corrective code that must be installed to augment an existing application program, similar to a patch that repairs a tear in a pair of trousers. Patches are almost always free of charge to registered users of the afflicted software, and readily available, often over the Internet. Despite the patches, the problems continue to be exploited over and over again. There are several reasons. First, a software patch cannot repair a vulnerability all by itself [37]. The correct patch must be identified for a given problem and then installed by an individual. Next, the modified system must be tested for accurate operations and that there are no new unintended malfunctions (regression errors). This generally takes much time, requires considerable attention to detail, and competes for the attention of personnel who are already inundated with routine work. Often, the growing number of patches become overwhelming [38]. A system running application software with known security flaws is an open invitation to an attacker. Few attackers will turn away. Common wisdom is to keep the software patched to the current level of release. This is easier said than done. For, patches once released are sometimes recalled or withdrawn by the manufacturer, stemming from subsequent discovery of flaws and errors in the patch. For obvious reasons, few administrators are keen to be the first to be victimized by such a situation, so there is little competition to be first to keep the software at the latest level of patching. The model of software patches is a holdover from a previous era when computers were few and software was simple; today, it is, at best, counterproductive. It must be changed. We realize that such a change will not be easy. First, the technology to enable it arguably does not exist today. Second, billions of dollars have been invested in software that is unlikely to be replaced simply to make it easier to patch.

5.3 Technical Approaches to Solving Security Problems

The suite of technical approaches include (1) antiviral software, (2) demobilizing code, (3) encryption, (4) firewalls, (5) intrusion detection systems, (6) virtual private networks, and (7) physical security measures. These have been technically detailed earlier, in Chap. 2 through Chap. 4 and we will touch on other, related issues here.

5.3.1 Antivirus Software

While antivirus software seeks to detect viruses, worms, and other forms of malicious code, and then prevents them from harming [39] the information system as well as spreading, it cannot prevent virus infection. Antivirus software is conceptually straightforward. It examines every file in the computer, and every data item coming and going from the computer. If any of the items match one of the stored signatures of a virus, the antivirus software raises an alert, takes action to contain the virus, or performs other acts. The dependence on comparing a virus to the signature of known viruses is the primary vulnerability of antivirus software. Clearly, antivirus software requires knowledge of a specific virus before it can be detected. Thus, it is essentially reactive, not proactive, and it is essential that the catalog of viruses be maintained with a high degree of currency. Viruses can be organized into two basic types, namely, those "in the wild," and those "in the zoo." Viruses in the wild are found on computers belonging to "real" users. They are the primary threat because they are in active circulation. Viruses in the zoo are viruses that have been written but never released into the wild [40]. So long as they remain captives in the zoo, they do not pose any threat. Most virus checkers do not check for zoo viruses, as they number ten to one hundred times more than those in the wild and that checking for them would noticeably compromise the performance of the system being examined. In theory, this compromise makes sense. In practice, there are flaws.

There are unknowns about the sanctity of the zoo perimeter and exactly who has access to zoo viruses is unclear. It is known that, in exchange for the rights to sell antivirus products in their countries, certain governments have demanded that antivirus software vendors turn over a number of zoo viruses to them, specifically to their military establishments. At least two of the major vendors are believed to have complied. This is a recipe for mischief. Should that government decide at some later time to undertake cyber hostilities, they will have gained potent ammunition. They also have seed stock, so to speak, which can be modified and improved, potentially producing a software supervirus. Identifying an unknown virus is a challenge. Many have argued that a virus may be detected through its malicious actions and then removed. If it acts like a virus, it must be a virus. The primary difficulty with this theory is that viruses read and write to files, an activity shared by many of the common applications. Significant effort and technology has been expended into predictive virus identification, so far without significantly improved results. Another vulnerability of virus checkers is their very versatility. Users can configure these tools in innumerable ways. The ability to customize is invaluable, but such versatility comes with a price. It makes it easy to misconfigure the tool. For example, all modern virus checkers can easily be configured to ignore checking certain categories of files. If a user configures an antivirus software to ignore precisely the type of file type that propagates hostile Visual Basic code, the software is rendered useless.

5.3.2 *Demobilizing Code*

To restrict the threat of mobile code, web browsers including the Internet Explorer provide a rich set of abilities to examine and limit mobile code activities. One can define different privileges for mobile code depending on its origin. This degree of customizability comes with the price of complexity. More often than not, user select default values for the security control parameters, which are rarely the proper choice for every system. The default values are also well publicized, so an attack against the default suite of privileges is more likely to succeed than a customized set of parameters.

Since the early days of operating systems design, it has been known that good security requires proper segmentation of the computer memory. In this model, user data is permitted to reside within a given range of memory addresses, while user executable code is restricted to a different range, and the operating system occupies a third address range. Writing of data from one memory segment to another is strictly controlled and usually disallowed entirely. The segmented memory model makes it much more difficult for malicious code that arrives as a Visual Basic script, say, to perform illegal operations on the operating system. Despite the obvious security advantages, memory segmentation is not widely used, primarily because the associated verification of memory writes slows down program execution. Although modern high-speed processors more than compensate for the time required for the additional memory verification there is little movement in the direction of requiring applications to conform to memory segmentation.

The Java programming language [41] successfully implements memory segmentation although it is far from perfect. Java was created with security in mind and it remains one of the few programming languages with an intrinsic security capability. Like BASIC, Java is an interpreted language, not compiled in that it does not produce pure binary code. Java is a platform-independent language, implying that it will run on any computer as long as the machine runs a Java Virtual Machine (JVM). The JVM is essentially an interpreter that presents a standard interface to Java and performs the necessary translations for it to run on that specific operating system. This makes Java a very desirable language in that programs need to be written only once and not multiple times, one for each and every operating system. On the other hand, JAVA is a potential security nightmare. Given its platform independence, cybercriminals can develop a single set of tools and use it to attack multiple information systems running on different platforms. Developed by Sun Microsystems, Java's security model works as follows. The user program in the high-level programming language is translated into bytecode, a compact representation that is suitable for interpretation by the JVM. While it is not executable binary code as found in a .exe file, it is less verbose than the source code written in Java. When the bytecode arrives at the target computer, it is presented to a verifier, which validates its digital signature. If affirmative, the bytecode is genuine and it is passed on for further inspection. Otherwise, no further processing is permitted. Following successful verification, the bytecode is checked by the Class Loader to determine if the code that is actually present purports to perform the same class of functions its digital signature indicates. Where this check passes, the bytecode is passed on to the JVM, where it is interpreted and the functions are performed. During execution, Java bytecode is prohibited from performing any functions such as disk access without first being examined by the Java Security Manager, whose primary objective is to prevent unauthorized access. Finally, the validated code is confined to a memory segment known as the Java Sandbox, and is precluded from accessing any code outside that memory segment. Neither is code outside the sandbox permitted direct access to the code inside the sandbox. All access is moderated by the Java Security Manager. The Java security model is evolving, as can be seen from the diagrams Figs. 5.2 and 5.3 below.

5.3.2.1 Java 1.1 Security Model

Although the security model adds credibility to Java, it is far from perfect. The elements of the security model comprise of more software, which can be modified, either permanently or in real time, by exploits including buffer overflows. It also turns out that it is possible to hand-craft Java bytecode and thereby bypass some or all of the security model. Similar to programming a computer directly in machine language, one can develop instructions for execution without first composing them in the Java language. Thus, while a superior approach to mobile code than ActiveX say, Java is still capable of mischief on the target machine.

5.3.2.2 Java 2SE Security Model

ActiveX differs from Java in that it is more of a collection of controls for execution on the target computer [42] and less of a programming language. ActiveX

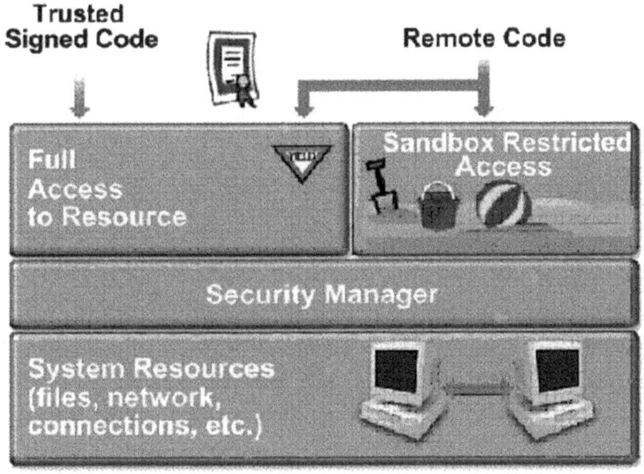

Fig. 5.2 Java 1.1 security model

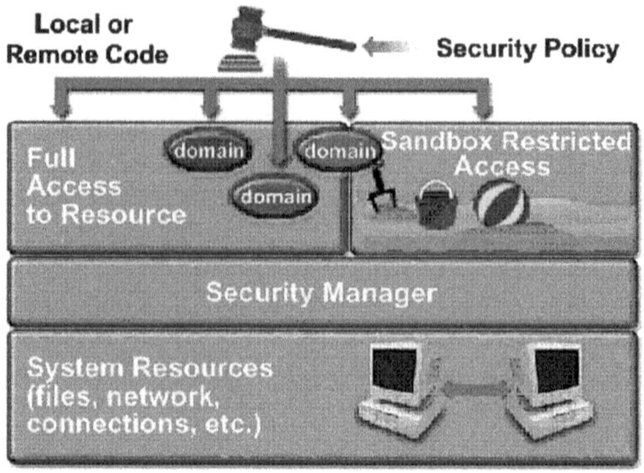

Fig. 5.3 Java 2SE security model

is Microsoft's response to Sun's Java, and was intended to replace Java in the Microsoft environment. Unlike Java, ActiveX lacks a security model. ActiveX controls may be utilized to perform literally anything on a target computer, including transmitting data to a distant location over a computer network, reformatting disk drives, deliberately running code that can physically damages monitors, etc [43]. Current security guidance relative to ActiveX is to disable it. However, as with the other kinds of mobile code, this "one size fits all" solution is unlikely to be suitable for any but the most straightforward information systems. Unlike most mobile code, it is far more difficult to control ActiveX simply because of its inherent capability.

The best way to control mobile code is to devise and implement strategies that can identify the code and confine it to a memory segment from which it cannot access critical machine functions. The more powerful the language, the more difficult the task, since the mobile code is capable of rewriting the instructions that were created to contain it. The problem is well-known and much effort is being devoted to the development of better ways to control mobile code.

5.3.3 Encryption

The key to security is to know which users are communicating between themselves and then constrain their interactions to a foreordained set of actions. This may be achieved by instituting encryption-based authentication. As pointed out earlier in this chapter, most internal networks are not encrypted. Through readily available software, any networked computer may be transformed into a packet sniffer, capable of reading all the details of any data packet on the network to which that computer is connected. There are commercial versions costing several thousands of dollars as well as freeware versions that cost nothing and offer essentially the same

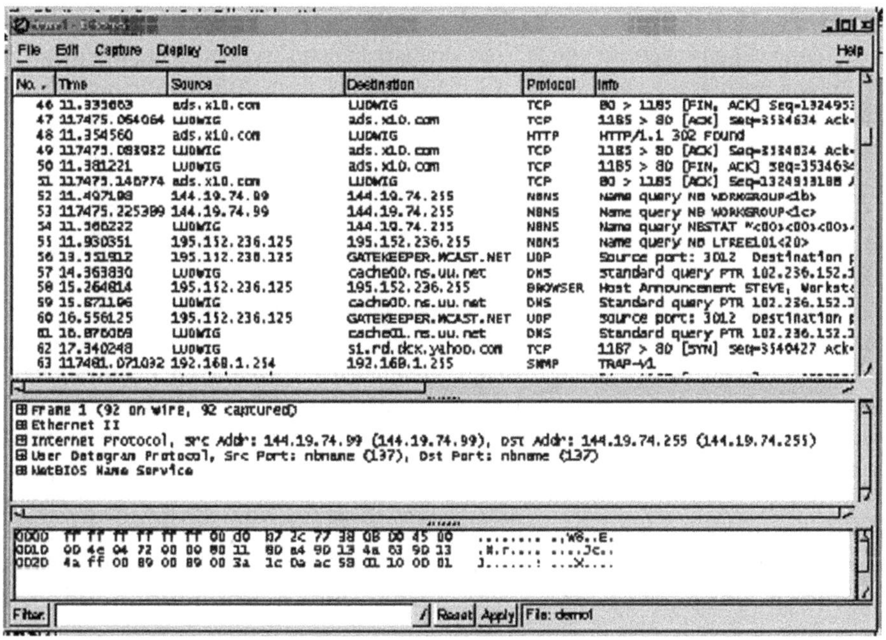

Fig. 5.4 Screenshot of network data captured with Ethereal freeware tool

functionality. A screenshot of data captured by one of the freeware tools, Ethereal (now Wireshark), is shown in Fig. 5.4. Anyone with basic network knowledge can use this data to map the network and to read the contents of every packet passing the computer running the capture tool. If the data were encrypted, this would not be possible.

To improve security in an organizational network, encrypted communications is recommended. Current protocols including Secure Sockets Layer (SSL), Transport Layer Security (TLS) [44], and IP Security (IPSec) [45] can accomplish secure communications with little impact on system performance. All these approaches can easily be made transparent to the user; applications operate as before without incurring any retraining costs, and it is not necessary to share any cryptographic information with the users. The protocols negotiate and establish the public-key cryptographic keys as needed. SSL requires an SSL-aware client, of which there are many, and digital certificates, but no preplanned security relationships. In contrast to SSL, IPSec requires a preexisting security relationship between the two ends of the connection but no digital certificates.

5.3.4 Firewalls

In building codes, a firewall is a physical structure that is installed to contain a fire for a predetermined time [46]. Built of components such as fire-resistant brick and steel, firewalls are effective at containing fires. Although not impervious to destruction, a firewall buys time in which to evacuate personnel and critical equipment and to attempt to suppress the fire, and it isolates the fire from critical functions within the building for at least the time for which it was designed. An information system firewall performs precisely the same function for the computer network it protects. It identifies threats that it has been programmed to identify, and prevents them from entering the protected network. Similar to its physical analog, an information system firewall can succumb to a determined attack. Figure 5.5 shows a pictorial description of a firewall.

Information system firewalls are typically deployed at the network edge, where the protected network meets the outside world. The Internet is usually seen as the enemy, but a better use of firewalls is to segregate each protected network segment from all other network segments. The smaller the segment the firewall protects, the better the security. Firewalls are not inexpensive. First, the cost of the firewall itself can range from a few tens of dollars for a software solution on an existing computer to several thousands of dollars for a dedicated hardware firewall. Second, firewalls reduce the speed of the transit traffic. Where the traffic is light, a software-only solution may suffice. It costs less and its relatively slow function won't be too noticeable. In the event of high traffic volume, a hardware solution may be warranted, which is both expensive and operates much faster.

A firewall inspects the data packets that are entering and leaving the protected network and compares each of them to a rule set of permitted operations [1]. Firewalls can be set up in one of two ways, either (1) everything not specifically prohibited is permitted, or (2) everything not specifically permitted is prohibited. The latter provides much better security, as efforts to define all threats are generally premature. Firewall rule sets are set up to enforce the principle of least privilege by

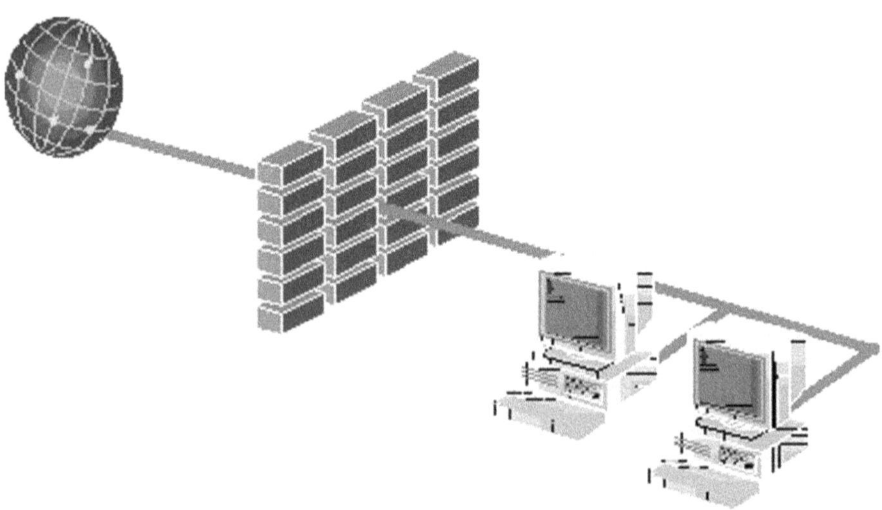

Fig. 5.5 Typical simple firewall deployment

permitting the minimum possible amount of data to enter and leave the protected network. A thorough knowledge of how networks operate is necessary to properly configure a firewall. The commonly held belief that simply acquiring a firewall and connecting it between the protected network and the outside world will provide security is a fallacy. The factory default settings of most firewall products will permit all traffic in either direction. Simply installing them changes nothing except the load on the power grid. For them to provide security, they must be configured, which involves creating and/or editing rule sets that can be voluminous and arcane. It therefore follows that the network professional that is responsible for the firewall truly has the keys to the kingdom, and should only be someone who is thoroughly trusted.

5.3.5 Intrusion Detection Systems

Intrusion detection systems (IDS) [47] examine traffic to uncover the signatures of known attacks on the network in contrast to firewalls that enforce rules on traffic packets. If an attacker were attempting to map the active services on a system by trying every possible port, a firewall would examine each query and determine on an attempt by attempt basis whether to allow the traffic. A properly configured and operating IDS, however, would recognize this pattern of queries as a form of attack and would raise an alert to the network security staff. IDSs can be configured not only to monitor and detect, but also to automatically initiate a response to an attack.

IDS also has its failings. First, the IDS must be able to keep up with the network. Otherwise, attacks will be missed and a false sense of security will prevail. Second, clearly, an IDS requires a priori knowledge of the attack structure, implying that it suffers from the same vulnerability as virus checkers. If the attack has not been seen before, it will probably not be detected. Third, there is the issue of false reports. In an ideal situation, an IDS detects all attacks and reports them. However, actual IDSs can and do generate false reports. The worst are false negatives, wherein the IDS fails to report an actual attack. Less problematic, but no less annoying, are the false positives, where the IDS reports an attack that in fact did not occur. False reports not only consume valuable management resources; they also reduce user confidence in the system. Intrusion detection technology has been available for far less than time than firewall technology. As expected, IDSs are less mature than firewalls and also more complex.

The author cautions that configuring an IDS to undertake an automatic response against a site that appears to be attacking the user is generally unwise. The automated response often takes the form of doing to others what the IDS believes was done to the user's system. Not only is that morally repugnant, it is usually illegal. This area is fraught with technical, ethical, and legal problems, and requires careful attention to policy. A superior use of the system is to generate prioritized alerts so the system operator can deal with the warnings on a case-by-case basis.

5.3.6 *Virtual Private Networks (VPNs)*

Through cryptographic technology, one may conceivably establish a secure communications link between two end points [48]. When correctly organized, such a connection can authenticate each of the terminal information systems to the other and can protect the information being transferred using encryption. As stated earlier in this chapter, the IPSec protocol allows the secure link to be implemented transparently so users need not be retrained on the use of their applications. The Microsoft Windows series of operating systems beginning with Windows 95 provide VPN client software, enabling VPNs to be implemented inexpensively. One may also acquire dedicated hardware to implement the VPN function. In that case, the VPN tends to be implemented from one network edge to another network edge. The tradeoff is that VPNs implemented exclusively in software tend to be two to ten times slower than dedicated hardware VPNs. For organizations with modest data transmission requirements and low budgets, the software solution is probably the method of choice. For high-volume users, the hardware is probably to be preferred. Functionally, both approaches provide VPNs of equivalent security. VPNs tend to be underutilized and poorly understood. Implementing a VPN between a wireless network client and the wired network can address the WLAN security problems that are of much concern. VPNs from machine to machine ensure the privacy, authenticity, and integrity of the data flow between those machines, and further protect the data from eavesdropping or illicit modification from desktop to desktop.

5.3.7 *Physical Security Measures*

Unlike traditional law enforcement professionals who are more attuned to the needs for physical security, the average information system administrator is generally unaware of the critical need for physical security. These professionals tend to be mathematically and technically oriented individuals who rarely consider that there are others who would physically interfere with their systems. The importance of physically securing computers and networks cannot be overstated. It is particularly important to control access by unauthorized persons to the physical information system assets. It is fruitless to employ high technology security solutions if the physical computing machinery is vulnerable to casual access. Bugs can be planted, data stolen or modified, illicit code installed, etc., by the most effective means possible. In the computing world, physical security gets little respect. This attitude needs to change. This area provides a great opportunity for traditional law enforcement and technologists to collaborate. Generally, law enforcers have need of the specific technical expertise that resides in the private sector. Similarly, technologists need the physical and personnel security expertise that tends to be found in the law enforcement sector. Ad hoc teams and task forces work, as evidenced by the success of the New York Electronic Crimes Task Force. Establishing even informal relationships between these two sectors brings benefits to both at low to no cost.

5.4 People Problems

Though nonintuitive, individuals constitute the greatest of all threats to information systems. After all, information is the only commodity that can be stolen and yet leave its rightful owner in possession of it. We have examined how attackers focus on technical problems that arise either from design or errors. The question remains, which people are the problem and where are they found?

Every year since 1995, the Computer Security Institute, a professional organization, and the US FBI conduct a survey of US businesses to determine the types of information security problems they have encountered and the cost associated with them. The results are promptly publicized, and available for reference and review. Although there are acknowledged problems with the structure of the survey and the extensibility of the statistics to the general case, the results represent the best empirical data that is currently available on the nature and magnitude of information security issues. One may legitimately dispute the accuracy of the figures; however, it is difficult to argue against the direction of the trends. A few of important trends gleaned from the 2002 CSI/FBI [33] study include:

- The average loss, measured by the mathematical mean of the losses reported by the respondents, exceeded two million, nearly double the $1.1 million figure reported in 2001, implying an accelerating trend. Superior reporting can only account for a part of the accelerated losses.
- The percentage of respondents reporting financial losses continues to rise, reaching 80% in 2002.
- The most serious category of financial losses continue to be loss of proprietary information and financial fraud.
- For the fifth consecutive year, more respondents reported external attacks exceeding internal attacks, 74% vs. 33%, and the disparity is growing. While in the past one could have confidently asserted that the largest threat lived within the firewall, it is no longer true.
- "WWW crime has become commonplace."

The CSI/FBI survey has been justifiably criticized for its many statistical shortcomings, which are acknowledged in the body of the report. However, a review of the past several years' data reveals that the situation is worsening. This report is recommended for anyone involved in detecting, investigating, or prosecuting cybercrimes.

Behind every attack is a person or a group of individuals, determined to commit a crime. While this is an obvious fact, the difficulty is how to mitigate the increasingly large impact these individuals bear on information systems? Little comfort should be taken from the increasing ratio of external to internal attacks. The worldwide proliferation of Internet has increased the number of people outside the private networks who possess the capability to launch attacks. One important statistic, not measured by the CSI/FBI survey, is the cost of attacks from outside versus internal attacks. One would suspect the latter to be much more costly, since authorized users not only have the best access to the design of the information systems, they also know in excruciating detail where the most lucrative targets are stored and how best to attack them.

A common problem in dealing with employees is failure to properly vet personnel. While it may be partly due to increasingly explicit privacy laws, many organizations fail to carry out even the most rudimentary background checks of those they hire. Hardly a week passes that one does not read about a doctor who has practiced with a valid license for years and found to lack a medical degree, or someone hired without even verifying their Social Security number. Background checks cost time and money and they annoy people. Many employers prefer not to know unsavory details about potential employees, to avoid later liability claims from either the rejected or fired employee or those whom the person might victimize after being hired. One school of thought holds that ignorance is bliss, for it reduces the potential cost of litigation. Perhaps. However, it is unwise not to run a credit check on the people to whom the corporate accounts will be entrusted. Information systems managers must be encouraged to be proactive in vetting their staff, both before hiring and periodically during their service with their organizations. Internal auditors, who should themselves be vetted by outside auditors, should oversee this function. The worst espionage cases of the twentieth century were due to people charged with detecting anomalous behavior in others, thereby giving those very people the benefit of the doubt. Human nature is to avoid giving offense, which certainly facilitates interpersonal relationships. However, we must establish and enforce uniformly applied standards of employee backgrounds and behavior. Experience shows that those who rebel at the imposition of such standards tend to be the ones who later prove to be problems.

We had earlier noted that the existing model to maintain the currency of software and hardware revisions is absurd. Failure to maintain software and hardware to current levels can lead to serious information security breaches. Although the model is flawed, it is the best we have and implementing it is an individual's task. Policies and procedures must be employed to ensure that the responsibilities for these tasks are clearly delineated and assigned to specific personnel. An audit function should be instituted to monitor that the policy is being implemented as written, while the policy must be periodically reviewed to ensure that it is both current and feasible. Nothing will create a lack of credibility faster than security demands that are unreasonable, unexplained, or not understood. The past decades have witnessed an increasing emphasis on doing more with fewer staff. Even in a bear market, the stock market has rewarded companies who have lowered costs dramatically by laying off employees. However, the work that was done by those who were laid off rarely goes away. Instead, it is redistributed among the remaining employees, resulting more often than not in information overload. People can handle only so much information at once, and their ability to prioritize diminishes rapidly as they become overwhelmed. It is critical that those charged with monitoring the security of information systems be given a workload that allows them time to review what they have seen and to think about whether there are patterns or anomalies there worthy of more detailed investigation. The best pattern recognition software ever built resides within the human cranium, and it is often misused or mistrusted.

It is generally accepted that the concept of mutual loyalty between employee and employer has long been dead in most of the world. Most notably in the US and in many parts of the world, employees serve at the pleasure of their employer. As they become more experienced, they can expect to be more, not less, likely to be dismissed and replaced by younger, less costly replacements. This trend has resulted in conflicting loyalties. Most workers are interested in doing a good job and they want to do the right thing according to their ethical system. Not sensing a reciprocal sense of commitment from their employer, however, employees are often at odds with themselves as to how to deal with problems that involve interpretation of less than explicit situations. More and more, employees are taking the understandable approach of protecting themselves first, as they fear retribution if they make the employer aware of conditions that might compromise security or safety. The employer may have a stated policy that they never shoot the messenger, but few employees who have been the bearers of unpleasant news will agree that the employers are sincere.

People are complex entities. Technologists are rarely trained in psychology, sociology, and the other "soft" sciences that help us understand how other human beings are likely to respond under different situations. Management courses tend to be results driven, not people driven, with predictable lack of transfer of any of these skills. Law enforcers, on the other hand, tend to have good "people skills." For example, it is important to have a good sense of when someone is lying. This is yet another area that can benefit from partnerships between information systems and law enforcement professionals.

5.4.1 Failure to Report Security Problems

According to the 2002 CSI/FBI Computer Crime and Security Survey, of those who experienced an intrusion into their information system, only 34% reported the intrusion to law enforcement. This is a substantial improvement over the 16% who had reported intrusions in 1996. It has not been a straight-line increase, so there is a long way to go. It is well known that not all crimes are reported; however, not reporting two-thirds of serious intrusions into information systems resembles failure to report two-thirds of felonies. Why is this so, and what can be done about it?

- First, many organizations do not have meaningful security policies in place. Policy is vital. Without a policy, there is no definition of what is permitted and what is forbidden. Absent that, anything goes. Furthermore, lack of policy leads to freelancing, or ad hoc decision making in the face of information system intrusions. Some intrusions may be reported to law enforcement under such a scheme, but not others, depriving both the police and the victim of data that could reveal a pattern that might lead to the perpetrator.
- Second, it is not uncommon for organizations to discover intrusions only after a long delay. It is human nature to regard "old news" as being of no interest to anyone, especially the police. After all, the police are supposed to be out catching

murderers. Why would they be interested in what had happened to my business's information system 3 weeks ago? It probably cost money, but the business is probably insured, too. Improved technical resources, such as those described in the previous section, can help mitigate this rationale.

- Third, reporting a security breach to a law enforcement agency conjures up images of standing under television lights in front of the organization's offices surrounded by reporters and police. It is not a pretty image. Few people seek to star on the five o'clock news. There is a clear conflict between the responsibility to report a crime and the fear of public embarrassment. Under such a conflict, avoiding public embarrassment usually wins. This happens in spite of the duty of corporate officers to report material failings, and it often happens because of a fear of retribution or blame. Few companies want to see their names on the front page associated with anything but good news. Having to report that one's company has just suffered a huge loss because the information system security was deficient does not meet the "good news" standard. It is worth noting that the only quote in the CSI/FBI survey that directly addresses this point states, "... concern over negative publicity remains a strong deterrent [33] to reporting [intrusions to law enforcement]."
- Fourth, a number of subtle incentives and disincentives are also at work when it comes to reporting information system intrusions. Many employees and even a few corporate officers may be able to convince themselves that there is no reason to believe a crime has occurred. It was an unfortunate event, but certainly not a crime. Thus, the police would not only be uninterested, they would castigate the organization for reporting the event. Everyone can recite some anecdote in his or her experience that gives the ring of truth to this, and changing this perception will take active outreach by law enforcement.
- Fifth, the average citizen has a positive aversion to picking up the telephone to report a crime to a local police force, much less picking up the phone to call the US Secret Service. There is a fear of being lumped in the public view, and perhaps in the perception of law enforcement, with the "criminal element." No upstanding citizen wants that sort of association to tarnish their reputation. The fear may be dismissed as unfounded, but it is real.
- Sixth, lack of faith in law enforcement has become a staple of common wisdom in most Western countries. The situation is not very different in other countries. The average citizen's opinion of law enforcement is unlikely to be favorable, and there are daily media stories that only reinforce that image. Good news does not sell newspapers or advertising space on the network news. "Good" coverage of law enforcement tends to revolve around prompt solution of particularly heinous crimes such as kidnapping or felony murder. Information systems intrusions don't make the grade in that comparison. As a result, many people are truly fearful that if they do report an information system intrusion to law enforcement, they will be not only be ridiculed by their peers and the police, they will be forced to work with incompetent officers who will only make matters worse. Little can be done about the past, but positive outreach and teaming can make a big difference in the future.

- Seventh, there is also a justifiable fear that if law enforcement, especially the FBI, becomes involved, that they will seize the computers, possibly interrupting the conduct of business for a long time so as to lead to bankruptcy, drive away customers by creating an impression that the company is somehow less than trustworthy, and consume the business's time, all without keeping the business informed about the progress of the investigation or the benefit to the business of having reported the intrusion. Few organizations outside law enforcement understand what happens after a cybercrime is reported, and this failing needs to be corrected. It is also true that one's experience with law enforcement is usually very much a function of which law enforcement agency becomes involved. Telling the average businessman to report suspected cyber crimes to the cognizant federal law enforcers is tantamount to advising him or her to antagonize their local police.
- Eighth, educational efforts need to be mounted to help the public understand what actually happens when cybercrimes are reported. Successful cases need to be judiciously publicized, even when investigations do not lead to indictments or convictions. Unsuccessful cases need to be analyzed to determine how to avoid the problems that were encountered in future. Business needs to understand that law enforcement is their ally, not the adversary. It is also incumbent on law enforcement to become more aware of the needs and fears, rational or otherwise, of the information security professionals, so that the degree of cooperation between the two groups can genuinely increase. This is a tough requirement, and not one likely to be solved quickly, but we must begin the process.

5.4.2 Policy

The need for a good security policy has already been stated. Brevity should not be taken for dismissal. If there is a single key to successful information system security, it would be a simple, logical, usable, and understandable security policy. One can attend industry conferences and buy "one size fits all, fill in the blanks" policies for $500–$1,000 [49]. In the author's professional opinion, these are unsuitable for most organizations as they attempt to cover all the possible needs of all possible types of organizations, public and private. As an educational tool, they are of great value. However, as the foundation of the actual policy for an organization, they are less useful and tend to spend their entire life on a bookshelf, unread, unused, and unhelpful. It is no mistake; writing, implementing, and maintaining a security policy is genuine hard work for which one can expect few thanks. But if policy is not thoughtfully prepared and enforced, security is a mirage. Policy defines what is allowed. Policy delineates who has what permissions. Policy specifies the actions to be taken when certain events occur. It covers natural disasters as well as cybercrimes, and should be as important a corporate document as the operational business plan. Thinking through a policy requires participants, each with a different view of the problems that may be encountered. All the potential problems will not come to light immediately, so the policy will need iterative revision. However, no attempt to implement and enforce information system security can succeed without a written policy.

Law enforcement agencies should also have policies in place, describing how they will respond to reports of cybercrime, and how should the case be systematically investigated following the initial report. This policy is useful not only to guide the agents charged with such investigations, but also to reassure the public as to what to expect when an information security breach occurs and is duly reported to the authorities.

5.5 Summary

In this chapter, we have discussed the nature of information system security problems at the application level. Technical solutions have been presented, along with their advantages and disadvantages. A proposal for collaboration between law enforcement and private sector technologists has been suggested. It turns out, however, that the greatest threat to information system security is not technical; it is people. The idea has been discussed, together with statistics on cybercrimes and the reluctance of a majority of victims to report them to law enforcement. Finally, the need for a security policy has been stressed.

References

[1] Gollmann, D. (1999). *Computer security*. New York, NY: Wiley.
[2] Lohr, S., & Markoff, J. (2006, March 27) Windows is so slow, but why? *The New York Times – Technology*.
[3] U.S. Department of Defense. (1985) *DoD trusted computer security evaluation criteria (The orange book)*. DoD 5200.28-STD.
[4] Bell, D., & Lapadula, L. (1996). Secure computer system: MITRE technical report 2547. *Journal of Computer Security, 4*(2/3), 239–263.
[5] Multics. Retrieved April 5, 2003, from http://wombat.doc.ic.ac.uk/foldoc/foldoc.cgi?Multics
[6] Everett, D. B. (2002, November 7). Trusted computing platforms. *Proceedings of the Trusted Computer Masterclass Conference*, QE2 Conference Centre, London.
[7] Moglen, E. (2002, August 11). *Free software matters: Untrustworthy computing*. Columbia University Law School. Retrieved from http://emoglen.law.columbia.edu/publications/lu-22.html
[8] Hulme, G. V. (2002, November 25). Trust this: Microsoft tries to secure Windows. *Information Week*.
[9] Festa, P. (1999, November 23). Study says 'buffer overflow' is most common security bug. *CNET News.com*.
[10] Bardon Data Systems. (2003, April 5). *How secure is the Windows operating system?* Retrieved from http://www.bardon.com/wp_windows.htm
[11] Malicious Code: Threats & Responses. Retrieved April 3, 2003, from http://www.infosec.spectria.com/av/malcode.html

[12] Malicious Code. Retrieved April 2, 2003, from http://csrc.nist.gov/publications/nistir/threats/section3_3.html
[13] Wikipedia The Free Encyclopedia. (2003, April 2). *Virus*. Retrieved from http://www.wikipedia.org/wiki/Virus_(biology)
[14] Buffer Overflow. Retrieved April 2, 2003, from http://searchsecurity.techtarget.com/sDefinition/0,,sid14_gci549024,00.html
[15] Delio, M. (2001, March 12). New kit renews e-mail worm scare. *Wired News*.
[16] Regan, T. (1999, October 7). Putting the dancing pigs in their cyber-pen. *Christian Science Monitor*.
[17] Stets, D. (2003, April 3). *A new browser could let others tap into your bank account*. Retrieved from http://www.iks-jena.de/mitarb/lutz/security/activex.pe.phillynews.html
[18] Abreu, E. M. (2001, August 6). *The cost is $1.2 billion, so far*. Chandigarh, India: The Tribune.
[19] Evers, J. (2001, September 27). Kournikova worm maker sentenced to community service. *IDG News Service*.
[20] Evers, J. (2001, September 13). Kournikova virus writer stands trial. *IDG News Service*.
[21] The Back Orifice 'Backdoor' Program. Retrieved March 31, 2003, from http://www.nwinternet.com/~pchelp/bo/bo.html
[22] Industry Canada. (2002, August 25). Government of Canada to review lawful access laws. *News Release*.
[23] Ian Hopper, D. (2002, April 7). FBI finds increasing reluctance to report computer crimes. *The Baton Rouge Sunday Advocate, 167*(67).
[24] Netgage, Inc. (2003, April 5). *Law, investigation, and ethics*. Retrieved from http://www.gonetgage.com/CISSP/legal.pdf
[25] KEYKatcher. Retrieved April 2, 2003, from http://www.chatworker.com/surge.htm
[26] KeyKey. Retrieved April 2, 2003, from http://www.cyber-007.com/keykey/screenshots.htm
[27] Rivest, R. (2001). *RSA security response to weaknesses in key scheduling algorithm of RC4*. Retrieved from http://www.rsa.com/rsalabs/technotes/wep.html
[28] Verton, D. (2001, July 16). Flaws in wireless security detailed. *Computerworld*.
[29] Retrieved April 5, 2003, from http://www.warchalking.org/
[30] Retrieved from http://www.netstumbler.com
[31] Retrieved from http://www.ethereal.com/
[32] Katz, J. (2000, May 15). Script kiddies – Who are these guys? *Time Europe, 155*(19).
[33] Computer Security Institute. (2002, April 7). *Cybercrime bleeds U.S. corporations, survey shows; financial losses from attacks climb for third year in a row*. Retrieved from http://www.gocsi.com/press/20020407.html
[34] CERT Coordination Center. (2001, June 4). Denial of service attacks.
[35] CERT Advisory CA-2000-01. (2000, January 3). Denial-of-service developments.
[36] Distributed Denial of Service (DDoS) Attacks/tools. Retrieved April 3, 2003, from http://staff.washington.edu/dittrich/misc/ddos/
[37] Lyman, J. (2002, August 16). *The trouble with software patches*. Retrieved from http://www.newsfactor.com/perl/story/19023.html
[38] Munro, N. (2002, January 4). Feds take minimal role in patching holes in cyberspace. *National Journal*.
[39] Kanish, B. (2003, April 2). *An overview of computer viruses and antivirus software*. Retrieved from http://www.hicom.net/~oedipus/virus32.html#update
[40] Molly Wood and CNET staff. (2000, July 13). The virus zoo: What's out there and how to avoid it.
[41] JavaTM Security. Retrieved from http://java.sun.com/security/
[42] Microsoft COM Technologies. (1999, March 30). *ActiveX controls*. Retrieved from http://www.microsoft.com/com/tech/ActiveX.asp
[43] McLain, F. (2003, April 6). *ActiveX, or how to put nuclear bombs in web pages*. Retrieved from http://www.halcyon.com/mclain/ActiveX/welcome.html
[44] Network Working Group. (1999, January). RFC 2246, The TLS protocol. *Internet Engineering Task Force*.

[45] Network Working Group. (1995, August). RFC 1825, security architecture for the Internet protocol. *Internet Engineering Task Force*.
[46] The Ontario (Canada) Fire Code, §1.2.1.2.
[47] Graham, R. (2000, March 21). *FAQ: Network intrusion detection systems*. Retrieved from http://www.robertgraham.com/pubs/network-intrusion-detection.html
[48] Virtual Private Network Consortium. Retrieved from http://www.vpnc.org/
[49] The SOS Information Security Policies. Retrieved from http://www.information-security-policies-and-standards.com/infopolicies.htm

Part III
Economic Impact of Cybercrimes

Chapter 6
Economic Consequences

Michael Erbschloe

6.1 Introduction

The economic impacts of computer crimes involving malicious code attacks, unauthorized intrusion into networks and computer systems, denial of service of attacks, and others are substantial. In testifying before the Senate Select Committee on Intelligence on 6 February 2002, Dale L. Watson, Executive Assistant Director, Counter-terrorism and Counterintelligence of the FBI, pointed out that during the past several years the FBI had identified a wide array of cyberthreats, ranging from defacement of Web sites by juveniles to sophisticated intrusions sponsored by foreign powers. Watson also pointed out that a few of these incidents pose significant threats, including the theft of national security information from a US government agency or the interruption of electrical power to a major metropolitan area in the US, which will imply grave consequences for national security, public safety, and the economy. Virtually every critical US national infrastructure, including energy, transportation, and government operations can be forcibly shut down through the clever use of cybertools, for the purpose of coercing or intimidating the government and civilian population. Even the less serious categories of threats have real consequences and, ultimately, can undermine public confidence in WWW-based commerce and violate privacy or property rights. An attack on a website that shuts down an e-commerce business can pose disastrous consequences for the company. An intrusion that results in the theft of millions of credit card information from an on-line vendor can result in significant financial loss and, more important, reduce consumers' willingness to engage in e-commerce. Watson stressed that the US cyberspace faces increasing threats from terrorist groups that are increasingly employing the Internet and new information technologies to formulate plans, raise funds, and spread propaganda through secure communications.

S. Ghosh and E. Turrini (eds.), *Cybercrimes: A Multidisciplinary Analysis*,
DOI 10.1007/978-3-642-13547-7_6, © Springer-Verlag Berlin Heidelberg 2010

6.2 Societal Benefits of Measuring Economic Impact of Cybercrimes

When the Department of Homeland Security (DHS) was established, following the terrorist attacks of 11 September 2001, one of its responsibilities was to implement the National Strategy to Secure Cyberspace (NSSC), which was released officially in February 2003. The document provided a framework to protect US technology assets from electronic and hacking attacks. It set forth the following priorities:

- Priority I: Establish a National Cyberspace Security Response System
- Priority II: Establish a National Cyberspace Security Threat And Vulnerability Reduction Program
- Priority III: Establish a National Cyberspace Security Awareness And Training Program
- Priority IV: Secure Governments' Cyberspace
- Priority V: Foster National Security and International Cyberspace Security Cooperation

Under each of these priorities is a list of initiatives in which DHS must take a leadership role. Clearly, the initiatives and the overall strategy constitute a long-term endeavor and very expensive, which can greatly benefit from an economic analysis of cybercrimes. The initiatives that can derive the greatest benefit from a formal approach to measuring the economic impact of computer crimes, include the following:

- Develop tactical and strategic analysis of cyberattacks and vulnerability assessments.
- Develop a public–private architecture for responding to national-level cyberspace incidents.
- Expand the Cyber Warning and Information Network to coordinate crisis management activities in the event of cyberspace incidents.
- Develop national public–private continuity and contingency planning efforts and mobilization exercises to test the plans.
- Deployment of new and more secure protocols and routing technology in order to reduce vulnerabilities.
- Deploy and upgrade software to reduce and remediate vulnerabilities.
- Establish a process to help prioritize federal cybersecurity research and development agendas and assess and secure emerging systems.
- Develop a national awareness program to help businesses, the general workforce, and the general population to secure their individual sections of the cyberspace.
- Improve capabilities for attack attribution and responses prior to, during, and post cyberspace incidents.

In pursuit of a strong cybersecurity effort, the DHS established the National Cyber Security Division (NCSD) and located it within DHS' Information Analysis and Infrastructure Protection Directorate. NCSD was mandated to provide round-the-clock functions, including carrying out cyberspace analysis, issuing alerts and warnings, improving information sharing, responding to major incidents, and assisting in national-level recovery efforts. The founding pillars of NCSD, in fact, came from the former Critical Infrastructure Assurance Office, National Infrastructure Protection Center, Federal Computer Incident Response Center, and the National Communications System. NCSD is staffed with 60 employees and is organized around three units:

1. Identify risks and reduce vulnerabilities to the government's cyberassets and coordinate with the private sector to identify and protect critical cyberassets.
2. Oversee a consolidated Cyber Security Tracking, Analysis, and Response Center (CSTARC), which will detect and respond to incidents on the Internet; track potential threats and vulnerabilities to cyberspace; and coordinate cybersecurity and incident response with federal, state, local, private sector, and international organizations.
3. In coordination with other appropriate agencies, foster cyber security awareness and establish educational programs and partnerships with consumers, businesses, governments, academia, and international communities.

6.2.1 Allocation of Funding and Expenses

Effective 2003, a consensus was reached that cybersecurity must constitute a public–private responsibility. There remains, however, a severe lack of structure and coordination for effort, especially funding for the study of the economic impact of malicious attacks. The National Strategy for the Physical Protection of Critical Infrastructures and Key Assets, identifies high priority, cross-sector security initiatives, which are designed to address planning and resource allocation; information sharing, indications, and warnings; personnel surety; building human capital; awareness, technology, research and development; and modeling, simulation, and analysis. The strategy clearly articulates that it is imperative that federal, state, and local governments and private-sector stakeholders cooperate in the planning and resource allocation process. It states:

- Define clearly the critical infrastructure and key asset protection objectives.
- Develop a business case for action to justify increased security investments.
- Establish security baselines, standards, and guidelines.
- Identify potential incentives for missing security-related activities in the marketplace.

The NSSC points out while the private sector is already structured and best equipped to respond to an evolving cyberthreat, the government's role in cybersecurity is warranted in cases where high transaction costs or legal barriers may lead to significant coordination problems. Thus, a public–private engagement must constitute the foundation of the NSSC. The engagement will take a variety of forms and address awareness, training, technological improvements, vulnerability remediation, and recovery operations.

The FY2004 budget request from DHS included $829 million to support information analysis and infrastructure protection. The budget is intended to support DHS's ability to analyze and identify potential threats, assess vulnerabilities, map the threats to the vulnerabilities, and provide information from which to organize protective measures. This budget allocates approximately $500 million to assess vulnerabilities in the critical infrastructure, which includes nuclear power plants, water facilities, telecommunications networks, and transportation systems, and address the highest priority vulnerabilities. It is unclear what priority DHS will assign to analyzing the economic impact of computer crime and malicious attacks over the years. The budget request represents an increase of $652 million (370%) over the FY2003 level.

Historically, representative organizations have allocated between 1.5 and 3% of their annual revenue on information technology (IT) services, while companies in the financial services industry have budgeted as high as 7% of their revenues for IT functions. Of the total IT budget, typical spending on information systems security and network security ranges from 1 to 5%, with very little, if at all, allocated to analyze the economic impact of malicious attacks. Most private organizations have adopted an informal approach to estimating a return on investment for their security related expenditure. In many cases, the actual cost of such analyses would exceed the entire budget allocation for information systems security and network security.

6.3 Malicious Code Attacks

The high-profile malicious code attacks, including Nimda, Code Red, SirCam, I Love You, Melissa, Explore, and Slammer disrupted computer operations and computer users, worldwide. The attacks required extensive clean-up operations where computer technicians and administrators expended tens of thousands of hours to detect and eradicate the malicious code, patch the vulnerable software to prevent future occurrences of the attack, and perform operational checks on computer systems and networks to return them to normal behavior. Tables 6.1 and 6.2 provide a partial record of the economic impact of malicious code attacks [1].

As vice president of research at Computer Economics, the author's efforts in compiling the loss data have been corroborated by other individuals in the media.

Table 6.1 Economic impact of malicious code attacks, by incident

Year	Malicious code	Worldwide economic impact ($US)
2001	Nimda	635 million
2001	Code Red(s)	2.62 billion
2001	SirCam	1.15 billion
2000	I Love You	8.75 billion
1999	Melissa	1.10 billion
1999	Explore	1.02 billion

Table 6.2 Economic impact of malicious code attacks, by year

Year	Worldwide economic impact ($US billion)
2001	13.2
2000	17.1
1999	12.1
1998	6.1
1997	3.3
1996	1.8
1995	0.5

When the Blaster worm struck the community in the summer of 2003, projection of economic loss ranged from a low of $35 million to a high of $300 million. Estimates of the number of systems infected ranged from 125,000 to 1.4 million systems. Attempts to analyze and compute the economic impact of malicious code attacks face three major obstacles:

- A lack of consensus on the number of machines infected, damaged, or disabled because of a given malicious code attack.
- Limited funding to carry out in-depth benchmarking of repair and restoration costs.
- Lack of public and government involvement in the analysis and computation of economic impact.

6.3.1 *Proposed Methodology to Measure Economic Impact*

The global nature of the Internet, the widespread use of computers, and societal dependence on computers pose a formidable challenge to accurately assessing the damage and impact of malicious code, economic and otherwise. When measuring the economic impact, we must take into account how computers and the Internet are integrated into the lives of individuals, business operations of for-profit companies, mandated activities of government organizations, and the societal contribution of non-profit organizations. We will focus on:

- Impact on an organization
- Impact on individuals
- Impact on societies

6.3.1.1 Measuring Economic Impact on an Organization

Table 6.3 enumerates the different avenues in which a malicious code attack can harm an organization. At the simplest level, the direct loss to a victimized organization's consists of the cost to repair damage and restore systems to normal, which

Table 6.3 Economic impact of malicious code attack on an organization

Direct damage to target organization's computer systems
Cost to repair damage or restore target organization's systems and functionality
Decrease in productivity of employees in target organization
Delays in order processing or customer service in target organization
Decrease in productivity in customer's organization because of delays in target organization
Delays in customer's business because of delays in target organization
Negative impact on local economies where target organization is located
Negative impact on local economies where target organization's customers are located
Negative impact on value for individual investors in target organization
Negative impact on value of investment funds holding target organization securities
Negative impact on regional economies where target organization, customer, or investor organizations are located
Negative impact on national economies where target organization, customer, or investor organizations are located

can be measured by the working time it requires technicians to perform the tasks necessary to return systems to their normal operational behaviors. For a given organization, the measurement of the loss is straightforward. However, the resources and techniques necessary to collect data from thousands of organizations and then compile it into a form that is usable for litigation purposes is not readily available to the criminal justice system. The situation becomes hopelessly difficult when attempting to collect data from organizations in dozens of countries around the world.

To most organizations, it is unclear how to measure the productivity decline that generally results from a malicious code attack. Furthermore, the need to restore computer and networking operations as quickly as possible is generally overwhelming and it overrides any desire to collect data on the loss of productive or in identifying other adverse impacts on the organization, if any. Regardless, the loss of productivity of an organization is directly proportional to the duration of the system outage.

We may also characterize the economic loss to an organization from the perspective of the actual timing of the impact of the cybercrime.

- The immediate economic impact will include damage to systems that require human intervention to repair or replace; disruption of business operations; and delays in transactions and cash flow.
- The short-term economic impact can include loss of contracts with other organizations in supply chains; loss of retail sales; negative impact on an organization's reputation; and obstructions to developing new business services.
- The long-term economic impact may include a decline in the market valuation of an organization, erosion of investor confidence, decline in stock price, and reduced goodwill value [2].

Table 6.4 Economic impact of malicious code attack on individual citizens

Direct damage to an individual's computer system
Cost to repair damage or restore individual's computer system and functionality
Decrease in productivity of individual
Loss of contribution to the employer of the individual
Loss of contribution to the family of the individual
Loss of contribution to the social groups to which the individual belong
Loss of contribution to the community of the individual
Decline in economic participation in the individual's local community
Decline in economic participation in the individual's region
Decline in economic participation in the overall e-commerce sector
Potential long-term decline in economic participation in the overall e-commerce sector

Table 6.5 Economic impact of malicious code attack on societies

Disruption of individual activities
Disruption of family activities
Disruption in educational participation
Disruption of social group activities
Disruption of community activities
Disruption of local commerce and e-commerce
Disruption of government operations and functions
Disruption of business activities
Disruption of seasonal social calendars

6.3.1.2 Measuring Economic Impact on Individual Citizens

Table 6.4 articulates the different ways in which a cybercrime may affect an individual. The damages are similar to those experienced by an organization. Individuals must also pay, either by expending their own time or hiring the services of consumer companies, to restore the computer and network functionality. Conceivably, unlike inanimate organizations, system outages may bear a more profound impact on the family, social groups, and communities to which the individual belongs. The home computer has become a significant tool and platform, facilitating participation in society and the workforce. Large numbers of people telecommute, at least on a part-time basis. This spans from working from home to responding to work-related e-mails at airports or when traveling. In addition, home computer systems allow individuals to participate in online degree programs and educational activities; assist in household management; check recreational schedules; and e-commerce.

6.3.1.3 Measuring Economic Impact on Society

Table 6.5 articulates the many avenues in which a cybercrime may bear impact on society. Computer attacks cripple computer systems and consume resources that could be otherwise expended for constructive purposes.

6.3.2 Data Acquisition and Computing Economic Impact

Though cumbersome and expensive, collecting data on the economic impact of malicious code attacks is achievable. For a given organization, the complexity of the data collection process is a function of the extent of the damage and the duration of the outage. In general, actual loss refers to the reasonably foreseeable pecuniary harm that resulted from the offense. In most computer crimes, however, actual loss includes the following pecuniary harm, regardless of whether such harm was reasonably foreseeable:

- Reasonable costs to the victim of conducting a damage assessment.
- Cost of restoring the system and data to their condition prior to the offense.
- Any lost revenue due to the interruption of service.

Table 6.6 lists the data required to determine the economic impact of malicious code attack in an organization. To assess the total cost of restoration, the hours spent on each of the applicable activity is multiplied by the corresponding cost, in $ per hour, as indicated in Table 6.7. Clearly, the time required for each of the necessary activities will depend on the nature of the attack, the type of systems compromised, and the extent of damage caused. The per hour costs will depend on the skill level required to perform each work, local salary levels, local benefits, and any overhead costs.

The complexity of determining the cost of lost productivity is a function of the organization. Many companies have a solid grasp on the productivity levels of individual employees or work groups, especially those that specify activity level in quotas, such as volume of sales call per hour. Others may determine the monetary value of an employee-hour through a risk- or cost benefit-analysis, utilizing

Table 6.6 Data required to compute economic impact of malicious code attacks on an organization

Time required to inspect systems to detect malicious code or deliberately placed code resulting from the attack
Time required to eradicate the malicious code or deliberately placed code resulting from the attack
Time required to apply patches to systems
Time required to certify systems and return to service
Time required to determine which if any files were damaged, altered, or stolen
Time required to restore files that were damaged or altered
Salaries, benefits, and overhead that comprise the per hour costs of technicians working on computer system restoration and file recovery
The value of stolen data or information
Salaries, benefits, and overhead that comprise the per hour costs associated with activities required as a result of data being stolen such as canceling credit card numbers and issuing new cards
Hours of lost productivity because of system outages
Salaries, benefits, and overhead that comprise the per hour costs of employees with reduced productivity
Lost revenue because of system outages

Table 6.7 Calculating the cost of restoring systems following malicious code attack

Activity	Measure
Time required to inspect systems to detect malicious code or deliberately placed code resulting from the attack	X hours
Time required to eradicate the malicious code or deliberately placed code resulting from the attack	X hours
Time required to apply patches to systems	X hours
Time required to certify systems and return to service	X hours
Time required to determine which if any files were damaged, altered, or stolen	X hours
Time required to restore files that were damaged or altered	X hours
	Total hours
Salaries, benefits, and overhead that comprise the per hour costs of technicians working on computer system restoration and file recovery	$ Cost per hour
Multiply the number of hours by the hourly costs	$ Total costs

the actual expenditures related to computer security and an expected return on investment. In the absence of such precomputed data, an organization may need to establish a data collection process from scratch, which can be both time consuming and expensive.

Measures of lost revenue stemming from system outages can be just as complex as calculating lost productivity. A quick way to determine loss revenue is to utilize the revenue from comparable days as a benchmark. It is important to take into account trends in revenue decline or growth. If the average daily revenue has increased or decreased by 10% over the last several months, compared to the prior year, this must be included in the analysis. It is equally important to examine the revenues of the week following the outage to determine what level of sales would have occurred on the days the system was unavailable.

In general, it is very difficult to establish the value of stolen data or information. If specific actions are required as a direct result of the data theft, the loss may be easy to compute. Under these circumstances, salaries, benefits, and overhead that comprise the per hour costs associated with necessary activities are utilized. As the first example, in the event of theft of credit card numbers, old cards must be canceled and new ones established. As a second example, fines may be levied and audits imposed as regulatory consequences of compromised data. As the third example, the Health Insurance Portability and Accountability Act of 1996 (HIPAA), for example, imposes mandatory fines for the unauthorized disclosure of an individual's medical information. In addition to reluctance to participate, many organizations do not have the resources to collect such data. Often, there is little motivation to spend time and money to establish the cost of stolen data when it is unlikely that the organization will be compensated for damages following the attack.

6.3.3 Incident Report to Facilitate Data Acquisition

This section presents a sample incident report that an organization that has been the subject of an attack may choose to complete to facilitate law enforcement investigations as well as to compute the economic impact of the crime [3].

- Date, time, and duration of the incident.
- The name, title, telephone number, fax number, and e-mail of the point of contact for law enforcement as well as the name of the organization, address, city, state, zip code, and country.
- The physical locations of the computer systems and networks that have been compromised.
- Whether the compromised systems and networks are managed in-house or by an outside contractor.
- Whether the affected systems and networks are critical to the organization's mission.
- If it is a part of the national critical infrastructure, which sector was affected:
  - Banking and finance
  - Emergency services
  - Gas or oil storage and delivery
  - Government operations
  - Electric power
  - Transportation systems
  - Telecommunications
  - Water supply systems
- The specific nature of the attack, which may include intrusion, system impairment, denial of resources, unauthorized root access, website defacement, compromise of system integrity, data theft, or data damage.
- Whether the problem had been experienced in the past.
- The suspected method of intrusion or attack, which may include virus, exploited vulnerability, denial of service, distributed denial of service, backdoor, or Trojan Horse.
- The suspected perpetrators and possible motivations of the attack, which may include a disgruntled employee, former employee, or competitor. If the suspect is an employee (or former employee), this report should note the type of system access privileges presently (or previously) assigned to the employee.
- An apparent source (IP address) of the intrusion or attack, if known, and any evidence of IP address spoofing.
- What computer system (hardware, operating system, or applications software) was affected.
- What security infrastructure had been in place, which may include an incident response team, encryption, firewall, secure remote access or authorization tools, intrusion detection system, security auditing tools, access control lists, or packet filtering.

- Whether the intrusion or attack resulted in either a loss or compromise of sensitive, classified, or proprietary information.
- Whether the intrusion or attack resulted in damage to systems or data.
- What actions were taken to mitigate the intrusion or attack, which may include the system being disconnected from the network, system binaries checked, backup of affected systems examined, or log files analyzed.
- What agencies had been contacted, which may include state or local police, CERT, or FedCIRC.
- When was the system last modified or updated along with the name, address, phone number, and point of contact of the organization that performed the work.

Where necessary to determine a dollar value of the damage, business loss, and the cost to restore the system to normal operating conditions, the following information may be very helpful.

- In the event that repairs or recovery were performed by a contractor, the charges incurred for the services must be recorded.
- If in-house staff were involved in determining the extent of the damage, repairing systems or data, or restoring systems to normal operating conditions, the number of hours staff expended to accomplish these tasks must be recorded along with the hourly wages, benefits, and overhead associated with each of the involved employee.
- If the business had been disrupted, the number of transactions or sales that were actually disrupted must be noted along with their cumulative dollar value.
- If the systems were impaired to the point that lost transactions or sales cannot be determined, the cumulative dollar value of the transactions or sales that would have occurred on a comparable day for the duration of the outage must be recorded.
- If the systems are used to produce goods, deliver services, or manage operations, the value of the loss caused by the disruption must be recorded. (The organization may have experienced similar disruptions due to inclement weather, fires, earthquakes, or other causes.)
- If the systems were physically damaged, the report must document how much was paid to acquire and install the systems.
- If the systems were physically stolen, the report must include how much was paid to acquire and install the systems and the cost of the actions adopted to ensure that the information on the stolen systems cannot be used for system access.
- Where intellectual property or trade secrets were stolen, the value of that property needs to be determined and recorded.
- If the stolen intellectual property or trade secrets were utilized by a competitor or another party, the report must determine and document the impact on the organization.

References

[1] Computer Economics. (2002, January 4). *Malicious code attacks had $13.2 billion economic impact in 2001*. Retrieved from http://www.computereconomics.com/article.cfm?id=133.
[2] Erbschloe, M. (2001). *Information warfare: How to survive cyber attacks*. Emeryville, CA: McGraw-Hill Osborne Media.
[3] Erbschloe, M. (2002). *Socially responsible IT management*. Elsevier Digital Press.

Chapter 7
Infosecurity Funding

Michael Caloyannides

While information security is a challenge encountered by practically every organization today, funding to develop new mechanisms to enhance it is not centralized and each institution has to fend for itself. The main problem in the Western world is that the information infrastructure is privately owned, and the governments cannot make decrees about information security enhancements without paying vast sums to the private sector to implement and maintain such enhancements. Thus, it is not surprising that organizations with R&D charters on infosec issues, listed subsequently, carry out their mission from a parochial perspective. They focus primarily on their own perceived needs and those of their customers. In essence, each funding organization understandably guards its prerogative and funds whatever it wants but is always accompanied by eloquent verbiage to justify its choice of funding decisions. The US government's leading organizations include:

- US DoD: Through the Defense Advanced Research Projects Agency (DARPA), the National Security Agency (NSA), and the research funding agencies and DoD laboratories, the US military conducts research to secure systems and networks that support war fighters. The DoD correctly views information security or infosec as a key component of information superiority for the war fighter. Infosec is a crucial building block in protecting the military's critical infrastructures. The reality of life is that even the US DoD must depend to a large extent on commercial telecommunications providers for meeting a significant portion of its own communications needs.
- The US Intelligence Community must assure that it maintains the integrity and confidentiality of the information it collects until it reaches the intended consumers, when and where needed. In addition to the operational requirements of overt users of information technology, such as the Department of Defense, the US Intelligence Community must also ensure that it also obscures the specific channels used, and often the mere existence of many of its communications.
- US Department of Energy (DoE): Along with the National Nuclear Security Administration and the Nuclear Regulatory Commission, the DoE is especially concerned with threats involving information and systems involving nuclear materials and the generation and distribution of electricity. DoE's mission includes providing the necessary energy resources, when and where required and

S. Ghosh and E. Turrini (eds.), *Cybercrimes: A Multidisciplinary Analysis*,
DOI 10.1007/978-3-642-13547-7_7, © Springer-Verlag Berlin Heidelberg 2010

in the correct measure. The provision of such resources necessarily requires the existence of a dependable and secure information and telecommunications infrastructure.

- US DoJ: The DoJ aims to detect, intercept, identify, and prosecute criminal acts involving computers and networks. As of the last decade, it also has the new responsibility of preventing terrorist acts against US persons and interests, and of prosecuting the culprits. DoJ focuses on computer and network forensics for the purpose of prosecution and its goal is to advance the investigative arts to meet the rapidly changing realities of the twenty-first century.
- The US Commerce Department: Through the National Institutes of Standards and Technology (NIST), the department is concerned with providing a sound basis for real-time, secure electronic commerce.
- The Federal Aviation Administration (FAA) must assure that the computers and networks, critical to the safe operation of the national air space, are highly available and provide accurate information. Threats to this needed availability are not only intentional acts but also configuration errors, acts of God, and any other causes of outages.
- The National Science Foundation (NSF) is responsible for advancing fundamental knowledge in Information Assurance, enhancing the universities' research capabilities, and educating researchers to address information assurance challenges. It does so largely through grants to universities on topics which include information security.

7.1 The INFOSEC Research Council

At a corporate level, the federal government views Infosec as a critical cog in its ability to provide efficient, effective, and private services to all of its citizens. Clearly, there is an increasing demand for effective and more affordable information assurance capabilities. The key questions that arise include: Where do we allocate the scarce infosec research resources for maximal effect? How do we minimize unnecessary duplication of government research efforts and share results effectively across all departments and agencies? How do we find creative ways to bring research results to bear on operational systems in a timely and cost effective manner? What is our vision for the future? The INFOSEC Research Council (IRC) was established to precisely address these questions. IRC's goals were as follows:

1. Describe, clearly and succinctly, the national level issues in Infosec and information assurance.
2. Document and summarize the R&D objectives and projects for each of the IRC members.
3. Relate the national issues to the programs and projects, identifying the synergies and potential gaps.
4. Suggest a research roadmap to help align each member's R&D programs with its information assurance vision.

The IRC consists of US Government sponsors of Infosec research from the Department of Defense, National Intelligence Community, and Federal Civil Agencies. The membership list includes the following but is far from exhaustive.

```
NSF
NIST
DTRA
DARPA
NSA
USAF
US Navy
US Army
FBI
Office of the Secretary of Defense
DoE
NRO
CIA
US Department of State
FAA
Institute for Defense Analysis (IDA)
ITRD
NRC
DoJ
Sandia National Labs
```

The IRC provides for its members a community-wide forum to discuss critical Infosec issues, convey the research needs of the respective communities, and describe current research initiatives and proposed activities for future research investments. Through participation in the IRC, sponsors obtain and share valuable information that helps focus their research programs, identify high-leverage, high-value research targets of opportunity, and minimize duplication of research. The IRC represents a collective effort for the mutual benefit and collaboration of all of the participating organizations and is intended to promote thoughtful Infosec investments. While it is clearly understood that each participating agency is free to choose its own research priorities, IRC will attempt to develop a common, shared appreciation of the important and challenging Infosec problems and help identify research areas of high priority for the members [1]. The IRC believes that coordination must begin with an accurate picture of the current state of research against the backdrop of the perceived information assurance needs of the US government. The picture must include a description of the long-term infosec visions of the member organizations, which is available to all of the participating IRC members. The roadmap will document progress in specific areas and identify those areas that may require additional investment or strategic realignment. It will remain unclassified and include indications of the level of effort devoted to different research areas by different organizations. It will also explain how IRC members are investing in key technologies to advance their specific goals. Last, by integrating information from different sources, the roadmap will provide a summary of what aspects of the problems are being addressed and what gaps may exist across the efforts of the IRC member agencies. The IRC notes that a comprehensive view of the current research will enable members to coordinate their individual R&D programs. They will be able to detect and eliminate duplicate programs in a timely manner and leverage the work done by other organizations.

While the stated goals and mission statements are laudable, the realities of human nature inevitably dilute them. When two different organizations come to realize that they are both funding very similar efforts, ideally one of them should back out. This rarely happens, however, since each of them create elaborate verbal justifications to keep its respective ongoing effort.

The community believes that the major national-level issues in Information Assurance include:

1. The existence of fundamental flaws in much of the nation's deployed information infrastructure, which renders the systems vulnerable and prone to exploitation.
2. Decreasing diversity in the software components of the nation's information infrastructure and diminishing multiple hardware communications paths imply that a single flaw is likely to cause wide-spread damage quickly.
3. There exists no effective means to detect the flaws and how they may be exploited, both tactically and strategically.
4. There exists no known mechanisms to offer a controlled and graduated response to exploitations.

While select sections of the nation's information infrastructure may be individually understood and modeled, the behavior of the overall infrastructure is far too complex and beyond reach. As a result, the infrastructure's response to a given stimuli cannot be predicted with any level of confidence. This, in turn, implies that given a sequence of unfolding events in the real world, one cannot decipher whether it represents benign activity or a precursor to a damaging attack. Infosec organizations have proposed possible solution to the problems. However, they are either too costly in terms of long development time; resource-intensive to the point of being unaffordable; or degrade the performance beneath the acceptable limit, where they become noncompetitive in the open market.

IRC's existence as a central coordinator but not an agency that dictates all Infosec funding centrally is based on the following realization. In theory, although the goals of the IRC member organizations are disparate, the knowledge and technology that can successfully address them is uniform. However, there are key human problems:

1. Each organization desires its own authority to decide what to fund and to what level of support.
2. Given that different organizations have unique needs, even if they are minimally different, a single centrally administered entity would be hard pressed to assess the relative importance of the different needs and decide how to divide a single large funding pie in an equitable manner.

The IRC's primary reason for existence is to assure that the government's R&D resources address the national needs in a technically coordinated manner. The IRC meet its objectives by facilitating awareness and fostering collaboration between the organizations and their research efforts.

7.2 The Current State of Infosec Research

7.2.1 Data Collection

Through one-on-one interviews and DoD-wide data calls, the IRC collected details on 300 projects from 26 government organizations. Of the collected data, more than two-thirds relate to the project-level, while slightly under one-third pertain to the program level. A program is a top-level effort, comprising of a number of individual projects. The disparity in the level of detail has constrained IRC's analysis. In cases where funding information was made available only at the program level, it is virtually impossible to infer which of the projects within a given program accomplished what specific goal and how much money was expended.

7.2.2 Projects and the List of "Hard Problems"

The nature of the data collected by IRC is highly multidimensional and posed difficulty in abstracting and tabulating it in a logical manner. To help understand the data, namely, the quality of the research efforts, two leading candidates for structuring the data were proposed:

(a) The "Defense in Depth" concept proposed by the DoD
(b) The "hard problem" list developed by the IRC

The list of hard problems included:

```
(a)  Intrusion and Misuse Detection
(b)  Intrusion and Misuse Response
(c)  Security of foreign and mobile code
(d)  Controlled sharing of sensitive information
(e)  Application Security
(f)  Denial of Service
(g)  Communications Security
(h)  Security Management Infrastructure
(i)  Information Security for Mobile Warfare
(j)  Secure system composition
(k)  High Assurance Development
(l)  Metrics for security
```

A few of the programs and projects reported which specific hard problem was addressed and the defense in depth area on which the research had focused. Often, multiple categories were listed and some project descriptions were sufficiently descriptive. However, for a large number of programs and projects, neither the defense in depth area nor the specific item from the hard problem list could be identified.

7.2.3 How Much Money is Being Spend and Where?

Strictly speaking, actual information on how much money is being spent on the programs and projects is unavailable for the following reasons:

1. Funding information is often available only at the overall program level and not at the project level.
2. In cases where funding information is available at the individual project level, one must often decipher nebulous language relative to:
    i. What is the exact objective of the project and the underlying reasons?
    ii. How does one project differ precisely from an apparently similar project funded by a different organization?
    iii. What is a realistic expected date of completion of a project?
    iv. What, if any, are the plans to transition the technology to an end user?
    v. To what extent is the technology likely to be useful to other end users?
3. There are legitimate concerns about the sensitivity and security classification of a document that might contain detailed funding information on the programs and projects of the US Government's infosec effort.
4. A number of organizations prefer not to disclose details of their internally funded efforts.

7.3 Research Goals

The Joint Vision 2010 stresses the need to, "...balancing the requirement to safeguard information with the seemingly opposite but necessary action of sharing information..."

The DoD Information Management Vision to, "Provide, in a secure fashion, the right information, at the right place and time from the right sources, in a form that users can understand and reliably use to accomplish their missions and tasks, effectively and efficiently."

The Joint Information Warfare envisions that, "Joint IW/IO must incorporate the actions and involvement of numerous non-DoD organizations and activities, to include elements of the private sector."

If we were to consolidate the three visions, stated above, into a single objective, it would assume the following form: "We want to ensure that the US government's information infrastructure will be secure in the foreseeable future from attacks. This goal can be achieved by identifying all relevant vulnerabilities and directing research towards eliminating such vulnerabilities."

To realize the objective, we must first differentiate between the present Infosec needs and those that are likely to arise in the foreseeable future, say, 10–15 years from today. This in itself is a challenge. While today's needs are well-known, efforts to address them are classified under development, not research. They receive a very small fraction of the total R&D funds, which are geared to address the more difficult and unknown problems of the future. Given the unprecedented rate at which information technology has been evolving, any prediction about the future Infosec needs is very likely to be premature. For obvious reasons, the federal government and the military will increasingly rely more on commercial, off-the-shelf software. There is little contention on this issue. Software has become the very lifeblood of the military and the functioning of our government and this trend is not likely to change. However, the entire infrastructure of commercial software is rife with vulnerabilities that threaten to bring the edifice crashing down.

If the federal government were to achieve the goal stated earlier, it stands to reason that we must begin to address this problem at its core. That is, we must develop superior software in that it is resistant to exploitation. In reality, this is highly unlikely for the following reasons:

- In terms of the dollar value of sales, the government constitutes a relatively small percentage of a commercial software manufacturer's market. The lion's share of the market is the commercial sector that is easily impressed with functionality as opposed to security.
- Any complex piece of software, say, Microsoft Office, is the result of the collective work of legions of different programmers, spread out all over the world and spanning over three decades. It is absolutely clear that the final product is a set of ad hoc patches on top of more patches, as distant as possible from a meticulously structured and documented program and where security and precision are guaranteed to be subordinate to functionality.
- The economic pressures of marketing are such that there are far stronger incentives to release software that has more features and dubious security than otherwise.

7.3.1 Recommendations

Against the backdrop of current activities, one would be very tempted to streamline the minimally structured US R&D efforts in Infosec by injecting greater efficiency. The author believes that, in reality, a streamlining attempt is unlikely to succeed for two reasons.

First, the independence that has characterized the different agencies of the US government in the past is likely to continue into the future. Given that each funding agency uses its own allocated monies to support R&D in Infosec, it is unlikely that organizations will genuinely embrace any kind of external guidance and directions on how to expend the funds. At best, an interagency coordinating organization such as IRC can serve as a "townhall meeting place," where attendees can become informed of everyone else's work so as enhance one's quality while avoiding any unnecessary duplication. At the same time, it cannot be overemphasized that while duplication is wasteful, it is far less dangerous than leaving security gaps unattended.

Second, much of the technical accomplishments in information technology is the result of the work by the commercial sector, not due to governmental decree or coercion. The reason is that the development cost and complexity of modern information technology is simply too high for the government to create its own hardware and software product. For instance, the typical cost of developing a new Intel microprocessor, namely, Pentium II, II, IV, or V, is a few billion dollars, with an expected lifetime of 2–3 years. The US government finds it affordable to use commercial hardware and commercial software.

When a new technology becomes a commercial success, including the WWW, web browsing, and public key encryption, it comes with its own set of security issues. It often introduces new security related problems and the commercial sector has always had a self-serving economic incentive to address them. The days when government spending had influenced technological directions are long gone in the information technology sector.

Most information security experts would offer a strong recommendation, along the lines of a caution, that the Government's legislative branch exercise extreme restraint in passing laws in the Infosec area. For, many laws, well intentioned as they may have been, have actually ended up crippling information security and US National Security.

As example 1, US Government legislation have criminalized attempts to reverse engineer the security features without understanding that the scientific process is absolutely critical to identifying and correcting security flaws and weaknesses before they may be exploited by a true adversary with disastrous consequences. While the intent to protect copyrighted material is noble, the reality is that it is now illegal to reverse engineer security features even for the purpose of demonstrating their weaknesses so that they can be properly redesigned.

As example 2, although DMCA is a US law on the surface, the underlying corporate funding is concerned with the international protection of US copyrights. New Zealand has been formally asked by Microsoft to further protect digital copyrights by updating New Zealand's Digital Technology Copyright Act of 1994. In contrast, the US Electronic Frontier Foundation (EFF) has been trying to convince New Zealand not to pass a law similar to the US's DMCA for it may hurt US national interests in the long term [2].

Under example 3, the activist Recording Industry Association of America (RIAA) had considered an offbeat scheme, namely, software to masquerade as a file-swapper online. Once it places itself in a computer that offers copyrighted music to others, the software would try to block others from downloading songs. Of course, the software would not be confined to the US. Ironically, this approach would run afoul of the new antiterrorism bills in the US. Since the software may potentially damage the computer it enters, the RIAA has lobbied for legal protection from any damage done by the software to other computers. In short, RIAA wanted legal license to attack file-swappers' computers without incurring any civil liability. "We refer to it as license to virus," according to a US congressional staffer [3].

As example 4, in mid-2001, at the request of Adobe Corporation, the FBI arrested 27 year old Dmitry Sklyarov, a Russian who had come to the US to deliver an academic presentation and charged him with crimes under the DMCA act. He was not accused of any copyright infringement but for developing software that enabled purchasers of electronic books view their eBooks. The software is legal in his native Russia where he developed it. What is prohibited by the DMCA is the act of providing the technology. Sklyarov had made the mistake of discovering and revealing a weaknesses in an encryption scheme that Adobe employs in its electronic book reading programs. He had composed software to unlock the Adobe eBook reader encryption system and his company, Elcomsoft, was selling copies of the decryption software for $99. Sklyarov was arrested for the specific violation of the DMCA, namely, in circumventing the protection measure that the copyright holder had placed around digital files to regulate access. As a result of intense pressure by Adobe product customers, Adobe subsequently asked that Sklyarov be released and refused to prosecute him [4]. Around the same time, Edward Felton, a professor of computer science at Princeton University was threatened with criminal prosecution when he announced his intent to discuss the findings of his encryption research that addressed the digital watermarking of music files. As a result, many US conferences with cutting edge technical content may move offshore or to Canada, in the end hurting US national interests.

As example 5, in November 2008, the Australian Federation Against Copyright Theft (AFACT), the Australian counterpart to the US RIAA, sued an Australian Internet Service Provider, iiNet, on behalf of the biggest Hollywood studios including Village Roadshow, Universal Pictures, Warner Bros, Paramount Pictures, Sony Pictures Entertainment, 20th Century Fox and Disney, as well as the Seven Network. AFACT alleged that iiNet, by virtue of being an ISP, facilitated the exchange of copyrighted material by its subscribers. AFACT claimed that iiNet was liable for "authorising" copyright infringement on its network because it did not warn or disconnect offending customers when repeatedly notified of the infringements by the movie studios. This was a novel legal concept with profound and widespread ramifications and was closely followed worldwide. The hearings ended in early December 2009, in which the author served as an expert witness on behalf of iiNet [5]. On 4 February 2010, Justice Dennis Cowdroy of the Australian Federal Court in Sydney found that the ISP was not liable for the downloading habits of its customers. In a summary of his 200-page judgment [6] read out in court this morning, Justice Cowdroy said the evidence established that iiNet had done no more than to provide an internet service to its users. He found that, while iiNet had knowledge of infringements occurring and did not act to stop them, such findings did not necessitate a finding of authorisation. He said an ISP such as iiNet provided a legitimate communication facility, which was neither intended nor designed to infringe copyright.

References

[1] Retrieved from http://www.infosec-research.org
[2] Retrieved from http://www.newsbytes.com/news/01/171435.html
[3] Retrieved from http://www.zdnet.com/zdnn/stories/news/0,4586,2818064,00.html
[4] Retrieved from http://www.cryptome.org/dmitry-eff.ag.html
[5] Ry Crozier. (2009, August 19). Forensics experts examine iiNet and Telstra facilities. In *itnews for Australian Business*. Retrieved from http://www.itnews.com.au/News/153360,forensics-experts-examine-iinet-and-telstra-facilities.aspx
[6] AFACT v iiNet: The judgement in full. In *itnews for Australian Business*. Retrieved from http://www.itnews.com.au/News/166365,afact-v-iinet-the-judgement-in-full.aspx, 4 February 2010.

Chapter 8
Information and Computer Security Risk Management

Emily Freeman

8.1 Private Industry Effectiveness: The Need for a Risk Management Perspective

Network based technology, either private or public networks, are continuing to bear dramatic impact on enterprises around the world, and a growing number of risk managers are recognizing the importance of understanding how these technologies are transforming every aspect of the business infrastructure.

Commerce and critical enterprise functions, including finance, accounting, human resources, supply-chain management and distribution, and marketing are being redesigned to integrate with the Internet, web portals, virtual private networks, Web 2.0., and web-enabled Enterprise Resource Management (ERM). New value propositions and relationships are being established between the enterprises, their customers, and critical business partners. All entities that either support or appear to have the potential to support enterprise revenue are being interconnected. In essence, except for organizations' creative people, every component of strategic value and importance is being stored on enterprise databases.

Besides the global change to networked systems, businesses routinely outsource major aspects of information technology (IT) functions such as program code development and maintenance, hosting, and in some cases, the entire IT department. Similarly business processes are outsourced ranging from customer service, credit card processing, finance, accounting, payroll, employee benefits management, debt collection, fulfillment, and many other infrastructure functions. The heart of the organization is now shared.

Risk management plays a crucial role in assessing, controlling, mitigating, and financing the risks an enterprise assumes when it employs and becomes dependent on computer and networking technologies. These systems represent an increasingly significant component of the organization's "operational risk" and become the central focus, not only for regulators, tax auditors, customers, regulators, and stakeholders, but the directors and officers of the organization as well.

Clearly, conventional thinking that the technology-related risks can be addressed only by technology or IT specialists is outdated and must be replaced by a recognition of these exposures as complex and evolving business risks. Such risks can

S. Ghosh and E. Turrini (eds.), *Cybercrimes: A Multidisciplinary Analysis*,
DOI 10.1007/978-3-642-13547-7_8, © Springer-Verlag Berlin Heidelberg 2010

best be managed by a cross-functional risk team or committee composed of senior representatives from risk management, legal, compliance, internal audit, IT, and operations.

8.2 Definitions of Risk and Enterprise Risk

In a given enterprise, a "risk" is any uncertainty about a potential future event that threatens the enterprise's ability to accomplish its mission, endangers its core assets, and limits the organization's ability to provide critical services.

The full scope of "enterprise risk" may be understood analytically through those of its four components, namely, strategic risk, financial risk, hazard risk, and operational risk. While strategic risk encapsulates issues relative to the competitive environment and positioning in the marketplace; financial risk relates to liquidity, cash flow, and access to the financial markets for the well-being of the enterprise; and hazard risk refers to natural disasters and other risks for which protection to the private industry is available from the traditional insurance offers.

Operational risk is defined as those concerns emanating from corporate IT and business processes (whether performed internally or partially or totally with third party vendors), other than market or credit risk. Thus, operational risk is increasingly centered on automated processes and information systems, which have migrated from the closed, stand-alone environment of legacy systems to the Internet and private network-based widely accessible systems. Clearly, operational risk is of the greatest relevant in this chapter. Other, more traditional elements of operational risk, including human resources, product development, legal and compliance, have witnessed significant impact by the use and dependence on networked technologies in an increasingly outsourced world.

Unlike in the past, where an enterprise's critical infrastructure consisted of its physical plant, equipment, and inventory, in the current technology-based environment, an enterprise's core operations involve electronic information and computer networks. Though an intangible asset, electronic information, notably knowledge databases and intellectual property, are key drivers of revenue and worth in today's economy. Electronic information assets include accounting information; intellectual property, i.e., trade secrets, know-how, patent information, design data, and source code; and customer, supplier, and other competitive information.

8.3 Risk Management and the Risk Management Process

Risk management is defined as a continual enterprise process; the objective being to address new challenges as the operations and applications change and new threats emerge over the life of the enterprise. For effectiveness, risk management must be accepted as integral to the business management process and never viewed as an obstacle or barrier. As an example, in the area of information technology security, risk management can no longer consist merely of annual penetration test, yearly security assessment, or an external required audit.

The adoption of new technologies, capabilities, applications, and changes in IT or business process management are a daily challenge for risk management. Too often, applications development and launching products in the marketplace have carried out in an atmosphere of speed, functionality, and cost, where security concerns may have not been incorporated into the business case, design, and testing phases of the systems development life cycle. Thus, inserting security risk management into the equation may not have appeared a priority to the application developers. However, today and in the future, failure to implement security risk management from the beginning of the business case analysis through the final launch of the products may result in near misses, security-related losses, and significant re-design costs as security flaws are discovered.

We present a risk management process that is equally applicable at the enterprise level, business unit, and application level. The elements include:

- *Analysis and assessment*: Defining threats, events, and consequences.
- *Risk prioritization*: Categorizing each risk based on defined frequency and severity metrics in order to concentrate on risks that bear the greatest impact on operations, assets, revenues, and reputational harm/brand equity.
- *Prevention*: Defining specific measures that would prevent the risk from occurring.
- *Mitigation*: Developing a plan to minimize the effects or consequences of a risk event that cannot be prevented or preempted, including crisis management, communication and incident response.
- *Transfer*: Protecting the enterprise by transferring all or part of the financial consequences, such as loss of revenue, litigation costs (defense costs and damages), and potentially other consequences (such as regulatory investigations and necessary costs of notification of affected individuals in the event of a data breach) to a third party through insurance and contracts. Contractual transfer is very relevant to downstream contracts with IT and business process outsourcing third party vendors.

For further details and additional resources on risk management principles and processes, especially related to information security, the reader is referred to [1–4].

8.4 Risk Management Analysis

In the world of IT security, the most important threats or risks surround:

- Personally identifiable non-public information (PII as defined by statute and/or regulation) including personal identifiers associated with bank/investment accounts and credit/debit cards.
- Personally identifiable health care information (PHI).

- Security of computer networks from attacks designed to disable or interrupt service and/or damage, delete or destroy key electronic information assets.

In any risk assessment, the five most important questions include:

- What are the risks or threats?
- What is the magnitude of exposure to PII and PHI?
- What are the impacts or effects of the identified risks if they actually transpired and how likely are they to occur?
- What prevention, mitigation, and financing have been put in place to address the most significant risks? How effective are these measures in addressing the severity risk potential?
- What critical business or IT functions are outsourced? What vendors have sensitive network access or process/host/store/transmit/hold customer or employee PII and/or PHI?

The risk analysis with a cross-functional risk committee or team generally attempts to identify potential threats or risk events and the resultant negative impacts on financials, namely sales, fees, license revenues, expenses, and litigation costs; brand equity, i.e., harm to reputation or company image and loss of customer trust or goodwill; and assets and operations. Assets may include both physical and non-physical assets, comprising of computer hardware, application software, data, and intellectual property rights. Operations span critical business infrastructure functions, productivity, production, and fulfillment. Mathematically, the formula for risk may be stated as:

$$\text{risk} = \text{threats} + \text{impact} + \text{likelihood of the threats.}$$

The following then are representative threat scenarios, including the risk events, affected assets, and consequences, which are likely to be prosecuted under cyber-crimes.

- Theft of credit card information carried out insiders and/or external perpetrators The results are notification costs, forensic costs, potential litigation (potentially in class), fines under PCI, regulatory investigations, loss of payments and revenue, legal costs, damage to reputation, loss of customer trust, and cancellation of services.
- Extortion threat based on confidential customer information unlawfully gained through a computer vulnerability exploitation, unlawful access to PII by various means, etc. The results are extortion payments, reputation harm, crisis management expenses, cancellation of services, and revenue loss.
- Unauthorized disclosure of confidential trade secrets and release of research data prior to public announcement, illegally gained through access to proprietary databases or source code in an industrial espionage scenario. The results may include litigation, loss of competitiveness, loss of revenue, loss of productivity, delay of market release, loss of investment value, and reputation harm.

A key difficulty with the mathematical formula for security-related risks is the lack of public, credible and quantitative information regarding the magnitude of loss or actual financial damages of security related incidents. In the U.S., there are a number of excellent sources of information regarding security incidents involving PII/PHI (what happened, when, and how many estimated persons) including web sites of Identity Theft Resource Center, Privacy Rights Clearinghouse, Federal Trade Commission, etc. The publication [5], which documents the findings of a survey conducted by the Computer Security Institute and the US FBI, is also of value. Despite the lack of credible, public data, a key measurement in evaluating severity is the number of records or transactions involving PII and/or PHI.

A few of the largest security breaches involved publicly traded companies that disclosed the magnitude of loss and/or reduction in future earnings caused by a major security breach. In other cases, out of court settlements with credit card companies or major banks have been documented in a number of instances. However, the vast majority of security breaches and the front end costs of mandatory notification as required by statute or regulation are not well documented.

The Ponemon Institute in the U.S. publishes an annual survey of data breach notification costs (www.ponemon.org) as these costs are a important financial component to a PII/PHI breach in the U.S. At the present time, the Ponemon annual Cost of a Data Breach study will be released for 2009. The trend has been to see incremental increases in the money spent by companies that experience a data security breakdown. In 2005, the first year the study was conducted, the average per-record cost was determined to be $138, with a total average incident cost of $4.45 million. Over the next 3 years costs rose steadily to a per-record average of $202 and an average total incident cost of $6.65 million for 2008. In 2008, the average cost per person of notification was $15; however, this is an average and depends on a number of factors related to the specific breach.

The reason the costs are increasing year on year with regard to data breaches involving particularly customer/employee/patient PII are due to:

- The growing sophistication of international criminal community focused on identity theft who target high value information – not necessarily large deposits of information, but smaller caches of data that can be used to reap large rewards at small risk – is all the rage with today's fashionable hacker (or insider as hacker).
- U.S. data protection laws and/or statutes follow the residency of the affected individuals and security breaches in many cases involve multi-state notification. The advent of strong data protection laws. Language in the new Massachusetts data protection law, effective March 1, 2010, for example, may well result in a shift from data breach as a cost of doing business and create serious liability for companies that fail to provide proper protections for personally identifiable information. Section 03 of Mass 201 CMR 17 describes a "duty to protect" personal information, and mandates that companies holding such information "shall develop" the necessary means of protection. For health care, Federal Health Care Data Breach Notification (Effective 9/23/09) and California Expansion of Notification Statute to Medical Data – AB1298 (Effective 1/1/2008) expanded notification requirements regarding PHI. Implementation of U.S. data breach requirements for PHI can expose a health care entity or provider to fines up to $1.5 million.

- Along with these statutes or regulations, there is the increasing role of regulators and their powers to investigate, fine, and compensate affected individuals after the public announcement of a significant security or privacy breach. In the U.S., the focus of this has been at the Federal Trade Commission and state attorney generals. For PHI, the focus is Health and Human Services at the federal level, state attorney generals and state medical regulators.
- Mandatory notification requirements are being considered around the world. In July 2009, Germany modified its Federal Data Protection Act. Additional provisions could be added to the EU Data Directive regarding mandatory notification, and EU Data Commissioners are also seeking more powers, especially the ability to audit and fine.
- The increasing tendency of significant or large data breaches to be followed by attempts to certify class actions in the U.S – either by affected individuals or financial institutions. Although unsuccessful in most cases to certify or pay out damages, the legal defense costs and out of court settlement costs can easily be in the millions. The U.S. legal precedent set by lawsuits filed against TJX and Heartland Payment Systems following data breaches involving millions of records will certainly up the ante for companies who fail to protect data and cause other commercial entities to lose money as a result. In 2009, TJX continued to pay out settlement money to banks and credit unions that were forced to cancel and re-issue their customers' credit and debit cards, and similar fallout from the Heartland breach is only just starting to settle.
- The role of PCI DSS (the standards for credit card security promulgated by credit card associations) establishes worldwide standards, as well as potential fines if these standards are violated.

Beyond financial costs, one cannot minimize the impact of reputational fallout generally associated with the public disclosure of these events. There is growing evidence in consumer facing industries of the impact a data breach has on customer loyalty and behavior. According to a respected survey conducted by the Javelin Research Survey, entitled Customer Survey on Data Breach Notification, Javelin Research & Strategy, June 2008, major findings were:

- For 40% of consumers, security breaches changed their relationships with the affected institution or business.
- Confidence and buyer behavior are severely impacted by security breaches, with 55% of victims trusting the affected organization less, and 30% choosing to never purchase goods or services again from that organization.
- Breach victims are beginning to expect fraud protection assistance from the institution, with 36% already having been offered some kind of identity fraud protection service.
- The majority of breach victims (56%) prefer a solution that prevents fraudulent use of their information, rather than detecting or resolving fraud after it has occurred.

8.5 Risk Prevention

IT security measures must be strong, continually improved, and evaluated both internally and externally against evolving threats. Considering the specific risk events or threats with severity potential, risk management (and by extension the risk committee or team) will need to evaluate whether the IT security and privacy controls are effective, somewhat effective, or not at all effective. The basic questions the need to be addressed by the risk management team, include:

- How does the organization identify critical information assets, defined by degrees or categories of confidentiality, as well as the risks to the identified assets?
- Does the frequency and scope of the risk evaluation adequately take into account evolving threats?
- Are the resources for IT security, namely, staff and funding, sufficient to meet the organization's needs and security challenges?

Risk control aims at preventing and preempting risk events. The unique nature of security related risks is the interaction of people, processes and technology in an atmosphere of survivability, not invincibility. There is no single measure that can be installed today that guarantees security. Even standards of security like ISO and PCI are not guarantees against successful attacks but best practices.

In evaluating risk control, it is critical to understand that security not only rests on internal efforts, but also the efforts of independent contractor or business associates who have sensitive network access or who process, store, host, transmit, or process PII and/or PHI.

Many corporate executives mistakenly believe that by outsourcing the work or process to vendors they have also transferred the liability that may arise from a data breach or system failure. Unfortunately, that is not the case. The legal and regulatory liability regarding security and privacy of personally identifiable non-public information, either medical or financial, primarily remains with the data owner, i.e., the client of the vendor. For this reason, it is critical that organizations understand the key risks associated with outsourcing and vendor relationships.

One important first step is to inventory and classify vendors as high risk, medium risk, or low risk based upon their exposure to the key risks identified in Sects. 8.3 and 8.4. This process is well known to IT security professionals who utilize a best practice called "data classification." A data classification scheme applies throughout the enterprise and is based on the criticality and sensitivity (e.g., public, confidential, top secret) of enterprise data and systems. Once a data classification scheme is in place, the IT professionals can further define security levels, protection controls, and develop a description of data retention policies and destruction requirements. It is used as the basis for applying controls such as access, archiving or encryption. This data classification scheme can be correlated for data protection risks to vendors, i.e., the "high risk" vendor accesses/utilizes/processes/stores the most sensitive levels of data (confidential and top secret).

Once high, medium and low data classification levels have been established and defined for the key risks, then the risk committee can establish due diligence processes and procedures, focusing initially on new "high risk" vendors and renewal of contracts with those "high risk vendors." The key principle at work here is that vendor selection criteria should include risk, as well as reward, and that front-end due diligence is the initial step towards effectively managing risks associated with vendors.

In any risk prevent effort, genuine support from senior management in the form of financial commitment is absolutely critical. During difficult economic times, applications are delayed and IT budgets are slashed. In the private sector, the information security portion of the IT budget is already small, generally in the range of 5–12%. When the IT budget is reduced even further, investment in information security can become totally inadequate, often resulting in eliminating positions or delaying the hiring of qualified security professionals. One alternative consists of outsourcing select information security functions to specialized managed security firms. However, firewall monitoring and intrusion detection does not eliminate the continuing need to manage the process and people issues, including access controls, security education and training, etc.

As stated, security risk prevention stands on the foundation of best practices pivoted around the interaction of technology, people, and processes. In planning prevention measures, consider the pattern of security events that have been documented through extensive surveys and forensic experience. The Verizon 2009 Data Breach Investigation report which is available on-line has been based upon 5 years and over 500 forensic engagements. The summary results are as follows:

Who is behind data breaches?

- 20% were caused by insiders.
- 74% resulted from external sources.
- 32% implicated business partners or vendors (rose fivefold over 5 years of the study).
- 39% involved multiple parties.

How do breaches occur (many in combination of causes)?

- 67% were attributed to a significant error.
- 64% resulted from hacking and intrusions (important causes – SQL injection attacks and default credentials).
- 38% incorporated malicious code or malware (growing with major target – the application layer).
- 22% involved privilege misuse.
- 9% were due to physical threats.

What commonalities exist in these events?

- 69% involved data the victim did not know was on the system (most common – did not know the data was on the compromised system, laptop, or other mobile device).
- 81% of victims were not Payment Card Industry (PCI) compliant – credit card security standard for merchants/processors.

- 83% of attacks were not highly difficult and 87% were considered avoidable through simple/intermediate controls.
- 99.9% of records were compromised from servers and applications.

Based upon the above, standards should be a "defense in depth" approach and include the following:

- Communication and training reinforcement with employees, managers, and outside contractors with penalties for non-compliance.
- Patching and vulnerability management.
- Baking in security considerations into new and updated applications.
- Encryption of PHI/PII at rest, in transit and on mobile devices.
- Credit and criminal background checks before hire and periodically with sensitive positions.
- Due diligence and management of vendors/outsourced partners.
- Internal and external assessments and penetration testing, including social engineering ruses.
- Continuous improvement of security posture to address evolving risks and business activities.

While risk control efforts cannot guarantee elimination of all of the numerous and evolving sources of threats, they can significantly reduce the likelihood of attacks and the associated financial losses. Perpetrators tend to prey on those who are least prepared. Risk managers must understand that cybercrime and security incidents are inevitable in the present era and that techniques to prevent or preempt attacks constitute a wise investment.

8.6 Risk Mitigation

Risk mitigation represents efforts to reduce the impact of losses that cannot be altogether eliminated.

With regard to threats against computer networks and electronic information assets from malicious code, denial of service attacks, and other methods, key questions to assess the effectiveness of risk mitigation include:

- Is a business continuity or IT disaster plan put in place to address the system availability requirements for critical applications?
- Is the plan regularly tested and found effective?
- Is there a single point of failure?

In developing a business continuity plan, the first step would consist of an analysis of the business impact should critical applications become unavailable as a result of the network failure and the time frame for recovery. The second step would consist of a cost/benefit analysis of the different solutions and available options.

8.7 The Need for a Security Breach Incident Response Plan

A well-established security breach incident response plan needs to be part of corporate contingency planning today, especially for industries where non-public personal information is an essential component of the business model. This need spans a large number of industries from financial services, healthcare, retailing, hospitality, public utilities, professional services, educational institutions, etc. For many industry verticals, having and maintaining a security breach incident response plan is not optional, but required. GLBA, HIPAA and PCI compliance standards are examples where this is the case.

Since financial and brand impacts can be severe, we recommend planning that involves a multi-functional team, rather than improvisation at the time of loss. This approach is utilized for natural disasters, terrorism, and other matters; although a coordinated plan for a data breach may be new to many companies. Some companies have an external contact list of experts, but a phone tree is a poor substitute for a predefined plan involving the key stakeholders. When an incident is first identified, the situation can (and usually does) get worse before it gets better, sometimes because of improvised reactions to the event. Operations personnel might not know when to escalate a security event to a security incident-which is a critical step of incident response planning.

Like other corporate contingency plans, the security breach incident response plan should be updated and maintained in a secure, globally accessible location, no matter the state of the enterprise infrastructure. Besides key internal people, there will be a need for external expertise in the areas of legal, public relations, crisis management, computer forensics, credit protection and credit services. In a significant security breach, expect there will be quite a few stakeholders potentially involved or affected: senior management, board of directors, law enforcement, financial markets, the affected individuals themselves, issuing banks of credit cards (if the breach involved such), employees (if not directly affected by the breach, nevertheless concerned about its impact), shareholders, and regulators.

8.8 Risk Financing

There are only two effective measures of transferring risk – through contracts and insurance.

As global insurance brokers, we are very involved with clients and their risk management team in understanding what specific insurance policies address (or do not address) security and privacy risks. A traditional insurance portfolio typically includes Property, Crime, Commercial General Liability and depending on the business activities, a Professional Liability/Errors & Omissions insurance policy.

With regard to first party coverage, crime policies do not address consequential damages nor do they address stealing data; rather these policies cover stealing things-money, security and tangible property. Property policies cover physical damages or loss to buildings and hardware; not operational mistakes and computer attacks directed at data and networks. One major property insurer offers a significant data protection sublimit on a property policy but with very limited coverage and a long waiting period (time retention) for paying business interruption losses.

For example, many insurance clauses in vendor contracts require the vendor to obtain "commercially reasonable insurance" or only General Liability Insurance. Coverage A of the Commercial General Liability policy (CGL) does not address financial loss or security risks arising out of data or the pure financial loss involved in performance failures. A number of courts have held that "electronic data" does not meet the test of being tangible property (a key requirement of coverage in a CGL policy). Many security incidents also involve intentional acts, which may not meet the definition of an "occurrence." Also, unless endorsed, the CGL is not a global policy.

Other vendor contracts may require "professional liability," which is a critical first step in getting the insurance clause right. However, professional liability policies also have significant limitations or more often than not, the vendor's policy does not affirmatively address security and privacy risks. The vendor's policy may contain inference coverage that may not step up when an identity theft class action suit has been filed. Even more problematic is that most professional liability programs do not have coverage or have only limited coverage for contractually based risks or exclude return of fees, service penalties or liquidated damages. Contractual liability is critical as a contractual indemnity for security breaches and notification costs need to be affirmatively covered.

One important risk management step is to completely redesign the vendor insurance clause around the unique nature of security and privacy risks and define the critical elements of coverage desired, including data breach notification costs.

We are also called upon to review the client's own insurance program or risks that cannot otherwise be effectively transferred. In the world of data protection risks, clients must protect themselves due to the ultimate responsibility of the data owner and the very real possibility that the vendor could commit a breach in security that could overwhelm them and their available insurance limits.

What if the vendor simply does not have the means to indemnify? What if the vendor has no incident response plan? What if they are located in a country where appropriate insurance cannot be obtained? What if the policy they purchased denies coverage or has inadequate limits? Even vendors with solid-looking financials can change in today's world. Vendors with security/privacy certifications can make mistakes or be exposed to an unanticipated threat.

There are robust insurance products designed to cover (1) direct business interruption and extra expense associated with a security breach/outage) and (2) security and privacy liability, either on a stand-alone basis or in come cases combined with professional liability. What is important to understand is that there is no standard industry wording for such coverages. Thus it is important to understand the specific coverages, terms, limitations, definitions and exclusions of alternative quotes, how claims will be managed, and the experience of the insurer/underwriter in providing such coverage.

In general, the security and privacy liability insurance program is structured typically as follows:

- Worldwide coverage.
- Defense costs within the policy aggregate limit.
- Claims made and reporting.
- Large limits available and retentions vary depend on size of company, industry, risk management, and exposure to personal data.
- Three Coverage Grants:
  - Civil Liability.
  - Privacy/Security Regulation Actions (aggregate sublimit) – defense costs and some insurers/underwriters also cover payment of a regulatory compensatory award and civil fine or penalty where insurable.
  - Notification and Crisis Management Costs (aggregate sublimit; reimbursement of costs including mailing, notification template, services to affected group including credit reports, credit monitoring, credit protection, identity theft insurance, etc.; computer forensics outside experts, outside PR and legal advice, and professional call center).

Typically, insurers will want to understand the IT security and privacy best practices through a combination of a written application and a conference call with the applicant's IT security lead to ask additional questions about security controls, typically surrounding encryption, mobile devices, and outsourcing controls.

From a first party perspective, the coverage offerings typically include:

- Cyber Extortion.
- Electronic information assets (data, programs, etc) damaged, corrupted, deleted, etc. by computer attacks. Coverage provides for cost of restoration or replacement.
- Cyber Business Interruption subject to a time period (waiting period) typically covering loss of income and extra expense due to a computer attack.
- The next generation of insurance products will likely delve more deeply into reputational harm impacts, not just financial loss.

8.9 Summary

In summary, identifying, preventing, mitigating, and transferring privacy/security is a major priority, particularly in high compliance industries (such as financial institutions), any company that accepts a debit or credit card as a form of payment, and publicly traded companies. Outsourcing and offshoring is a fact of life, but definitely increases data protection risks. Vendor management process is needed which includes due diligence, contract protections, and vendor insurance requirements. This is a risk of survivability, not invincibility. It is recommended that one develop a team and plan for a data breach incident response, similar to contingency plans for other threats. The client should consider insurance protection, either on a combination with professional liability coverage or stand-alone coverage. Insurance is not a substitute for best security practices, but deals with the potential severity risk that the client cannot prevent. Quality of coverage and management of claims are very important, as well as the experience of the underwriter. One should be a thoughtful buyer.

References

[1] Retrieved from http://www.aignetadvantage.com
[2] Retrieved from http://www.symantec.com
[3] Retrieved from http://www.exodus.com
[4] Retrieved from http://www.plus.org
[5] Retrieved from http://www.gocsi.com

Chapter 9
Trend Analysis for Digital Risk Management

Dan Geer

The importance of measurement had been stressed by philosopher-scientists over the millennia and more recently by Galileo. Lord Kelvin had stated it succinctly, "When you can measure what you are speaking about, and express it in numbers, you know something about it; but when you cannot measure it, when you cannot express it in numbers, your knowledge is of a meager and unsatisfactory kind: it may be the beginning of knowledge, but you have scarcely, in your thoughts, advanced to the stage of science." The idea holds true in the field of digital computing and, more importantly, in the risks associated with all products and services supported by digital computing and networking.

We will define a term, "digital risk," to describe all forms of risks that relate to a digital asset, per se. As explained earlier, the computing engine is a discrete device, implemented through digital electronics and is the foundation for all major systems consisting of computer systems, networks, and software. These systems are referred to as digital assets. The objective of this chapter is to understand the trends in digital risk analysis, especially the critical role that scientific measurement of security will play on the precise quantification of the risk in monetary terms.

The digital, information-centric world is characterized by unprecedented flexibility in that it may be adapted to virtually every endeavor of our lives. While this capability implies great strength, this inherent power can be employed for constructive as well as destructive purposes. It is this potential for undoing the constructive gains that represents a great source of difficulties in the business world and has led to the introduction of risks and risk management. Analysis reveals the following key trends:

- The most important recent development has been that risk management has assumed the form of a major business proposition, overtaking all other forms of information security concerns. Security has become a valuable commodity. Unlike academia and government that continue to be focused on provable security, the practical business world already realizes that provable security is rarely affordable and that affordable security is rarely provable. Economics ultimately dominates.
- The demand for quantitative methods in information security is growing, but tools and products are slowly becoming available in the market. Clearly, not every

S. Ghosh and E. Turrini (eds.), *Cybercrimes: A Multidisciplinary Analysis*,
DOI 10.1007/978-3-642-13547-7_9,

aspect of information security can or will be rendered quantifiable. However, once quantification takes hold, it will replace qualitative security methods and begin to steer the field. The need is overwhelming and the practical products long overdue.
- Since September 11, 2001, the business world has come to accept that while it is not embarrassing to have suffered an information security attack, it is shameful to turn an ostrich eye and ignore the incursions. Unlike in the past, when information security officers were driven to uphold the image of flawless public record, whether or not factually true, today, a demonstrated willingness to take overt action against information bandits has become the expected norm.
- A major change on the horizon is a growing market for quantitative digital risk management, bolstered by an unwillingness to passively absorb risk. In business terms, this implies a need for a hybrid mix of loss prevention insurance and portfolio management, which, in turn, will require new models and possibly shared data.

By definition, an industry is considered matured when it offers products and services with a given assuredness or reliability, thereby stimulating expectations. In information rich fields, the onset of maturity must coincide with a given level of security [1] of the data and all that may be derived from it. Greater information security translates into greater data reliability, the core attribute of information systems businesses. The need is clearly visible in the financial services sector, energy distribution, telecom, government, healthcare, etc. In each of these cases, however, information and data are not the end but a means to other, more important goals. In essence, information and data are powerful enablers of extraordinarily valuable objectives. For example, the data on the health of a city's residents is crucial for government health officials to stockpile essential medicines in the event of emergencies. Also, whenever an entity, in our case data, is not in itself an end but a means, it may be substituted by any other means, overtly or covertly, whenever and wherever economic, regulatory, and opportunity conditions dictate. The field of data security encompasses the "any other means," in that the actual deliverable, i.e., the native data, may be substituted for with data sequestration, obscurity of access method, mechanisms that disambiguate identities and authorities, surveillance-based criminal justice, contractual assignment of liability, redundant provisioning, professional licensure and certification, or risk transfer in the insurance style, and so forth.

For a decision-maker, to whom the native data represents "the end" and not "the means," the author suggests pursuing a logical path of digital risk management. This path encourages the decision-maker to ask the following questions:

- How secure am I?
- Am I better off than I was this time last year?
- Am I spending enough on security?
- How do I compare with my peers?
- What risk transfer options do I have?

The answers are likely to lead to the following risk management options, which may be adopted individually or combined.

1. Bear the risk, as the cost of doing business.
2. Mitigate the risk, i.e., fundamentally reduce or eliminate it, if and where possible.
3. Transfer the risk, i.e., hedge it.

The remainder of this chapter will be devoted to digital risk management, especially option 3 focusing on how to transfer the risk through hedging. Of the three, this is possibly the best option, for the following reasons. For option 1, we point out that it is very difficult to know precisely all of the digital risks a priori. With respect to option 2, we note that the sheer number of risks and mitigation techniques may render it difficult to possess adequate knowledge at all times. Option 3 offers the greatest freedom and leverage to structure the business.

In the digital risk management world, the risk transfer theme is gaining popularity and the number of available sub-options is growing. First, as the most transparent example, consider that a company, XYZ, resorts to "managed services," which is backed by errors and omissions insurance. The "managed services" is realized through a security monitoring firm that is responsible for the data security. In the event the firm itself fails to interdict an information security attack in progress, the insurance provides for any stop loss coverage. This is a pure risk transfer paradigm and it appeals most to the middle tier of companies, who on one hand can suffer substantial loss from data insecurity but on the other hand lack sufficient staff to realistically provide "eternal vigilance." Money and surveillance data flow out of the client firm (XYZ) and, in return, the security monitoring firm provides an expanded lead time to XYZ to address any problem. The security monitoring firm adds value by aggregating client intelligence, processing it, and disseminating warning messages with the highest possible precision and timeliness. From XYZ's point of view, the risk of sending out surveillance data is hedged by the insurance contract and traded for expanded risk mitigation handling time. From the managed security service provider's point of view, its margin is preserved and defended if it invests in tools for labor productivity of its own staff while its value proposition enjoys a net positive effect determined by the size of its client base, explicitly for common mode failures, including organized crime automation.

Information security becomes a risk transfer exercise when failures of data and information security are categorized as specific perils within business continuation coverage, especially for those firms where security is understood to be a key subset of reliability. As a second example of digital risk management, consider the following illustration. A primary underwriter of e-commerce business continuation coverage has accumulated a sufficiently large portfolio and begins to sell tranches or components of the portfolio into the re-insurance market. Potential re-insurance buyers ask the standard questions, namely, (1) describe the quality of the insureds that make up the portfolio, (2) the loss history, and (3) the risk aggregation characteristics of the portfolio. The insureds are unremarkable and hence acceptable. However if, as is likely, the loss history in this portfolio has been effectively zero, the re-insurer focuses on one question, namely, whether the lack of a loss history might be due to hidden or overlooked risk aggregation in the portfolio. In other words, does the absence of loss history imply a warning that losses would be aggregated when they do occur? For this portfolio, risk aggregation would have to come through mechanisms of failure in e-commerce infrastructure outside of the idiosyncratic practices at any particular insured. A commissioned white paper on possible risk aggregation connectors between and among the insureds found two foci: (1) common mode failure of major Internet structures such as top level naming services or peer-to-peer points between major ISPs, and (2) the pervasive Microsoft monoculture on the desktops, given the universally abject history of exploitability and exploitation. Thus, in this scenario, risk transfer had become an exercise in model-based risk bounding. In the absence of actuarial data, the margin of error in risk estimation must expand to include joint and cascade failures as well as individual failures.

A third example of information security as a risk transfer exercise consists of the apparent inevitable expansion of Directors' and Officers' (D&O) liability and liability coverage to include failures of information handling primarily denominated in terms of failures of information security apparati, policies, and investment levels. Though litigation is perhaps the poorest of all alternatives for societal change management, it is nevertheless undeniable that assigning responsibility for information security failings to those individuals with whom the buck stops represents an intra-organizational risk transfer mechanism that may then involve D&O insurers as they are simply the next stage of the responsibility chain. In case it is not obvious, we point out the following. It is already true that nearly all privacy regulation has D&O penalties implicit, while nearly all privacy compliance relies on information security apparati, policies, and investment levels. In essence, information security is already in-scope for D&O insurance and the bounding perimeter for the D&O insurance market will only grow to include it.

As a fourth example, consider that much of the current control apparatus of an information-centric enterprise begins with authentication and there are numerous examples of risk transfer in outsourced authentication services. Most notable are the variations on the public key infrastructure (PKI). While far from pervasive, identification services that offer performance guarantees of any sort amount to a risk transfer in that for a consideration the identification provider takes on at least some of the risk of mis-identification. While the exact measure of "at least some" is subject to contractual limitation and will someday inevitably be the basis for a body of case law, the Identrus consortium [2] serves as a good example. Intended for the banking sector, it is nevertheless an identification hierarchy in which full deployment would cover high value e-commerce of all types, not just financial transactions. Identrus is noteworthy in that, by design, it is a risk transfer mechanism. That is, should a mis-identification occur, there would be a fixed-value warranty payment to the relying party. More broadly, should the Identrus consortium proposed model become pervasive, it would represent a securitization of the principle risk of electronic commerce, leading, it is hoped, to a liquid market in packaged risk in the digital economy.

As a fifth example, consider that product liability promises to play a central role in digital risk transfer. Software failures underwrite information security breaches including failures to effectively provide any of the classic triad of information security, namely, data confidentiality, integrity, or availability. If and when a member of the plaintiff's bar succeeds in extracting stiff penalty over contingent losses due to failure of security functions embedded in a software product, every software vendor will be looking at both risk minimization and risk transfer. Risk mitigation must focus almost entirely at the design stage of the software development process [1]. The author and colleagues are already able to prove that return on investment in application security strongly favors the earliest feasible intervention in the development process, not an afterthought. The risk transfer alternative might consist in changing software license paradigms toward mandatory upgrade as a condition of license, probably with an automatic approach as the default. In other words, if a software vendor is liable for failures of its product, the vendor will naturally endeavor to retain control of the product in its fielded state, including the right to either repair it when needed in situ, or to force the risk transfer onto its user should the user refuse the repair. The mobile device market is sorting this out as we speak.

While the sixth and final example of information security as a risk transfer exercise is more speculative, it is perhaps the most important example, given that banks are the longstanding bellwether of security futures. Details notwithstanding, major banks have long had regulatory minimum levels of capital reserves that they must set aside to hedge against loan defaults among their loanee base. The regulatory reserves are to protect the banking system from a cascading failure of individual banks. Under the long delayed but seemingly inevitable "Basel II Capital Accord" [3] the consolidated banking industries of the G8 countries will move to a regime where the minimum regulatory capital is a tripartite equation, first part set aside against credit risk or loan defaults; second part set aside against market risk, i.e., downside price exposures of assets; and third part set aside against operational risk. Operational risk encompasses the entire reliability spectrum including information security, both in its raw form and in such derivative forms as internal fraud unblocked by adequate information security measures. Operational risk can be insured, it can be mitigated by investment in technology and procedures, and it can be counter-balanced with set aside capital. Thus, operational risk management forces an explicit business decision driven by quantitative analysis. There is an additional issue. Record keeping over a long baseline duration will play a central role in regulatory assessment of the unhedged operational risk a bank holds and hence how much capital will and must be set aside. When combined, these records will norm pricing of digital risk at least within the sub-sector from which the numbers are obtained. It is the pricing of risk that is ultimately the arbiter of tradeoffs.

The list of six examples presented in this chapter is not exhaustive. The author nor any other is in complete possession of all the facts. The facts are unstable in any case. It is merely indicative of the many ways in which information security may be viewed as a risk transfer exercise. We will summarize by stating that complexity is the primary enemy of certainty, i.e., complexity of information structures is the source of information insecurity. When software vendors disclaim the liability of their products while at the same time increasing the complexity with each release, they are engaging in a subtle and substantial risk transfer game. Given that there is now more information security risk sloshing round the economy than can actually be accepted were it exposed, the challenge now turns to who can minimize their risk the best, i.e., who can mitigate what they can and externalize the rest of their downside information security costs. The weapons to mitigate security risks are perhaps as simple as the wisdom of Delphi, "Know thyself" and "Nothing to excess" – know thyself in the sense of quantitative rigor and a perpetual propensity toward designing information systems with potential failures in mind; nothing to excess in the sense of mimicking the biological world's proof by demonstration that species diversity is the greatest bulwark against a fragile ecosystem.

References

[1] Ghosh, S. (2002, April). *Principles of secure network systems design*. New York, NY: Springer.
[2] Retrieved from http://www.identrus.com
[3] Basel Committee on Banking Supervision. (2003, April). *Basel II: Overview of the New Basel Capital Accord* (pp. 1–18). Retrieved from http://www.bis.org

Part IV
Critical Infrastructure Protection and Cybercrimes

Chapter 10
Evolutionary History of Critical Infrastructure Protection in the USA

Sumit Ghosh

According to Scott Charney, Former Chief of the Computer Crime and Intellectual Property Section for Microsoft, "The notion that only States have access to weapons of war is no longer correct, at least not if information warfare is considered. Simply put, we have distributed a technology that is far more powerful than most that are placed in the public domain. Traditional vigilance regarding states that support terrorism, political unrest, or are otherwise considered rogue, i.e., nations of concern, are now supplemented by threats from individuals of concern, a far larger pool, and one that is harder to identify and police [1]."

The idea that specific services and functions in our society are so essential that they must be protected from natural and artificial disruptions is not new. Indeed, the government, owners, and operators of critical infrastructure facilities have managed the risks arising from service disruptions as long as such infrastructures have existed. For example, when the northeast power system suffered the largest blackout in US history on 9 November 1965, leaving 30 million people without electricity for up to 13 h [2], President Lyndon Johnson wrote to the chairman of the Federal Power Commission, "Today's failure is a dramatic reminder of the importance of the uninterrupted flow of power to the health, safety, and well being of our citizens and the defense of our country. This failure should be immediately and carefully investigated in order to prevent a recurrence. You are therefore directed to launch a thorough study of the cause of this failure. I am putting at your disposal full resources of the federal government and directing the Federal Bureau of Investigation, the Department of Defense and other agencies to support you in any way possible. You are to call upon the top experts in our nation in conducting the investigation. A report is expected at the earliest possible moment as to the causes of the failure and the steps you recommend to be taken to prevent a recurrence."

While concerns about such infrastructure failures have long existed, the challenge to prevent them has become much more complex in the "Information Age." The United States of America relies increasingly upon new information technologies and the Internet to conduct business, manage industrial and governmental activities, engage in personal communications, and perform scientific research. These technologies have (1) enabled unprecedented gains in efficiency, productivity, and communications, (2) spurred tremendous growth in the US economy, and (3) become essential to our nation's ability to function. Ironically, the diverse and

S. Ghosh and E. Turrini (eds.), *Cybercrimes: A Multidisciplinary Analysis*,
DOI 10.1007/978-3-642-13547-7_10,

interdependent information technology systems that assist in managing and controlling the infrastructure are inherently vulnerable. Information systems are prone to accidental disruption. The May 1998 failure of the Galaxy 4 communications satellite, for example, disrupted 90% of the pagers in the US [3]. It also disrupted credit card purchases, ATM transactions, and the communications of health care providers and emergency workers [3]. The disruption demonstrated that interdependencies can trigger cascading failures that can spread into multiple sectors of the critical infrastructure. Information systems can also be intentionally disrupted for nefarious purposes. The September 11, 2001 terrorist attacks on the World Trade Centers destroyed 1,600 telephone lines in the immediate area of the attack, disrupting telecommunications for residences, businesses, and government offices in southern Manhattan [4]. An estimated 50 million people across eight States in the USA and the Canadian province of Ontario were left without electrical power in August 2003 when a utility in Ohio experienced problems that began a chain reaction of events leading to power outages lasting, in some places, several days. This incident, known as the "Northeast Blackout of 2003," cost roughly $6 billion and caused at least 265 power plants to shut down [5]. In November 2008, the compromised payment processors of an international bank unwittingly permitted fraudulent transactions at more than 130 automated teller machines in 49 cities within a 30-min period, [6,7]. The ultimate goal of critical infrastructure protection (CIP) is to understand and prevent cascading failures that can trigger major nationwide disruptions of entire infrastructures and industries.

Today, CIP efforts are largely motivated by concern about the potential for deliberate disruption of the infrastructure. Many nations have instituted "information warfare" programs that can target vulnerable infrastructure networks for cyberattacks. Furthermore, since 11 September 2001, the cyberthreat from non-state actors, including terrorist groups, has garnered greater attention, although the degree of danger posed by such groups using cyber techniques remains the subject of debate. Even though CIP efforts have been underway since the mid-1990s, CIP policy is still in its infancy, and policymakers and CIP stakeholders continue to work to reach consensus on a host of CIP issues.

10.1 What is "Critical Infrastructure"?

Currently, a number of definitions of the "critical infrastructure" are being used by policymakers. Congress has codified a framework for defining the critical infrastructure. US law defines the "critical infrastructure" as "systems and assets, whether physical or virtual, so vital to the United States that the incapacity or destruction of such systems and assets would have a debilitating impact on security, national economic security, national health or safety, or any combination of those matters." However, efforts to reach consensus on identifying the companies, entities, and sectors that fall within this definition are yet to converge. In 1996, a presidential commission identified eight sectors that were so vital to US society that their incapacitation or destruction would have a debilitating impact on US defense and economic security. The Presidential Decision Directive (PDD) enumerated the sectors as transportation, oil and gas production and storage, water supply, emergency services, government services, banking and finance, electrical power, and telecommunications. However, the subsequent US administration has abandoned this definition. The White House's National Strategy for Homeland Defense, released on July 16, 2002, identifies 13 critical infrastructure sectors. The new definition adds agriculture and food, public health, defense industrial base, chemical industry, and postal and shipping sectors to the existing list. The National Strategy for Homeland Security, released October 2007 [8], expanded the scope of critical infrastructure and key resources (CI/KR) to 17 and included information technology; commercial nuclear reactors, materials, and waste; dams; and national monuments and icons. The 60-day Cyberspace Policy Review [6], conducted by the current US Administration, broadens the scope of CIP and recognizes that "cyberspace touches practically everything and everyone." The Review candidly admits that the Federal government is not presently organized to effectively address the growing problem with breaches in cyberspace now or in the future. The responsibilities for cybersecurity are distributed across a wide area of balkanized federal bureaucratic departments and agencies, many with overlapping authorities, and none with complete awareness and sufficient decision authority to direct actions that deal with often conflicting issues in a consistent way. The government must integrate competing interests, develop a holistic vision, underwrite policies, processes, people, and technology to mitigate cybersecurity-related issues confronting the USA. The review took into account the Center for Strategic and International Studies (CSIS)' Cybersecurity Commission report [9] and one of its recommendations was that the National Security Council be restructured to address cyber issues and that a position be created for a Whitehouse cyber security advisor who would answer to the National Economic Council (NEC) and National Security Council. The advisor, Howard Schmidt, was appointed in December 2009.

Clearly, specifying the sectors of the critical infrastructure is vital to CIP efforts. After all, it is difficult to protect a target of indiscriminate scope or dimension. However, limiting the definition has been difficult because "critical" is often a matter of perspective. In general, the critical infrastructure has been defined too broadly. While certain sectors are universally acknowledged to be crucial to society, the disruption of others might amount to a monumental inconvenience, but not immediate peril. Thus, if we lose access to electrical power or potable water, lives would be immediately endangered. On the other hand, it is possible to survive without immediate access to postal and shipping services. Yet, the definition of the critical infrastructure has grown more expansive and currently includes sectors that may not meet the statutory definition of a critical infrastructure. It is important to note that an imprecise definition of critical infrastructure can undermine CIP's mission. If the critical infrastructure is defined too broadly, CIP efforts assume the quixotic mission of preventing the disruption of all information networks rather than focusing on key networks. This may not be practically realizable. The US CIP policy continues to be in a state of flux and any inadvertent over reaching efforts may be trimmed.

10.2 US CIP Policy

Our newfound reliance on information networks has unwittingly furnished criminals, terrorists, and hostile foreign nation-states with many new opportunities to steal money and proprietary data, intrude upon private records, invade sensitive computer networks, and disrupt vital infrastructures. CIP policy addressing such dangers has evolved from initial efforts that were government-directed to more recent efforts that seek to forge a government/private industry partnership to address the vulnerabilities. Over the years, CIP has spawned the creation of a government agency, namely, the National Infrastructure Protection Agency; White House staff devoted to the CIP issue, namely, the Office of Cybersecurity; and executive orders governing CIP policy. This focus on CIP is the product of new anxiety over the potential dangers posed by an attack on the critical infrastructure.

10.2.1 The Threat

The Internet's vulnerability to deliberate disruption was presaged by a 1988 incident involving the Department of Defense's Advanced Research Projects Agency Network (ARPANET), the progenitor to today's Internet. ARPANET was a large, wide-area network created by the United States Defense Advanced Research Project Agency (ARPA) in 1969 [10]. ARPANET was an experiment in networking technologies that linked universities and research centers [11]. On November 2, 1988, the ARPANET had its first automated network security incident caused by a computer worm commonly referred to as "the Morris worm." A student at Cornell University, Robert T. Morris, wrote a program that could connect computer A to another computer, say B; find and use one of several vulnerabilities to copy itself to computer B; and begin to run the copy of itself at the new location. Both the original code and the copy would then repeat these actions indefinitely, seeking out other computers on the ARPANET [12]. He released the worm through the computers at the Massachusetts Institute of Technology to hide his tracks. The Morris Worm spread in a geometric progression across the ARPANET, consuming so much of the system resources that the attacked computers could no longer function. As a result, 10% of the US computers connected to the ARPANET, including university, military, and medical research computers, effectively stopped operating. The estimated cost of remedying the damage caused by the worm at each site ranged from a low of $200 to a high of $53,000.

The networks that comprise today's Internet are no less susceptible to attacks by programs that resemble the Morris Worm. A detailed assessment of attacks may be found under Part II of the book. Indeed, in 2001 the Code Red and Nimda Worms worked in similar fashion to impair access to computers across the World Wide Web (WWW). The Code Red Worm infected more than 250,000 computers in just 9 h [13]. The worm was written to spread itself by creating a sequence of random IP addresses to infect, infiltrate the computer, inspect the infected computer's system time clock, and trigger a DoS attack at midnight July 20, 2001 on the www.whitehouse.gov website [13]. The Nimda Worm reportedly infected at least 150,000 computers and knocked many business websites and e-mail servers offline for days [14]. These worms are only an example of the mischief and, perhaps the mayhem, that may be caused by attacking the infrastructure through the Internet. The Confiker virus is estimated to have already affected, by the end of 2009, between 6 and 11 million computers. The compromised machines can essentially be turned into Botnets capable of being orchestrated to launch massive DDOS attacks. The Domain Name Services (DNS) that translate website names into computer addresses have been increasingly under attack. While simple mischiefs such as defacing websites are common, a serious DNS attack may have untold consequences. As a hypothetical example, consider that a DNS attack successfully reroutes an unsuspecting remote operator of a nuclear power plant to a bogus website which has been carefully designed to accurately mimic the regular website with which the operator is intimately familiar. While the operator reacts normally to the controls of the otherwise fictitious website, the actual plant receives no instructions from the operator and any misbehavior will remain uncorrected, potentially leading to dangerous consequences. A detailed discussion of attacks on the Internet infrastructure including the DNS occurs in Sect. 13.2.

While such incidents provide anecdotal evidence of the potential peril, they do not yield certain and quantitative proof of the threat posed by cyberattacks against our critical infrastructure. Although there is agreement that Internet vulnerabilities exist and are being maliciously exploited, there is no consensus about the potential consequences of cyberattacks or even that an effective cyberattack on the critical infrastructure is possible. Policymakers have characterized the threat to the critical infrastructure as a ticking "electronic Pearl Harbor," and the number of cyberattacks executed every year continues to grow. Former CIA Director John Deutch claimed in June 1996 [15] that an "electronic Pearl Harbor" was a possibility and that hackers had offered their services to Iran, Iraq, and Libya with plans to break into American computers to gain information and to commit sabotage. In order to escalate the seriousness of potential infrastructure attacks, Paul Kurtz, a former US Whitehouse cybersecurity official [16] and US senators, Rockefeller and Snowe, drafters of pending Cybersecurity legislation [17], have used the term "cyber Katrina" to emphasize that the US financial markets, power grid, and the World Wide Web may all be abruptly shut down by cybercriminals. Kurtz has even proposed the establishment of a Federal Emergency Management Agency (FEMA) for the Internet, citing that the current balkanized federal bureaucracies cannot deliver a coordinated and timely response to attacks. A few cybersecurity experts maintain that the danger has been grossly overstated and that the likelihood of triggering sustained damage to a critical infrastructure facility through a cyberattack is remote [18]. These skeptics have noted that it would be easier to mount a physical attack using explosives to disable a facility than to attempt to marshal the resources and expertise needed to launch an effective cyberattack. Arguably, even a successful cyberattack would likely only be effective for a limited period of time before security and remediation efforts curtailed it.

There is considerable debate whether entities that possess the technical sophistication to execute complex cyberattacks would ever attempt them. The entities capable of marshalling the skills and expertise to execute an effective cyberattack are nation-states. Indeed, it has been reported that many nation-states are developing capabilities to conduct and defend against cyberattacks [19]. Yet, a true cyberattack, launched by a nation-state, would be tantamount to an act of war and would likely be attempted during an armed conflict or as a precursor to an armed conflict. Conceivably, however, many nations are already currently engaged in cyber-espionage, which is similar but distinct from a cyberattack. While a cyberattack may cause extensive damage to an infrastructure, the goal of cyber-espionage is covert information gathering. It is unlikely that most nations would unleash their cyberattack capabilities, except during conventional wars. In contrast, terrorist organizations may desire to launch a cyberattack, but lack the resources and skill to successfully mount a cyberattack on a critical infrastructure [20]. It is axiomatic that almost any computer is capable of causing a serious cyberincident, especially since tools used to conduct cyberattacks are all too easily available online. Interpol estimates [21] that as many as 30,000 websites provide some form of automated hacking tools. The ability to stage an effective cyberattack requires up-to-date intelligence about the target network and its architecture, which would likely require stealthy intrusions conducted over a period of time. While nation states are likely to invest in such expensive intelligence-gathering efforts, most terrorist organizations may lacks the resources.

To-date there have been no intentional cyberattacks on a critical infrastructure that may be equated to an "electronic Pearl Harbor." Nevertheless, there is cause for concern about the possibility of a serious cyberincident involving a critical infrastructure. Terrorist groups in particular have exhibited a propensity for targeting critical infrastructures for attack. Terrorists have launched physical attacks on telecommunications networks [22], electric power systems [23], oil and gas pipelines [24], and banking and financial systems [25, 26]. In 1987, the LTTE [22] attacked a telecommunications complex north of the Jaffna tower, severely damaging the sophisticated computer systems. Their strategic goal was to deprive the residents of Jaffna of the basic amenities, including public libraries and telephone services. In 1997 IRA terrorists [23] sought to bomb six National Grid Group substations, which would have cut off all power to the city of London and the south-east UK. If the plot was successful, it would have crippled hospitals, transportation, emergency services, and vital computer links, requiring months to return to full service. In Colombia [24], the FARC and the ELN achieved great success in targeting the nation's oil and gas pipelines, carrying out a majority of the 152 attacks against Cano Limon, Columbia's second largest crude oil pipeline and forcing Occidental Petroleum to halt exports through August and September of 2000. In 1992, the IRA bombing of London's Baltic Exchange [25] cost three lives and caused over $1 billion in damage, while in April 1996, the LTTE drove a truck laden with explosives into the Central Bank [26] in Colombo, the capital of Sri Lanka, killing 91 people. A former head of the FBI's National Infrastructure Protection Center notes, "We have seen a clear decision by terrorist groups like al Qaeda to focus on critical infrastructures, financial networks and power grids. And they have developed expertise with computer systems for secure communications and planning attacks. The next step is to put the two together" [27].

Furthermore, the incidence of politically-motivated cyberattacks has been growing over the last few years. Many recent international conflicts have been accompanied by cyberattacks against information networks belonging to the parties involved in the conflicts [28]. During the Israeli and Palestinian tensions in late 1999 and early 2000, while pro-Israeli hackers attacked web sites of the Palestinian Authority, pro-Palestinian hackers retaliated by crippling web sites of the Israeli Parliament, Israeli Defense Forces, the Foreign Ministry, and the Bank of Israel. Following the U.S. air strikes against the Former Republic of Yugoslavia in 2000, the North Atlantic Treaty Organization web servers hosting NATO's international website and e-mail traffic suffered sustained cyberattacks. The U.S. and China spy plane incident in early 2001 triggered a free-wheeling exchange of cyberattacks between U.S. hacker groups and Chinese hacker groups, including the Honker Union of China and the Chinese Red Guest Network Security Technology Alliance. There have also reportedly been exercises suggesting that an intentional cyberattack against a critical infrastructure is indeed feasible. In 1997, the Pentagon conducted "Eligible Receiver," an information warfare exercise that illustrated some of the implications of infrastructure interdependence. During the exercise, which simulated a rogue state attempting to attack US information systems, a team of National Security Agency (NSA) computer specialists successfully used off-the-shelf technology and software to simulate attacks against city power grids and 911 emergency systems. The success of their attacks and the ease with which they might have successfully breached system security was reportedly sobering [29]. According to one account, the NSA team could have shut down the US electric-power grid within days and rendered impotent the command-and-control elements of the US Pacific Command [30].

Potential targets for a cyberattack whose disruption would cause a serious critical infrastructure incident also exist. Backbone operations systems for utilities called SCADA (supervisory control and data acquisition) systems that control vehicular traffic, dams, electric grid, and the flow of gas, water, and oil supplies are among the infrastructure networks that have prompted the greatest concern. SCADA is a category of software application program for gathering data in real time from remote locations in order to control equipment and operations. SCADA systems are used in power plants as well as in oil and gas refining, telecommunications, transportation, and water and waste control. The hardware gathers and feeds data into a computer running the SCADA software. The computer processes the acquired data and calibrates and operates the equipment accordingly. Security firms have raised concerns about SCADA system vulnerabilities, noting that SCADA networks and corporate IT systems are often interlinked. According to Riptech, a network security firm, these systems are often linked without a full understanding of the associated security risks [31]. The lack of adequate barriers between the systems can facilitate unauthorized access and control of SCADA systems [31]. The concerns are heightened by the fact that the knowledge required to access and control SCADA systems is relatively easily available. Several standards for the interconnection of

SCADA systems have been published in the open literature and many are available on the Internet [32,33]. Furthermore, SCADA providers publish the design and maintenance documents for their products and sell toolkits to help develop software that implements the various standards used in SCADA environments. In January 2002, the FBI issued a warning that al Qaeda may had scrutinized information on SCADA systems available on multiple SCADA-related websites, seeking information about water supply and waste management practices in the US. At a SCADA conference in January 2008, CIA analyst, Tom Donahue [34] confirmed successful cyberattacks and intrusions over the Internet on foreign electrical power systems, which cause power outages across multiple cities. The attacks were immediately followed by extortion demands. The interfering with, or disruption of SCADA controls may have far reaching consequences. In the USA, over 85% of the CI/KR are controlled through SCADA. A recently recorded demonstration conducted by USA government researchers, labeled the Aurora Generator Test, investigated a dangerous vulnerability in the computers at USA utility companies. The test illustrated the potential destruction caused by seizing control of a crucial part of the USA electrical grid, namely, an industrial turbine spinning wildly out of control until it becomes a smoking hulk and the power shuts down.

Notwithstanding the debate over the probability and consequences of a cyberattack, it is prudent for the government to prepare for possible attacks. In the aftermath of the 11 September 2001 terrorist attacks, policymakers would find it difficult, possibly irresponsible, to ignore the threat posed by a cyberattack on the critical infrastructure. As one commentator offered in an analysis of the government's failure to prevent 11 September 2001 attack, "... The terrorist attack was not the product of a failure of intelligence-gathering; it was the product of a failure of imagination [35]." Since the potential consequences of a cyberattack are too serious to ignore, CIP efforts that began in the mid 1990s have culminated in a large government-wide effort to create a coherent and effective CIP policy.

10.2.2 The Structure and Evolution of US CIP Efforts

Following the 1993 World Trade Center and 1995 Oklahoma City bombings, the federal government examined the vulnerabilities of the nation's critical infrastructures to terrorist attacks. Pursuant to Presidential Decision Directive (PDD) 39, the Attorney General assessed the vulnerability of those critical infrastructures and recommend measures to protect them. The Attorney General concluded that with the advent of the Information Age, US infrastructures were vulnerable, not just to traditional, physical terrorist attacks, but also to cyberattacks on the computer networks and communications systems that are embedded in and connect the infrastructures [36].

In July, 1996, by Presidential Executive Order 13010, a presidentially-appointed panel, dubbed the "President's Commission on Critical Infrastructure Protection" (PCCIP), was created to formulate a comprehensive national strategy for protecting the infrastructures we all depend on from physical and cyber threats. The PCCIP consisted of two full-time members from ten executive branch departments and agencies whose respective jurisdictions included critical infrastructure facilities. These included the Department of the Treasury; Department of Justice; Department of Defense; Department of Commerce; Department of Transportation; Department of Energy; Central Intelligence Agency; Federal Emergency Management Agency; Federal Bureau of Investigation; and the National Security Agency. Robert T. Marsh served as the Chairman of PCCIP and the committee consisted of the following commission members: Merritt Adams, American Telephone & Telegraph; Richard P. Case, International Business Machines Corporation (IBM); Dr. Mary J. Culnan, Georgetown University; Peter H. Daly, U.S. Treasury; John C. Davis, National Security Agency; Thomas J. Falvey, Department of Transportation (DOT); Brenton C. Greene, Department of Defense; Dr. William J. Harris, Texas Transportation Institute; David A. Jones, Department of Energy; William B. Joyce, Central Intelligence Agency; Stevan D. Mitchell, Department of Justice; Dr. Irwin M. Pikus, Department of Commerce; Dr. John R. Powers, Federal Emergency Management Agency; Paul Rodgers, National Association of Regulatory Utility Commissioners; Susan Simens, Federal Bureau of Investigations; Dr. Frederick M. Struble, Board of Governors of the Federal Reserve System; and Nancy J. Wong, Pacific Gas and Electric Company. In addition, the commission included representatives from academia, state agencies, and industry. The commission's mission included:

- Determining and categorizing the range of threats to critical infrastructures
- Identifying vulnerabilities within and among critical infrastructures
- Finding and assessing options for protecting infrastructures
- Assuring continuation and restoration of service
- Developing a strategy for protecting critical infrastructures
- Recommending an implementation plan for protective and assurance measures, including the policy, legislative and other changes required

In October 1997, the PCCIP issued a report that prompted the creation of PDD-63, a framework for initial CIP efforts. PDD-63 assigned overall responsibility for policy development and coordination for critical infrastructure assurance to the National Coordinator for Security, Infrastructure Protection, and Counter-Terrorism at the National Security Council. It also created the National Infrastructure Protection Center (NIPC) at the FBI which united representatives from FBI, DoD, USSS, Energy, Transportation, the Intelligence Community, and the private sector in an unprecedented attempt at information sharing among agencies in collaboration with the private sector. Furthermore, PDD-63 established the Critical Infrastructure Assurance Office (CIAO) as an interagency office located at the Department of Commerce to support the National Coordinator in carrying out these policy development and coordination functions. Following The Homeland Security Act of 2002 [37], the Department of Homeland Security (DHS) was established as an executive department of the USA within the meaning of title 5, United States Code. Its primary mission was to (1) prevent terrorist attacks within the USA, (2) reduce the vulnerability of the USA to terrorism, and (3) minimize the damage and assist in the recovery from terrorist attacks that do occur within the USA. The NIPC was absorbed into DHS in 2002 and it no longer exists. Although the National Cyber Security Division (NCSD) at DHS was established under the HSPD-7 [38, 39] and has a comparable purpose, there is nothing that has precisely the same mission as the NIPC.

In October 2001, President George W. Bush signed Executive Order 13231 establishing a new entity to further U.S. CIP efforts and initiatives. The Order amended some of the bureaucratic structure created by PDD-63 and established the President's Critical Infrastructure Protection Board (PCIPB) as a part of the White House's Office of Homeland Security and the National Security Council. The Board has responsibilities for Federal programs involving:

- Cooperation with, and protection of, private sector infrastructure, state and local governments' critical infrastructure, and supporting programs in corporate and academic organizations
- Protection of Federal departments and agencies critical assets and information systems
- Continuity of operational and continuity of government for the Federal government
- Related national security programs

It also, inter alia, created the position of the Special Advisor to the President for Cyberspace Security who chairs the PCIPB. Since virtually every US department and agency in the federal government contributes to the objective of CIP, the PCIPB includes every cabinet secretary and adviser, as well as other senior government leaders. The PCIPB has emphasized building government/industry cooperation. For, in the US, an estimated 85% of the critical infrastructure is owned by private industry [40]. The PCIPB's policies eschew government regulation and seek to make market forces work to improve information security. In the simplest of terms, current US CIP efforts are organized into four categories:

- *Prevention*: efforts to develop and implement practices and strategies to eliminate or limit vulnerabilities through activities such as robust government and industry information sharing and promulgation of best practices; analysis, watch, and warning functions; intelligence gathering; training; research and development efforts; and deterrent sentencing.
- *Prediction and detection*: attempting to forecast hostile capabilities with sufficient warning to prevent them from being exploited and identifying that a cyber incident is occurring on the Internet that warrants preventative measures.
- *Response*: identifying the source of a cyber incident and terminating the incident.
- *Reconstitution*: the rapid resumption of services and rebuilding of the systems following a cyber incident that damaged critical infrastructure facility or impaired service from such a facility.

Different federal and private entities are responsible for the discrete areas of CIP. Until it was absorbed in the DHS in 2002, the entity with the most multi-faceted role was the NIPC, which was comprised of representatives from law enforcement, intelligence community, and the military. NIPC was a national focal point for gathering information on threats to critical infrastructures in the US. It plays a central role in facilitating and coordinating the federal government's response to a cyberincident, mitigating attacks, investigating threats, and monitoring reconstitution efforts. The NIPC had included investigators and analysts experienced in computer network intrusions and infrastructure protection.

The NIPC had also worked to improve the exchange of information between industry and the government through its Infragard [26] Initiative. Infragard expands upon the FBI's direct contact with the private sector infrastructure owners and operators and is a vehicle through which information about cyber intrusions and vulnerabilities can be shared. All 56 FBI field offices have Infragard chapters and Infragard has 34,084 members [26]. Infragard has addressed a key issue that has been an obstacle to robust information sharing, namely, confidentiality. A reporting entity edits out any identifying information on the notices that are sent out to other members of the Infragard network for discussions on vulnerabilities and exploits that may have been encountered. Clearly, from the perspective of preventing cyberattacks, information about the attack and tools used in the crime are more important than the identity of the victim. This measure continues to build trust between industry and the government and encourage companies to report cyberattacks to law enforcement.

A number of non-profit organizations and entities associated with US academic institutions also play a significant role in CIP and cybersecurity. As a first example, the Computer Emergency Response Team Coordination Center (CERT/CC), located at Carnegie Mellon University studies Internet security vulnerabilities, handles computer security incidents, publishes security alerts, investigates long-term changes in networked systems, and develops information and training to improve cybersecurity. It is funded primarily by the US Department of Defense. As a second example, the System Administration, Networking and Security Institute (SANS) is a cooperative research and education organization through which more than 150,000 security professionals, auditors, system administrations, and network administrations share lessons they have learned and attempt to seek solutions to problems that arise.

The shock of the 11 September 2001 terrorist attacks had re-invigorated CIP efforts. Funding for CIP increased from $1.14 billion in FY1998 to $2.03 billion in FY2001. In addition to the Executive Branch of the government, US Congress has also enacted legislation recognizing the importance of CIP. In Section 1016 of the USA PATRIOT Act, Congress declared that it is now the policy of the United States, "that any physical or virtual disruption of the operation of the critical infrastructures of the United States be rare, brief, geographically limited in effect, manageable, and minimally detrimental to the economy, human and government services, and national security of the United States." The pronouncement [42] is unusual in a federal statute. Congress also declared that this policy would be achieved in a public-private partnership involving corporate and non-governmental organizations. While there have been significant steps forward in CIP outreach and education, other difficult CIP issues persist. One of the most vexing problem relates to which government agency should lead the response to a critical infrastructure incident and what authorities might the agency invoke to handle the incident.

In addition to the establishment of the NCSD at DHS under HSPD-7, as described earlier, the National Counterterrorism Center was created to serve as a fusion center to encourage cross-agency and cross-community information sharing. The Homeland Security Presidential Directive 5 (HSPD-5) [43, 44] established the Secretary of DHS as responsible for the National Incident Management System, which coordinated the USA Government (USG) response to large-scale domestic incidents. In response, US-CERT, the CERT for USG systems, was established [45].

Following the National Security Presidential Directive 54 (NSPD-54) on 8 January 2008 [46], the Comprehensive National Cybersecurity Initiative (CNCI) was established in January 2008 but both its operations and budget had been classified. According to the Washington Post of 21 July 2008, the single-largest request for funds in the fiscal 2009 intelligence budget was for CNCI. On February 1, 2010, the current administration has released CNCI's budget at $3.6 billion and will soon release an unclassified summary of the initiative [47].

10.3 Criminal and Intelligence Authorities and CIP

An attack on the critical infrastructure may be classified as a criminal issue, national security concern, or a combination. As a result, CIP poses a unique challenge for the federal government. The government's authority to investigate and respond to CIP incidents is divided between criminal law enforcement and national security agencies, two functions that have historically been segregated. Thus, at times, the intelligence and law enforcement divide can impede an effective government response. Following the 11 September 2001 terrorist attack, the US government is attempting to improve the exchange of information and coordination of activities between intelligence and law enforcement. Without thoughtful coordination, CIP efforts are destined to be parochial, duplicative, and ineffective.

10.3.1 CIP and National Security

A broad array of actors are responsible for cyberattacks. The perpetrators have different motives and, as a result, pose different degrees of threats to the critical infrastructure. The actors include:

- *Conventional Criminals*: Individuals or groups interested in using cyberattacks to further conventional crime, namely seek extortion money from a business by threatening to interrupt service to its customers. A disgruntled employee may also seek revenge on the employer by damaging the organization's network.

- *Hactivists*: Similar to terrorists, hacktivists are driven by political convictions to carry out disruptions on the Internet. Unlike terrorists, however, their activities are typically limited to conduct that is not life threatening.
- *Hackers*: Thrill-seekers who commit computer intrusions and website defacements, driven by intellectual challenge, not political agenda. Hackers are responsible for most of the computer intrusions.
- *Terrorists*: Individuals or groups pursue the use of computers and malicious code to harm a nation's population or to retaliate against a government for its policies or perceived activities.
- *Nation States*: Hostile foreign countries that seek to harm US interests by disrupting infrastructure, usually to prove military or intelligence superiority.

Cyber incidents that trigger national security threats are of particular concern to the government and those initiated by a terrorist organization or nation state will almost always be deemed a national security concern. While indications that terrorist groups are deploying cybertools as weapons against critical infrastructures are lacking, there is growing evidence that the technical sophistication of these groups is increasing [48]. Clearly, when adequate expertise has been amassed, a cyberterrorism incident may be unleashed. A former director of Central Intelligence, George Tenet, has testified before Congress that terrorist groups, "including Hizbollah, Hamas, Abu Nidal organization, and Bin Laden's al Qaeda are using computerized files, e-mail, and encryption to support their operations." According to Thomas [49], evidence strongly suggests that terrorists had used the Internet to plan their operations for 9/11. Computers seized in Afghanistan have reportedly revealed that al Qaeda had been collecting intelligence on targets and sending encrypted messages via the Internet. As of 16 September 2002, al Qaeda cells operating in America reportedly had been using Internet-based phone services to communicate with cells overseas. During the trial of Younes Tsouli in London in January 2008, anti-terrorist detectives and forensic science officers revealed the [50] sophisticated IT activities of the accused and linked it to al Qaeda's efforts to recruit computer savvy geeks to boost its Internet and computer capabilities. According to Hagmann [51], analysis of the information obtained from Major Hasan's digital files, downloaded from al Qaeda and Islamic terrorist websites, indicates a pattern of deliberate and willful planning to conduct some type of attack against the USA military.

10.3.2 Identifying Whether a Cyberattack Poses a National Security Concern

Unfortunately, the government's ability to identify the exact nature of a cyberattack is limited. At the outset of any cyberincident, it is typically impossible to determine with certainty who is responsible and what might be the underlying motive. This fact was illustrated during a cyber incident, dubbed "Solar Sunrise." In February 1998, a series of apparently related computer intrusions into government and private industry systems sounded an alarm. A joint task force consisting of investigators from both criminal law enforcement and national intelligence agencies was quickly assembled and tasked to determine the source of the cyber intrusions. While the identity of the perpetrators was unknown, the attacks appeared to have been executed in preparation for a coordinated strike on the Defense information infrastructure [52]. The timing, nature, and apparent source of a few of the attacks raised concerns in the Pentagon that the intrusions could represent a concerted effort by Iraq to interfere with US troop deployments. The incident occurred during Iraq's attempts to deny United Nations weapons inspectors access to key facilities in Iraq. NIPC had coordinated a multiagency investigation that included the FBI, Air Force Office of Special Investigations, National Aeronautics and Space Administration, Department of Justice, Defense Information Systems Agency, National Security Agency, and the Central Intelligence Agency. Within several days, the investigation converged on their finding that the intrusions did not emanate from Iraq but that several teenagers in the US and Israel were responsible. They had committed the attacks for sport. Two juveniles in California pleaded guilty to the intrusions and several Israelis were prosecuted in Israel.

The Solar Sunrise incident taught the government three valuable lessons. First, hasty conclusions about the source and purpose of a cyberattack may be dangerous. Even a moderately simple attack may be routed through several computers around the globe, disguising the true origin of the incident and creating a false image that it had been launched by a hostile foreign nation. Second, the motive may not always be accurately inferred from mere context. Third, the incident underscored the susceptibility of the Defense Department's systems to relatively simple computer exploits.

10.3.3 The Criminal Law Enforcement and National Intelligence Divide

Both criminal law enforcement and national intelligence authorities may be employed by the government to quickly track down the source of a cyber incident. These authorities facilitate the government to conduct wiretaps and other electronic surveillance, collect personal information, and otherwise focus its resources on predicated targets. However the use of the authorities in the same investigation often requires close coordination between the law enforcement and national intelligence communities, given that historical abuse of domestic intelligence-gathering and subsequent embarrassment of the government had led to tight restrictions on the government's ability to investigate US citizens. Since the 1970s, barriers have been erected between the law enforcement and national intelligence agencies to prevent them from freely sharing information. The restrictions have become firmly entrenched in the policy and culture of the law enforcement and national intelligence communities.

National security laws were developed in the 1970s in the wake of several incidents that undermined the public's confidence in the government's exercise of its authorities. From 1956 until 1971, the FBI carried out domestic security investigations under the Counter-Intelligence Programs (COINTELPRO), through which the FBI Director, J. Edgar Hoover, intended to disrupt the US Communist Party, perceived by many in the 1950s as a rising domestic security threat. COINTELPRO was expanded in the 1960s to target a range of other "subversive" organizations. COINTELPRO-New Left, for example, targeted college campus groups and those who opposed America's involvement in the Vietnam conflict, including non-violent, anti-war groups. COINTELPRO-Black Nationalist targeted Black civil rights groups, including those involved exclusively in non-violent political expression [53]. The investigations included the illegal wiretapping of Rev. Martin Luther King, Jr., illegal break-ins committed by FBI agents, and disinformation campaigns intended to discredit organizations and individuals [54]. Following the death of J. Edgar Hoover in 1972, practices in FBI's COINTELPRO investigations started to surface. NBC and CBS were ultimately responsible for exposing COINTELPRO's activities by forcing the FBI to release documents under the Freedom of Information Act [55]. The disclosures relative to the COINTELPRO investigations triggered congressional hearings and a successful lawsuit against the FBI by groups and individuals who had been subjected to illegal investigations. In 1974, the Department of Justice conducted its own investigation of the FBI's conduct in COINTELPRO and Attorney General William Saxbe released a public report. He characterized some of the tactics used by the FBI during COINTELPRO as "abhorrent in a free society" [56].

The Justice Department promulgated new guidelines governing criminal and domestic security investigations in response to the COINTELPRO abuses. In 1976, the FBI changed the character of domestic security investigations by treating investigation of domestic terrorism as a criminal law enforcement matter, as opposed to a political intelligence matter [56]. Accordingly, supervision of domestic terrorism investigations was shifted from the FBI's Intelligence Division to its Criminal Investigative Division. International terrorist groups, however, would be investigated by FBI's Intelligence Division, under the classified foreign counterintelligence guidelines. The revised Intelligence Division devoted its attention to investigating hostile foreign intelligence operations, including Soviet efforts to influence domestic politics through the Communist Party and other front organizations [56]. In essence, the criminal law enforcement and domestic intelligence operations within the FBI were split into two separate components. Subsequent reforms would further institutionalize the segregation of these two functions.

While revelations about COINTELPRO were unfolding, the activities of other components of the US intelligence community also came under public scrutiny. On December 22, 1974, Seymour Hersh published an article in The New York Times bearing the headline, "Huge C.I.A. Operation Reported in U.S. Against Anti-War Forces." According to the article, the CIA was engaged in massive domestic spying activities against "subversive" interests opposed to the Vietnam War. Reportedly, the allegation took President Gerald Ford and the White House by surprise and

President Ford established a blue-ribbon panel, the Rockefeller Commission, to investigate "whether any domestic CIA activities exceeded the Agency's statutory authority and to make appropriate recommendations" [57]. The Rockefeller Commission scrutinized the CIA's activities and found a variety of abuses, including illegal mail openings and unwarranted collection of information on US citizens [57].

In light of the abusive CIA's activities, the Rockefeller Commission recommended adoption of a new framework for assessing the propriety of intelligence activities. If an activity was undertaken by the intelligence community and its primary objective was to further the prosecution of crimes or protect against civil disorders or domestic insurrection, the activity must be transferred over to law enforcement and the intelligence community must consider itself prohibited from any further engagement. In contrast, where the principal objective of an activity relates to foreign intelligence or protection of the intelligence community, the activity could permissibly be undertaken on behalf of the intelligence community, within limits [57]. The framework closely resembles the the one that was ultimately adopted by the US government as Executive Order No. 12333, which redefined the intelligence community's goals, directions, duties, conduct and responsibilities. Today, Executive Order No. 12333 remains the chief authority regarding the scope and jurisdiction of the intelligence community's activities [58].

The COINTELPRO revelations and the scrutiny of the CIA triggered a wave of government reform that placed limits on the manner in which criminal law enforcement, intelligence community, and the Executive Branch utilized their power to investigate and disseminate information on US citizens. Ultimately, free-flowing information sharing among criminal law enforcement and national intelligence entities in the government ceased. A body of national security law was developed and, today, serves as the basis for apportioning responsibilities and jurisdiction in matters that constitute both national security and law enforcement matters.

Attacks on critical infrastructures may constitute either a national security or a law enforcement matter. However, the methods used by law enforcement and the intelligence community to investigate the same cyberattack differ, stemming from the authorities such as Executive Order No. 12333. As an example, the interception of an intruder's online electronic communications during the commission of a cyberattack can provide important information about the intruder's location. However, the legal authorities used by law enforcement and the intelligence community to trace and identify the cyber intruder differ and the authorities dictate how the intercepted information must be handled and disseminated. Under federal law, the legal authority to conduct a wiretap can be obtained under two different statutes, namely, a criminal statute and an intelligence statute. A criminal wiretap may be obtained from a federal court under Title III of the Omnibus Crime and Control and Safe Streets Act of 1968 [59] upon a showing based on an affidavit submitted by the government that there is probable cause to believe that a crime has been, is being, or is about to be committed, in violation of one of the predicate felony offenses enumerated in the wiretap statute [60]. In contrast, the Foreign Intelligence Surveillance Act of 1978 (FISA) permits electronic surveillance against a person located within the United States after the intelligence agency obtains a court order from the Foreign Intelligence Surveillance Court (FISC) located in Washington, D.C. In general, to obtain a FISA warrant, there must be probable cause that the target of a FISA intercept is an agent of a foreign power. In addition, the information sought by the surveillance must be foreign intelligence, as opposed to criminal investigative information, which cannot be obtained by any other less intrusive collection techniques. Prior to the USA PATRIOT Act amendment, the purpose of the FISA intercept had to be intelligence collection as opposed to the "significant purpose." The USA PATRIOT Act Amendments enabled FISA wiretaps to collect both intelligence and criminal information.

Under the FISA statute, the significant purpose of a FISA surveillance must be to gather intelligence [61]. While information obtained under FISA can be used for criminal purposes [62,63], wherever a law enforcement purpose supplants the intelligence purpose, authorization for conducting FISA surveillance will be withdrawn by the FISC. The evidence gathered under FISA authority after investigation was no longer primarily for the purpose of intelligence gathering and were inadmissible [64]. The Office of Intelligence Policy and Review, the component of the Department of Justice that supervises FISA warrants, has historically adopted a cautious approach to sharing with criminal investigators any intelligence and evidence that may have been collected under FISA surveillance. The intent is to avoid any appearance that the FISA intercept had been primarily conducted for a criminal purpose. While this has ensured that the intelligence authorities were not compromised, it has also meant that FISA-derived intelligence information is typically not shared with the criminal investigators. Much of the institutional difficulty involving the sharing of FISA information may be remedied by a USA PATRIOT Act amendment to 50 USC §1804. The amendment abandons the requirement that "the purpose" of FISA warrant be foreign intelligence gathering. Instead, FISA surveillance is permissible if "a significant purpose" of the investigation is foreign intelligence gathering. The change will likely permit law enforcement to receive more intelligence information without concerns that such sharing will permit the FISC to withdraw authorization for the FISA surveillance. This may provide for greater coordination of intelligence and criminal investigations in all matters, including those involving CIP.

Even where information sharing is approved by law, cultural impediments may frustrate efforts to coordinate joint law enforcement and national intelligence matters. At times, parochial interests and efforts to protect the sources and methods underlying the intercepts may prevent the flow of information between the two communities. At other times, legitimate and countervailing incentives prompt law enforcement agents and intelligence officers to use information in different ways. As an example, consider that the successful conclusion of a law enforcement agent's work is a prosecution in which the evidence must be publicly disclosed. In contrast, an intelligence officer seeks to gather covert information and often requires secrecy to protect the source. As a result, the intelligence officer would eschew disclosing information from a valuable source publicly from legitimate concern that it might reveal the source.

Fortunately, coordination between the law enforcement and intelligence communities may be easier in CIP investigations than it is with other cross-jurisdictional matters. Institutions like the NIPC, which included representatives from both the national intelligence and criminal law enforcement communities working on CIP matters, had facilitated national security investigations involving critical infrastructures. Furthermore, many of the government's CIP prevention and detection efforts have brought together select elements of the law enforcement and intelligence communities, which has helped forge valuable relationships within the CIP community and are likely to encourage joint efforts in the future.

According to David Kris and J. Douglas Wilson [65], while the divide between FISA and other areas of law enforcement and makes national security more challenging, the the government's bypassing of the FISA Act of 1978 by wiretapping USA citizens without a proper warrant following the terrorist attacks of 11 September 2001, became a serious issue. They claim that FISA Amendments Act passed by Congress in 2008, which offered retroactive immunity to telecommunications companies that had participated in warrantless wiretapping after 11 September 2001, has made FISA even more complex.

10.3.4 U.S. Military CIP and Cyber Activities

The US DoD has a natural and unique interest in CIP/KR for a number of reasons. First, it is a government system that is heavily dependent on information systems. Computing software is a key component in nearly every critical system. According to the DoD, it relies on over 2.5 million unclassified computer systems; 10,000 local-area networks; and hundreds of long-distance networks for mission-critical operations. These systems and networks run on multiple hardware and software platforms consisting of interconnected mainframes and network operating systems that often utilize public and commercial telecommunication lines [66]. Second, DoD systems are expected to be the most likely targets of any hostile nation or terrorist groups. Third, evidence shows that the DoD infrastructure has been a premier target of cyberattacks. The General Accounting Office reports that, "in 1999 and 2000, the Air Force, Army, and Navy recorded a combined total of 600 and 715 [serious] cyber attacks, respectively." Fourth, the DoD's interest in CIP transcends the mere concern of being a target of cyberattacks. The newfound global reliance upon information systems provide the DoD with tools that represent unprecedented military arsenal. The DoD has been instrumental in developing the government's capability to use cyberattacks in both offensive and defensive roles. Information technologies have long been used in armed conflicts to accomplish military objectives. The deployment of radio frequency jamming and other electronic countermeasures date back way into the past.

Schaap [67] observes that the CIA has reported detecting the appearance of doctrine and dedicated offensive cyber-warfare programs in other countries. The report added that the countries developing cyber programs "recognize the value of attacking adversary computer systems, both on the military and domestic front. NATO's Chief of Cyber-Defense concurs, stating that "cyber terrorism [and] cyber attacks pose as great a threat to national security as a missile attack." In April 2007, important websites in Estonia, including the website of the president, parliament, ministries, political parties, major news outlets, and Estonia's two dominant banks, were hit by a series of DDoS attacks. These attacks continued until mid-June of 2007. A Defense Ministry spokesman of Estonia reported that websites that usually received 1,000 visits a day were buried under as many as 2,000 a second. Similar DDoS attacks against Georgia in 2008 illustrate that this new form of warfare is operational.

The USA military is justifiably concerned that cyberattacks can interfere and disrupt SCADA systems, which control elements of the power grid, air traffic control networks, and nuclear power plant safety systems. The consequences may have far reaching and there is the potential to cause physical damage, injury, and death. Cyberattacks can focus on dual-use targets that are used for both military and civilian purposes, including power plants that provide electricity to both civilian institutions as well as military command and control centers; specific research facilities; air traffic control networks that regulate both civilian and military aircraft; computerized civilian logistics systems upon which military supplies will be moved; electronic power grid control networks; communications nodes and systems, including satellite and other space-based systems; railroad and other transportation systems; civilian government networks; oil and gas distribution systems; and others.

Several countries have openly stated [67] that they retain the right to use nuclear weapons first against the means and forces of information warfare, and then against the aggressor State itself. A 2007 Department of Defense report indicated that the People's Liberation Army (PLA) of the People's Republic of China had established information warfare units to develop viruses to attack enemy computer systems and networks, and tactics and measures to protect friendly computer systems and networks. Like all offensive cyber strategies, Russia's includes the capability to disrupt the information infrastructure of their enemies and includes strategies that would disrupt financial markets and military and civilian communications capabilities as well as other parts of the enemy's critical infrastructure prior to the initiation of traditional military operations.

In the mid 1990s, a study by the RAND Corporation found the costs of developing the cyber weapons needed for conducting cyber warfare to be extremely modest and within financial reach for nearly every country. It is now estimated that about 140 nations have active operational cyber weapons development programs in place. In the Moonlight Maze incident [67], hackers from Russia penetrated Department of Defense computers for over a year, stealing vast amounts of sensitive information. According to Pentagon and FBI officials, Moonlight Maze was a state-sponsored Russian intelligence campaign to secure USA technology, which targeted not just the Department of Defense, but also the Department of Energy, NASA, military contractors and military-linked civilian universities. Experts view Moonlight Maze intrusions as pre-war reconnaissance where half a dozen nations are busy scanning each other's networks to get a good map of where the key things are and what are the key vulnerabilities of those networks.

Military and legal experts acknowledge [67–69] significant difficulty in analyzing cyberattacks, including attributing an attack to the responsible party and determining with certainty whether the attack was intentional or accidental. Serious questions arise, namely, when does a cyberattack constitute "use of force" under Article 2 of the United Nations (UN) Charter?; when does a cyberattack constitute an "armed attack" under Article 51 of the UN Charter?; when can a state respond in self-defense with a cyberattack of its own?; when can a state respond in self-defense with physical force to a cyberattack?; and what is the appropriate, proportional response to a cyberattack? While no consensus has emerged relative to these questions, it is troubling that different experts hold widely divergent views with respect to these basic questions. Even the European Union's Convention on Cybercrime focused on criminal acts, but declined to address cyberattacks as possible acts of war.

In response to growing cyber threats, in the USA, the Joint Task Force-Global Network Operations (JTF-GNO) [70] has been directed to carry out operations in the defense of the Global Information Grid (GIG) to assure timely and secure Net-Centric capabilities across strategic, operational, and tactical boundaries in support of DoD's full spectrum of war fighting, intelligence, and business missions. As of January 2009, Lieutenant General Carroll F. Pollett serves as the commander of JTF-GNO. The JTF-GNO achieved initial operational capability on 30 December 1998 and full operational capability by June 1999 [71]. In the fall of 2000, in accordance with DoD doctrine, JTF-CND became the Joint Task Force-Computer Network Operations (JTF-CNO). In October 2002, the new Unified Command Plan, Change 2, re-aligned JTF-CNO under the United States Strategic Command (USSTRATCOM). The JTF-CNO initiated its most comprehensive transformation in April 2004 when the Commander of US Strategic Command approved the Joint Concept of Operations for Global Information Grid Network Operations. This "NetOps CONOPS" provided the common framework and command and control structure to conduct the USSTRATCOM Unified Command Plan-assigned mission of Global Network Operations, combining the disciplines of enterprise systems and network management, network defense, and information decision management. The Secretary of Defense signed a delegation of authority letter on 18 June 2004, designating the Director, Defense Information Systems Agency (DISA) as the new Commander of the JTF-GNO. With this designation, the new command assumed the responsibility for directing the operation and defense of the GIG. The transformation enhanced the JTF-GNO's mission and objectives in achieving the Joint Vision 2020 Objective Force and the evolving concept of Net-Centricity.

Of key relevance to this chapter is the specific approach the USA military adopts to fight cyberattacks. The DOD's Joint Publication 3-13 [72] provides the doctrine for information operations planning, preparation, execution, and assessment in support of joint operations. The publication comments that computer network operations (CNO) "is one of the latest capabilities developed in support of military operations" and stems from the "increasing use of networked computers and supporting IT infrastructure systems by military and civilian organizations." It also notes that CNO, along with electronic warfare, are used to attack, deceive, degrade, disrupt, deny, exploit, and defend electronic information and infrastructure. Furthermore, for the purpose of military operations, CNO are divided into three categories: computer network attack (CNA), computer network defense (CND), and related computer network exploitation (CNE) enabling operations. CNA is defined [73] as a set of actions realized through the use of computer networks to disrupt, deny, degrade, or destroy information resident in computers and networks themselves; while CND consists of actions adopted to protect, monitor, analyze, detect, and respond to unauthorized activity within the DOD information systems and computer networks; and CNE is a set of enabling operations and intelligence collection capabilities that are conducted through the use of computer networks to gather data from target or adversary automated information systems or networks. The USSTRATCOM is one of ten unified commands under the Department of Defense. Part of USSTRATCOM's mission is to ensure freedom of action in cyberspace and to deliver integrated kinetic and non-kinetic effects, including information operations, in support of Joint Force Commander operations. USSTRATCOM helps plan and coordinate offensive computer operations across military and defense agencies through what it calls the Joint Functional Component Command for Network Warfare (JFCC-NW).

The CND mission is carried out across multiple disciplines, including network operations, intelligence, counterintelligence, and law enforcement components. Conceivably, CNA operations have multiple useful purposes, including helping US military forces prevail on the battlefield and facilitating military operation to reduce loss of life and physical destruction. The boundary between CND and CNA is not always clear. Defensive tactics that the DoD might contemplate in defending its information systems may in fact be so aggressive that they may be rightly classified as offensive. For example, "Active Network Defense" measures under CND may easily reach into CNA territory. Active Network Defense includes tactics such as "hackback," where the apparent source of an attack becomes a target for the DoD [74, 75].

Since 2003, there has been a gradual development of incorporating cyber-warfare into military doctrine and in creating an organizational structure for managing cyber warfare operations, highlighted most recently by the establishment of the 24th Air Force, a new numbered air force focused solely on the cyber mission. In 2005, the Air Force mission statement expanded to reflect that cyberspace was now an official Air Force domain: "to fly and fight in air, space, and cyberspace."

With no universal agreement on what constitutes the equivalent of an armed attack in cyberspace and no international agreements in place, the entire discipline of cyberwarfare is very unsettling. Regardless of the claims, there is no known scientific mechanism that can trace an attack on a computer system or network back to the true source with certainty. In addition, everything in cyberspace is expressed as an identifier expressed in 0s and 1s, lacking any semantics. As a result, a nation's computers may be hijacked and employed, unbeknownst to them, to perpetrate a crime. This ambiguity is a fundamental attribute of cyberspace, as we will see throughout the book. Thus, a retaliatory attack, launched in the time scale of computers and networks, always carries with it the potential to hurt innocent nations and their citizens.

10.3.5 Changes in Federal Law in Support of CIP

Following the attacks of 11 September 2001, Congress enacted the USA PATRIOT Act, intended to be a comprehensive legislation directed towards homeland security. The legislation contains measures to provide additional law enforcement tools such as increased surveillance of suspected terrorists, border protection, anti-money laundering programs, increased information sharing, enhanced criminal sanctions against terrorists, and cooperation among law enforcement officials and with the intelligence community. The USA PATRIOT Act also expanded key critical infrastructure protection provisions.

US federal criminal statutes have long held the position that unauthorized access to a computer system is a criminal offense. The Computer Fraud and Abuse Act ("CFAA"), codified as 18 USC §1030, was first enacted in 1984 and substantially amended in 1986, 1994, and 1996 to protect the confidentiality, integrity, and availability of data and computer systems. The PATRIOT Act included provisions to bolster law enforcement's CIP efforts by increasing the scope of federal statutes that apply to cyberattacks and the penalties for committing cyberattacks. The Act also expanded the types of computers protected by the CFAA and specifically included key critical infrastructure systems. The amended section 1030 now states that a hacker is in violation of federal law if he or she damages a computer "used by or for a government entity in furtherance of the administration of justice, national defense, or national security," even where the damage does not result in provable loss over $5,000. Under section 1030, previously, damages to computer systems must exceed $5,000 to establish criminal liability. The inclusion of critical infrastructure systems enhances the ability of law enforcement to prosecute cyberattacks against select portions of US infrastructure. The PATRIOT Act amendments also doubled the sentence from a potential 5 years of imprisonment to 10 years for violating 18 USC §1030(a)(5). Furthermore, if the offender had previously violated 1030(a)(5), the potential sentence is 20 years.

In 2002, Congress established the Department of Homeland Security (DHS) under The Homeland Security Act of 2002 [37]. In February 2003, the HSPD-5 [43, 44] established the Secretary of DHS as responsible for the National Incident Management System, which coordinated the USA Government (USG) response to large-scale domestic incidents. Later, in December 2003, the NCSD was created under HSPD-7 [38, 39], followed by the establishment of the National Counterterrorism Center.

To better coordinate CIP, especially against the backdrop that an estimated 85% of the critical infrastructure is owned by private industry in the USA, Congress had been contemplating measures to encourage industry to share sensitive cybersecurity information with the government. The private sector and industry are not confident that any shared vulnerability related information can be protected by the government [76]. The first area of concern is the requirement that, under Freedom of Information Act (FOIA), the Federal government make certain information in its possession public. FOIA permits any person, including foreign citizens, partnerships, corporations, associations, and foreign governments, access to existing, unpublished agency records on any topic, possibly including the vulnerability and trade secrets that the private sector may share with the government. The private sector is uncertain whether the FOIA may force the government, at a future time, to disclose sensitive and proprietary information to the public. This justifiable concern has reportedly deterred private sector and industry participation in information sharing with the government [76]. Under the second concern, the US industry believes that US antitrust law[1] does not clearly permit the private sector to share information and vulnerabilities between themselves. That is, they may potentially face liability for antitrust violations if they share CIP information with other industry partners. Although the DOJ has already declared information sharing and cooperation between businesses does not violate the antitrust law [77], industry believes that a statutory change is necessary, beyond the promotion of the Information Sharing and Analysis Centers (ISACs) forums, to protect the participating corporations.

In 2002, Congress passed the Critical Infrastructure Information Act of 2002 [78], in response to which the DHS established the The Protected Critical Infrastructure Information (PCII) Program [79]. PCII enables the private sector to voluntarily share sensitive information about critical infrastructure with government entities. The act protects information validated as PCII from public release under the FOIA, state sunshine laws and local disclosure laws, and from use in civil litigation. On 1 September 2006, the DHS released the final procedures for handling PCII [80]. These procedures, updated in April 2009, govern the receipt, validation, handling, storage, marking and use of critical infrastructure information voluntarily submitted to the DHS. The rule applies to all federal agencies, all US government contractors, and state, local and other governmental entities that handle, use, store, or have access to critical infrastructure information that is protected under the Critical Infrastructure Information Act of 2002.

References

[1] Charney, S. *The Internet, law enforcement and security*. Internet Policy Institute. Retrieved from http://www.internetpolicy.org/briefing/charney.html

[2] Conroy, D. (2002, April 30). *The Great Northeast Blackout of 1965*. Central maine power. Retrieved from http://www.cmpco.com/about/system/blackout.html

[3] Files, J., & Dickinson, J. (1998, May 20). Up to 90% of pagers in U.S. crash; Wayward satellite's full impact unknown. *The Dallas Morning News*.

[1] The Sherman Antitrust Act, 2 July 1890; The Clayton Antitrust Act, 1914; and The Robinson-Patman Act, 1936

[4] AIDT Corporation Reports Over 99% of Long Distance Customers Have Full Service Following Attack on World Trade Center Company Continues to work at Restoring Full Service to All Lines and to aid in World Trade Center Relief Efforts. (2001, September 21). *IDT Press Release*.
[5] Department of Homeland Security, USA. (2002, July). *The National Strategy for Homeland Security*. Retrieved from www.dhs.gov/xlibrary/assets/nat_strat_hls.pdf
[6] The Whitehouse, USA. (2009, May). *Cyberspace policy review: Assuring a trusted and resilient information and communications infrastructure*. Retrieved from http://www.whitehouse.gov/assets/documents/Cyberspace_Policy_Review_final.pdf
[7] Retrieved February 5, 2009, from www.bankinfosecurity.com/article.php?art_id=1197
[8] Department of Homeland Security, USA. (2007, October). *The National Strategy for Homeland Security*. Retrieved from http://www.dhs.gov/xabout/history/gc_1193938363680.shtm
[9] The Center for Strategic and International Studies (CSIS). (2008, December). *Cybersecurity Commission Report*. Retrieved from http://csis.org/publication/securing-cyberspace-44th-presidency
[10] Bellis, M. (2002, April 28). *Inventors of the modern computer ARPAnet – The first Internet*. Retrieved from http://www.inventors.about.com/library/weekly/aa091598.htm?pid'2821&cob'home
[11] Webopedia. (2002, May 1). *ARPANET*. Retrieved from http://www.webopedia.com/TERM/A/ARPANET.html
[12] Hafner, K., & Markoff, J. (1991/1995). *Cyberpunk: Outlaws and hackers on the computer frontier*. New York, NY: First Touchstone Books/Simon and Schuster.
[13] Wiser, L. G., Jr., Section Chief, Training, Outreach, and Strategy Section, National Infrastructure Protection Center, FBI. (2001, August 29). Statement before the House Committee on Government Affairs, Subcommittee on Government Efficiency, Financial Management, and Intergovernmental Relations.
[14] Lemos, R. (2001, September 20). Nimda winds down; Companies recover. In *CNET News.com*. Retrieved from http://www.news.com.com/2100-1001-273286.html?legacy'cnet
[15] Laqueur, W. (1999). *The new terrorism, fanaticism and the arms of mass destruction*. New York, NY: Oxford University Press.
[16] Retrieved February, 2009, from http://www.businessweek.com/the_thread/techbeat/archives/2009/02/fearing_cyber_k.html
[17] Retrieved April, 2009, from http://www.wired.com/threatlevel/2009/04/vowing-to-preve/
[18] Weisman, R. (2001, May 15). Senator compares cyber war to nuclear attack. In *NewsFactor Network*. Retrieved from http://www.newsfactor.com/perl/story/9739.html
[19] National Infrastructure Protection Center. (2001, October). Cyber protests: The threat to the U.S. information infrastructure.
[20] National Infrastructure Protection Center. (2001, November). Cyber protests related to the war on terrorism: The current threat.
[21] Vizard, F. (1999, July). A hacker attack against NATO spawns a war in cyberspace. In *Waging War.Com*. Retrieved from http://www.silkroad.com/papers/pdf/war_reprint1.pdf
[22] Cilluffo, F. J., Co-chairman, Cyber Threats Task Force, Homeland Defense Project, Center for Strategic & International Studies. (2001, October 4). Critical infrastructure protection: Who's in charge, statement before the U.S. Senate Committee on government reform.
[23] Verton, D. (2002, January 7). Critical infrastructure systems face threat of cyberattacks.
[24] Office of the Coordinator for Counterterrorism. (2001, April 30). *Latin overview*. U.S. Department of State.
[25] Centre for Defence and International Security Studies (CDISS). (1998). *Terrorism: 1990–1998*. Retrieved from http://www.cdiss.org/terror_1990s.htm
[26] Wilcox, P. C., Jr. (1997, April). U.S. Department of State: Patterns of global terrorism. In *HR-NET: Hellenic resources network*. Retrieved from http://www.hri.org/docs/USSD-Terror/96/year.html
[27] Quinn-Judge, P. (2002, June 17). Cracks in the system. *Time Europe*. Retrieved from http://www.time.com/time/eu..rticle/0,13005,901020617-260664.html

[28] Institute for Security Technology Studies at Dartmouth. (2001). Cyber attacks during the war on terrorism: A predictive analysis.
[29] Lieutenant General Kenneth Minihan. (1998, June 24). Statement to the senate governmental affairs committee hearing on vulnerabilities of the national information infrastructure.
[30] Stidham, J. (2001, September 26). *Can hackers turn your lights off: The vulnerability of the US power grid to electronic attack*. SANS Institute.
[31] Private communications with Riptech. (2001, January). *Understanding SCADA system security vulnerabilities*. RIPTECH.
[32] Retrieved from http://www.wstnres.com/pdf/Elec_Ops.PDF
[33] Retrieved from http://www.azpsoasis.com/oasis/unsecure/docs/PSEI/PSE%20Intercon.pdf
[34] Retrieved January, 2008, from http://blogs.baselinemag.com/security/content001/corporate_espionage/hackers_gain_real_power_over_electric_grid.html
[35] Friedman, T. (2002, May 19). *New York Times*.
[36] Vatis, M. A. (1999, July 29). Recovery and cyber-reconstitution: Understanding the role of the information coordination center. *Y2K Response*.
[37] The Homeland Security Act of 2002. Retrieved 2002, from http://www.dhs.gov/xabout/laws/law_regulation_rule_0011.shtm
[38] Homeland Security Presidential Directive 7. Retrieved December 17, 2003, from http://www.fas.org/irp/offdocs/nspd/hspd-7.html
[39] Retrieved from http://www.dhs.gov/xabout/laws/gc_1214597989952.shtm
[40] Press release of Senator Bob Bennett. (2001, September 24). Bennett introduces bill to protect critical infrastructure through information sharing.
[26] Retrieved from http://www.infragard.net
[42] USA PATRIOT Act. Pub. L. No. 107-56 " 1016(c)(1) and (2).
[43] Homeland Security Presidential Directive 5. Retrieved February 28, 2003, from http://www.fas.org/irp/offdocs/nspd/hspd-5.html
[44] Retrieved from http://www.dhs.gov/xabout/laws/gc_1215444247124.shtm
[45] US CERT. Retrieved from http://www.us-cert.gov/
[46] nextgov: Technology and the Business of Government. The Comprehensive National Cybersecurity Institute. Retrieved June 1, 2009, from http://www.nextgov.com/the_basics/tb_20090601_8569.php
[47] Government Information Security. (2010, February 2). *CNCI budget request set at $3.6 Billion*. Retrieved from http://www.govinfosecurity.com/articles.php?art_id=2151
[48] Testimony of Leslie Wiser, at 15 (supra n. 8).
[49] Thomas, T. L. (2003, Spring). *Al Qaeda and the Internet: The danger of "cyberplanning"*. Retrieved from http://www.usamhi.army.mil/USAWC/Parameters/03spring/thomas.htm
[50] Recruits reveal al Qaeda's sprawling web. Retrieved July 31, 2009, from http://www.cnn.com/2009/CRIME/07/30/robertson.al.qaeda.full/index.html
[51] Hagmann, D. J., Director. Retrieved November 9, 2009, from http://homelandsecurityus.com/?p=3250
[52] The President's National Security Telecommunications Advisory Committee. (1998, September). Information infrastructure group report.
[53] Select Comm. to Study Governmental Operations with Respect to Intelligence Activities. (1976). Final report, Book II: Intelligence activities and the rights of Americans and Book III: Supplementary detailed staff reports on intelligence activities and the rights of Americans.
[54] Churchill, W., & Vander Wall, J. (1990). The COINTELPRO papers: Documents from the FBI's secret war against dissent in the United States.
[55] Weisberger, B. A. (1995, September 1). The FBI unbound. *American Heritage*.
[56] Elliff, J. T. (1984). The Attorney General's guidelines for FBI investigations. *69 Cornell L. Rev. 785*.
[57] Commission on CIA Activities Within the United States. (1975). Report to the President, pp. 62, 115, 149–150, 250.
[58] 3 C.F.R. 200 (1982), reprinted in 50 U.S.C. " 401 note (1994). 1982/1994.
[59] 18 U.S.C. '2510-2521.

[60] 18 U.S.C. '2511, et seq.
[61] 50 U.S.C. "1804 (a) (7)(B).
[62] Exec. Order No. 12,333, 3 C.F.R. 200, 211 (1982), reprinted in 50 U.S.C. '401. 1982/1994.
[63] United States v. Humphrey, 456 F. Supp. 51 (E.D. Va. 1978), aff'd sub nom. United States v. Truong Dinh Hung, 629 F.2d 908, 913 (4th Cir. 1980), cert. denied, 454 U.S. 1144 (1982). 1978/1980/1982.
[64] United States v. Truong Dinh Hung, 629 F.2d 908, 916 (4th Cir. 1980). 1980.
[65] Kris, D., & Douglas Wilson, J. (2007). *National security investigations and prosecutions*. Thompson West.
[66] GAO Report. (2001, March). Information security challenges to improving DOD's incident response capabilities.
[67] Schaap, A. J. (2009, December 1). Cyber warfare operations: Development and use under international law. *Air Force Law Review*. Retrieved from http://findarticles.com/p/articles/mi_m6007/is_64/ai_n42124173/?tag=content;col1
[68] Todd, G. H. (2009, December 1). Armed attack in cyberspace: Deterring asymmetric warfare with an asymmetric definition. *Air Force Law Review*. Retrieved from http://findarticles.com/p/articles/mi_m6007/is_64/ai_n42124171/?tag=content;col1
[69] Franzese, P. W. (2009, December 1). Sovereignty in cyberspace: Can it exist? *Air Force Law Review*. Retrieved from http://findarticles.com/p/articles/mi_m6007/is_64/ai_n42124169/?tag=content;col1
[70] Joint Task Force-Global Network Operations. Retrieved January, 2009, from http://www.stratcom.mil/factsheets/gno/
[71] United States Space Command. (2000, September 29). Press release no. 15-00, U.S. Space Command take charge of computer network attack.
[72] DoD Joint Publication 3-13. Retrieved February 13, 2006, from http://www.fas.org/irp/doddir/dod/jp3_13.pdf
[73] US DOD Dictionary. Retrieved October 13, 2009, from http://www.dtic.mil/doctrine/dod_dictionary/
[74] Mills Abreu, E. Computers under attack can hack back, expert says. *Forbes Magazine*. Retrieved August 3, 2002, from http://www.forbes.com/business/newswire/2002/08/03/rtr685622.html
[75] Radcliff, D. (2000, April 29). Hack back: Virtual vigilante or packet pacifist? Network executives have mixed feelings about whether to retaliate against an attack. In *Network World*. Retrieved from http://www.nwfusion.com/research/2000/0529feat2.html
[76] Malcolm, J. G., Deputy Assistant Attorney of the Criminal Division, National Infrastructure Protection Center, FBI. (2002, May 8). Statement before the Senate Committee on government affairs.
[77] US DoJ Antitrust Division. Retrieved from http://www.usdoj.gov/atr/public/busreview/6614.htm
[78] Retrieved 2002, from http://www.dhs.gov/xlibrary/assets/cII_Act.pdf
[79] Protected Critical Infrastructure Information Regulations (PCII). Retrieved from http://www.dhs.gov/files/programs/editorial_0404.shtm April 2004; December 2005.
[80] Final Rule: Procedures for Handling Protected Critical Infrastructure Information. Retrieved from http://www.rjhresearch.com/SecurityGuide/S2unclas/Pcii.htm 1 September 2006; April 2009.

Chapter 11
Critical Infrastructure Protection Policy in the US

Melanie Schneck-Teplinsky

Critical infrastructure protection has been a hot topic in homeland security policy circles for nearly a decade, yet the definition of the term "critical infrastructure" (CI) remains fluid. In 1996, President Clinton became the first to formally define CI when he issued Executive Order 13010 identifying eight "critical infrastructures" whose incapacitation or destruction would have a debilitating impact on U.S. defense and/or economic security.[1] Since then, CI repeatedly has been defined and redefined in executive orders, statutes, and high-level policy documents.[2] Most recently, President Obama defined CI as "the assets, systems, and networks, whether physical or virtual, so vital to the United States that their incapacitation or destruction would have a debilitating effect on security, national economic security, public health or safety."[3] Properly defining the scope of CI is important to assure, on the one hand, that key infrastructure vulnerabilities are not overlooked, and, on the other, that limited public resources are not spread unnecessarily thin.

Regardless of the precise definition of CI, it is generally acknowledged that the private sector owns an estimated 85% of CI in the U.S., and largely voluntary

[1] EO 13010 - Critical Infrastructure Protection. Federal Register, July 17, 1996. Vol. 61, No. 138. pp. 37347–37350 (identifying telecommunications, electrical power system, gas and oil storage and transportation; banking and finance; transportation; water supply systems; emergency services (including medical, police, fire, and rescue); and continuity of government as critical infrastructures).

[2] In 1998, the Clinton Administration expanded "critical infrastructure" to include information systems and the public health sector. See Presidential Decision Directive 63 (PDD-63). After 9/11, the Bush Administration expanded the definition of CI even further to include a total of thirteen sectors (adding agriculture/food supply, defense industrial base, chemical industry, and postal/shipping). See Executive Order 13228. In 2002, the USA Patriot Act (Section 1016(e)) defined CI as the "systems and assets, whether physical or virtual, so vital to the United States that the incapacity or destruction of such systems and assets would have a debilitating impact on security, national economic security, national public health or safety, or any combination of those matters." The Bush Administration's National Strategy on Homeland Security further broadened the definition of CI to include those assets, systems, and functions vital to our national security, governance, public health and safety, economy, and "national morale."

[3] White House Office of the Press Secretary, Presidential Proclamation - Critical Infrastructure Protection Month, December 2, 2009, available online at http://www.whitehouse.gov/the-press-office/presidential-proclamation-critical-infrastructure-protection-month.

S. Ghosh and E. Turrini (eds.), *Cybercrimes: A Multidisciplinary Analysis*,
DOI 10.1007/978-3-642-13547-7_11, © Springer-Verlag Berlin Heidelberg 2010

public-private partnerships have served as the centerpiece of U.S. CIP policy for the past decade.[4] One of the key components of public-private partnerships is sector planning, a concept which calls for one federal agency (known as a "sector-specific agency" or SSA) to be responsible for coordinating public and private CIP efforts within each CI sector. For example, the Department of Energy is the SSA responsible for the energy sector. The "sector planning" approach was set out in the National Infrastructure Protection Plan (NIPP) issued by the Department of Homeland Security[5] in 2006 and updated in 2009. Pursuant to the NIPP, SSAs were required to develop sector-specific plans (SSPs) addressing how their sectors would implement the NIPP, including how their sectors would improve their cybersecurity (e.g., network security) and physical security. SSPs also were to identify risk management practices that could improve the security of CI that relies on cyber and to identify approaches to protect critical cyber infrastructure. Although the "sector planning" approach to public-private partnerships has been credited with doing valuable work, it also has been criticized, inter alia, for spawning duplicative and sometimes inconsistent efforts, and failure to clearly define the responsibilities of involved parties.

At present, U.S. CIP policy is in a state of flux. While the Obama Administration has signaled that it remains committed to the general concept behind the public-private partnership model, the Administration's Cyberspace Policy Review (the result of President Obama's February 9, 2009 order directing a 60-day review of all U.S. cyber policies and structures) states: "[t]here are many ways in which the Federal government can work with the private sector," and recommends that alternative approaches be explored. With respect to existing public-private partnerships, the report recommends optimizing the ability to "identify priorities and enable efficient execution of concrete actions" and ensuring that these partnerships have "clearly defined institutional mission[s]" and "well-defined roles and responsibilities for participants."[6] Significantly, the report also recommends that the Federal government "identify procurement strategies that will incentivize the market to make more secure products and services available to the public."[7] Exercising federal government market power through procurement could have substantial implications

[4] Over the past decade, government regulation of industry generally has been eschewed in favor of reliance on market forces to improve information security, however a number of pro-industry regulations have been enacted, including, for example, a Freedom of Information Act (FOIA) exemption deemed necessary to facilitate private sector sharing of CI information with the government, and various legislative provisions expanding protections for CI (e.g., USA Patriot Act provisions expanding the scope of computer crime laws to cover certain CI attacks).

[5] Shortly after the events of 9/11, the then-newly-created U.S. Department of Homeland Security (DHS) was tasked with leading, integrating, and coordinating efforts to protect both physical and cyber CI. See Homeland Security Presidential Directive 7.

[6] Cyberspace Policy Review at 18.

[7] Cyberspace Policy Review at v.

for CIP policy, especially as it relates to cyber. It remains to be seen if, when, and how these recommendations will be translated into action, and many of these decisions could depend on positions taken by President Obama's new cybersecurity coordinator, Howard Schmidt, who was appointed in December 2009 to assist in developing a new U.S. cyber policy. Accordingly, it is premature to speculate as to the contours of future CIP policy, particularly as they relate to cyber.

Chapter 12
Scientific and Technological Nature of Critical Infrastructure Vulnerabilities

Sumit Ghosh

To gain a better appreciation of why and how we must protect our CIs, we need to understand briefly the fundamental scientific and technological underpinnings of their vulnerabilities.

12.1 The Electric Power Grid

As the primary supplier of energy today, the electric power grid represents a significant advancement of our civilization. Given that energy is the life blood of any society, today, the electric power grid is perhaps the most critical of all CIs in every nation on earth. The grid suffers from its inherent and unique set of vulnerabilities and we will describe a few of the key reasons.

Electricity is generated through electric generators which transform other sources of energy, namely the flow of water; coal, oil, and gas; wind; and nuclear fission into electrical energy. The corresponding plants are labeled hydroelectric, thermal power generators, wind power generators, and nuclear reactors. For a number of reasons, including the availability of natural resources and safety, electric power generating stations are generally located far from population centers and industries, where the generated power is consumed. Thus, electric power must be transported from the generating to the consuming stations and this task is carried out via the overhead transmission lines and towers that dot the countryside and the surrounding regions of any major metropolitan city.

Electricity comes in two forms, namely, direct current (DC) and alternating current (AC). To transport electric power with minimal losses, we must use the AC form, which assumes the shape of a periodic sinusoidal wave of a given frequency. In the USA, we use 60 Hz. Thus, as the electricity flows from the generating to the consuming station, its amplitude or magnitude changes from the positive to the negative territory, 60 times every second. Other countries use a frequency of 50 Hz.

Furthermore, the electrical appliances that we use for our comfort and convenience, namely, the incandescent bulb, fluorescent bulb, LED bulb, fan, air conditioner, refrigerators, dishwasher, washing machine, electric dryer, air handler, etc. all resolve to a set of three basic electrical components. These are called resistors

S. Ghosh and E. Turrini (eds.), *Cybercrimes: A Multidisciplinary Analysis*,
DOI 10.1007/978-3-642-13547-7_12,

(R), inductors (L), and capacitors (C). The incandescent bulb is primarily a R; while the refrigerator compressor is a combination of R and L; and the fluorescent bulb is a combination of R, L, and C. Under AC, the values of the R, L, and C become dependent on the frequency of the AC wave. This also causes a secondary effect, namely, when AC electricity travels from the generator to a consuming station over the transmission line, a part of it is reflected back toward the generator. This is analogous to a powerful tsunami wave that travels straight from its origin to a rocky beach and is then reflected toward an island that may not have been in a direct line with the point of origin of the tsunami. The strength of the reflected electric power wave depends on the values of the R, L, and C that the AC wave encounters at the power consuming station. Of great importance is the fact that the reflected wave can cause harm to the generator, so proper precautions must be taken to protect it. A key precaution is that the amount of power generated and transported from the generator along the transmission line must match closely with the power needs of the consuming station. This implies careful and continuous monitoring of the power generated and the power consumption. If a power generator continues to send normal power to city of Phoenix, Arizona, but, unbeknownst to it, Phoenix had decided to sever itself abruptly from the power supply, a huge power wave will be reflected back to the generator, possibly causing severe damage to the expensive generator. As an added aggravation, the speed with which the wave travels is close to the speed of light, namely 3×10^8 m/s. Thus, if the power generator is located 300 km away from Phoenix, the wave will reflect back from Phoenix and hit the generator in $\frac{300 \times 10^3}{3 \times 10^8} = 1$ ms. That isn't enough time for an operator to react, given that human reaction time is in the range of 0.5–1 s. Clearly, the generator can withstand the temporary pressure from a few reflected power waves but a sustained assault will inevitably damage the generator. This yields two inferences. First, we need a computer to continually monitor the system status, namely, the power generated and transmitted by the generator as well as the power needs of the consuming station. The power needs of a city during a hot and muggy afternoon when everyone turns on their air conditioners is vastly different from the nighttime when it may turn comfortably cool. Second, as an emergency precaution, the generator may need to be quickly disconnected from the electric transmission lines so as to avoid the impact from a reflected power wave. This is achieved by means of circuit-breakers, which must also be controlled by computers. Under certain circumstances, the consuming station may also require protection from a huge power wave arriving through the transmission line. This implies the deployment of circuit-breakers at the power consuming stations. Often, the strength of the reflected waves can be controlled by deploying matching impedances. In extreme cases, errant power waves can be dissipated by wasting the energy to heat up resistors.

In essence, a single system that monitors and controls both the generator and the consuming station is necessary for smooth operation. When the consumer station's power needs are low, the generator must be adjusted precisely and quickly to generate and transmit less power. Conversely, during peak demands, either the generator must develop and transport more power to the consuming station or additional generators must be brought online. There is the danger of instability whenever the power generated and transmitted differs from the power consumed, beyond a threshold. Given that turbines are difficult to turn ON and OFF, power generating stations prefer to generate power at a constant rate, day or night. In contrast, a power consuming station's demand undergoes considerable fluctuation during a 24-h period. To balance out, more and more power generating stations and power consuming stations over a wider geographical area are brought together under the umbrella of a single super-system, giving birth to the idea of the current power grid. In essence, the grid is an immense network of transmission lines spanning a wide geographical area. Utilizing the grid, excess power from a generator during the nighttime can be channeled to a distant industry or factory that runs throughout the night at 100% capacity or more. While the science and technology of power generation and transmission is nearly a 100 years old, the use of power semiconductors to safely channel power along select transmission line conduits and computers to automatically coordinate the balancing act with great precision are new.

The computers transform the power grid into an immense centralized control facility. As the geographic reach of the power grid grows in order to utilize every unit of energy produced in the entire system, the complexity of centralized control increases. Throughout the entire system, the power generated, transmitted, and consumed must remain within a narrow tolerance. In the massive power grid system, precise real-time demands of the power consuming stations are very difficult to obtain on a timely basis. As a result, operations are mostly based on past data and future predictions, which can and do go wrong at times, leading to discrepancies, which become difficult to mitigate. When a power consuming station senses an errant incident power wave from the transmission lines, it trips the circuit-breaker and disconnects itself from the grid. The corresponding town or city experiences an immediate power loss, either partial or total blackout. The subsequent reflected wave may be sensed by the generating station and it too will trip its circuit-breaker to disconnect the generator and protect it from damage. The huge surge of energy in the transmission lines will then approach the remaining generators and power consuming stations that are connected to the grid, causing them to also trip their circuit-breakers for safety. All throughout the grid, the circuit-breakers are tripped, like out-of-control dominos, and within a very short time, sometimes as quickly as 10 s [1], large portions of the grid becomes deactivated. The energy surge will reflect back and forth in the power grid until it dissipates.

There is yet another challenge encountered by the grid. The frequency of the electricity generated is closely linked to the speed of rotation of the AC generator machine. Any change in the rotational speed of the turbines, etc. may affect the AC power frequency. Given that the magnitude of the impedances depend on the AC frequency, even small fluctuations in the frequency may upset the matching impedance settings. In turn, this may cause a significant disbalance between the power generated and power consumed, which will subsequently lead to tremendous power loss and trigger the onset of instability. The challenge becomes even formidable when we consider the need to maintain the frequencies of hundreds of AC power generating machines within a very narrow tolerance. Any departure from the standard frequency of 60.000 Hz will cause the power consuming elements, matching impedances, etc. to operate outside the realm of the design parameters, implying significant power loss [2], inefficiencies, and instability.

In summary, the principal challenge encountered by the grid is the lack of system-wide precise and timely knowledge of the fluctuating demands of the power consuming stations, changes in the status of the power generators, and frequency variations. The solution, from the perspective of the power grid operators, is a centralized control system that continually collects every necessary data from all power consuming stations, circuit-breakers, transmission lines, and generators and utilizes them to compute the "globally optimum" settings of all of the entities in the power grid. The centralized computer control is expected to keep the entire system in balance at all times. Over the past decades, the geographical reach of the grid has increased tremendously, the amount of power transmitted has grown significantly, and the number of power generators and power consuming stations have multiplied several fold. The result has been an overburdened centralized control, which is increasingly unable to maintain a system-wide balance. Research in electric power have focused on the use of parallel computers to address both the computational needs as well as faster system-wide control of all of the elements of the power grid. As further aggravation, the existing transmission lines are being continually driven to 100% of their design capacity and beyond, while engineering safety rules dictate a maximum use of 50% of design capacity. As a result, the transmission lines are heating up, sagging down and often coming in contact with trees, and inadvertently subject to accelerated aging. The circuit-breakers are required to detect whether an incident power wave is potentially threatening. However, this determination is complex and time consuming and, often, the circuit-breakers are set to predetermined values based on past experience, and not necessarily on immediate needs.

In reality, the expectation that centralized control systems can yield "globally optimum" settings of all of the entities in the power grid, may be misplaced. Research shows [3] that as the frequency of the data collection increases and as the system gets larger, dynamic, and more complex, the decisions may no longer be precise. The problem is far more complex, involving fundamental computer science issues, asynchronous distributed algorithms, and the physics of information propagation and processing and may not be solved through fast, parallel computers alone. The desire to render the power grid into a single, tightly-synchronized system, as noted by Lerner [2], is formidably challenging.

While Marks [4] reports that cascading failures may be triggered and the power grid successfully brought down through a strategic attack on lightly loaded nodes, this chapter has clearly revealed an appreciable number of fundamental, native vulnerabilities of the electric power grid. Of serious concern is that the network deployed to collect data and control the different elements of the power grid is either a subset of the global Internet or a proprietary network that is built along the same principles as the Internet. In either case, the networks are unreliable and inappropriate [1] for the needs of the power grid and, worse, they suffer from serious vulnerabilities, which will be discussed further in Chap. 13.

The greatest concern lies with clever perpetrators who may combine their knowledge of the basic vulnerabilities of the power grid and the networks to formulate a highly destructive attack plan. As a hypothetical example, consider that false demands and power generation values are synthesized and sent to mislead the operators and cause them to channel exceptionally large currents through specific transmission lines. The high currents are transmitted and sustained for precise time durations, enough to cause accelerated fatigue at a number of transmission line (cable) locations, but without setting off any alarms or causing breakages. The process is repeated for a large number of strategic transmission lines. Thus, the scenario is set up and the final attack causes a system-wide cascading crash of both physical transmission line cables as well as the AC generating equipment, from which recovery is difficult and may require an extended period of time.

12.2 Other Critical Infrastructures

Leaving aside the power grid which we had discussed in Sect. 12.1, all other CIs may be broadly classified into two categories, namely, (1) those that are primarily derived from computers, networks, and the Internet, collectively representing the cyber infrastructure, and (2) the remaining subset, which merely utilizes the cyber infrastructure to yield unprecedented conveniences and great operational efficiencies. Given the immense advantages, this trend will continue to grow in the USA and other technologically advanced nations. There are, of course, undeniable overlaps between the two categories. Thus, emergency services, government facilities, information technology, and banking and finance sectors may be classified under category (1). The remainder of the CI sectors, including the power grid, would fall under category (2). Thus, although agriculture and food come from the earth, their inventories, reserves, and distribution are all managed through computers and networks. The stockpiles of the seeds and their labeling are all located in the computers. Similarly, the water distribution and treatment facilities are controlled via the cyber infrastructure. The sterilization and purification treatment procedures, including the knowledge and operational use of specific chemicals are all controlled through computers and networks. A significant portion of the health sector, especially electronic medical records for individual patients and the nation's population as a whole will be managed through computers and networks. Nearly all of the medical scanners, instruments, and intravenous drips are controlled through the computers and intra-hospital networks. In the transportation sector, the traffic lights are controlled through SCADA. The same reasoning would apply to the defense industrial base, energy and chemical sectors, nuclear reactors, dams, and postal facilities. Even for the national monuments and icons, security policies and operations are all managed through computers and networks.

In any event, today, virtually all of the CIs have become inadvertently and uniformly accessible via the Internet. In Chap. 13, we will examine the vulnerabilities of the Internet, which will reveal how the CIs have become targets for hackers and cybercriminals and why the threat will keep rising in the future.

References

[1] Doug Page. (2006, January 15). '03 Blackout finally trips grid-hardening effort. In *Homeland Technology*. Retrieved from http://www.homeland1.com/print.asp?act=print&vid=349971

[2] Lerner, E. J. (2003, October/November). What's wrong with the electric grid? In *The Industrial Physicist*. USA: American Institute of Physics.

[3] Ghosh, S. (2003, September). *Algorithm design for networked information technology systems: Principles and applications*. New York: Springer.

[4] Marks P. (2009, September 11). How to short-circuit the US power grid. Retrieved from http://www.newscientist.com/article/mg20327255.900-how-to-shortcircuit-the-us-power-grid.html?full=true&print=true, Issue 2725.

Chapter 13
Internet Infrastructure Attacks

Alan Boulanger

The bulk of the cyber-attacks today target the endpoints of the Internet, namely, web servers, personal computers, and mobile devices. While they are highly damaging, should attacks target the constituent components of the Internet itself, the results can be far more destructive. Attacks on the Internet infrastructure can deliver a devastating blow to private and government organizations and potentially impact entire economies. Given the increased reliance on the Internet and related technologies, many commercial, financial, and government organizations would be effectively shut down in the event of a major incident that disrupts service for an extended period of time. This represents a significant vulnerability within our communication fabric and is clearly a major target for cyber-terrorism.

As in most infrastructure systems, efficiency is built on trust between the different constituent components of the Internet. Ironically, this inherent and implicit dependency on trust can be leveraged by cybercriminals and exploited to cause enormous service disruption and compromised systems. Attacks on Internet routers and Domain Name Services (DNS) constitute two major modes of assault on the Internet or cyber infrastructure. The third mode of attack focuses on the links of the cyber infrastructure, which can comprise of severed electric cables and optical fibers and wireless links jammed via artificially synthesized noise across specific electromagnetic bands.

13.1 Internet Router Attacks

Routing is a key element of the Internet and is responsible for the transmission and delivery of information from the originating systems to the desired destination points. When a user's data leaves the local area network and enters the Internet, a group of systems, labeled routers, are entrusted with the responsibility of guiding the data toward its intended destination. To fulfill their responsibility in the most efficient manner, the routers cooperate among themselves to deliver the data in the shortest amount of time. Logically, for fast and efficient cooperation, the Internet routers must implicitly trust each other, i.e., they must assume that the information received from their peers is authentic, reliable, and has not been modified with any

S. Ghosh and E. Turrini (eds.), *Cybercrimes: A Multidisciplinary Analysis*,
DOI 10.1007/978-3-642-13547-7_13, © Springer-Verlag Berlin Heidelberg 2010

malicious intent. While cooperation is rooted in trust, where trust is lacking, the routing process will slow down considerably, and may even come to a grinding halt. Armed with the knowledge that cooperation is founded on trust, perpetrators will exploit this trust and attempt to insert false and misleading information in order to influence how the router or group of routers will manage the Internet traffic. By falsifying router control information, a cybercriminal can deliberately redirect network traffic away from the legitimate destinations systems, thereby causing an outage, or intercept and alter legitimate network traffic through hostile systems.

As a simple example of how to redirect traffic away from a targeted site, consider the following. An attacker deliberately compromises a router "A" and causes it to transmit a lie about the traffic load on a specific link to router "B." By design, the routers cooperate to determine the shortest path to any intended destinations. When router "A" transmits a lie about the load of a particular network link, router "B" will trust and act on the information and choose to route network traffic around the alleged overloaded link. Assume that B chooses to redirect the traffic to router "C." When a large number of routers are similarly deceived and their number exceeds a threshold, router "C" can quickly become overwhelmed with traffic, leading to a serious outage. If router "C" happened to be a principal unit, responsible for managing the network traffic for a large enterprise system, users would be denied access to the system via the Internet. The denial will persist until the attack ceases or it is successfully neutralized.

Often, a perpetrator will compromise specific routers on the Internet in order to redirect network traffic to a given router or system that it owns and controls, where any plaintext traffic data will be intercepted and either copied, i.e., stolen, or maliciously altered. In the event the traffic data is encrypted through SSL or other mechanisms, its vulnerability is lowered but never completely eliminated. Other, more sophisticated techniques of attacking Internet routers include routing table poisoning, packet spoofing, and packet based DOS attacks. The ultimate consequences of all of these techniques are identical in that they all adversely influence the flow of network traffic, leading to loss of service, unauthorized stealing of network data, or maliciously modifying of traffic data.

History notes a number of reported incidents, representing inadvertent Internet traffic routing mishaps. For instance, in February 2008, while attempting to restrict access to the popular video web site, YouTube.com, strictly within the physical boundaries of Pakistan, the Pakistan Telecom had accidentally transmitted incorrect routing information via the Border Gateway Protocol (BGP) to an Internet Service Provider (ISP) in Hong Kong. The Hong Kong ISP's routers assumed the information was trustworthy and relayed the erroneous information worldwide, without analyzing it for accuracy or realizing the potential consequences. This resulted in YouTube.com being knocked offline for 2 h throughout the world. A second significant incident occurred in 2004 when the Turkish ISP, TTNet, inadvertently transmitted a routing table with incorrect routing information to the worldwide Internet via BGP. As a consequence of the error, most of the global Internet traffic was routed though TTNet's systems for the several hours.

13.2 Domain Name Services (DNS) Attacks

Along with routing, Domain Name Services (DNS) constitutes the fundamental suite of functions of the Internet. It too suffers from vulnerabilities. Thus, as a component of the Internet cyber infrastructure, DNS unwittingly becomes a candidate for malicious attacks. DNS is the translation mechanism that is used to associate the English-readable domain name of a network accessible server or system, that we human beings understand, with the Internet Protocol (IP) address, which is ultimately expressed in binary and precisely understood by the computers. Thus, an user can type in the address of a service, say, "www.amazon.com," and the DNS will first lookup the numeric IP address of the system as "72.21.207.65" and then substitute the binary address in subsequent processing. In essence, DNS is equivalent to the telephone directory for the Internet and access to websites.

An obvious and clear vulnerability is that the user typing in an English-readable website address and attempting to communicate with it has no way of ensuring that the IP address returned from DNS is, in fact, valid. As we have stated throughout the book, the fundamental problem is that the computer neither understands nor cares for the semantics of any identifier; to it, the identifier is a mere sequence of binary bits. The user's system will subsequently attempt to connect to the system in cyberspace at the IP address that had been returned from the DNS query. If the DNS systems can be successfully manipulated into returning a false IP address, it will bear impact on both the requested service as well as the system initiating the request.

Consider a scenario where a user wishes to connect to an online bookstore. If an attacker can fake or "spoof" the DNS reply, the client system will attempt to connect to the system at the IP address the attacker has deliberately specified. Since DNS is organized hierarchically, should a higher level DNS server be compromised, a significant amount of traffic can be misguided into connecting to the system that the attacker owns and controls. As a result, users become vulnerable to theft of their personal credentials and are also denied service to the legitimate destination systems. Furthermore, the destination services will be impacted in that legitimate traffic will now be diverted to the attacker's system, resulting in a potential loss of business revenue.

A serious incident of a successful DNS attack occurred in December 2008, when a unknown attacker was able to access and alter the DNS records for the financial company CheckFree, the largest electronic bill paying service in the USA. This was accomplished by using the legitimate access credentials of CheckFree's domain registrar, namely, Network Solutions. After the DNS record was successfully altered, customers were misredirected to computer systems, physically located in the Ukraine, which attempted to install password stealing malware. This incident impacted around 160,000 known victims, worldwide, out of a total of five million customers.

DNS is susceptible to a number of known attacks of different types. We will subsequently describe three of the attack modes that are common and representative, but by no means exhaustive.

The first type of attack is labeled, DNS cache poisoning. Under the DNS cache poisoning attack, a perpetrator will send false messages to the DNS server, which the latter will accept as the most up-to-date information and quickly store it in its cache to enhance performance. Since the message is implicitly trusted, for obvious reasons, the DNS server neglects to assess its validity against the information that is currently held in a non-cache memory unit. In fact, most often, the cached information is used to overwrite the information stored in the non-cache unit, which is then lost forever. Subsequently, when a legitimate DNS request is received, the DNS server will return the false data from the poisoned cache and the requesting user will be unwittingly misdirected to an IP address that the attacker had specified. The deployment of secure socket layer (SSL) that utilizes encryption can alert a user to this type of attack, especially when a sensitive service is involved, including banking. For services that are not cryptographically protected, the requesting system will automatically connect to the erroneous system in cyberspace at the IP address that has been returned by the DNS, without the mere suspicion that it had fallen prey to an attack.

The second type of attack is labeled DNS spoofing attack and represents a variation of the cache poisoning attack, described earlier. Under the DNS spoofing attack, an adversary will carefully monitor the network for any DNS requests. As soon as it identifies a DNS request that is transmitted by a user's system to the DNS server for address translation, the attacker springs into action. It causes the DNS server to be flooded with bogus networks traffic, thereby overloading it and degrading its performance. Thus, the DNS server will incur a significant delay before it can respond to the requesting system. The perpetrator immediately sends a bogus DNS query response, pretending to be a legitimate DNS server, to the requesting system. If the perpetrator can time the attack precisely, the spoofed DNS response will arrive before the legitimate DNS response, causing the user's system to be misdirected to the system specified by the spoofed IP address. When the legitimate DNS response does arrive, late, it will very likely be discarded. Clearly, the DNS spoofing attack is a highly localized attack and the perpetrator's timing is of utmost importance. However, where combined with a simultaneous Internet routing attack, described in Sect. 13.1, the impact may be devastating.

Under the third type of attack, the cybercriminal targets the system providing the DNS service directly. If successful in breaking into and compromising a DNS server, the perpetrator will have gained the ability to modify the DNS translation tables and exploit, with full impunity, the higher level trust between the compromised DNS server and other DNS servers in the worldwide cyber infrastructure. Under these circumstances, the attacker will gain the potential to redirect any request for any service to any IP address of its choosing. It can also launch attacks onto other, non-DNS systems. Many information services rely on the domain name of the connecting hosts to permit connections and authentication. An attacker commanding a compromised DNS server will have the capability to alter any DNS response, causing the attacking system to appear as a legitimate authorized system and potentially bypassing network security precautions such as firewalls, filtering bridges, and application access control lists. As an example, assume that a specific service restricts access to its protected systems. By design, it only permits access from a specific domain, say, "goodsystem.com." Following the successful compromise of a DNS server, the attacker reassigns the IP address of a legitimate system to that of an attacking computer system. When the supposedly protected service is accessed by the attacking computer, the accessing system's IP address will resolve to "bob.goodsystem.com," and access will be immediately granted.

In summary, the basic foundation of today's Internet and the cyber infrastructure that have been developed around it, are highly fragile and susceptible to attacks. The Internet and the DNS designs were originally developed in research laboratories as experimental technologies and never took into account the many ways in which the system could fail, either inadvertently or otherwise. While attempts to secure the Internet infrastructure is a important topic and currently being addressed by the security communities and nations, we may want to remember that it has become an essential and indispensable part of the global economy and well being. Therefore, it is imperative that we retrofit the existing Internet infrastructure, where possible, or replace it with a practical system that can withstand the rigors and challenges of the real world.

Part V
Psycho-Social Impact of Cybercrimes

Chapter 14
The Psyche of Cybercriminals: A Psycho-Social Perspective

Marcus K. Rogers

14.1 Introduction

The onset of the widespread new technology of computers and networks has unfortunately attracted cybercriminals, whose actions are primarily destructive. It is important to understand the psychological mindset of the individuals so we may integrate key insights about human behavior along with technical solutions to develop superior mitigation techniques. This chapter focuses on the nature of the individuals who are drawn to commit cybercrimes. We will examine who is involved in criminal activity, why are they drawn to commit crimes, and how may we effectively reduce criminal behavior. The chapter is organized as follows. First, we will propose a model to classify the different types of cybercriminals, provide a taxonomy, and analyze the characteristics of two specific types of criminal behaviors. We will also state the limitations of the taxonomy. Second, we introduce two traditional theories of criminal behavior, namely, social learning theory and moral disengagement, and examine them in the context of cybercrimes. We will also analyze the influence of anonymity on cybercrimes. Third, we will present a detailed discussion on the utility of deterrents to reduce criminal behavior, including laws, social sanctions, and education, and provide insights on how to make the strategies more effective. While an exhaustive examination of the nature of cybercrimes is beyond the scope of this chapter, we will also limit our discussions to criminal behaviors targeted or directed at computers and networks.

14.2 Who is Drawn to Cybercrimes

It has been posited that human beings possess free will, from which flows the ability to choose how we behave, albeit with heredity and environmental influences. As supposedly rational beings, how is it that some of us "choose" to be involved in aberrant and destructive activities, including cybercrimes? This is the proverbial "$64000.00" question and in order to provide answers, we must examine who is currently engaged in this behavior. This exercise can help us identify common

S. Ghosh and E. Turrini (eds.), *Cybercrimes: A Multidisciplinary Analysis*,
DOI 10.1007/978-3-642-13547-7_14, © Springer-Verlag Berlin Heidelberg 2010

characteristics such as socio-demographics and personality traits that are logically likely to be correlated with this type of deviance. These commonalities can be used to develop categories or taxonomies of the offenders and help develop profiles of individuals within these categories. The effort can also help us measure the effectiveness of our current strategies, aimed at reducing cybercrimes, and develop effective and practical approaches.

14.2.1 *Taxonomy*

Drawing upon the discipline of biology, we first develop a rudimentary one dimensional taxonomy or classification scheme to organize the nature of cyber criminals. This simple continuum based taxonomy is expanded upon later to form a two dimensional circumplex model [1]. A taxonomy is defined as a scientific classification, in accordance with a pre-determined system, and the resulting catalog is then used to provide a conceptual framework for further analysis or discussion. The criteria utilized in developing our taxonomy includes technical expertise, overt behaviors, motivation, and moral development. Examination of the case studies and anecdotal evidence collected over several years by different information security practitioners and researchers yield a total of seven high-level categories of criminal behaviors. These include script kiddies, cyber-punks, hacktivists, thieves, virus writers, professionals, and cyber-terrorists, as show in Fig. 14.1. The categories are placed on a continuum to reflect behaviors that range from novices and amateurs only interested in causing mischief, to state sponsored terrorism.

Script Kiddies (SK) refer to individuals with limited technical knowledge and abilities who run precompiled software to create mischief, without truly understanding what the software is accomplishing "under the hood." Immaturity, ego boosting, and thrill seeking primarily motivate this group. To them, attacking a system is a thrill ride of sorts and provides an adrenaline rush. Given their immaturity, the SK group either does not grasp the consequences of their actions or do not care. They tend to possess an underdeveloped sense of morality and would be viewed at stage 2 of Kohlberg's morality scale – naive instrumental hedonism. The SK group routinely brags about their exploits and seeks attention and ego stroking from others. This group is the most easily apprehended by law enforcement due to their lack

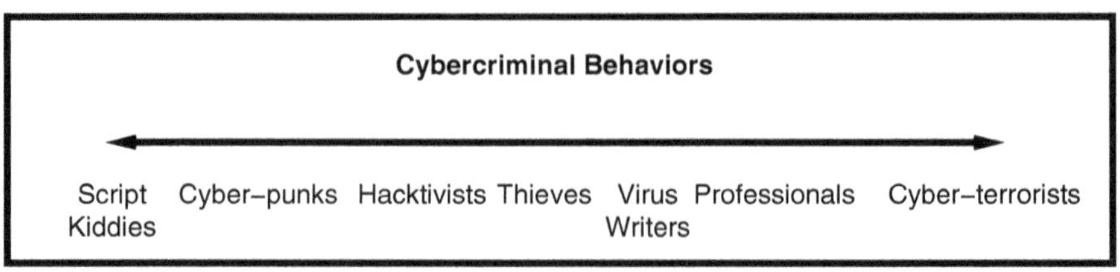

Fig. 14.1 A taxonomy of cybercriminal behaviors

of sophistication and propensity to draw attention to themselves. Kohlberg's model includes three levels of morality, namely, pre-conventional, conventional, and post-conventional, and there are two stages within each level. We pass through these stages as we mature cognitively and morally. For most well functioning adults, the norm is between stage 4, representing acceptance of authority; and stage 5, implying flexible judgments. Stage 6 is rare and indicates an unusually high degree of cognitive maturity.

The Cyber-punks (CP) group extends the real-world "punk" mentality into cyberspace. These individuals have a clear disrespect for authority and its symbols and a disregard for societal norms. They are driven by the need for recognition or notoriety from their peers and society. Although they are able to comprehend the consequences of their actions, given their predominant demographics, namely, 12–18 year old males, they have learned that they are likely to receive only a slap on the wrist, if and when apprehended. Similar to the SK group, the CP group is characterized by an underdeveloped sense of morality. Fear of apprehension is not a deterrent. On the contrary, getting arrested is synonymous to a badge of honor and it raises them to the level of folk hero within the computer underground. The need for public attention and the bragging rights associated with a successful attack are the primary motivators. While the CP group tend to be more sophisticated and technical than the SK group, their members often rely on attack software developed by others. The group members tend to be drawn toward defacing webpages and other activities that generate the maximum public attention. These criminal are the second most likely to be apprehended.

The inclusion of a hacktivist (H) category has been somewhat controversial. It is unclear whether the individuals constitute a unique group or are merely individuals from other categories who are simply trying to hide their actions behind semantic camouflage, namely, employing morally neutral terms to disguise aberrant behavior [2]. Calling oneself a hacktivist sounds more respectful than a petty criminal. The individuals tend to justify their destructive behavior, including defacing websites, by labeling them civil disobedience and ascribing political and moral correctness to it. Empirical data indicates that political motivation is usually a distant second to other, more base motives, including revenge, power, greed, marketing, or media attention. Given the difficulty of relating their actions to their intent, this group's moral development may, at best, be characterized between stage 2 and 3.

The thieves (T) category includes common criminals. These individuals commit cybercrimes and hide behind labels to deflect their feelings of guilt. They are primarily motivated by money and greed. The T group targets systems for financial gain and, as such, is attracted to credit card numbers and bank accounts that can be used for immediate personal gain. This group may be accurately labeled petty criminals, given that the activities of the members are usually not sophisticated, namely, simple wire transfer fraud and fraudulent use of credit card numbers; and that their sole livelihood is generally not dependent on these criminal acts. It is no surprise that this group's moral development had ended at stage 2. A disturbing trend with this group is the increased involvement in identity theft. This cybercriminal endeavor involves gathering enough information about a target to assume the victim's identity and then falsely obtain credit cards, loans, and even mortgages. In the US, there had been close to 1.2 million reported incidents of identity theft in the beginning of this decade and growing [3]. Of course, the debts are never repaid and the poor, hapless victim, is left holding the proverbial bag. The victims are also left with the daunting task of clearing their names and credit ratings with the different financial institutions and credit bureaus.

The next group, the Virus Writers (VW), may in fact represent a continuum within a continuum. This category of individuals can include both the technically proficient as well as the "Click Kiddies." At most, the technical acumen required of the "Click Kiddies" is to use a mouse. Their moral development would span stages 2 through 5, depending on the specific individual involved. In her seminal work on virus writers, Sarah Gordon, concluded that VW was never a homogeneous group and discussed four sub-categories, namely, the adolescent, college student, adult, and the ex-virus writer. Gordon indicates that there is an "aging out" process, in which the virus writer starts as an adolescent and progress through to the ex-virus writer category, as he or she matures both chronologically and cognitively. The thrill for individuals at the end of the sub-spectrum stem from the mental challenge and the academic exercise involved in the creation of the viruses. Unfortunately, the intellectual exercise is associated with "real world" consequences once the virus gets into the wild. Often, the person who creates the virus, not referring to the Click Kiddies, is not the one who introduces it to the world. The individual who actually releases the virus shares characteristics and motivations similar to the CP group, who desire attention, raw thrill, and are not deterred by any anticipated sanctions. Despite being around in one form or another for nearly decades, viruses continue to drive a very lucrative market for anti-virus software.

The professional group (P) is the most elite of the cybercriminal groups and are often linked with the terms, competitive intelligence and white and grey activities. These individuals may be involved in sophisticated swindles or corporate espionage. They will sell information and intellectual property to the highest bidder. Very little is known about this clandestine group as they use strict anonymity to cloak their activities. To them, their criminal activities are jobs and they are consummate professionals. It is believed that this group is made up of a large number of ex-intelligence operatives. When the former USSR and several of the Eastern Bloc countries fell apart in the mid 1990s, a large number of instantly displaced intelligence people reportedly became mercenaries. For these individuals, neither morality nor the ethics of their actions figure into the equation. They have been very well indoctrinated against such self-regulatory mechanisms by their previous intelligence and espionage training. They are most likely at the post-conventional stages of moral development where ethics are dictated by self-chosen principles.

The last category includes the Cyber-terrorist (CT) individuals. On the surface, this group's activities mimic those of the other categories. They may be part of the military or paramilitary of a nation state and are viewed as soldiers or freedom fighters in the new cyberspace battlefield. Their goal is no different from that of the traditional military, namely, to win the battle or war by whatever means possible. Computers and computer-related technologies are logical targets as they now play

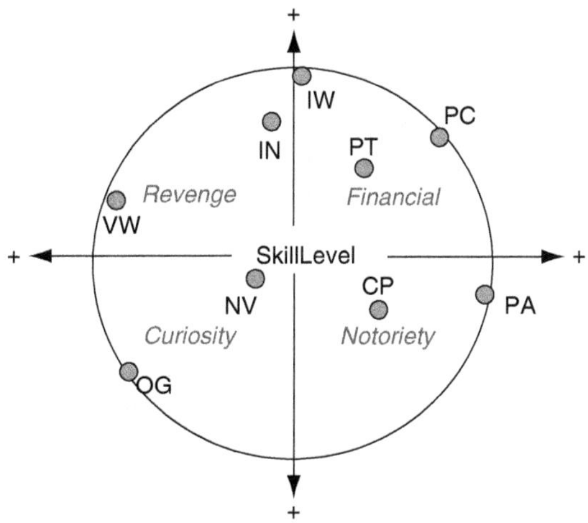

Fig. 14.2 A circumplex model (novice (NV), cyber-punks (CP), petty thieves (PT), virus writers (VW), old guard hackers (OG), professional criminals (PC), information warriors (IW), and political activists (PA) are included as a discussion point only)

a crucial role in the military and nations' well being. Computers are employed to process vast amounts of information upon which command and control decisions are predicated. The motivation of the CT group is simple, namely attack systems just as it is the military pilot's job to maneuver an aircraft and drop bombs. Members of the CT group are always trying to disrupt the enemy's society or defense systems or protect their own systems from similar attacks from the other side.

Using the continuum as a base, we can expand the model to include not only the skill of the individuals in question, but also the motivation for carrying out their behavior [1]. In this circumplex model, shown in Fig. 14.2, the position of variables relative to each other represents the motivation component using the standard circular ordering criteria (e.g., opposite and orthogonal).

The position of the variable relative to the origin is used to represent the skill level (i.e., variables farther out from the center on the radius indicate a higher skill level).

The four motivational quadrants are (1) Revenge, (2) Financial, (3) Notoriety, (4) Curiosity. These motivational categories were chosen as they capture the sum total of the primary motivations for criminal behavior expressed by both general criminals and cyber criminals [4].

In the circumplex model, the categories of cyber criminal types has been modified to better reflect the hypothesized effect of the two principal components of skill and motivation. In this newer model, hacktavist is replaced by the term political activist (PA). Thieves in the older model (continuum) are referred to as petty thieves (PT) and professionals are now termed professional criminals (PC). Cyber terrorists are now referred to as information warriors (IW) to better capture the diversity of this sub-group.

The new model also adds the categories of internals (IN) and old guard (OG). Internals (IN) represents the greatest risk. Historically, internals or insiders, have been the most costly attackers from both an impact and cost perspective. The internals group is primarily made up of disgruntled employees/ex-employees/contractors/consultants who violate the level of trust they have been given (or had been given), and using elevated system/access privileges inherent to their job functions, attack their own organization's systems [1]. The skill level for this group is somewhat elevated due to the fact that individuals in this category are often IT professionals and sometimes administrators. The motivation most often reported is revenge centered; internals feel they have been slighted, wrongfully terminated or overlooked by management and rationalize that their actions are justified.

Old guards (OG) appear to have no criminal intent although there is an alarming disrespect for personal property [1]. The OG embraces the ideology of the first generation hackers and appears to be interested in the intellectual endeavor. This group has deep technical skills and often writes the code and scripts that are used by the less skilled individuals. Although these individuals rarely use the scripts themselves, they readily post them and indirectly encourage their use by the other members of the hacker society. The primary motivations for this group are curiosity and the need for intellectual challenge [1].

14.2.2 Limitations

As with any social science, a limitation of the proposed taxonomy is that human beings are complex and the individual categories are not necessarily mutually exclusive, even when plotted in a two dimensional method. Thus, an individual in the CP category may, at times, display a skill level similar to persons in the VW category, namely, deploying one of the numerous "virus tool kits" to author a virus and then releasing it on the Internet. In this case the tool is very "skilled" not necessarily the individual using the tool. Also, like general criminals, cyber criminals often have more than one motivation for committing their illegal activities. In some cases the criminal activity is motivated for financial gain as well as revenge or notoriety.

Despite the usefulness of the taxonomy in providing a reference, we face a major hurdle. The majority of the computer criminal categories have never been the subject of an extensive, formal study. The SK and CP categories have had some formal, albeit limited examination, primarily due to the fact that the corresponding individuals have been frequently apprehended by law enforcement. Generalizing the characteristics learned from only two types of cybercriminals is risky but it is the only data available to serve as the starting point of the study. There is a saying in law enforcement that only the stupid and the unlucky criminals are apprehended. If affirmative, these are hardly the groups that we want to use as the sole source of data.

Documented cases of cybercrimes, primarily derived from the SK and CP categories, point to greed, fraud, embezzlement, theft, jealousy, revenge, hubris, and the desire for power as the key motivating factors. Although the computer underground would like everyone to believe that their primary motivation for hacking is the desire for knowledge, historical evidence refutes their claim and reveals that their motivations had been propaganda and attempt to rationalize their errant behavior. The evidence is subject to limited samples.

The lack of serious research has resulted in stereotypes being substituted for meaningful, investigative profiles of the cybercriminals. The present stereotype is a male, 12–28 years old, single, and socially dysfunctional, possibly from a dysfunctional family. These characteristics generally match those of an individual involved in deviant and delinquent behavior, but do not betray any unique cybercriminal characteristics.

14.3 Why are Cybercriminals Attracted to Commit Crimes

Armed with the general characteristics of cybercriminals, we will examine why specific individuals choose to become involved in cybercrimes. The disciplines of sociology, psychology, and criminology have put forward a number of theories to help determine the etiology of criminal behavior in general. These theories have postulated that criminal behavior is the result of diverse factors, including industrialization, social control, class strain, physiological deficiencies, psychopathologies, and learning. While no single theory has been proven to be superior than any other, empirical research findings tend to favor two popular theories, namely, social learning theory and moral disengagement. In its basic form, cybercrime is yet another form of general criminal behavior, so it is logical that we utilize the traditional theories of crime etiology to help us understand the cybercrime problem.

14.3.1 Social Learning Theory

The basic premise of social learning theory is that the same, high-level learning process can produce both deviant as well as conforming behaviors. The learning process operates in the context of social structure, interactions, and situations. Thus, the resulting criminal or conforming behavior is a function of the underlying variables of the social learning process, especially reinforcement. Ronald Akers presented the theory in terms of four testable hypotheses. According to him, an individual is more likely to commit violations, under the following circumstances:

1. He or she differentially associates with others who commit, model, and support violations of social and legal norms.
2. The violative behavior is differentially reinforced in contrast to behavior that conforms to the norm.
3. He or she is exposed to more deviant than conforming models.
4. His or her own learned definitions are favorable toward committing deviant acts.

According to the social learning theory, the primary learning mechanisms include differential reinforcement and imitation. It is believed that the mechanisms operate through a process of differential association and are influenced by definitions. First, differential association occurs, creating a social environment. Second, within the social environment, exposure to definitions and imitation of models occur. Definitions are acquired through imitation and observational learning. Differential reinforcement can originate from internal and external sources. Reinforcement can assume the form of tangible rewards of the activity itself, namely, money, or social rewards, including increase in peer status. Over time, however, imitation becomes less important and reinforcement or consequences of the actions determine the probability with which the activity will continue.

Recent studies indicate that individuals involved in cybercriminal behavior have higher rates of differential association and differential reinforcement, compared to the non-criminal public. Cybercriminals have been found to associate with people who hold similar opinions about the ethics and morality of engaging in deviant behavior. These associations occur in the real world as well as the cyberworld via computer-mediated communication (CMC). For cybercriminals, the CMC associations usually outnumber those in the real world. The CMC associations can occur in a number of scenarios, namely, chat channels in Internet Relay Chat (IRC), ICQ, instant messaging news groups, and e-mail. CMC may be organized into two categories, namely (1) synchronous, where communication occurs in real-time as with chat groups or MUDS, and (2) asynchronous, where the interactions are non real-time such as e-mail, newsgroups, or list-servers.

To the cybercriminal, the CMC relationships are just as important as the real world associations of ordinary people. The strong reliance on CMC by cybercriminals has been largely overlooked by numerous studies and it bears interesting implications for research in this area. The prevailing opinion among experts has been that computer "hackers" possess poor or under-developed social skills. This opinion has been based on the traditional definition of social skills, namely, face-to-face interactions and communications. However, when the definition is expanded to include CMC, the opinion cannot be supported by evidence. In general, cybercriminals have a highly active, non-traditional social life. They possess superior CMC social skills, namely, "netiquette," than the ordinary public who are generally unfamiliar with online communications. In the computer underground, CMC and consequent online relationships form the basis for the peer groups. These individuals are very comfortable in the realm of non face-to-face interactions. Many of them maintain friendships; engage in mentoring, namely helping newer comers understand the technology and software; and some even find romance online. Many IRC channels serve as virtual "cafes," where users visit, exchange pleasantries, argue, and share information. These channels can also be used to coordinate attacks; trade illicit items, including credit card numbers and stolen account information; and discuss the different exploits and efforts by the authorities to apprehend them. While cybercriminals maintain a robust CMC social life, there is an important distinction with respect to face-to-face communication. Research indicates that the real world is high-bandwidth in that people who communicate face-to-face employ multiple modes of interchange in real time, including speech, gestures, facial expression, the entire gamut of semiology. In contrast, CMC is low-bandwidth in nature in that communication is restricted to a few lines of text on a screen at any given time. Thus, CMC runs the risk of missing important information that may be necessary to comprehend the other party completely. The limited cues can and has led to numerous misunderstandings, misinterpretations, arguments, implying a volatile social foundation.

Socializing and peer relationships in the computer underground are not solely restricted to CMC. There are face-to-face gatherings in the real world, including the Chaos Computer Camp in Europe, DEFCon in Las Vegas, and Blackhat Briefings. The gatherings often attract more law enforcement officers and corporate recruiters than individuals from the computer underground. The conferences mirror the CMC gatherings in that the individuals trade information, discuss attacks in formal or quasi-formal lectures, and gossip. Careful observations of the interactions at these events reveal that the majority of the underground feel more at ease with CMC than with face-to-face interactions. CMC establishes the primary social context in which the other facets of social learning exert their influence. While CMC provides the opportunity to associate with other members of the underground and mentored by some of them, it also constitutes the primary environment in which reinforcement and punishment are served. Since the CMC community is of great significance to the hacker, the community's opinions and reactions influence the individual's continued involvement in criminal behavior. Positive reinforcement will increase the cybercriminal tendencies, while punishment will decrease the likelihood of continued engagement in the computer underworld. Positive reinforcement includes praise, encouragement, a virtual pat on the back, and gaining "folk hero" status in the underground community. Punishments may include being ostracized, ignored, shut out of the flow of information, and locked out of a specific chat channel. For cybercriminals, reinforcement and punishment are not limited to CMC. Events in the real world also influence their behavior. Examples of positive reinforcement in the real world include testifying before a government hearing; media attention, including movies chronicling one's exploits; and obtaining high paying jobs in the technology sector despite being convicted of a cybercrime offense. Often, the degree of punishment a cybercriminal receives in the real world fails to counteract the positive reinforcement obtained from the computer underground. Even today, most countries have ineffectual or non-existent laws against cybercrimes and a judicial system that neither understands the nature of the offense nor believes that there are real victims of the crimes.

According to the social learning theory, where the overall ratio of positive reinforcement to punishment is very high, errant behavior will continue unabated, and in many cases, increase. Data from the CIS/FBI and Australian computer crime surveys confirms this trend, namely, that criminal behavior is rising, year after year, both in severity and frequency. Criminal behavior is influenced by the traditional learning mechanisms, including classical and operant learning. Furthermore, the varying ratios of positive reinforcement to punishment result in a very resilient learning paradigm, rendering it difficult to neutralize the errant behavior.

The deviant behavior is quick to return once positive reinforcement is reintroduced back into the environment.

14.3.2 Moral Disengagement

A computer security expert, Eugene Spafford of Purdue University, has opined that the activity of "hackers" should be evaluated not in terms of the ends or the justifications but by the acts themselves. However, by studying the espoused justifications and rationalizations of individuals engaged in aberrant behavior, we are indirectly able to obtain insight into the underlying psyche of these people. Cybercriminals have evoked an undeniable mystique in our culture. They are commonly portrayed as modern-day "Robin Hoods," who are carrying out a valuable function in society. Numerous articles, editorials, interviews, and web pages claim that without hackers, there would be no "real" security. Interviewed "hackers" contend that they serve as society's watchdogs, maintaining a vigilant eye on unscrupulous vendors and tyrannical governments. Publications such as "Phrack" and "2600" commonly carry editorials validating the illegal activity of "hackers" and urging others to join the "cause." Sadly, many sections of society have accepted the rhetoric of the cybercriminals at face value. To many in the younger generation, cybercriminals have become role models whose activities and exploits are to be emulated. This has undoubtedly led to a variety of "copy-cat" and "one-upmanship attacks," a trend that could account for the increased frequency of attacks over the past years. The media has added fuel to the fire by inadvertently associating the benign term "hacker" with the ruthless cybercriminals. This mistake has been exploited by the criminals who hide behind the facade. As we had mentioned earlier, the original definition of hacker had little or nothing to do with criminal activity. The term "hacker" does not share the negative connotations with the term "criminal."

It is normal for cybercriminals to feel the need to justify their aberrant behavior in terms of fulfilling a noble and higher societal imperative. For, human beings usually do not engage in reprehensible conduct unless they have successfully convinced themselves their actions are right. The process of moral justification permits a detrimental conduct to be rendered personally and socially acceptable by portraying it as a valuable social service or fulfilling a higher moral purpose. The complex process can be best understood through Albert Bandura's social cognitive theory and the concept of moral disengagement. According to the social cognitive theory, human beings tend to naturally refrain from behaviors that violate their own moral standards and bring about feelings of self-censure and guilt. The standards are derived from the moral agency and manifested in terms of self-regulatory mechanisms, which comprises of three major sub-functions, namely, self-monitoring, judgmental, and self-reactive. The first step to exercising control over one's conduct is self-monitoring. Second, following an action by an individual, a judgmental function evaluates the conduct against the internal standards and situational circumstances. This gives rise to self-reactions.

In theory, criminals can defeat the self-regulatory system by decoupling the internal moral control from their detrimental conduct through one of four mechanisms. These include, (1) re-construing the conduct, (2) obscuring the personal causal agency, (3) misrepresenting or disregarding the negative consequences of the action, and (4) vilifying the victims and blaming and devaluing them. These are detailed as follows:

1. Language can play an important role in helping an individual re-construe his or her conduct and shape the perception of the actions. Reprehensible conduct can be successfully masked by euphemistic language and, in many cases, permit the conduct to be viewed as respectable. For example, the act of hacking a system appears distant from committing a crime. Destructive conduct can also be masked by comparing it to other, more injurious behavior. This enables the individual to rationalize that their activities are relatively minor in the grand scheme of things. The advantageous or palliative comparison increases in effectiveness when even more flagrant activities are considered. For example, the act of breaking into the computer system of a large multinational corporation is insignificant compared to their deliberate attempts to poison the environment.
2. Criminals can successfully obscure the personal causal agency by distorting the relationship between their own conduct and the consequent effects. By displacing their personal responsibility, individuals can view their actions as stemming from social pressures, including socio-economic status, and other compelling circumstances. An individual who steals food because he or she is hungry is clearly not at fault. Self-censure is immediately reduced since the individual is no longer the actual agent of the reprehensible actions. An equally effective mechanism to obscure personal responsibility is by diffusing it among all members of the group, couched in the form of segmentation of duties. Each segment's actions are, by itself, benign; however, the totality of the entire group's actions is harmful. Group decisions also diffuse responsibility, since the individual no longer assumes personal responsibility for the group's final decision., and thus, is not at fault.
3. Self-censure can also be grossly minimized by disregarding or distorting the consequences of an action. By ignoring the negative consequences of the actions, as in selective inattention or through cognitive distortion, the feelings of guilt are reduced. When individuals minimize the harm that they have caused, there is little chance of self-censure.
4. The final mechanism of disengaging the self-regulatory system focuses on the recipients of the acts. Stripping the victims of their human attributes through dehumanization can reduce feelings of guilt or remorse. This is probably the most common mechanism deployed in moral disengagement. It reduces the victims to sub-human status, and not a person with feelings or worthy of empathy. Often, the blame is transfered to the victim or circumstances. Through attribution of blame, the perpetrators view themselves as victims who had been needlessly provoked to commit the reprehensible conduct, thereby rendering their actions as defensive. The victims are blamed and accused of bringing the actions upon themselves.

It has become clear that cybercriminals routinely use combination of the four techniques of moral disengagement to reduce self-censure. Several studies and articles, quote "hackers" as stating that their activities represent pure intellectual activity and that information should be freely available to everyone anyway. They continually minimize or misconstrue the consequences. Hackers [5] claim that they never truly damage any files, since companies either have backups of their data and systems anyway. Any loss incurred by a business is its own fault for not taking prudent precautions. Other hackers dehumanize the victims, referring to them as impersonal multi-national corporations, faceless bureaucracies, and simply inanimate networks and systems. It is ironic that the cybercriminals never comment on the adverse impact to the end users and system administrators, the cost to potential consumers, and the long-term effects. As we had indicated earlier, the most common mechanism used by cybercriminals is to blame the victims. Court transcripts, media interviews, and self-report surveys quote cybercriminals blaming systems administrators, software developers, and programmers for poor code-writing practices and lax security. They even go so far as to state that the victims deserved to be attacked.

14.3.3 Anonymity

A possibly unique factor in the field of cybercrimes is anonymity. The Internet protocols permits a person to operate virtually anonymously. A popular cartoon depicts a dog sitting behind a computer and talking to a cat standing in front. The caption reads, "On the Internet no one knows you're a dog." This anonymity and the consequent ability to take on any persona has been leveraged by pedophiles and cyber-predators who often pretend to be young females in order to gain the trust of their victims. The technology and underlying protocols enable criminals to obfuscate their physical locations, thereby rendering them impossible to trace and track. Studies on online behaviors have found that people behave very differently in cyberspace than in the real world. Online, individuals tend to be more aggressive, less tolerant, more promiscuous, and their opinions tend to be polarized at the extreme ends of the continuum. Researchers hypothesize that anonymity tends to bring out the worst personalities in individuals when they are online, given that they believe with certainty they are anonymous and can assume any fictitious persona. In essence, online behavior may reflect an individual's true nature, in the absence of self-control and visible societal norms and pressures. In the real world, most individuals moderate their behavior based on a social identity that incorporates social norms and the cultural morality. Thus, behaviors in the real world are more conservative to fit within the prescribed societal tolerances.

The hypothesis that anonymity encourages permissiveness finds support in the social control theory, which states that in general, people will refrain from deviant and criminal behavior because of the presence of social controls, including police, laws, social ostracize, etc. Where the controls are missing or the assumed power of these controls is diminished, deviance grows. If it highly unlikely or even impossible to correctly identify the individual responsible for a deviant behavior, the fear of sanctions will disappear and the controls will fail. The diminished fear of sanctions stemming from anonymity may account for the unexpected finding that a majority of cybercriminals convicted of deviant online behaviors would not otherwise engage in traditional criminal acts. Clearly, there is an undeniable disconnect between overt behaviors in the real world and those in cyberspace [6]. Unfortunately, at this point in time, the exact influence of anonymity on the etiology of criminal computer behavior is unknown, as little if any research attention has been focused in this area. We are left with suppositions and educated guesses and more research needs to be pursued.

14.4 Strategies to Contain Cybercriminal Behaviors: Deterrence and Rehabilitation

Knowledge of the psychological characteristics of cybercriminals and the possible etiology of cybercriminal behavior constitute one important element of the equation in dealing with the serious social issue of cybercrimes [7]. The second element is one of developing meaningful approaches to deter such destructive behavior and possibly rehabilitate the offenders. The conventional models for deterrence include laws and law enforcement, social norms, education, market forces, and physical controls. In this chapter, we will confine ourself to laws, social sanctions, and education, as they offer the highest probability of success. Market forces, namely controlling consumer demand, contains a plethora of concomitant factors and identifying and measuring the effectiveness of each of the factors is extremely difficult. Physical controls tend to restrict the outward expressions of behaviors; however, they fail to directly address the underlying causal factors.

14.4.1 Cybercrime Laws

Today, the legal system serves as one of the primary mechanisms to control aberrant behavior in society. While opponents criticize the legal system as reactive and void of preventative controls, proponents argue that the system achieves vicarious deterrence by metering out swift justice with appropriate punishments. Vicarious deterrence is viewed as the primary process through which others are persuaded not to engage in similar deviant and criminal behaviors. Relative to cybercrimes, a number of key factors influence the effectiveness of legal sanctions. They include the global nature of cybercrimes, lack of cybercrime laws at the international level, many nations with no cybercrime laws, and absence of coordination between cyberspace law enforcement agencies in different nations. The global nature of the Internet coupled with the international reach of cybercrimes have effectively rendered the traditional national borders irrelevant in cyberspace.

Thus, when prosecuting cybercrimes across national boundaries, issues of jurisdiction and extradition become highly complex. The alleged author of the "I Love You" virus escaped prosecution as his native country of Philippines had no laws pertaining to the creation and/or distribution of computer viruses.

Even for countries that have enacted cybercrime laws, the adequacy, precision, and effectiveness of the legislation is suspect. In Canada and the United States, current legislation lacks real "teeth." The punishments metered out by the courts, which become precedent, are simply not proportional to the damage resulting from the criminal behavior. Recent studies note that cybercriminals are likely to receive a far lighter sentence than most other types of criminals. In Canada, for example, on average, cybercriminals receive sentences that are half as long as those charged with offenses of similar severity, including assault, forgery, and theft under $5,000. The most common punishment for adults convicted of cybercrime offenses is a 1 year suspended sentence. For youths, i.e., those under the age of 18 years, the average sentence is alternate measures and the incident does not even appear on their record as a conviction.

Many have argued that an effective alternative to criminal sanctions might lie in civil remedies. That is, since the criminal courts are not metering out effective punishments, suing cybercriminals for monetary compensation against the damages they have inflicted on the victims appears logical. However, a majority of the individuals apprehended for cybercrimes under the SK and CP categories are young people with little or no assets. In many cases, the offenders are under the age of 18 and they have no means of paying a judgment against them. In many countries, the courts have ruled that parents and legal guardians cannot be named in a lawsuit and that they are not responsible for their children's behavior. This leaves open the question, whom does one sue? A number of imaginative litigators are beginning to focus on third party liability, namely punish the owners of systems that had been hijacked by the perpetrator and used to launch the attack. Evidently, owners of the compromised systems have been negligent in securing their systems, thereby facilitating the attacker to obtain a "toe hold" to launch their attack against the victim's assets. Clearly, the deterrent effect of civil remedies on the offender is nil.

Surprisingly, the mere effort to track accurate computer crime rates is extremely difficult. This stems from the fact that a majority of victims never report the incident to authorities. Most businesses and organizations refuse to report, fearing that public knowledge will generate negative publicity. Negative publicity resulting from a News of a successful attack may lead to a decrease in stock holder and consumer confidence. For publicly traded companies, share prices may fall. If customers feel unsafe, business can experience a sharp drop. The net effect of the reluctance is an under-reporting of cybercrimes and a consequent under-estimation of its true impact. Despite the apparent under-estimation, surveys reveal that the frequency and seriousness of cybercrimes is increasing. Clearly, deterrence is not working.

One of the important reasons why the justice system is ineffectual in dealing with computer-related offenses lies in the fact that nearly all politicians, judges, and senior lawyers belong to the pre-computer generation. They are neither familiar with the computing principles, computer technology, nor the Internet. As such, they struggle with even basic concepts, including the potential impact of online and computer deviance. Thus, it is not surprising that criminal laws are struggling to keep up with the expanding technologies in cyberspace, while ambiguous and erroneous definitions of cybercriminal activities are stirring problems throughout the world. For the cyberspace laws to keep pace with technology, they must succeed in defining what constitutes a criminal act. The adversarial legal system in North America places the burden on the State to prove, beyond a reasonable doubt, each of the required elements of the offense, namely, jurisdiction, competence and intent, along with the actions of the accused which constitutes the criminal offense. Merely defining cybercriminal acts has been difficult, given that virtually all legislators neither understand the technology nor the ramifications of security breaches, i.e., loss of confidentiality, integrity of data, and availability of data and systems. Historically, legislators have reacted conservatively to new and unique needs. While the courts have turned to common law concepts of crime in an attempt to define legal and illegal activities in cyberspace, legislators have attempted to cast cybercriminal activities into traditional offenses and processes. Ironically, the courts and legislators have often relied on analogies and metaphors to represent computer and Internet events. Unable to grasp technological concepts, many legislators compare computer break-ins to a burglar breaking into a house and e-mail monitoring to wire-tapping. This strategy clearly does not work with activities that are unique to technology, namely, virus authoring and denial of service attacks. Highly specific laws and precise definitions are required when addressing cybercriminal activities involving computers, systems, networks, or application vulnerabilities. For legislation to be effective, a clear understanding of both the technology and the individuals engaged in exploiting them are absolutely essential. In the past, the courts have been reluctant to view computer attacks as crimes, largely due to the fact that the object of the attack had been something intangible, namely data. In Canada, until just a few years ago, the term, data, was not even defined in the Criminal Code. Without a definition, data could not even be criminally attacked. Data has been subsequently defined as a document and is now offered protection by the Criminal Code.

In conclusion, it is clear that society cannot solely rely on the current justice system and criminal sanctions to control deviant behavior in cyberspace. Other methods, including social sanctions, altering the social environment, and education need to be deployed in conjunction with legal sanctions. A few of these methods have been utilized to fight the "war on drugs" and curb gang involvement, with differing degrees of effectiveness.

14.4.2 Social Sanctions

When words and actions don't go hand-in-hand in society, an atmosphere of hypocrisy arises. As a society we have supposedly frowned upon cybercrimes and cybercriminals. We hear our law enforcement officials and various others condemning those who engage in this type of deviant activity. Businesses cry foul when they fall victim to destructive behavior. Yet, in the next breath, the same businesses or government agencies hire former or still "practicing" cybercriminals as information security specialists charged with the responsibility of protecting the business's assets. The irresponsible media places "hackers" on a pedestal and turns them into folk heroes. Our politicians reference wild and outrageous statements that now "famous hackers" spew forth as the gospel truth. Computer criminals have books and movies made of their exploits. Thus, our actions fail to not match our words. It would appear that, deep down, society actually idolizes these criminals and condones their activities. If we are to truly deter destructive, cybercriminal behavior, we must be consistent. Society needs to act in accordance with what the spoken words, namely, that cybercriminal behavior is not acceptable and will not be tolerated. Social sanctions can serve as a powerful tool here. The sanctions may be as straightforward as refusing to hire individuals who either admit to or have been convicted of serious cybercrimes, or as severe as socially ostracizing cybercriminals. A logical starting point would be for the media to stop elevating convicted cybercriminals to "pop star" status. Publishers and conference organizers should rethink the practice of allowing criminals to capitalize on their criminal behavior by authoring books on their supposed area of expertise. Most of these books constitute thinly veiled attempts to circumvent the restrictions imposed by the courts on the criminals so they may not profit from their crimes.

A second, effective strategy would be to focus on the social environment, which serves as the foundation upon which the forces and factors interact. As we had explained previously, differential association and imitation and modeling play a key role in both attracting individuals to cybercrimes and in prolonging their association with the computer underground. If we can only modify the underlying social environment and increase the contact between a cybercriminal and members of the "mainstream" computer community, who consider criminal behavior inappropriate, we might succeed in pushing the ratio of positive reinforcement to punishment higher by exposing the individuals to opinions and attitudes that are counter to the ones held by the underground. This might go a long way into rehabilitating the cybercriminals.

Under a third strategy, convicted cybercriminals must be forced to witness, first hand, the consequences of their actions. In traditional criminology, a constructive punishment consists in forcing the offender understand the impact that their actions have had on the victims. It is hypothesized that through personalizing the impact of the criminal conduct, it will be difficult for the offender to continue rationalizing the aberrant behavior and that it should lead to a reduction in recidivism. There is no reason why the same approach could not be applied to cybercriminals. The cybercriminals must meet with the system administrators whose systems have been damaged and cost them countless hours of work and worry as well as merchants who have lost money from the illegal use of credit card numbers. They must be forced to experience, first hand, how much effort is involved in recovering from a breach and realize that it is not merely an intellectual game. Although modifying the social environment and exposing the convicted criminals, up front, to the consequences of their actions will never be 100% effective or appropriate for all offenders, given the makeup of the most commonly arrested cybercriminals, namely, script kiddies and cyber-punks, this approach may bear significant positive impact. The courts need to seriously consider these approaches as alternatives to probation, parole, and the sentencing procedure.

14.4.3 Education

Education is probably our best tool in the fight against cybercrimes. It is a powerful resource and has proven to be a significant factor in reducing deviance. For maximal effectiveness, education must be deployed during the critical periods of the individuals's developmental process. The general rule is to initiate the education process during the early formative years and continue the process through the later developmental stages, namely, adolescence and early adulthood. During the formative years, the individual is open to new ideas, different concepts, and constructive approaches, which will serve as the "seeds" for later opinions on morality, ethics, and righteousness.

In the context of reforming cybercriminal behavior, education relates to the following concepts:

1. Understanding the link between online or cyberspace actions and their real world manifestations
2. Developing cyber morality and ethics that mirror the morality and ethics of the real world
3. Internalizing positive societal, cultural, and parental norms that relate to technology and cyberspace

The key toward successful education is to target children who are just venturing into the world of technology and cyberspace. Our traditional educational system which, for better or worse, is currently focused on instilling our societal and cultural norms, must be expanded to include related concepts in the cyberworld.

A number of academicians have pointed out the widespread lack of ethics and morality in cyberspace as well as with the use of technology. This is hardly surprising, given that we have focused intently on the impersonal and technical aspect of the information revolution while ignoring the philosophical side of the overall education equation. We currently face an imbalance between what is technically feasible and what we philosophically believe as morally correct. Many of the leading computer science and engineering schools today offer courses in ethics. While they appear, at first glance, a worthwhile endeavor, a deeper examination reveals a serious flaw. By the time most individuals are at a university, their personalities are fairly well developed and the cast set. They have already internalized their individual notions of right, wrong, moral, and immoral and it is too late to instill any new, constructive ideas. At this late stage of development, any effort is negligible at best. The education process must begin in the early grades, namely, KG through 6, if we wish to influence their behaviors in the late teen years and early adulthood.

Research confirms that cybercriminal behavior tends to manifest itself in teenagers, similar to criminal behavior in general. Clearly, education prior to this period is critical. The specifics of educational programs aimed at reducing computer crime is beyond the scope of this chapter. However, it will suffice to say that the concept is presently being used with other types of deviance and should be easy to adapt it to fit computer crime.

14.5 Conclusions

As society becomes increasingly dependent on computer technology and the Internet, the impact of cybercrimes will increase exponentially. The Internet has been described as the "wild west," with no Sheriffs, Marshalls, nor governing body. It has been portrayed as both the great equalizer in terms of access to information and as chaotic, since many of our real world concepts no longer apply. In particular, borders, jurisdictions, and geographical distances no longer seem to be relevant.

As with any new frontier, the first settlers will be responsible to establish and maintain law and order informally. Definitions of acceptable and unacceptable behavior need to be agreed upon and, more importantly, diligently enforced. The new frontier has also attracted the unsavory side of society. While a few individuals view this an opportunity to further indulge their selfish and deviant tastes, others see it as an opportunity to further their criminal endeavors. The same features that make computer technology attractive for businesses and other organizations also render it lucrative to the criminal element. These features include the anonymity of the Internet, ability to communicate with vast numbers of people and systems quickly, irrelevance of borders and physical distance, abstraction, and the naivety and trust of users on the Internet.

The fact that cybercrime exists should surprise no one; what is shocking is that we know so little about its genesis and the criminals. Before society can cogently deal with computer crime, we need a far better understanding of the who and why of this criminal activity. We need to move beyond mere anecdotes and cultural myths and adopt a scientific approach toward understanding cybercrimes and cybercriminals. Hype and hyperbole sell security products and help obtain budget money, yet they rarely help us develop a true understanding of computer crime. Knee jerk reactions based on limited information and the "more of approach" to cybercrime are not acceptable answers. We need to apply the same scientific rigor to computer criminals that we have applied in our attempts to understand general criminal behaviors. The "more of approach" simply refers to increasing potential punishments for criminal activity, without understanding what factors truly influence criminal behavior.

In our quest to understand cybercrimes, we need to crawl before we walk and walk before we run. There are still several unanswered fundamental questions, namely, is cybercrime merely a part of the overall continuum of criminal activities or is it unique? And do cybercriminals pick victims at random or is it based on opportunity? Although preliminary research indicates that cybercriminals do not represent a homogeneous group, we have little to no information on how they are unique. We still lack a commonly agreed upon terminology for whom we are examining. For example, does the term hacker refer to programmers, script-kiddies, or credit card thieves? Clearly, the study of this area is in its infancy, but the importance of gaining a better understanding is clear. If we understand what motivates the individuals involved in criminal activity, we can begin to understand the who and the why. Examining the victims of cybercrimes will also shed light on the behavioral characteristics of these criminals.

It is only through a superior understanding of the individuals involved in deviant behavior that we will succeed in developing practical strategies to deal with the problem of cybercrime [1,4,7]. Simply treating the symptoms is not adequate; we must deal effectively with the root causes of the behavior. We need to craft and support legislation with clearly defined social norms and attitudes that will be punitive toward cybercriminal activities. We also need to ensure that we educate our young people on ethical behavior in cyberspace.

As many of today's cybercriminals age, cybercrimes will not spontaneously disappear. Others will willing take their place. Presently, we are losing the battle on cybercrime. The frequency and impact of this criminal activity is increasing every year. To-date, our strategy has been to focus on technical solutions to the problem, namely, superior firewalls, intrusion detection systems, and stronger passwords. We have ignored the fact that we are dealing with human behavior and that individuals, not technology, are the true source of the problem.

As we move into the not too distant future, the need to effectively deal with cybercrime will become paramount. As technology and computers become even more ubiquitous in our society, our ethics and morality must gain commensurate maturity or we will find ourselves in a desperate situation. It is time for society to come to grips with the problem of cybercrime and make a concerted and coordinated effort to arrive at a long-term solution. A band-aid approach, as we currently seem to be embracing, is doomed to failure and will ultimately result in frustrating any true efforts to deal with this long-term societal issue.

References

[1] Rogers, M. (2006). The development of a meaningful hacker taxonomy: A two dimensional approach. *Digital Investigations*, 97–102.

[2] Private communications with Dr. Bruce Hoffman.

[3] US Federal Trade Commission. (2003). Report on identity theft.

[4] Rogers, M., Siegfried, K., & Tidke, K. (2006). Self-reported computer criminal behavior: A psychological analysis. *Proceedings of the Digital Forensics Workshop* (pp. 116–120). Elseiver.

[5] Levy, S. (1984). *Hackers: Heroes of the computer revolution.* New York, NY: Doubleday.

[6] Baggili, I. (2009). *Effects of anonymity, pre-employment integrity and anti-social behavior on self-reported cyber crime engagement: An exploratory study.* Unpublished Dissertation, Purdue University.

[7] Rogers, M. K., Smoak, N., & Jia, L. (2006). Self-reported criminal computer behavior: A big-5, moral choice and manipulative exploitive behavior analysis. *Journal of Deviant Behavior, 27*(3), 245–268.

Part VI
Cybercrime Regulation Through Civil and Criminal Penalties

Chapter 15
Spurring the Private Sector: Indirect Federal Regulation of Cybersecurity in the US

Stewart Baker and Melanie Schneck-Teplinsky

The US federal government has long understood the importance of securing cyberspace and the private sector's essential role in that effort. Over the past decade, the government consistently has eschewed direct federal mandates regarding private sector cybersecurity practices and instead has favored indirect regulation to achieve cybersecurity goals. Indirect regulation is a regulatory approach that seeks to encourage behaviors that lead to increased cybersecurity and prohibit/discourage behaviors that lead to decreased cybersecurity.

This chapter explores how the government's efforts to secure cyberspace through indirect regulation have evolved over the past decade. Initial government attempts at indirect regulation nibbled around the edges of the cybersecurity problem, but as the government has become more sophisticated in its approach to indirect regulation and the political climate has become more amenable, indirect regulation has become a powerful tool in the government's effort to secure cyberspace.

15.1 Introduction

In the 1980s, the federal government revised the US criminal code to address the nation's cybercrime problem.[1] Among the government's most significant milestones in this regard was the Computer Fraud and Abuse Act (CFAA) of 1986,[2] which criminalized unauthorized access to certain computers and computer networks.[3] CFAA has since been amended multiple times[4] to broaden its scope[5] and increase

[1] In 1984, Congress chose for the first time to address federal computer-related crimes in a single new statute, 18 U.S.C. §1030, rather than to add new provisions to existing criminal laws.

[2] The CFAA of 1986 amended 18 U.S.C. §1030.

[3] 18 U.S.C. §1030.

[4] CFAA was amended in 1988, 1989, 1990, 1994, 1996, 2001 and 2002.

[5] In its current form, CFAA outlaws a variety of activities, including hacking into a government computer (18 U.S.C. §1030(a)(3)); hacking that results in exposure of certain governmental, credit, financial, or commercial information (18 U.S.C. §1030(a)(2)); and damaging a computer through cyberattacks, cybercrime, or cyberterrorism (18 U.S.C. §1030(a)(5)).

S. Ghosh and E. Turrini (eds.), *Cybercrimes: A Multidisciplinary Analysis*,
DOI 10.1007/978-3-642-13547-7_15, © Springer-Verlag Berlin Heidelberg 2010

the severity of the penalties available under the statute,[6] and other criminal statutes also have been invoked in the fight against cybercrime.[7] By themselves, however, criminal laws have proven insufficient in the fight against cybercrime, let alone in the greater fight for cybersecurity, largely because they focus on wrongdoers and fail to confront the more significant problem – our nation's security vulnerabilities.[8]

For nearly a decade now, the federal government has recognized the importance of addressing security vulnerabilities and has recognized the private sector's essential role in this effort since cyberspace technology and processes are largely owned by the private sector. Throughout this period, the federal government has avoided direct federal mandates regarding private sector cybersecurity practices for both practical and political reasons, including concerns that legislation putting the federal government or its agencies in the position of picking "winners and losers" in technological development could stifle private sector innovation in cybersecurity, stimulate industry backlash, impose substantial costs on the private sector, and potentially result in less secure systems over the long-term. The federal government instead has pursued its cybersecurity goals largely through indirect regulation.

The federal government first explicitly embraced indirect cybersecurity regulation in the 2003 National Strategy to Secure Cyberspace, the cybersecurity strategy born out of the September 11, 2001 terrorist attacks. Shortly after the attacks, President Bush issued an Executive Order establishing the Critical Infrastructure Protection Board (CIPB) to coordinate federal cybersecurity efforts related to critical infrastructure protection.[9] One of CIPB's most important responsibilities was to develop a national cybersecurity strategy in coordination with the private sector. CIPB's first chairman, Richard Clarke, developed and, in September 2002, released for public comment a draft report entitled "The National Strategy to Secure Cyberspace." [1] The draft outlined a number of initiatives designed to "secure US information systems against deliberate, malicious disruption."[10]

---

[6] Congress increased the penalties available under CFAA when it passed the Cyber Security Enhancement Act of 2002 as part of that year's Homeland Security Act.

[7] For example, (1) the Electronic Communications Privacy Act (18 U.S.C. §§2510-2521, 2701-2710), which criminalizes interception of electronic communication, has been used to prosecute hackers; (2) the Economic Espionage Act of 1996 (18 U.S.C. §1831, et seq.) has been interpreted as sufficiently broad to criminalize theft of trade secrets through computer intrusion; (3) the Wire Fraud Act has been interpreted to criminalize computer-aided theft involving the use of interstate wires or mails; and (4) there have been a limited number of prosecutions pursuant to state computer crime statutes such as those in force in Arizona, Florida, Illinois (criminalizing computer tampering and computer fraud), and Vermont.

[8] The federal government has long recognized the inadequacy of criminal laws standing on their own. See, e.g., President's Critical Infrastructure Protection Board, Draft National Strategy to Secure Cyberspace (Draft National Strategy), September 2002 at 4 ("[T]hose who rely on networked computer systems need to identify and remedy their vulnerabilities now, rather than wait for an attacker to be stopped or until alerted of an impending attack.").

[9] Executive Order 13231, "Critical Infrastructure Protection in the Information Age," October 16, 2001.

[10] Draft National Strategy at 1.

Clarke's draft strategy revealed the tension between CIPB's regulatory inclinations and industry's deregulatory desires. A central focus of the strategic effort was to find mechanisms to modify industry behavior without direct regulation. The government indicated that it was exploring ways to motivate companies that owned and operated the Internet's infrastructure but were ill-prepared to accept external regulations [2]. The draft essentially was a conglomeration of different approaches to indirect regulation, reflecting the government's efforts to influence the conduct of private sector companies without direct regulation [2].

When President Bush approved the final version of the "National Strategy to Secure Cyberspace" in February of 2003, it largely reflected industry's deregulatory stance, stating: "[F]ederal regulation will not become a primary means of securing cyberspace. Broad regulations mandating how all corporations must configure their information systems could divert more successful efforts by creating a lowest-common-denominator approach to cybersecurity, which evolving technology would quickly marginalize. Even worse, such an approach could result in less secure and more homogeneous security architectures than we have now. By law, some federal regulatory agencies already include cybersecurity considerations in their oversight activity. However, the market itself is expected to provide the major impetus to improve cybersecurity."[11]

The Bush Administration subsequently avoided direct federal mandates regarding cybersecurity in keeping with the pro-industry stance taken in the National Strategy, but it recognized the pressing need for cybersecurity (including critical infrastructure protection) and relied heavily on indirect regulation to pursue its cybersecurity objectives.

In 2010, with the economy in a serious recession, and with the election of President Obama, the political climate is quite different, and various forms of federal cybersecurity regulation are under consideration. However, the Obama Administration has signaled that the federal government will continue to favor indirect over direct regulation to achieve its cybersecurity objectives. In his May 29, 2009 speech addressing cybersecurity issues and announcing the release of his administration's Cyberspace Policy Review (CPR), President Obama stated: "My administration will not dictate security standards for private companies. On the contrary, we will collaborate with industry to find technology solutions that ensure our security and promote prosperity."[12] The CPR delicately suggests in its Executive Summary that some federal cybersecurity regulation may be necessary to spur private sector cybersecurity, stating: "the government should explore ... adjustments to liability considerations (reduced liability in exchange for improved security or increased liability for the consequences of poor security), indemnification, tax incentives, and

[11] The National Strategy to Secure Cyberspace (2003) (National Strategy) at 15, available online at https://www.dhs.gov/xlibrary/assets/National_Cyberspace_Strategy.pdf.

[12] Remarks by the President on Securing Our Nation's Cyber Infrastructure, May 29, 2009 (Obama Cybersecurity Remarks), available online at http://www.whitehouse.gov/the_press_office/Remarks-by-the-President-on-Securing-Our-Nations-Cyber-Infrastructure.

new regulatory requirements and compliance mechanisms."[13] Reviewing the CPR in the context of President Obama's speech favoring indirect regulation, it appears that any "adjustments to liability" would be achieved through indirect, rather than direct, cybersecurity regulation. This reading of the CPR is bolstered by the fact that other CPR recommendations also embrace an indirect approach to regulation. For example, the CPR recommends that the federal government "can assist" the private sector in making "a business case to justify the resource expenditures needed for integrating information and communications system security into corporate risk management and for engaging partnerships to mitigate collective risk [by] considering incentive-based legislative or regulatory tools to enhance the value proposition [for participation in information-sharing arrangements] and fostering an environment that facilitates and encourages partnership and information sharing."[14] As discussed in more detail in Sect. 15.3.2, these recommendations embrace the idea of indirect regulation – i.e., they seek to encourage behavior leading to increased cybersecurity as a means of achieving the administration's stated cybersecurity goals.

The remainder of this chapter describes the evolution over the past decade of various US federal government efforts to enhance cybersecurity in the absence of direct federal mandates.

15.2 Indirect Regulation Through Law

15.2.1 Intellectual Property Law

More than a decade ago, the federal government recognized that advances in our information technology and communications infrastructure were facilitating theft of intellectual property (IP). One of the earliest federal efforts to address the issue of IP theft was the Digital Millennium Copyright Act ("DMCA"), which was signed into law by President Clinton in October 1998. DMCA is a classic example of indirect federal regulation. Unlike pre-existing laws criminalizing actual copyright infringement, the DMCA prohibits certain action that can lead to copyright infringement, specifically, circumvention of copyright protection mechanisms and trafficking in the tools used to circumvent copy-protection technology [3]. DMCA prohibits the manufacture, importation, or distribution of "devices, products, components" or services used for circumvention of copy-protection technologies [4]. DMCA's provisions have been criticized as overbroad, criminalizing certain behaviors that do not contribute to copyright infringement. For example, "the DMCA . . . makes it a crime (subject to complex exceptions) to manufacture code to circumvent a copyright

[13] Cyberspace Policy Review: Assuring a Trusted and Resilient Information and Communications Infrastructure, May 29, 2009 (CPR), at 5.

[14] CPR at 17.

protection mechanism, even if the use of the underlying material itself would be a fair use" [5]. Since passage of the DMCA, the government increasingly has recognized the importance of achieving cybersecurity not through sanctions on cybercriminals, but by addressing cyber vulnerabilities and largely has shifted its attention to that end.

15.2.2 Financial and Medical Privacy Law

In the late 1990s, the U.S. financial and health sectors were storing massive amounts of sensitive consumer data electronically. The government attempted to ensure the privacy and security of this information through two landmark pieces of legislation: (1) the Gramm–Leach–Bliley (GLB) Act [6] financial privacy rules; and (2) the Health Insurance Portability and Accountability Act (HIPAA) medical privacy rules, which recently were expanded by the Health Information Technology for Economic and Clinical Health (HITECH) Act of 2009.

15.2.2.1 GLB Financial Privacy Law

GLB was the ground-breaking financial services modernization law adopted in 1999 that repealed various Depression-era legal provisions requiring the strict separation of the banking, brokerage and insurance industries. GLB permitted these businesses to cross-sell each other's products and services. Concerned about the impact of this massive deregulation on consumer privacy, Congress included privacy provisions limiting the collection and sharing of customers' personal financial information and information security provisions requiring financial institutions to maintain safeguards to protect customer information.[15] Congress directed the federal bank regulatory agencies[16] and the Federal Trade Commission (FTC) to promulgate regulations implementing the law's privacy and information security provisions. These regulations are known as the GLB Privacy Rules[17] and the GLB Safeguards Rules[18] (collectively, the GLB Rules).

The GLB Rules require private sector companies to adopt adequate safeguards to protect against unauthorized disclosure of certain consumer data that they hold in their possession. The rules do not direct private sector companies to adopt specific

[15] 15 U.S.C. Sec. 6801(a)-(b).

[16] The federal bank regulatory agencies are the Office of the Comptroller of the Currency, Office of Thrift Supervision, Federal Deposit Insurance Corporation, Federal Reserve Board, and the National Credit Union Administration.

[17] See e.g., Federal Trade Commission Privacy of Consumer Information, May 12, 2000 (GLB Privacy Rule).

[18] See, e.g., Federal Trade Commission Standards for Safeguarding Customer Information; Final Rule, 67 Fed. Reg. 36484, May 23, 2002 (GLB Safeguards Rule).

information security technologies; rather, they regulate cybersecurity indirectly. They are designed to increase private sector investments in cybersecurity in order to reduce the incidence of cybercrimes, including unauthorized access to electronically stored consumer data. The rules require corporate boards of directors to devote special attention to security practices and to assume direct responsibility for the adequacy of data security measures [6]. The requirement that boards of directors allocate a portion of their scarce attention to privacy and security issues has the practical effect of requiring CEOs to be prepared to discuss them, which, in turn, forces higher levels of attention all the way down the corporate chain of command. This intervention in corporate organization was expected to drive security spending and attention without the need for a direct government mandate. The GLB Privacy Rules also require financial institutions to notify their customers of their privacy policies, including steps the institutions have adopted to protect select sensitive customer data. The disclosure requirements, coupled with the knowledge that the market might punish companies with weak privacy policies, are designed to drive necessary increases in security spending.

15.2.2.2 HIPAA Medical Privacy Law

On the medical front, the federal government indirectly regulates cybersecurity through President Clinton's Health Insurance Portability and Accountability Act (HIPAA) of 1996, the primary federal medical privacy law in the US today.[19] HIPAA's security provisions are set forth in three distinct places: (1) HIPAA statutory provisions;[20] (2) the HIPAA Privacy Rule;[21] and (3) the HIPAA Security

[19] Various state medical privacy laws are beyond the scope of this article, however two California laws, Assembly Bill 211 (AB 211) and Senate Bill 541 (SB 541) adopted in September of 2008 are worthy of mention. These laws took effect January 1, 2009 and give Californians rights that are much more expansive than those granted under HIPAA. The laws impose privacy and security standards not only on HIPAA "covered entities" but on other "health facilities" as well. See Civil Code §§56.05 and 56.06. In addition, the laws make it a misdemeanor to unlawfully access, use, or disclose protected information (Civil Code §56.36(a)); and impose fines of up to $250,000 for disclosures of protected information made for financial gain (Civil Code §56.36(c)(3)). The full text of AB 211 may be found online at: http://info.sen.ca.gov/pub/07-08/bill/asm/ab_0201-0250/ab_211_bill_20080930_chaptered.pdf. The full text of SB 541 may be found online at: http://info.sen.ca.gov/pub/07-08/bill/sen/sb_0501-0550/sb_541_bill_20080930_chaptered.pdf.

[20] HIPAA's statutory provisions themselves require reasonable security. Specifically, covered entities that use, store, maintain, or transmit certain patient health care information known as protected health information (PHI) must maintain "reasonable and appropriate administrative, technical, and physical safeguards" to (1) ensure integrity and confidentiality of PHI; (2) protect against any reasonably anticipated threats or hazards to the security, integrity, or unauthorized uses or disclosures of PHI; and (3) ensure HIPAA compliance by officers and employees of the covered entity. HIPAA, Section 1173(d)(2). Additional security provisions are set forth in the HIPAA Privacy Rule and the HIPAA Security Rule, the federal regulations implementing HIPAA.

[21] Standards for Privacy of Individually Identifiable Health Information, 45 CFR part 160 and part 164, subparts A and E (HIPAA Privacy Rule). The security provisions of the HIPAA Privacy Rule,

Rule.[22] All three sets of security provisions apply when so-called covered entities[23] (which include healthcare providers and health plans) transmit or maintain protected health information (PHI)[24] in electronic format.

The HIPAA Security Rule has the most detailed security provisions. It requires covered entities that transmit or maintain PHI in electronic format to ensure the confidentiality, integrity, and availability of that PHI. Toward that end, the Security Rule requires covered entities to have a written security plan that includes three types of safeguards: administrative, technical, and physical. The Security Rule's administrative safeguards require covered entities to engage in "risk analysis" to assess risks and vulnerabilities to PHI and to engage in "risk management," including adopting security measures sufficient to reduce the risks and vulnerabilities to PHI. The administrative safeguards also require mandatory reporting for all "security incidents" (regardless of success) and adoption of security incident response procedures. The technical safeguards required by the Security Rule include access controls (i.e., technologies that limit access to PHI to those persons having access rights); audit controls (to record and examine activity in systems that use electronic PHI); and integrity controls (to detect and protect electronic PHI from alteration and destruction). Finally, the physical safeguards of the Security Rule require covered entities to adopt measures necessary to prevent physical access to electronic PHI.

Also worth nothing are the "Business Associate" provisions of the Security Rule which extend HIPAA's already expansive reach far beyond the healthcare sector. Pursuant to these provisions, covered entities must, by contract, require their contractors who handle electronic PHI to implement the same kinds of administrative, physical and technical safeguards as the Covered Entity. Moreover, business associates must extend the same requirements to their own subcontractors.

Finally, as if to add an exclamation point to HIPAA's requirements, HIPAA violators may be punished with a big stick: criminal penalties for the most serious, intentional violations of HIPAA consist of up to 10 years in prison and $250,000 in fines;[25] civil penalties are up to $25,000 per year for each requirement violated;[26] and while HIPAA does not create a private right of action (i.e., HIPAA does not give individuals the right to sue under HIPAA for privacy violations), civil suits for

(45 CFR 164.530(c)), also known as the "mini-security rule," require covered entities to implement general security measures to protect PHI. Under the Privacy Rule, covered entities must "adopt appropriate administrative, technical, and physical safeguards to protect privacy of [PHI]" and "safeguard PHI from any intentional or unintentional use or disclosure that is in violation of the Privacy Rule." HIPAA Privacy Rule, Sec. 164.530(c).

[22] The Security Rule took effect April 20, 2005 for large entities and 1 year later for small businesses.

[23] The term "covered entities," as defined under HIPAA (45 CFR Part 160.103), is not limited to health care companies; it also includes "health plans," a term which itself includes many employer-sponsored group health plans.

[24] PHI refers to certain individually identifiable health care information. 45 CFR 164.501.

[25] HIPAA, Section 1177(b)(3).

[26] HIPAA, Section 1176(a)(1).

violations of state medical privacy law potentially could reference the HIPAA Privacy and Security Rules to establish the appropriate standard of care and result in large judgments.

HIPAA's security rule is much more detailed than the GLB safeguards rule applicable in the financial sector, and its provisions drive cybersecurity spending not only in the health care sector but beyond as a result of HIPAA's business associate provisions. HIPAA-required "risk analysis" and "risk management" together operate to encourage covered entities to allocate resources to cybersecurity in an efficient manner. Finally, like GLB, HIPAA has privacy notice requirements that are intended to drive necessary increases in security spending since the market might punish companies with weak privacy policies.

15.2.2.3 HITECH Act

Recently, the scope of HIPAA was expanded significantly with passage of the Health Information Technology for Economic and Clinical Health Act (HITECH Act), which was embedded in the stimulus bill that President Obama signed into law on February 17, 2009.[27] The HITECH Act imposes new rules on how covered entities[28] and their business associates (e.g., web-based vendors that store medical data) must handle a breach of protected health information (PHI). The HITECH Act requires that covered entities notify affected individuals of breaches of "unsecured" (i.e., unencrypted) PHI if the security and privacy of that PHI is compromised. The Department of Health and Human Services (HHS) recently published an interim final "breach notification" rule clarifying the requirements of the HITECH Act and providing the mechanics of when and how the breach notification requirements will apply.[29] The Federal Trade Commission (FTC) issued companion breach notification regulations[30] that apply to vendors of personal health records (including web-based vendors that store medical data) and certain others not considered covered entities under HIPAA.

The HITECH Act and its implementing regulations encourage covered entities to invest in securing PHI, and thereby serve as yet another example of federal government efforts to improve cybersecurity through indirect regulation. In this respect, the

---

[27] American Recovery and Reinvestment Act of 2009 (Public Law 111-5). The Stimulus Law included a section on health information technology (Title XIII) and allocated up to $19 billion to establish a system of electronic health records by 2014.

[28] As noted above, the term "covered entities" is defined under HIPAA (45 CFR Part 160.103) and is not limited to health care companies; it also includes "health plans," a term which itself includes many employer-sponsored group health plans.

[29] HHS Breach Notification for Unsecured Protected Health Information; Interim Final Rule (HHS Rule), 74 Fed. Reg 42740 (August 24, 2009). The HHS Rule technically applies to any breach discovered on or after September 23, 2009; however, HHS has said that enforcement will be delayed until February 22, 2010, to allow time for covered entities to come into compliance with the rule. HHS Rule, 74 Fed. Reg. at 42757.

[30] FTC Health Breach Notification Rule, 74 Fed. Reg. 42962 (August 25, 2009).

most important part of the breach notification rules may be what they do not require. Notification is not required where there has been a breach of "secured" PHI. PHI is considered "secured" under HHS' interim rule when protected in certain ways. For example, PHI is "secured" when it is encrypted using specific processes approved by the National Institutes for Standards and Technology (NIST).

The Act effectively creates a safe-harbor from breach notification requirements when PHI is encrypted using NIST-approved processes. Thus, it provides a strong incentive for covered entities and their business associates to maintain electronic PHI in NIST-approved encrypted form at all times. The legislation and its implementing regulations tilt the scales so that as covered entities determine where to put their security dollars, investments in securing PHI through NIST-approved encryption appear more favorable than they would in the absence of the legislation. It is expected that many covered entities will conclude that safe harbor compliance is cost-effective in the long-run; despite the upfront costs of securing PHI, safe-harbor compliance minimizes the costs of compliance with HITECH's breach notification rules down the road.

Outside of the financial and medical sectors, the federal government has abstained from legislation and/or regulations specifically addressing private sector cybersecurity levels. The private sector generally opposes government regulation of this type on the grounds that it will have a detrimental effect on innovation, and it is expensive to implement. In lieu of such legislation/regulation, the government is expected to continue its indirect regulation of the cybersecurity problem.

15.2.3 Identity Theft Law

Another example of federal government efforts to secure cyberspace through indirect regulation is the Fair and Accurate Credit Transactions Act of 2003 (FACTA) and its implementing regulations. By its terms, FACTA requires certain "financial institutions" and "creditors" to develop identity theft programs. However, the quoted terms are so broadly defined that the rules not only could be read to apply to mortgage brokers, utility companies, and telecommunications companies, but also potentially to doctors and other professionals that provide goods and services and bill later.[31] Indeed, FACTA's definition of "creditor" includes any entity that regularly extends or renews credit and all entities that regularly permit deferred payments for goods or services.

The federal financial regulatory agencies and the FTC jointly issued their so-called "Red Flags" rules and accompanying interagency guidelines implementing FACTA on November 9, 2007.[32] The rules require the creation of identity theft

---

[31] As noted below, the U.S. District Court for the District of Columbia has ruled that the FTC's rule implementing FACTA does not apply to attorneys.

[32] Identity Theft Red Flags and Address Discrepancies Under the Fair and Accurate Credit Transactions Act of 2003; Final Rule, 72 Fed. Reg. 63718 (Nov. 9, 2007).

prevention programs. Specifically, financial institutions and creditors with covered accounts must develop a written identity theft prevention program to identify the warning signs of identity theft. Taking a line from the GLB implementing regulations, red flag programs must be approved by the Board of Directors of the financial institution or creditor, or, if there is none, a senior employee.

Pursuant to the rules, red flags programs must: (1) identify relevant red flags (i.e., relevant patterns, practices, and specific forms of activity that are "red flags" signaling possible identify theft); (2) incorporate those red flags into its program; (3) detect red flags that have been incorporated into the program; (4) respond appropriately to red flags that are detected in order to prevent and mitigate identity theft; and (5) ensure that the program is updated periodically to reflect changes in risks arising from identity theft. The Interagency guidelines implementing FACTA provide additional details on formulating a red flags program that complies with each of these requirements. Notably, as with GLB, the Red Flags rules do not specify what red flags programs must look like. Instead, they set forth the requirements that any red flags program must meet and attempt to give businesses the flexibility to create programs that suit them.

The Red Flags rules became effective on January 1, 2008, and covered financial institutions and creditors were required to comply with the rules by November 1, 2008, with one exception: the FTC repeatedly has delayed enforcement of its Red Flags rule for a variety of practical and political reasons, most notably, to allow more time for compliance and to give US Congress additional time to consider the issue of whether FACTA's provisions apply too broadly. Most recently, on October 3, 2009 the FTC agreed to delay enforcement of its Red Flags rule until June 1, 2010 in response to a request from members of US Congress who are considering legislation to exempt from the Red Flags rules certain small businesses including health care, accounting, and legal entities with fewer than 20 employees. With respect to exempting lawyers from the rule, the U.S. District Court for the District of Columbia appears to have beaten Congress to the punch with its October 30, 2009 ruling that the FTC's Red Flags rule cannot properly be applied to all attorneys, however, the Court left open the question of whether lawyers in the financial sector potentially could be subject to the rule.[33]

For our purposes, the Red Flags rules are important because they are yet another excellent example of the federal government's indirect regulation in the cyberspace arena. Through FACTA, the federal government not only encourages business practices that help prevent identity theft, but also requires corporate boards of directors in a wide range of businesses to pay attention to identity theft, thereby driving increased security spending on, and corporate attention to, identity theft without a direct government mandate.

[33] Memorandum Opinion, American Bar Ass'n. v. Fed. Trade Comm'n, Civil Action No. 09-1636 (RBW) (U.S.D.C. Oct. 30, 2009) at 40.

15.2.4 Indirect Regulation Through Laws Imposing Liability and Through the Establishment of Best Practices and Standards

15.2.4.1 Laws Imposing Liability

The threat of massive consumer lawsuits is likely to influence how companies behave, so another means of indirect regulation is to subject companies to liability for losses arising out of a security breach. Imposing liability likely would be an effective way to "encourage" companies to bolster their cybersecurity efforts. Exceptions notwithstanding, Democratic administrations tend to favor corporate liability for security lapses[34] while Republican administrations do not welcome the imposition of liability on corporate interests.

The Obama administration does not appear to present an exception to the above-stated tendency. The President ordered a comprehensive 60-day review of US cybersecurity policies on February 9, 2009, and the resulting Cyberspace Policy Review, released by the While House on May 29, 2009, recommends that the government explore "adjustments to liability considerations."[35] Specifically, the CPR recommends that government explore "increased liability for the consequences of poor security [or] reduced liability in exchange for improved security."[36] With the Obama Administration apparently signaling that some form of increased government intervention may be necessary to protect the nation's critical digital networks, the possibility of a private right of action for cybersecurity breaches cannot be ruled out.

The idea of imposing corporate liability for security lapses is not new. Back in April of 2002, Senator Hollings (D-S.C.) introduced S. 2201, a privacy bill creating a private right of action for improper release of certain sensitive information.[37] Largely opposed by industry, S. 2201 provided that "[i]f an internet service provider, online service provider, or commercial website operator . . . fails to provide . . . reasonable security for . . . sensitive personally identifiable information . . . then that person may bring an action in a district court of the United States. . . ".

Imposing liability for security breaches is just one option for bolstering cybersecurity, and a politically difficult one at that. Over the past decade, the government also has explored (1) encouraging the adoption of best practices; and (2) imposing standards for Federal networks. Notably, either best practices or federal standards could serve as de facto standards for liability in private tort cases.

---

[34] In this regard, it is noteworthy that plaintiffs' lawyers are a major Democratic party constituency and fund-raising engine.

[35] CPR at 28.

[36] CPR at 28.

[37] S. 2201, the Online Personal Privacy Act, 107th Congress, 2d Session (available at http://frwebgate.access.gpo.gov/cgi-bin/getdoc.cgi?dbname=107_cong_bills&docid=f:s2201is.txt.pdf).

15.2.5 Best Practices

Richard Clarke, former chair of the CIPB, viewed liability as a lever to improve corporate security. However, his 2003 National Strategy to Secure Cyberspace did not call for expanded corporate liability because of the lack of widespread agreement on this point. Instead, it focused on the adoption of industry "best practices," stating that "[t]he software industry is encouraged to consider promoting more secure 'out-of-the-box' installation and implementation of their products, including ... where feasible, promotion of industry guidelines and best practices that support such efforts."[38] Obama's 2009 Cyberspace Policy Review similarly touts "best practices," stating that, as part of the challenge of securing cyberspace, the federal government in collaboration with the private sector should "continue to develop and promote best practices."[39]

From industry's point of view, once "best practices" are established, failure to follow them may lead to liability. In essence, once a specific conduct has been endorsed as a "best practice," it is likely to become a de facto standard, and failure to follow the practice may result in liability. This view is reinforced by the fact that cyberinsurers offer discounts to companies that comply with certain "best practices," as explained in more detail in Sect. 15.3.1 below.

15.2.6 Federal Cybersecurity Standards

Industry also has long been concerned that, in lieu of direct regulation, the federal government will try to wield its substantial purchasing power to contractually impose federal cybersecurity standards on a significant portion of the private sector by imposing cybersecurity standards not only on federal government agencies but on private sector companies that enter into contracts with the agencies.[40] Once private contractors have incurred the expense of meeting federal cybersecurity standards in the course of supplying products and services to the government, they are more than likely to apply the same standards to products and standards provided to other customers. Thus, federal cybersecurity standards have the potential of becoming de facto cybersecurity standards for the private sector generally.[41]

Both the Bush and Obama Administrations have given the nod to such an approach. The Bush Administration's 2003 National Strategy to Secure Cyberspace

---

[38] National Strategy at 33.

[39] CPR at 17.

[40] As with best practices, private sector companies also are concerned that federal standards inevitably will be cited as the "standard of care" in tort cases and, accordingly, private sector companies likely will be compelled to comply with federal security standards even in the absence of legislation requiring compliance.

[41] As discussed in more detail in Sect. 15.3.1 below, the federal government similarly could require its contractors to insure against cyberrisks to accelerate private sector adoption of cyberinsurance.

provided that: "With respect to investment in cyberspace security, government can lead by example by fostering a marketplace for more secure technologies through large procurements of advanced information assurance technologies."[42] The Obama administration's Cyberspace Policy Review expands upon the procurement strategy set forth in Bush's National Strategy. It recommends that the government "should identify procurement strategies that will incentivize the market to make more secure products and services available to the public."[43] Specifically, the CPR recommends that the President's cybersecurity policy official should "[d]efine procurement strategies through the General Services Administration... for commercial products and services in order to create market incentives for security to be part of hardware and software product designs, new security technologies, and secure managed services" and should "expand partnerships with State, local, and tribal governments and international partners to maximize the market influence of these procurements."[44]

The CPR's recommendations are in line with the December 2008 report of the Commission on Cybersecurity for the 44th Presidency (Presidential Commission) which recommended that the government use federal acquisitions to drive security in products and services.[45] The Presidential Commission was quite blunt, explaining that: "[t]he federal government is the largest single customer of information technology products. We recommend that the United States buy only secure products and services; standards and guidelines for secure products should be developed in partnership with industry."[46] The Commission further explained that: "[f]ederal acquisitions mandates could rapidly drive the market and provide benefits beyond the federal government."[47]

Industry also continues to be concerned about the possibility that the government will legislatively impose cybersecurity standards not only on federal government agencies and their contractors, but on private sector network owners and operators. This is more than mere speculation. The proposed Cybersecurity Act of 2009 (S. 773), introduced by Senators John D. Rockefeller (D-WV) and Olympia Snowe (R-ME) on April 1, 2009, would empower NIST to establish software standards not only for networks owned and operated by the Federal government, but those owned by contractors and those solely owned and operated by the private sector.[48] Critics are concerned that imposing software standards on the private sector would be costly, stifle innovation, and potentially reduce security because any vulnerabilities

---

[42] National Strategy at 4.

[43] CPR at v.

[44] CPR at 34.

[45] Securing Cyberspace for the 44th Presidency: A Report of the CSIS Commission on Cybersecurity for the 44th Presidency (Presidential Commission Report), December 2008 at 50, 55–59.

[46] Presidential Commission Report at 2.

[47] Presidential Commission Report at 59.

[48] Cybersecurity Act of 2009, S. 773, (111th Cong., 1st Sess) introduced April 1, 2009 (hereinafter, Cybersecurity Act of 2009), Section 6(a).

could affect many entities.[49] Industry also is concerned that any such federal standards could be cited as the applicable standard of care in litigation. By imposing cybersecurity standards on private sector network owners and operators, the provisions of the Rockefeller–Snowe bill fly in the face of the administration's stated opposition to mandatory security standards and are likely to trigger serious industry backlash. For these reasons, we believe that they are unlikely to be adopted in their current form.

15.3 Indirect Regulation Through Market Forces

Government manipulation of market forces to influence private sector behavior is one of the most important forms of indirect federal regulation. In the cybersecurity context, the government may encourage desired behavior through subsidies, discourage unwanted behavior through taxation (just as the government discourages smoking by imposing a luxury tax on cigarettes), or otherwise influence market forces to obtain the desired private sector response.

15.3.1 Cyberinsurance Markets

Insurance markets are potentially one of the most important means by which the government can influence private sector cybersecurity practices without direct government mandates. Over the past decade, the insurance industry's response to cyberrisks has evolved significantly. Initially, many standard business insurance policies were worded broadly enough to cover losses arising out of cybersecurity breaches. However, insurance companies quickly recognized this and moved to exclude cyberrisks from their standard coverage. To fill the resulting gap in coverage, insurers began marketing specialized cyberinsurance policies. Industry has been slow to purchase these policies in part because they are quite expensive.

Specialized cyberinsurance coverage is expensive for several reasons. First, considerable uncertainty remains about the appropriate pricing of cyberinsurance policies due to the lack of empirical data necessary to construct actuarial tables, yet insurers understand well that there is a risk of very large losses. Second, because networked information systems are particularly vulnerable to a major disaster that could result in a large number of claims, the cost of re-insurance for cyberinsurers is high.[50] Finally, barriers to entry into the cyberinsurance market reduce competition.

---

[49] Center for Democracy & Technology, Analysis of S. 773 Cybersecurity Act of 2009, May 2009 at 9, available online at http://www.cdt.org/security/20090511_rocksnowe_analysis.pdf. See also Presidential Commission Report at 51.

[50] Internet Security Alliance Comments to Hathaway on Cyber Insurance, available online at http://www.isalliance.org/index.php?option=com_content&task=view&id=192&Itemid=365.

One significant barrier to entry is that a catastrophic event could occur before an insurer has built up sufficient cash reserves to pay out on its policies.[51]

Specialized cyberinsurance coverages have become increasingly sophisticated as insurance companies have come to better understand the nature of cyberrisk. For example, some large cyberinsurers now require companies to implement specific security practices as a prerequisite to obtaining cyberinsurance and offer reduced rates on cyberinsurance policies to companies that comply with industry "best practices." The Chubb Group of Insurance Companies, to take one example, offers a premium discount for its cybersecurity insurance to organizations that adopt NIST's "best-practice" testing methods which, among other things, evaluates a network's ability to protect information from unauthorized access. From Chubb's perspective, the required testing improves customers' security and lowers their risk profile.[52]

Such sophisticated cyberinsurance coverages encourage companies to make necessary investments in cybersecurity. First, requiring a certain level of security as a precondition of coverage pressures would-be-cyberinsurance buyers to maintain a specified level of cybersecurity. Second, there is the possibility that security requirements adopted by cyberinsurers will become de facto industry standards that all companies will strive to meet, especially if failure to meet them could lead to tort liability. Third, offering lower rates for companies with better security practices forces companies to internalize not only the benefits of good security but also the costs of poor security, thereby encouraging companies to make appropriate investments in cybersecurity.

Although cyberinsurance products are available, the market for cyberinsurance has been slow to materialize. Industry has been slow to adopt cyberinsurance as a risk management tool, both (1) because it lacks the data with which to decide whether insuring against a cyberrisk is worthwhile;[53] and (2) because of the high cost of cyberinsurance coverage.

Some insurers foresee a system in which (1) civil liability is imposed for cybersecurity breaches (possibly with safe harbors or other limitations on cybersecurity liability where industry has made a reasonable effort to conform to insurer-adopted best practices); (2) private insurers cover associated industry losses; and (3) the government offers backstop reinsurance for cyberinsurers to help reduce the price of cyberinsurance thereby improving private sector access to cyberinsurance and, arguably, leading to improved cybersecurity.[54]

---

[51] Internet Security Alliance Comments to Hathaway on Cyber Insurance, available online at http://www.isalliance.org/index.php?option=com_content&task=view&id=192&Itemid=365.

[52] Chubb Encourages Adoption of New Information Security Best Practices, Offers Premium Credit for Organizations That Implement Testing, December 3, 2007 available online at http://www.chubb.com/corporate/chubb7880.html.

[53] This is an issue the federal government is attempting to address by promoting public–private information sharing, as discussed in Sect. 15.3.2.

[54] Since insurance markets are driven by fear of liability, industry may be wary of any federal government interest in insurance that may signal the dawn of new liability regimes.

Others may even go so far as to suggest that the federal government use its market power to promote cyberinsurance by requiring its contractors and subcontractors to carry cyberinsurance. This approach obviously would increase demand for cyberinsurance. Also, companies that purchase cyberinsurance to meet federal contracting requirements presumably would tout their coverage as a competitive advantage when bidding on private contracts. This likely would lead their competitors to purchase cyberinsurance. Accordingly, it is argued that this approach would ultimately bring about improved security, more insured companies, and, potentially, reduced costs for insurance coverage.[55]

Interested industry observers would be wise to keep an eye on the federal government's treatment of the fledgling cyberinsurance industry. The federal government understands that insurance markets are an effective means of driving future private sector cybersecurity without direct regulation, and some Congressional leaders may have a strong interest in satisfying powerful insurance constituencies seeking to tap into the cyberinsurance market.

15.3.2 Public–Private Information Sharing Initiatives

Public–private information sharing initiatives are another avenue for indirect regulation of cybersecurity. The federal government has long promoted private sector information sharing initiatives as a means of improving cybersecurity by, among other things, facilitating risk management. Risk management (i.e., managing the risk of loss due to cybercrime/cybersecurity) is a central element of information security because it is exorbitantly expensive, if not impossible, to achieve perfect security. The federal government has touted information sharing with the expectation that corporate decision makers armed with up-to-date information about cybersecurity risks will allocate additional private sector investment in security measures and engage in partnerships to mitigate collective risks, thereby bolstering cybersecurity. Similarly, improved information could serve as the basis for standardized actuarial data on the costs and frequency of cyberattacks. Such data would enable the insurance industry to further develop cyberinsurance coverage, as discussed in more detail in Sect. 15.3.1.

The Clinton, Bush, and Obama administrations have all touted public–private information sharing as an important element in any cybersecurity strategy. For example, nearly a decade ago, John Tritak, former director of the US government's Critical Infrastructure Assurance Office (CIAO) [7], explained in testimony to Congress: "Encouraging the appropriate exchange of information within and among the infrastructure sectors and between the sectors and government provides infrastructure operators with a more accurate and complete picture of their

---

[55] See, generally, Internet Security Alliance Comments to Hathaway on Cyber Insurance available online at http://www.isalliance.org/index.php?option=com_content&task=view&id=192&Itemid=365.

operational risks, as well as the techniques and tools for managing those risks. It is also an invaluable tool to enable the government to direct resources to assist the private sector and to undertake appropriate law enforcement and other activities against wrongdoers."

More recently, Obama's Cyberspace Policy Review recommended that government "work creatively and collaboratively with the private sector to identify tailored solutions that take into account both the need to exchange information and protect public and private interests and take an integrated approach to national and economic security. These solutions should identify clear, actionable objectives for the sharing of data and define standards for incident reporting."[56]

The positions taken by recent administrations reflect an understanding of the fact that businesses need additional data to properly manage their cybersecurity risk. While businesses need to balance the costs of added cybersecurity measures, financial and otherwise, against the benefits of those measures, there are few metrics available to help decision makers most effectively spend their cybersecurity dollars. When it comes to cybersecurity, we are missing key data about the following: the frequency of cyberattacks; the severity of cyberattacks; and the effectiveness of current mitigation techniques. As Lord William Thompson Kelvin the great nineteenth century Scottish mathematician and physicist once said, "When you measure what you are speaking about and express it in numbers, you know something about it, but when you cannot express it in numbers, your knowledge about it is of a meager and unsatisfactory kind."

Although we increasingly understand the importance of measuring the return on our information security investments, we lack the data to do so. First, we lack complete and accurate information on the incidence of cybercrimes and cyberattacks at least in part because of corporate reluctance to report cybersecurity breaches. Second, we also lack information about the costs associated with cybercrimes and cyberattacks both because of corporate reluctance to report and because of the difficulty measuring some costs, such as loss of customer trust. Thus, companies are unable to take into consideration the probability with which cybercrimes and cyberattacks are likely to strike and the costs resulting arising out of them, including loss of reputation, loss of privacy, and other tangible and intangible costs. Third, the effectiveness of current technological mitigation methods is unknown [8]. Consequently, businesses are unable to calculate the resources necessary for mitigation. As a result, businesses are unable accurately to calculate their return on information security investments, potentially resulting in under- (or over-) investment in information security.

In a recent interview, Bruce McConnell, Cybersecurity Counselor to the DHS National Protection and Programs Directorate Deputy Undersecretary, described the problem confronting businesses as follows: "Today, if you own a small business or manage a large business, and you go to your Chief Information Security Officer and say, 'I have another dollar to spend on cyber security, where should I spend

[56] CPR at 19.

it in order to be most effective? Should I spend it on employee training? Should I spend it on stronger firewalls? Should I spend it on better authentication?' there are no metrics that the CSO can give that business manager to tell him, 'this is where we see the most cost effective use of the marginal dollar of investment in cyber security.'... Until we get those metrics, our decisions about investments in cybersecurity are going to be based on anecdote and unclear criteria, rather than a more rigorous and scientific data based approach to those decisions."[57]

The Obama White House has framed the issue as follows: "If the risks and consequences can be assigned monetary value, organizations will have greater ability and incentive to address cybersecurity. In particular, the private sector often seeks a business case to justify the resource expenditures needed for integrating information and communications system security into corporate risk management and for engaging partnerships to mitigate collective risk. Government can assist by considering incentive-based legislative or regulatory tools to enhance the value proposition and fostering an environment that facilitates and encourages partnership and information sharing."[58]

The CPR reiterates the importance of private sector engagement and public–private information sharing and specifically encourages the private sector to "engag[e] in enterprise information sharing and account for the corporate risk and the bottom line impacts of data breaches, corporate espionage, and loss or degradation of services.... Businesses need effective means to share detection methods, information about breaches and attack methods, remediation techniques, and forensic capabilities with each other and the Federal government."[59]

Information sharing has enormous potential not only to facilitate improved cybersecurity among participants, but also to (1) facilitate industry cyberrisk management thereby contributing to efficient allocation of cybersecurity dollars; and (2) contribute to the efficient workings of the cyberinsurance market (e.g., by facilitating more accurate pricing of cyberinsurance coverage), potentially enabling insurers to charge lower premiums and attract more buyers.

15.3.2.1 Potential Practical Obstacles to Information Sharing

When viewed from a practical viewpoint, a number of obstacles to information sharing emerge. First, out of genuine concern for their reputations, companies may understandably hesitate to share information regarding security breaches or vulnerabilities. Public exposure of a company's vulnerabilities has the potential to undermine investor and consumer confidence. Second, companies seeking to protect their trade secrets and proprietary information are likely to be reluctant to share

---

[57] http://thenewnewinternet.com/2009/11/17/bruce-mcconnell-of-dhs-looks-to-long-term-solutions/ at 4.

[58] CPR at 17-18.

[59] CPR at 17-18.

sensitive information with competitors. Critics claim that these obstacles are simply red herrings designed to deflect attention from companies that avoid participation in information sharing initiatives because they believe it is unlikely to materially benefit their bottom line. Private sector companies generally recognize that investments in security can prevent destructive activities, but in many instances, the prevailing corporate viewpoint is that security does not contribute to revenue. Specifically, bolstered security, including increased participation in information sharing activities designed to reduce cybercrimes, is not a source of revenue that will increase the company's "bottom line."

Moreover, participation in information sharing initiatives is not without legal risks. Private sector participants must be aware of the potential antitrust, Freedom of Information Act (FOIA), and liability issues discussed in more detail in Sect. 15.3.2.2.

15.3.2.2 Potential Legal Obstacles to Information Sharing

1. *Antitrust issues*: Participation in ISACs and other information sharing arrangements that involve collaboration among competitors may have antitrust implications. The US DoJ has indicated that there are minimal antitrust concerns involving properly structured joint industry projects for dealing with externalities and that any entity created to share information regarding common threats to critical infrastructure should fall under this category [9]. Specifically, antitrust enforcement agencies have been willing to review proposals for ISACs and issue "business review letters" confirming that the agencies do not intend to challenge the ISAC on antitrust grounds so long as it is formed and operated in accordance with the companies' proposals.[60] This reflects the view espoused years ago by Harris Miller, then-President of the Information Technology Association of America, that ISACs "should be in compliance with the antitrust laws because they are not intended to restrain trade by restricting output, increasing prices, or otherwise inhibiting competition, on which the antitrust laws generally focus. Rather, ISACs facilitate sharing of information relating to members' efforts to enhance and protect the security of the cyber infrastructure, so the antitrust risk of such exchange is minimal."

   If necessary, Congress could take action to ensure that antitrust law does not impede information sharing efforts. Such action might take the form of proposed legislation similar to the CyberSecurity Information Act of 2001,[61] which provided that antitrust law would not apply to conduct undertaken solely for the purpose of, and limited to (1) facilitating the correction of cybersecurity-related problems; or (2) communicating or disclosing of information to help correct or

[60] Mark F. Grady and Francesco Parisi, eds., The Law and Economics of Cybersecurity, (2006), Amitai Aviram, Chapter 5, Network Responses to Network Threats: The Evolution into Private Cybersecurity Associations at 158.

[61] H.R. 2435, 107th Cong. (2001).

avoid the effects of a cybersecurity related problem. If Congress were to deem an antitrust exemption necessary to facilitate information sharing, legislation of this sort could be revived.

2. *FOIA*: Another obstacle to information sharing is FOIA. The private sector initially was reluctant to enter into information-sharing arrangements with the government, in part due to concerns that the government might be required to disclose to the public any information received from businesses, proprietary or otherwise, pursuant to a proper FOIA request. Industry's concerns were not allayed by the existing FOIA exemption for proprietary information. Although the exemption potentially would have given the government a sufficient basis for refusing to release cybersecurity information to the public pursuant to a FOIA request, industry wanted assurances that it was fully protected before sharing information. Congress eventually concluded that legislation was necessary to overcome industry reluctance to share information with the government.

   In the Homeland Security Act of 2002 (HSA), Congress created a new FOIA exemption in exchange for private sector cooperation in sharing information with the government regarding vulnerabilities in the nation's critical infrastructure. The FOIA exemption covered "critical infrastructure information," a broadly defined term that included information covering a wide variety of facilities (e.g., privately operated power plants, bridges, dams, ports, and chemical plants) that might be targeted for a terrorist attack. During the 2002 HSA negotiations, which took place against the backdrop of the 9/11 terrorist attacks, House Republicans and the Administration are said to have "promoted the broadly worded FOIA exemption on the grounds that it was necessary to encourage owners of critical infrastructure facilities to identify vulnerabilities in their operations and share that information with DHS ... to ensure that steps could be taken to ensure the facilities' protection and proper functioning."[62]

   As many in industry are aware, the language of the FOIA exemption has since been attacked as overbroad. Senator Leahy (D-Vt.) has argued that the HSA's "disclose and immunize" approach "is subject to abuse" by businesses that want to "exploit legal technicalities to avoid regulatory guidelines that are designed to protect the public's health and safety."[63] Leahy has criticized the FOIA exemption for "shield[ing] from FOIA almost any voluntarily submitted document stamped by the facility owner as 'critical infrastructure'... no matter how tangential the content of that document may be to the actual security of a facility. The law effectively allows companies to hide information about public health and safety from the American people ... simply by submitting it to DHS."[64]

---

[62] Statement of Senator Patrick Leahy on Introduction of the Restoration of Freedom of Information Act (Leahy Statement) March 15, 2005, available online at http://leahy.senate.gov/press/200503/031505.html.

[63] Leahy Statement at 3.

[64] Leahy Statement at 2-3.

In 2005, Senators Leahy, Feingold, Levin and Leiberman introduced "Restore FOIA" to limit the scope of the FOIA exemption in several ways.[65] First, Restore FOIA would limit the FOIA exemption to "records" pertaining to the vulnerability of and threats to critical infrastructure rather than exempting from FOIA any critical infrastructure "information." Second, it would provide for agency review to permit release of those portions of records not covered by the exemption. Finally, it would not forbid use of voluntarily submitted records in civil court cases to hold companies accountable for wrongdoing, whereas the original HSA provisions prohibited direct use of the information in civil suits by government or private parties and made it more difficult to use the information in civil suits even if the information was obtained independently.

Restore FOIA has never been adopted, and at this time, the FOIA exemption created in 2002 remains intact.

3. *Cybersecurity Liability*: Another risk of ISAC participation is that companies potentially could be subject to liability for harm arising out of cybersecurity flaws disclosed to the government. As discussed in item 2, Congress addressed this concern when it created DHS. Pursuant to the DHS charter legislation, when a private company shares critical infrastructure information with the DHS, third parties and the government will be prohibited from using that information in a civil action against the company. However, critics seek to rollback this liability protection.
4. *Other Liability*: ISAC participants also may incur liability for providing inaccurate information, failing to protect sensitive ISAC information, failing to heed a warning issued by the ISAC, or failing to disclose information that could have prevented a cybersecurity attack. The ISACs themselves could potentially incur liability for providing inaccurate information to members, failing to detect a breach, failing to share or disclose information, failing to protect anonymity (raising privacy concerns), or failing to protect proprietary data. The liability may be minimized through a written contract, namely, via ISAC membership agreements and member operating rules, and participants should investigate whether their ISAC is structured to minimize these risks.

15.3.3 Federally-Funded Research and Development

Federally-funded research and development is another good example of the federal government encouraging desired behavior – in this case cybersecurity research – through subsidies. When the federal government provides financial support to government agencies, academia, and the private sector for cybersecurity research and development, it effectively subsidizes the cost of securing the nation's networks (whether public or private) against would-be cyberattackers and cybercriminals, thereby loosening the constraints of the market on cybersecurity investment.

---

[65] Leahy Statement.

Over the past decade, the federal government has funded numerous cybersecurity research and development initiatives. An early example of such government action is the 2002 Cyber Security Research and Development Act,[66] passage of which was triggered by the September 11, 2001 attacks. The Act authorized approximately $900 million in long-term cybersecurity research and development grants to government agencies, academia, and the private sector over 5 years in an effort to strengthen the security of critical computer networks, both public and private.

In February 2005, the President's Information Technology Advisory Committee (PITAC) released a report urging the federal government to substantially increase "[f]ederal support for fundamental research in civilian cybersecurity" in ten high-priority areas; "increase[] support for the rapid transfer of [f]ederally developed... cybersecurity technologies to the private sector;" and strengthen the coordination of federal cybersecurity R&D activities.[67]

The Report explained that while NSF, DHS, NIST and DOJ all play key roles in cybersecurity, at the time, only NSF had a substantial federal cybersecurity research program, with nearly $60 million dedicated to cybersecurity research in FY 2004.[68] The bulk of that money supports individual and university researchers through NSF's CyberTrust program. In contrast, DHS's Cyber Security R&D program was funded at $18 million in FY 2004 with $1.5 million dedicated to long-term research. NIST's cybersecurity research program, which focuses on short-term research, was slated to receive nearly $20 million for FY 2005, and DOJ had a $7 million budget to fight cybercrime.[69]

The Rockefeller–Snowe bill seeks more than $1 billion in government funding over the next 5 years for cybersecurity research and development programs. The legislation would continue to fund federal cybersecurity R&D at NSF,[70] authorizing $800 million in NSF grants for FY 2010–2014 (i.e., an average of $160 million annually). However, the bill would require NSF to prioritize specified types of research (including, e.g., how to design and build complex software-intensive systems that are secure and reliable when first deployed).[71]

Supporters of federally funded research programs contend that they fill a gap that would not be filled by the private sector because "companies have little incentive to invest significantly in activities whose benefits will spread quickly to their rivals."[72] In addition, they contend that government-funded R&D is more likely to lead to open standards than industry R&D since "industry is more likely to

---

[66] Cyber Security Research and Development Act of 2002, (P.L. 107-305, 107th Congress, 2d Session, November 27, 2002), 15 U.S.C. 7402, et seq.

[67] President's Information Technology Advisory Committee, Report to the President–Cyber Security: A Crisis of Prioritization, February 2005 (PITAC Report), p. iv, available online at http://www.nitrd.gov/pitac/reports/20050301_cybersecurity/cybersecurity.pdf.

[68] PITAC Report at 21.

[69] PITAC Report at 21-22.

[70] The Cybersecurity Act of 2009, Section 11.

[71] The Cybersecurity Act of 2009, Section 11.

[72] National Research Council, Innovation in Information Technology, 2003, p. 4.

invest in proprietary products and will diverge from a common standard if it sees a potential competitive or financial advantage."[73] In contrast, critics contend that the government may wind up picking technological "winners and losers" when it takes the lead in R&D, thereby stifling innovation, and that government research priorities may trump those of the private sector when the government funds research. Regardless of the merits of federal funding, it is clear that federally-funded R&D is another important avenue by which the federal government indirectly regulates cybersecurity.

In fact, the Rockefeller–Snowe bill separately directs NIST to establish cybersecurity competitions and challenges with cash prizes to attract talented individuals for the federal IT workforce and stimulate innovation in cybersecurity research and development that potentially could be applied to benefit federal information technology activities.[74] To fund these efforts, the bill authorizes annual appropriations of $15 million for 2010–2014. Once again, the proposed legislative provisions reflect federal government efforts to spur private sector innovation without direct government mandates by providing incentives for increased cybersecurity research and development.

15.3.4 Federally-Funded Educational Programs

Cyber Corps is a scholarship-for-service program sponsored by DHS and NSF that initially was designed to encourage engineering students, at the undergraduate and graduate levels, to accept government jobs to help protect the nation's defense, information, and telecommunications networks against cyberterrorism [10–12]. The program provides scholarships to students specializing in information technology in return for a commitment to serve the federal government. Through the Cyber Corps program, the federal government influences the information technology job market by fostering a market-based incentive for students to consider a specified career path.

Cyber Corps originally was created to help protect the nation's critical infrastructure from terrorists. It now serves to bolster cybersecurity more generally as Cyber Corps participants use their expertise to improve federal agency cybersecurity and many, after fulfilling their service obligation, continue their cybersecurity work in the private sector.

The pending Rockefeller–Snowe bill would expand and extend the Cyber Corps program sponsored by NSF. The bill creates full scholarships for 1,000 students to pursue undergraduate or graduate degrees in cybersecurity in return for serving in the Federal information technology workforce for a period equal to the length of

[73] CRS Report for Congress, The Federal Networking and Information Technology Research and Development Program: Funding Issues and Activities, Updated October 23, 2008, CRS-12 available online at http://ipmall.info/hosted_resources/crs/RL33586_081023.pdf.

[74] The Cybersecurity Act of 2009, Section 13.

the scholarship. In addition, the bill provide for summer work, internship programs, and other initiatives to promote early recruitment of federal information technology employees. To fund these efforts, the bill authorizes annual appropriations of approximately $60 million to NSF through 2014.

15.4 Indirect Regulation Through Social Norms

15.4.1 Cybercitizen Partnership

Finally, through the Cybercitizen Partnership, the federal government has partnered with the private sector to influence social norms in an effort to reduce cybercrime. The Cybercitizen Partnership is a public–private venture funded by DoJ that was designed to create awareness of appropriate on-line conduct in children. DoJ and the Information Technology Association of America (ITAA) partnered to establish the program with the hope that early intervention will deter children from falling prey to cybercrimes when they mature into teenagers and young adults. The Partnership is "designed to establish a broad sense of responsibility and community in an effort to develop in young people smart, ethical and socially conscious online behavior [13]." The expectation is that a continuing effort to instill proper behavior in today's children will be a good defense against the growing number of reported cybercrime incidents [9].

15.5 Conclusions

Consistent with the 2003 National Strategy to Secure Cyberspace, the federal government once sought to secure cyberspace through voluntary industry efforts and private sector partnerships with government. As a matter of policy, the National Strategy rejected prescriptive regulatory efforts in favor of minimal indirect regulation, explicitly stating that federal regulation would not become a primary means of securing cyberspace.

Now, 7 years later and with at least as many expert reports on cybersecurity having crossed the Chief Executive's desk (including the PITAC Report, the Presidential Commission's Report and the Cyberspace Policy Review), indirect regulation has become the norm and is far more pervasive and forceful than it once was. To give just one example, indirectly regulating cybersecurity by imposing private sector liability for security breaches – a concept that was considered and rejected during the Bush years – now appears to be under serious consideration at the highest levels of the Administration and Congress. Most importantly, a new consensus appears to be emerging around the need to spur, rather than wait for, industry action through a combination of voluntary cooperation, market-based incentives, and a regime of targeted – albeit indirect and decidedly not prescriptive – regulation.

References

[1] Clarke, R., President's Critical Infrastructure Protection Board. (2002, September). The National Strategy to secure cyberspace: Draft.

[2] Krebs, B. (2002, June 10). *White House stressing unorthodox in it security fight.* Retrieved from http://www.washingtonpost.com/wp-dyn/articles/A27682-2002Jun10.html

[3] Pub.L. 105-304, 112 Stat 2877 (1998). 1998.

[4] Public Law 105-304, 112 Stat. 2860 (1998), codified in various sections of 17 U.S.C. 1998.

[5] Lessig, L. (1999). *Code and other laws of cyberspace.* New York, NY: Basic Books.

[6] Gramm–Leach–Bliley Financial Services Modernization Act of 1999, 12 U.S.C. §1811 (1999). 1999.

[7] Tritak, J. S. (2001). Director, Critical Infrastructure Assurance Office, Bureau of Industry and Security, United States Department of Commerce. (2002, June 24). *Statement before the House Committee on Science.* Retrieved from http://www.ciao.gov/publicaffairs/tritak6.24.02.html

[8] Geer, D. E., Jr. (2001). Making choices to show ROI. *Secure Business Quarterly, 1*(2), 7.

[9] Miller, H. N., President, Information Technology Association of America. (2001, July 16). *Testimony on Internet security before the Senate Committee on commerce, science and transportation subcommittee on science, technology and space* (p. 6).

[10] The National Education and Training Program. Retrieved from http://www.ciao.gov/education/index.html

[11] Mark, R. *GOVNET aims to protect critical it functions from attacks.* Retrieved from http://dc.internet.com/news/article/0,1934,2101_900961,00.html

[12] Gillham, O. (2002, January 21). *Cybercorps students to fight terror.* Retrieved from http://www.cis.utulsa.edu/InTheNews/cybercorpsstudentstofightterror.asp

[13] Retrieved from http://www.cybercitizenship.org/aboutus/aboutus.html

Chapter 16
Criminal Regulations

Jessica R. Herrera-Flanigan and Sumit Ghosh

In the 1980s, an entirely new type of criminal began to surface on law enforcement's radar screen. Unlike a traditional criminal who would engage in wanton destruction of life and property, this criminal, often male, was technologically-savvy and had discovered that he could gain information, wealth, and power through the use of computers and networks. Often he would act alone but, at other times, he would organize groups with cryptic names including 414s, the telephone area code for the city of Milwaukee; Legion of Doom; and the Chaos Computer Club [1, 2]. These individuals would use their technological knowledge and skills to primarily break into computers and networks to either steal proprietary information or fraudulently obtain telecommunications services at no cost. This new group of cybercriminals challenged our legal system and forced Congress and state governments to enact new laws to fight them. This chapter analyzes the substantive and procedural laws that Congress had to enact to combat crimes involving the use of technology and computers. It looks examines the challenges posed by cybercrimes, in particular the difficulties encountered by law enforcement in investigating and prosecuting cybercrimes.

16.1 Substantive Laws Addressing Digital Crimes

16.1.1 Computer and Network Crimes

Prior to 1984, the US did not have laws specifically prohibiting computer and network crimes, including hacking, malicious code dissemination, and denial of service attacks. Applicable laws that came anywhere near cybercrimes included the wire and mail fraud statutes. In the first known federal prosecution for computer hacking, U.S. v. Seidlitz, 589 F.2d 152 (4th Cir. 1978), the government convicted the owner of a computer company of wire fraud. The individual had made two of the 50 access calls across state lines in the process of stealing confidential software by hacking into his previous employer's computers. Clearly, wire and mail fraud provisions proved useful; however, many law enforcement officials convinced Congress that

S. Ghosh and E. Turrini (eds.), *Cybercrimes: A Multidisciplinary Analysis*,
DOI 10.1007/978-3-642-13547-7_16, © Springer-Verlag Berlin Heidelberg 2010

these provisions could not match the forms of criminal activity that were beginning to perpetrated through new technologies [3]. Congress responded to the law enforcement community's urgent request by including in the Comprehensive Crime Control Act of 1984 provisions to address the unauthorized access and use of computer networks by providing "law enforcement community, those who own and operate computers, as well as those who may be tempted to commit crimes by unauthorized access to them" ... "a clearer statement of proscribed activity [4]."

In 1986, Congress solidified its commitment to cybercrimes by enacting the 1986 Computer Fraud and Abuse Act (CFAA), which amended 18 USC §1030. The statute provided the means to protect the confidentiality, integrity, and availability (CIA) of computers and networks. Protection of the "CIA" has remained the focus of the statute, despite extensive amendments in 1990, 1994, 1996, and the 2001 USA Patriot Act.

The CFAA addressed a number of objectives. First, Congress addressed federalism issues by balancing the federal government's interest in cybercrimes and the states' interest in punishing such offenses. In the CFAA, Congress limited federal jurisdiction to cases in which there is a compelling federal interest, namely national security, interstate nexus, or adverse impact on interstate commerce [5]. Second, a number of the provisions in the original 1030 were clarified and a number of additional activities were criminalized in the CFAA. It included a provision to penalize theft of property via computer when it constitutes a part of a scheme to defraud. To prohibit activities including malicious codes and denial of service attacks, the CFAA incorporated a provision to penalize those who intentionally alter, damage, or destroy data belonging to others. Congress also included in the CFAA a provision classifying traffic in passwords illegal. Additional changes were made by Congress to the CFAA over the next 15 years, the most significant ones being National Information Infrastructure Protection Act of 1996 and the USA Patriot Act of 2001. We will not explore the intricacies those changes and the reader is referred to the US DoJ website, namely, www.cybercrime.gov [6]. The CFAA includes seven types of criminal activity, per 18 U.S.C.A. '1030, and Table 16.1 outlines the various offenses found in the CFAA.

Any attempt to commit these crimes are also addressed by the Act. 18 USC §1030(b). Authorized "hacking" is explicitly excluded from the section, 18 USC §1030(f). In addition, USC §1030(g) permits any person who suffers damage or

Table 16.1 Offenses in CFAA

OFFENSE	18 U.S.C. §
Obtaining National Security Information	1030(a)(1)
Compromising the Confidentiality of a Computer	1030(a)(2)
Trespassing in a Government Computer	1030(a)(3)
Accessing a Computer to Defraud and Obtain Something of Value	1030(a)(4)
Damaging a Computer	1030(a)(5)
Trafficking in Passwords	1030(a)(6)
Threatening to Damage a Computer	1030(a)(7)

loss from a violation of the CFAA to bring a civil action against the violator for compensatory damages and injunctive relief, subject to specific limitations.

In this chapter, we will explain how each of the sections in the CFAA may be applied to the different types of known network crimes. We will also explain how other federal statutes may be applicable to other types of digital crimes. To understand how the CFAA addresses different types of network crimes, it is important to examine key definitions found in the statute.

For the most part, the CFAA covers "protected computers," which are defined, per 18 USC §1030(e)(2)(B), as all government and financial institution computers and any other computers which are used in "interstate or foreign commerce or communication of the United States." Thus, virtually all computers that are connected on the Internet are protected by the CFAA. The inclusion of computers used in "foreign commerce or communication of the United States" in the CFAA makes it possible for domestic law enforcement agencies to pursue international violations as natural extensions of domestic offenses. In theory, the CFAA potentially covers hackers from the US who attack foreign computers as well as foreigners who route communications through the United States to attack computers in the US and other countries. The reader is referred to Chap. 17 for further details on international dimension of cybercrimes.

In 18 USC §1030(e)(8), damage is defined as, "any impairment to the integrity or availability of data, a program, a system or information." The definition of damage is broad and only requires that an individual's intent to impair integrity or availability. Specific provisions of the CFAA, however, relate damage to "loss." While loss is not linked to the intent of the crime, it is the outcome of the damage caused by an individual. The CFAA defines loss to include, "any reasonable cost to any victim, including the cost of responding to an offense, conducting a damage assessment, and restoring the data, program, system, or information to its condition prior to the offense, and any revenue lost, cost incurred, or other consequential damages incurred because of interruption of service."

Throughout the CFAA, the occurrence of the phrase, "Without authorization or exceeding authorized access,"is intended to address two types of computer incursions, namely, intrusions by outsiders, who gain access to computers "without authorization" and insiders, who are authorized to access certain areas of a network yet abuse their privilege to obtain, alter, or damage information that the individual is not entitled to obtain, alter, or damage. One of the first lawsuits to explore the difference between "without authorization" and "exceeding authorization" was United States v. Morris, 928 F.2d 504 (2nd Cir. 1991). The prosecution of Robert Tappan Morris in 1989 represents one of the defining moments in the history of cybercrime prosecution. Morris, the son of a former NSA employee, was a Cornell University graduate student who on November 2, 1989 released a stealth "worm" on a networked computer. Unfortunately, Morris miscalculated the rate at which the worm would spread and how much damage it would cause. His actions caused a massive melt-down of the academic, government, and industry computers connected to the Internet. Among the arguments that Morris presented to the 2nd Circuit on appeal, he explained that since he was permitted to send mail to other computer users, he should be considered an "authorized" user and permitted "access" to other computers. The Court rejected his argument and ruled that he had acted without authorization.

Several civil cases have addressed the notion of "exceeding authorized access," most of which involve accessing credit reports of consumers or employees. In LeBlanc v. Allstate Insurance Co.,[1], the plaintiff alleged that Allstate Insurance Company exceeded its authorized access by using his consent form to obtain a credit report for the improper purpose of defending a lawsuit the plaintiff had filed against the company. The court dismissed the plaintiff's section 1030 claim, holding that Allstate was authorized to obtain the report and that they could not have had an unauthorized purpose since the litigation for which Allstate allegedly obtained the report had not been initiated at the time they requested the report. Id. In Edge v. Professional Claims Bureau, Inc., 64 F.Supp.2d 115, 116, 119 (E.D.N.Y. Sep. 10, 1999), aff'd 234 F.3d 1261 (2nd. Cir. 2000), process server claimed that a debt collection business obtained his credit report for an improper purpose, namely, retaliation. The court dismissed the complaint for failure to prove unauthorized access, finding that the company had made an authorized "social search" of his credit report to obtain his address so that they could contact him about a hospital debt. In Letscher v. Swiss Bank Corporation,[2] the plaintiff had authorized Swiss Bank to obtain his credit report prior to his employment there. Many years later, while responding to an IRS subpoena for the plaintiff's personnel file, a Swiss Bank employee requested a current credit report, thinking she was authorized to do so because the file had been mistakenly filed in the "active" employees drawer.[3] The plaintiff sued, claiming that Swiss Bank had obtained his credit report without authorization in violation of 18 USC §1030(a)(2) and §1030(a)(5).[4] The court dismissed these counts, finding that the Swiss Bank employee, who thought she could legally obtain the credit report, did not have the requisite mens rea to "knowingly," "recklessly," or "intentionally" obtain the credit report without authorization.

In United States v. Riggs, 739 F. Supp. 414 (N.D. III 1990), the 18 USC §2314 that prohibits the transport of stolen, converted, or fraudulently obtained material across state lines also applies to computer data files.

16.1.1.1 Computer Fraud, Intrusions, and Abuse

A number of provisions of the CFAA are applicable to the first category of network crimes addressed by the CFAA, namely, intrusion or hacking. In essence, intrusions constitute attempts by individuals to gain access to computer networks and systems without authorization or exceeding authorization. Where an individual deliberately

---

[1] 2000 WL 825683, at *1-3 (E.D. La. June 22, 2000).

[2] 1997 WL 304895, *5-6 (S.D.N.Y. June 5, 1997).

[3] Id. at *2.

[4] Id. at *1.

breaks into a computer and obtains information relevant to national defense or foreign relations, which can bring injury to the United States if disclosed or passed on to a foreign nation, the individual has potentially violated 18 USC 1030(a)(1). The aforementioned activity may also be prosecuted under section 793(e), which targets the unauthorized possession of, access to, or control over classified information. For further details, the reader is referred to The National Information Infrastructure Protection Act of 1995, P.L. 104-294, Economic Espionage Act of 1996, S. Rep. No. 357, 104th Cong., 2nd Session 1996. The key difference is as follows. While 1030(a)(1) pertains to the use of the computer to gather the classified information, the 793(e) focuses on how classified information is utilized. The first violation of 1030(a)(1) carries a fine of $250,000 or imprisonment for not more than 10 years, while a second offense is punishable with up to 20 years of imprisonment.

Section (a)(2) of the CFAA was intended to protect the confidentiality of data contained in the computers. The premise behind the section's enactment was to protect from computer intrusions (1) individual privacy by protecting computerized credit records and computerized information relating to customers' relationships with financial institutions and (2) information on government computers. The section does not require a minimum specific damage amount for a violation to occur. In addition, as upheld in U.S. v. Tanimowo, 199 F.3d 1324 (2nd Cir. 1999) (unpublished), even merely "viewing" the information online is treated as "obtaining" information under the section, even if the information is never downloaded.

The severity of a 1030(a)(2) violation determines whether the crime is classified as a misdemeanor or felony. For the most part, merely obtaining information worth less than $5,000 is a misdemeanor, punishable by up to a year in prison and a $100,000 fine, as upheld in U.S. v. Carron, 928 F.2d 1137 (9th Cir. 1991) (unpublished). The crime is elevated into a felony, punishable by a fine and up to 5 years imprisonment for a first offense, where the offense is committed to gain commercial advantage or private financial gain, the perpetration is a criminal or tortuous act in violation of the Constitution or laws of the United States or of any State, or if the value of the information obtained exceeds $5,000. A second offense under 1030(a)(2) is punishable by 10 years and $250,000 fine. The phrases, "for purposes of commercial advantage or private financial gain" and "for the purpose of committing any criminal or tortuous act," are adopted from copyright law (17 USC §506(a)) and the wiretap statute (18 USC §2511(1)(d)), respectively.

Section (a)(3) of the CFAA addresses computer intrusions into any nonpublic computer of the federal government. The section refers only to those crimes that are "without authorization" and, as such, does not address insider attacks into government computers. Unlike 1030(a)(2), an intruder does not have to obtain information to violate '1030(a)(3). A hacker who merely violates the "integrity" of a government computer is liable, even where there has been no access to private or confidential information. The first offense for a '1030(a)(3) violation is a misdemeanor, punishable by a year in prison and a $100,000 fine. A second offense is punishable by a 10 year prison term and a $250,000 fine.

Section 1030(A)(4) criminalizes any act of breaking into a computer with the intent to defraud, where the conduct furthers the fraud and the individual obtains anything of value. This section contains a "computer use" exception that exempts any fraudulent conduct intended to obtain only the use of a computer, where such use is valued at less the $5,000 during any 1-year period. A first offense of '1030(a)(4)is punishable by a $250,000 fine and imprisonment for up to 5 years. A second offense is punishable by a 10 year term and a $250,000 fine.

The "computer use" exception was originally crafted in 1986 to punish as felonies only the most serious of computer crimes, namely, those involving fraud. Congress was concerned that without the computer exception clause, even simple acts of trespassing would be treated similar to serious crimes. Per S. Rep. No. 99-432, 99th Cong., 2nd Sess. 10 (1986) and H.R. Rep. No. 99-612, 99th Cong., 2nd Sess. 12 (1986), Congress did not want to "treat every trespass as an attempt to defraud a service provider of computer time." In 1996, Congress further amended '1030(a)(4) to carve out of the exception clause any trespasses that cost a computer provider more than $5,000 during any 1 year period, as stipulated in S. Rep. No. 357, 104th Cong., 2nd Sess. (1996). Congress was prompted by reports that hackers were breaking into Cray supercomputers for the purpose of running password cracking programs, often amassing computer time worth thousands of dollars.

Section (a)(5)(A) addresses damages to a computer and is probably the most widely used section of the CFAA. It is organized into three subparts. Subsection (a)(5)(A)(i) is the workhorse of the CFAA and protects against many of the network crimes. It classifies an act as criminal when one knowingly causes "transmission of a program, information, code, or command" and intentionally damages a protected computer without authorization. Despite the inclusion of the sub-clause, "without authorization," the provision covers both insiders and outsiders as the wording of the section focuses on the intentional damage inflicted on the computer as opposed to the means by which the system is accessed. This provision has been misconstrued and misunderstood by a few as applicable only to outsiders. In reality, insiders pose a serious threat to computers and will often use computer hacking and malicious code disseminations, including logic bombs, to retaliate or cause damage to their employer's computers.

Since a computer hacker has to type commands or compose code in order to break into another computer, (a)(5)(A)(i) may be applicable. In April 2003, Alan Giang Lee pleaded guilty in the Central District of California to an 18 USC 1030 (a)(5)(A)(i) charge for hacking into the computers of Airline Coach Service and Sky Limousine Company and deleting critical data. Tran, a former network administrator for the companies, hacked into the systems and deleted the companies' customer database, as well as shut down the companies' servers, credit card processing system, and website [7].

Section (a)(5)(a)(ii) makes it a crime for an individual to intentionally access a computer without authorization and recklessly inflict damage. The provision is relevant only to outsiders and is classified a felony. Section (a)(5)(a)(iii) refers to individuals who intentionally access a computer without authorization and, regardless of intent, inflict damage to the computer. The provisions charge the violators with a misdemeanor.

In addition to the provisions contained in the CFAA, other federal laws are applicable in many computer intrusion cases. The "Wiretap Act," found in 18 USC 2510 et seq, can be used against computer hackers who break into systems and monitor others' computers. Under 18 USC 2511, it is illegal to intentionally intercept any wire, oral, or electronic communications. The latter includes communications that travel over the Internet. A hacker is considered to have violated the Wiretap Act and could face up to 5 years in prison and/or a $250,000 fine if he or she breaks into a system and intercepts any communications in "realtime" or uses a sniffer or keystroke capture device after the system has been compromised. The Wiretap Act is further detailed in 16.1.4.

The Electronic Communications Privacy Act (ECPA), 18 USC 2701 et seq., is also applicable to computer intrusion attempts. ECPA makes it illegal to intentionally access, without authorization or in excess of authorization, a facility through which an electronic communication service is provided and thereby gain access, alter, or prevent others from accessing communications that might be stored on that system. Thus, when a hacker breaks into hotmail, gmail, Yahoo, AOL, or any other Internet Service Provider and gains access to subscribers' information, shuts down the system so individuals cannot get to their e-mails, or otherwise modifies the system, he or she has potentially violated 18 USC 2701. An individual violating the provision faces a misdemeanor charge, unless the person sought commercial gain or advantage or caused damage, in which case serious charges are levied.

The federal wire fraud statute, codified at 18 USC 1343, may be used to prosecute computer intrusions or, for that matter, many network crimes. Often referred to as the "workhorse of federal prosecutors," the provision is used to prosecute any fraud perpetrated through interstate electronic communications. It prohibits using the wires in "furtherance of a scheme or artifice to defraud, or for obtaining money or property by means of a false or fraudulent pretenses." Today, the bulk of the Internet's operations are carried out in whole or part by a "wire" within the meaning of the wire fraud statute. While this may change in the coming years, as wireless communications technology advances, key aspects of the Internet operation are likely to utilize a wire for a long time to come. Violators prosecuted under this statute face up to 5 years of prison and a $250,000 penalty. For further details, the reader may consult [8] the United States Attorneys' Manual which provides extensive guidance regarding wire fraud charges[5] and the manual for Identity Theft and Social Security Fraud (2004).

A demonstration of how a computer crime can be charged under the wire fraud statute is United States v. Scheier, 908 F.2d 645, 646 (10th Cir. 1990), cert. denied, 498 U.S. 1069 (1991), in which the defendants were successfully convicted under the wire fraud statute for accessing American Airlines' computer reservation system. While on the system, the defendants replaced the names of real passengers with a non-existent person whom they enrolled in American's frequent flyer program. Unfortunately, a number of prosecutorial efforts under section 1343 have

[5] see USAM §9-43.000.

failed, which may be attributed to the inadvertent underestimation of the seriousness of the substantive component of wire fraud statute, when applied to computer fraud. In U.S. v. Czubinski, 106 F.3d 1069, 1072-74 (1st Cir. 1997), the defendant-appellant, Richard Czubinski, who had been an employee of the Internal Revenue Service, serving as a Contact Representative in the Boston office of the Taxpayer Services Division, was convicted by a magistrate judge and the district court through two separate orders for wire fraud. The government had proved beyond doubt that, while Czubinski had authorization to look at taxpayers' files in the Integrated Data Retrieval System (IDRS) in the course of his job, he had exceeded his authorization by accessing unrelated taxpayers' files, despite a IRS rule that IRS employees were not permitted to access files on IDRS outside of the course of their official duties. The IDRS "master files" were located in Martinsburg, West Virginia, so data was retrieved onto Czubinski's terminal screen in Boston across state lines. The First Circuit Court dismissed Czubinski's wire fraud conviction on the grounds that the government had failed to prove that (1) Czubinksi had disclosed any of the confidential information that he had accessed by knowingly disregarding IRS's rules and that (2) he had intended to deprive the IRS of its property right in the IDRS information. In the trial, one single witness testified that Czubinski had once remarked at a social gathering that he intended to build dossiers on potential Ku Klux Klan informants. It is well established that to be convicted of wire fraud, the defendant need not successfully carry out an intended scheme to defraud. The government did not need to prove that Czubinski had actually created dossiers on select individuals using the information or used it for other nefarious purposes. However, the fatal flaw in the government's case, according to the First Circuit, was that it had failed to show beyond a reasonable doubt that Czubinski intended to carry out a scheme to deprive the IRS of its property interest in confidential information. This proof of intention constitutes the substantive element of the wire fraud statute, 18 USC 1343, and the CFAA, 18 USC 1030(a)(4).

In Shurgard Storage Centers, Inc. v. Safeguard Self Storage, Inc., 119 F. Supp. 2d 1121 (W.D. Wash. 2000), the Seventh Circuit Court adopted a broad interpretation of the term, "without authorization," in the language of the Computer Fraud and Abuse Act. Shurgard, the plaintiff, had developed sophisticated business and marketing plans, constituting electronic trade secrets. As part of his employment, a former employee was allowed full access to the confidential plans. The defendant, Safeguard, a competitor, had offered the former employee a position with its company. While still employed by the plaintiff, the former employee sent e-mails containing the electronic trade secrets to the defendant and continued to provide the plaintiff's confidential plans even after beginning employment with the defendant. The court opined that the former employee's authorized access ceased to exist the moment he acted against his employer for the defendant's benefit and ruled, "Unless otherwise agreed, the authority of the agent terminates if, without knowledge of the principal, he acquires adverse interests or if he is otherwise guilty of a serious breach of loyalty to the principal." In International Airport Centers, L.L.C., v. Citrin, 440 F.3d 418 (Seventh Circuit, 2006), a progeny of Shurgard, Citrin was employed in his real estate prospecting job at International Airport Centers (IAC). He quit his job to go into business for himself. However, prior to returning his company-issued laptop computer, Citrin used a secure-erasure program to delete all the data pertaining to IAC ventures as well as all data pertaining to his improper conduct while he was employed at IAC. Of great importance, IAC did not have duplicates of the files that Citrin had deleted. AC sued Citrin for destroying data through the transmission of the erasure program and also for recklessly causing damage to the computer data without authorized access. The Seventh Circuit ruled that Citrin had exceeded his authorized access the moment he acted in an adverse manner to his employment.

In Sect. 16.1.1, we had described the US v. CDT case. Although not found in the Court's ruling, it is clear that the government agents had clearly exceeded their "authorization" in accessing data from the seized computers and could be held in violation of the Computer Fraud and Abuse Act, 18 USC §1030.

At issue in the U.S. v. Czubinski; Shurgard v. Safeguard and its progeny; and US v. CDT cases, detailed in this chapter, are the definitions of "authorized access" and "exceeds authorized access." While the Seventh Circuit has employed a broad definition, other courts have adopted a narrow interpretation of CFAA [9], limiting themselves strictly to the plain and unambiguous statement of the statute and refusing to consider the subjective mindset of the accused while engaged in access of data to which they have been authorized. In Lockheed Martin Corp. v. Speed, 81 USPQ.2d (BNA) 1669 (M.D. Fla. 2006), the court dismissed charges against three former employees who, according to Lockheed, had copied confidential and proprietary information before resigning from Lockheed and joining L-3, a major competitor, and had committed three violations of the CFAA. In so doing, the court refused to adopt the principles outlined in Shurgard, Citrin, and progeny.

The authors believe that the continued oscillation in the federal courts, whether to interpret CFAA's authorized access and exceeds authorized access with a broad definition or a narrow interpretation, independent of the merits of any specific case, reflects a much deeper problem. There are two issues. First, in our normal, daily world, the notion of authorization carries with it an undeniable subjective element. Every natural language, by definition, is imperfect, so we are often expected to search, utilizing our intellect and experience, for the precise definition of authorization in cases that are out of the ordinary. In contrast, in the computing world, functions are far more specific and precise. When a user, as in the case of US v. Czubinski, is provided with a username and password by the IRS to access the IDRS, all taxpayers' data and files within the IDRS come into view of the user, exceptions notwithstanding. Therefore, logically, the user may be assumed to have been granted complete access to all data within IDRS, without exceptions. If the IRS had wanted to restrict Czubinski's access to specific files relevant to his business at hand, appropriate computing functions should have been instituted within the IDRS. The computing world indeed permits this possibility, far more precisely than possible in our normal world of discourse. Second, in contrast to the well established principles, where a principal is required to adopt prudent measures to protect and safeguard his property, rights, etc., there is absolutely no mention in the case laws of the courts requiring a principal to have adopted some form of prudent measures to safeguard his confidential data when he had granted authorized access to it to an employee or someone else. The Economic Espionage Act, 18 U.S.C. §1839(3), requires that the owner adopt reasonable measures under the circumstances to hold the trade secret information confidential. A number of security measures are outlined in [10]. These protections will be a critical component of the case or the decision not to prosecute. In summary, the oscillation can only be settled through a different avenue, namely approaching the problem from a technical, computer science perspective.

If a hacker attacks U.S. military computers or systems, he might be in violation of 18 USC 1362, which makes it a crime to interfere with US computers or systems for military and civil defense functions. While this statute is not used often, it remains a tool to prosecute attempts at computer hacking, intrusions, etc. A violation of this section is a felony, punishable by a fine, imprisonment for not more than 10 years, or both. For further discussions, the reader is referred to Sect. 10.3.4.

The Identity Theft Enforcement and Restitution Act of 2008, under Title II, H.R. 5938, amends Section 1030 of title 18, United States Code, to strengthen the law against malicious spyware, hacking, and keyloggers. An offense under subsection (a)(5)(B) would include, (I) loss to 1 or more persons during any 1-year period (and, for purposes of an investigation, prosecution, or other proceeding brought by the United States only, loss resulting from a related course of conduct affecting one or more protected computers) aggregating at least $5,000 in value, (II) the modification or impairment, or potential modification or impairment, of the medical examination, diagnosis, treatment, or care of one or more individuals, (III) physical injury to any person, (IV) a threat to public health or safety, (V) damage affecting a computer used by or for any entity of the United States Government in furtherance of the administration of justice, national defense, or national security, and (VI) damage affecting ten or more protected computers during any 1-year period. The Act also directs the US Sentencing Commission to review its guidelines and consider increasing the penalties for those convicted under sections 1028, 1028A, 1030, 2511, and 2701 of title 18, United States Code.

16.1.1.2 Password and Access Device Theft

The trafficking of passwords and theft of other access devices in computer networks is a fast increasing cybercrime that law enforcement is committed to fight. They can culminate in identity theft and provide criminals unfettered access to computer systems. A number of federal laws offer protection from password theft.

Ten separate activities [8] relating to access devices are criminalized in 18 USC §1029. The term "access device" is broadly defined to mean "any card, plate, code, account number, electronic serial number, mobile identification number, personal identification number, or other telecommunications service, equipment, or instrument identifier, or other means of account access that can be used, alone or in conjunction with another access device, to obtain money, goods, services, or any other thing of value, or that can be used to initiate a transfer of funds (other than a transfer originated solely by paper instrument)."[6] Access devices related to network crimes might include passwords, electronic banking account numbers, and credit card numbers.

Section 18 USC §1030(a)(6) of the CFAA prohibits trafficking in computer passwords knowingly and with an intent to defraud. A violation of the provision can result in 1 year of prison and a $100,000 fine.

In 1984, Congress included section 1029, entitled "fraud and related activity in connection with access devices" to Title 18 in the same bill that encapsulated the CFAA. Section 1029 was enacted to primarily address the increasing amount of credit and debit card fraud that the US witnessed in the early 1980s [11]. Congress learned about widespread occurrences of sophisticated national schemes exploiting stolen cards, counterfeit cards, account numbers, and card-making equipment. Prior to 1980, credit card fraud primarily involved misuse of actual cards, both stolen and lost. Post 1980, credit card related transactions were increasingly carried out through telephone and network services, rendering it unnecessary for the cybercriminals to acquire the physical cards. All the perpetrators needed were the account numbers and other data.

Section 1029, however, is more than just a "credit card" fraud statute and is often used in the prosecution of other cybercrimes. Per U.S. v. Mitnick, 145 F.3d 1342 (9th Cir.), cert. denied, 525 U.S. 917 (1998), the infamous hacker Kevin Mitnick was charged and pled guilty to violating 18 USC §1029(a)(3) for his possession of unauthorized access devices with the intent to defraud. Furthermore, in United States v. Brewer, 835 F.2d 550 (5th Cir.1987), a hacker called into a telephone company's toll free phone number and repeatedly tried out his guesses, eventually coaxing out valid access codes which gave him access to free long distance service. The individual was charged with violating 18 USC §1029(a)(1)). The United States v. Brewer case also clarified the definition of "counterfeit" for the purposes of section 1029. The Fifth Circuit ruled that Brewer's guessing of valid codes did meet the section 1029 definition of "counterfeit" in that they were "forged;" the defendant had "fabricated codes that just happened to be identical to the [company's] codes."

Subsection 1029(e) contains important definitions relative to the access device statute. The most significant is that for "access device," which had been constructed to include computer passwords. This was evidenced in United States v. Hughey, 147 F.3d 423 (5th Cir. 1998). "Congress intended that the definition of an access device be broad enough to include devices that were not then contemplated, but which by way of technological development might become available as a means of affording unlawful account access." The inclusion of this broad definition of "access device" and its application to cloned cell phones and long distance telephone access codes renders section 1029 a viable prosecutorial tool against password theft and other access device fraud.

Charges under section 1029 [8] would be useful in many types of "phishing" cases, where a defendant uses fraudulent e-mails to obtain various types of

---

[6] 18 USC §1029(e)(1).

passwords and account numbers, and "carding" cases, where a defendant purchases, sells, or transfers stolen bank account, credit card, or debit card information. Penalties for violations of section 1029 range from a maximum of 10 or 15 years' imprisonment depending on the subsection violated.[7] Second and later offenses are subject to 20 years' imprisonment.[8] Forfeiture is also available in many cases.[9]

16.1.1.3 Malicious Code Dissemination

In subsection (a)(5)(A)(i) of the CFAA, Congress has attempted to address the malicious code crime. As stated earlier, this provision makes it criminal to knowingly cause the "transmission of a program, information, code, or command" and intentionally damaging a protected computer without authorization. As we had also stated earlier, the provision is applicable to both insiders and outsiders. Relative to malicious code, it is important to note that a perpetrator may be prosecuted even if the person did not directly disseminate the code. Thus, a virus writer who merely places a virus code in a chatroom for subsequent dissemination by others can be charged for violating the "knowingly cause" clause of the provision.

A question that has been continually raised is whether federal law should be amended to prosecute the mere creation and/or possession of malicious code. After all, there is no legitimate purpose to create a piece of malicious code and that it is no different than a dangerous weapon or chemical, which is generally subject to regulation or banned. In response to this line of argument, critics have claimed that any code, malicious or otherwise, is speech, which is protected by the First Amendment. In Universal City Studios v. Corley, 273 F.3d 429, 445, 448 (2nd Cir 2001), the Second Circuit found that "communication does not lose constitutional protection as 'speech' simply because it is expressed in the language of computer code…Computer programs are not exempted from the category of First Amendment speech simply because their instructions require use of a computer." Where one accepts the premise that malicious code may be protected by the Constitution, restrictions on malicious code may be acceptable if it can be shown that limiting the creation of such code serves a compelling state interest and there are no lesser restrictive means available. As malicious code becomes increasingly severe, especially across many platforms and in new technologies, it would not be surprising to see the free speech resurface again.

There are two practical problems with regulating the creation of malicious code. First, it may be impossible to precisely define a malicious code, which would be crucial to banning its creation. Is a program that goes berserk, works improperly, and consequently causes damage a piece of malicious code, regardless of its creator's intent? Second, if mere possession was outlawed, it would be difficult to determine

---

[7] See 18 USC §1029(c)(1)(A).

[8] See 18 USC §1029(c)(1)(B).

[9] See 18 USC §1029(c)(1)(C), (c)(2).

with any certainty whom to prosecute if the virus or worm had already spread. Under these circumstances, all the victims would be in possession of the malicious code and potentially in violation of the law.

16.1.1.4 Denial of Service Attack

Subsection (a)(5)(A)(i) of the CFAA protects against a denial of service attack, as follows. First, the sub-clause, intentionally causing damage without authorization to a protected computer, is applicable. Again, the provision is applicable to both insiders and outsiders. Second, as described in Chap. 2, an actual denial of service attack is often preceded by the perpetrator gaining access and control of other computers through spreading malicious codes on the victim computers or through network intrusions. These constituent activities of the overall denial of service crimes are already covered by the provisions.

16.1.1.5 Excessive Unsolicited E-mails, Commercial or Otherwise

The CAN-SPAM Act of 2003, Pub. L. No. 108-187, 117 Stat. 2699 (2003), which became effective on January 1, 2004, provides a means for prosecuting those responsible for sending large amounts of unsolicited commercial email (also known as "spam") [8]. Although civil and regulatory provisions are the primary mechanism by which the CAN-SPAM Act's provisions are enforced, it also created several new criminal offenses at 18 U.S.C. §1037. These offenses are intended to address more egregious violations of the CAN-SPAM Act, particularly where the perpetrator has taken significant steps to hide his or her identity, or the source of the spam, from recipients, ISPs, or law enforcement agencies.

In addition to section 1037, the CAN-SPAM Act contains another criminal provision, codified at 15 USC §7704(d), which prohibits sending sexually explicit email that does not contain a label or marking designating it as sexually explicit. A knowing violation of this section is punishable by a fine, imprisonment for not more than 5 years, or both. It is pointed out that section 1037 only criminalizes conduct involving "multiple" commercial email messages:The term "multiple" means more than 100 electronic mail messages during a 24-h period, more than 1,000 electronic mail messages during a 30-day period, or more than 10,000 electronic mail messages during a 1-year period.

16.1.2 Intellectual Property Violations

The emergence of new computer technologies have brought into light a number of issues in intellectual property protection. The Internet and related technologies allow individuals to share and disseminate digitized information easily, quickly, and en masse. The information, however, does not always belong to the disseminator and could be others' property that is protected by copyright, trade secret, or other laws. The recent years have witnessed a proliferation of cheap, if not entirely free, music, software, and other digital media on the Internet, many of which pose serious violations of intellectual property ownership rights. We will devote the remainder of this section to briefly explain US federal laws relative to the violations of criminal copyright and economic espionage. For additional details, the reader is referred to Sect. 15.2.1.

16.1.2.1 Criminal Copyright

The widespread illegal distribution of stolen software and music is increasingly becoming a key focus of law enforcement agencies. In particular, law enforcement has devoted resources to investigate and prosecute "warez" groups, which deal in stolen or illegally copied software, music, and movies.

Under 17 USC §506 and 18 USC §2319, it is a crime for any person to willfully infringe a copyright for commercial advantage or private financial gain or to reproduce or distribute during any 180-day period, one or more copies of a copyrighted work (or works), whose retail worth exceeds $1,000. A first offense can result in a prison term of up to 5 years or a fine if the reproduction or distribution consists of ten copies of copyrighted work (or works) that is worth more than $2,500. Since 1997, per the No Electronic Theft (NET) Act of 1997, Pub. L. No. 105-147, 111 Stat. 2678, even where an individual does not personally profit from the distribution or reproduction, he or she may still be liable in large scale cases. Congress enacted the NET Act in response to United States v. LaMacchia, 871 F. Supp. 535 (D. Mass. 1994), in which a Massachusetts District Court held that the defendant, a MIT student, could not be prosecuted under the existing copyright laws since he distributed software for free and not for any commercial advantage.

Perhaps the most controversial application of the copyright laws to the digital electronics arena involves prosecuting those who share music on Peer-to-Peer (P2P) networks. By permitting individuals from around the world to share files, Napster, Gnutella, and KaZaA may have facilitated criminal violations of the copyright law. If an individual or individuals are found to trade files with retail worth exceeding $1,000, the NET Act has been violated. In the summer of 2000, John Malcolm, Deputy Assistant Attorney General, Criminal Division, U.S. Department of Justice, stated that criminal prosecutions of individuals who engage in file sharing on the Internet is necessary. "There does have to be some kind of a public message that stealing is stealing is stealing" [12].

The 17 USC §117 provides a limited exception to the blanket rule against copying, by allowing one who owns a copy of a computer program to copy the program as necessary to use the program or do machine maintenance or repair, and as an archival backup, subject to certain limitations [10].

16.1.2.2 Trafficking in Counterfeit Trademarks, Service Marks, and Certification Marks

Trademarks and service marks appear on many items that are purchased by consumers, including clothes and cars, and they are advertised on the street, in magazines, on television, and at websites. They are protected by the criminal counterfeit marks statute, 18 USC §2320, which was amended effective March 16, 2006, pursuant to the Stop Counterfeiting in Manufactured Goods Act, Pub. L. No. 109-181, §1, 120 Stat. 285, 285-88 (2006), and the Protecting American Goods and Services Act of 2005, Pub. L. No. 109-181, §2, 120 Stat. 285, 288 (2006) [10].

The statute has yet to play a key role in the cybercrime arena. However, its emergence is inevitable, given that online business is increasing rapidly and that Congress's goal in 18 USC §2320 is to ensure fairness in business. The statute will require significant revisions in the future so it may address the significantly more complex scenarios that will stem from exceptionally quick and deceptive claims and misrepresentations in cyberspace.

16.1.2.3 Circumvention of Protections on Digital Work

The US Congress enacted Title I of the Digital Millennium Copyright Act (DMCA) [10] on October 28, 1998, with the dual goals of protecting copyrighted works from piracy and promoting electronic commerce.[10] Congress accomplished these goals by enacting prohibitions relating to the circumvention of copyright protection systems as set forth in 17 USC §1201, and the integrity of copyright management information pursuant to 17 USC §1202. As a tool for the criminal prosecution of intellectual property theft, the DMCA has generated much interest.

The DMCA prohibits anyone from willfully and for purposes of commercial advantage and private financial gain to circumvent a technological measure that effectively controls or safeguards access to a work protected under the copyright laws. Thus, an individual or a group of people are liable under the DMCA if they circumvent encryptions placed on a dvd or discover a way to crack protections on software. A violation of the DMCA can result in up to 5 years of prison and a $500,000 fine.

In one of the first significant tests of the DMCA's applicability to criminal cases, a jury in December 2002 rejected the government's charges against a Russian company for composing and selling a program that could circumvent Adobe's eBook reader security protections. ElcomSoft, of Moscow, had released the software but pulled it from the market after only 5 days and having sold 25 copies. The company had stated that it earned a few thousand dollars. The jurors apparently believed that while the product was illegal, the company did not intend to violate the DMCA [13]. It is unclear how the ElcomSoft case will affect future criminal DMCA prosecutions.

[10] See H.R. Rep. No. 105-551 (II), at 23 (1998); S. Rep. No. 105-190, at 8 (1998).

Critics will continue to use the argument of "fair use" against the DMCA. Under copyright law, fair use allows for the limited copying or distribution of copyrighted works, with the copier/distributor infringing on the rights of the owner of the works. Although there are no "hard" rules the precisely define fair use, there are four key factors that must be considered, namely, (1) the purpose and nature of the use, (2) the nature of the copyrighted work, (3) the nature of the material used, and (4) the effect of the fair use on the market value of the work. A few of the critics argue that since the DMCA is written in such broad terms, any method of circumventing a copyright protection without explicit consent from the copyright owner, constitutes a violation.

Furthermore, serious concerns have been raised on the adverse impact of DMCA on research and academia. In 2001, Ed Felton, a Princeton professor, filed a lawsuit against the Recording Industry Association of America (RIAA) after he and a team of researchers felt that the association had used the DMCA to keep the team from releasing a research paper describing the defects in a proposed "lock-down" schemes for audio CDs. Per Felton v. RIAA (CITE) (Nov. 28, 2001), a federal district court judge dismissed the lawsuit in November 2001, finding for RIAA and the DoJ. Felton threatened to appeal the decision, but later decided otherwise, citing papers filed by the RIAA and Department of Justice, which stated that "scientists attempting to study access control technologies" are not subject to the DMCA [14].

Section 1201(f) contains a limited number of reverse engineering or "interoperability" defenses for individuals using circumvention technology "for the sole purpose of trying to achieve 'interoperability'" of computer programs through reverse engineering.[11] At least one court has upheld that reverse engineering can satisfy the statutory fair use exception.[12]

For further details, the reader is referred to Chaps. 4 and 7.

16.1.2.4 Economic Espionage

In 1996, Congress enacted the Economic Espionage Act (EEA) to criminalize the theft or misappropriation of trade secrets. The term "trade secret" [10] refers to all forms and types of financial, business, scientific, technical, economic, or engineering information, including patterns, plans, compilations, program devices, formulas, designs, prototypes, methods, techniques, processes, procedures, programs, or codes, whether tangible or intangible, and whether or how stored, compiled, or memorialized physically, electronically, graphically, photographically, or in writing. As an example, a computer software system used in the lumber industry constitutes a trade secret.[13]

---

[11] Davidson & Associates v. Jung, 422 F.3d 630, 641-42 (8th Cir. 2005).

[12] Bowers v. Baystate Techs., Inc., 320 F.3d 1317, 1325 (Fed. Cir. 2003).

[13] Rivendell Forest Prods., Ltd. v. Georgia-Pacific Corp., 28 F.3d 1042, 1046 (10th Cir. 1994).

The two constituent provisions of the EEA have wide applicability and can also be utilized to prosecute individuals for stealing digital works or secrets from others, including their employers (or former employers). The first provision, section 18 USC 1831(a), is intended to punish individuals who engage in foreign economic espionage in order to benefit a foreign government, instrument, or agent. Anyone who steals or fraudulently appropriates without authorization a trade secret to benefit a foreign entity is deemed to have committed an offense. The provision renders it a felony to copy, duplicate, sketch, draw, photograph, download, upload, alter, destroy, photocopy, replicate, transmit, deliver, send, mail, communicate, or convey any trade secret to a foreign government or entity. The provision also makes it illegal to receive, buy, or possess a trade secret, knowing that the said secret had been stolen or otherwise obtained without authorization. Violations of this provision can result in fines up to $500,000 and 15 years of imprisonment.

The second provision of the EEA, section 18 USC 1832, makes it a crime to steal trade secrets for purely economic or commercial advantage. If an entity or individual steals or otherwise obtains without authorization a trade secret that is related or included in a product produced for or placed in interstate or foreign commerce, an EEA violation might exist. Likewise, it is a crime to copy, duplicate, sketch, draw, photograph, download, upload, alter, destroy, photocopy, replicate, transmit, deliver, send, mail, communicate, or convey a trade secret; as well as receive, buy, or possess the trade secret, if it is known that the trade secret had been stolen or obtained without authorization. Violators of 18 USC 1832 face fines up to $250,000 and 10 years in prison. Organizations can also be found guilty of violating either provision of the EEA and face fines up to $10 million for violating section 1831 and $5 million for violating section 1832.

In May 2003, the U.S. Attorney's Office for the Northern District of California indicted Brent Allan Woodward on an 18 USC 1832 (Theft of Trade Secrets) charge, demonstrating that the EEA can be used in cybercrimes. Woodward allegedly stole trade secrets, which had been stored on backup computer tapes, from his former employer, Lightwave Microsystems, and attempted to sell them to JDS-Uniphase, a competitor of Lightwave [15].

On December 13, 2006, the U.S. Attorney's Office for National Security indicted Xiaodong Sheldon Meng for violation of the EEA of 1996 (18 USC Section 1831), which led to conviction and sentencing on 18 June 2008 for a term of 24 months. He was also ordered to serve a 3-year term of supervised release following his prison term; pay a fine of $10,000; and forfeit computer equipment seized in the case. Mr. Meng misappropriated a trade secret, known as "Mantis 1.5.5," from his former employer with the intent to benefit the People's Republic of China Navy Research Center in Beijing. The product is used to simulate real world motion for military training.

The U.S. Attorney's Office for National Security filed its fifth indictment under EEA Section 1831 on 6 February 2008 in the Central District of California in United States v. Dongfan "Greg" Chung, No. SA CR 08-00024. Chung was convicted and remanded into custody on 16 July 2009. During his trial, the government proved that Mr. Chung took and concealed Boeing trade secrets relating to the Space Shuttle and

Delta IV rocket for the benefit of the People's Republic of China. On 8 February 2010, he was sentenced to 16 years of prison.

A key difference between 18 USC §1831 and 18 USC §1831 is as follows [10]. When an individual misappropriates a trade secret but does not intend for anyone to gain economically from the theft, he or she cannot be prosecuted under 18 USC §1832. However, where the scenario involves economic espionage for a foreign-government, the 18 USC §1831 applies, regardless of the economic or non-economic nature of the misappropriation.

Examination of the EEA's legislative history reveals [10] that the owner of a trade secret, unlike the holder of a patent, does not have "an absolute monopoly on the information or data that comprises a trade secret."[14] Other companies and individuals have the right to discover the information underlying a trade secret through their own research and hard work; if and when they do, there is no misappropriation under the EEA.

16.1.3 Crimes Against Persons & Other Unlawful Digital Conduct

It is nearly impossible to list every single form of cybercrime that exists today and is committed on any given day. Numerous cybercrimes, including unlawful gambling, child pornography, money laundering and unlawful sale of goods are simply "physical world" crimes that have migrated online. In essence, they are the exact same crime but committed in a different medium. While there may be unique evidentiary and procedural issues related to online investigations, the general aspects occur in almost all the cybercrimes described in this chapter. A good resource on the different types of unlawful cyberconducts and how federal law enforcement are engaged in combating them can be found in the 2000 government report [16], The Electronic Frontier: The Challenge of Unlawful Conduct Involving the Internet. Of the different types of unlawful conducts [16], crimes against individuals such as identity theft and harassment have unique aspects and are analyzed in the remainder of this chapter.

16.1.3.1 Identity Theft

Identity theft is a growing menace and the Federal Trade Commission received over 86,000 reports of identity theft in 2001. Within the broad category of identity theft, the most prevalent crime reported was credit card fraud, with the average age of the victims being in the thirties [17]. Recognizing the increasing problem of identity theft as early as 1998, Congress passed the Identity Theft and Assumption

[14] 142 Cong. Rec. 27,116 (1996).

Deterrence Act of 1998. The Act amended 18 USC 1028, making it illegal for someone to knowingly transfer or use, without authority, any means of identification of another person with the intent to commit any violation of Federal laws or a felony under any applicable State or local law. The identification means may include e-mail addresses and any other electronic identifier.

The Identity Theft Penalty Enhancement Act [8], codified in 18 USC §1028A, took effect July 15, 2004 and established a new offense of aggravated identity theft. Section 1028A adds an additional 2-year term of imprisonment in cases where a defendant "knowingly transfers, possesses, or uses, without lawful authority, a means of identification of another person" during and in relation to any felony violation of certain enumerated federal offenses, including 18 USC §1028 (but not 1028(a)(7)), 1029, 1030, 1037, and 1343.[15] In cases of terrorism-related aggravated identity theft, including that related to section 1030(a)(1), the section imposes an additional 5-year term of imprisonment.[16] In most cases, the additional terms of imprisonment will run consecutively, not concurrently.[17]

The Identity Theft Enforcement and Restitution Act (ITERA) of 2008, under Title II, H.R. 5938, offers victims in the case of an offense under section 1028(a)(7) or 1028A(a) a restitution amount equal to the value of the time reasonably spent in an attempt to remediate the intended or actual harm from the offense. The Act also amends Section 1030(a)(2)(C) by removing the past restrictions that the conduct must involve an interstate or foreign communication. Under the Act, federal courts will be able to prosecute even when the victim and the cybercriminal reside in the same state.

As of February 2010, 45 states plus the District of Columbia, Puerto Rico, and the U.S. Virgin Islands have data breach reporting statutes. Spurred by the accidental compromise of social security and other personal information of over 250,000 state employees from the California state website, California was the first state to enact the Database Security Breach Notification Act in 2002,[18] which took effect on 1 July 2003. Missouri is the 45th and most recent state to enact legislation along the lines of the California statute. The main focus at the present is in the area of notification of a data breach, although many states are increasingly expanding the scope and definition of data breach to include any data that might put an individual at risk of identity theft. While each state's laws governing data breach notification differ, they all generally impose the following requirements: (1) The statutes generally apply to state residents or entities conducting business in the state. Thus, if an entity does business in more than one state, it will have to comply with multiple reporting agencies. (2) "Personal" information is usually defined to mean some combination of a person's name in combination with other identifying information such as social security number, driver's license number, financial

[15] See 18 USC §1028A(a)(1).

[16] 18 USC §1028A(a)(2).

[17] 18 USC §1028A(b).

[18] Civil Code Sec. 1798.80-1798.82.

account number, and credit card information. In Arkansas, personal information is expanded to include medical information, while Wisconsin law explicitly protects personal electronic records and old fashioned written information or hard copy that is lost or stolen [18, 19]. (3) The statutes often apply if unencrypted information is lost or it is believed that it has been acquired by an unauthorized person or entity. (4) When a breach is discovered, expedient notification to state residents is usually required. (5) Parties that maintain, but do not own personal information, must notify the owner of the information of the occurrence of the breach, and it then falls on the data owner to inform customers and state authorities. While some states explicitly provide for private enforcement actions (e.g., New Hampshire), others specifically limit enforcement to their Attorney General (e.g., Arizona). States are beginning to implement other requirements including protecting data and destruction of personal information. The recently released 2009 Verizon Business Data Breach Investigations Report confirms that more and more electronic records are being breached and point to two factors: the direct targeting of the financial services industry by cybercriminals and the involvement of organized crime. For additional information, the reader is referred to Chap. 15.

16.1.3.2 Harassment, Cyberstalking, and Cyber-Extortion

Just as technology has made it easier for individuals to communicate across great distances, quickly and easily, it has also made it easier for criminals to stalk and harass others. Technology has made it possible to perpetrate crimes against victims located anywhere in the world. An individual committed to harass or cause harassment to another person can easily accomplish it over the Internet by posting messages about the victim or, in certain circumstances, from the victim that incite others to attack him or her.

A number of federal laws make it a crime to harass or cyberstalk. Section 18 USC 875(c) makes it a crime, punishable up to 5 years in prison and a maximum fine of $250,000, to transmit any communication in interstate or foreign commerce that contains a threat to injure another person. While useful, the provision is limited in that it requires an "actual threat" to be communicated. Mere harassment alone does not satisfy the statute's requirement.

Where no direct threats are made, charges may still be brought under section 47 USC 223. The provision makes it a crime to use any telecommunications device, including the telephone, Internet, or e-mail to annoy, abuse, harass, or threaten any person located at the called location. The provision applies only to situations where the perpetrator, having hidden his or her identity, makes direct communications with the victim.

In 1996, Congress passed the Interstate Stalking Act, 18 USC §2261A, that renders it a crime for any person to travel across state lines with the intent to injure or harass another person and, in the course thereof, places that person or a member of that person's family in a reasonable fear of death or serious bodily injury. The provision may be relevant to cyberstalking cases, where a perpetrator initially harasses his or her victim from far and then travels to the victim's state to continue on with the perpetration. In October 1998, Congress enacted a similar law, 18 USC 2425, that specifically protects children by making it criminal to use any means of interstate or foreign commerce to knowingly communicate with any person with the intent to solicit or entice a child into unlawful sexual activity.

The Identity Theft Enforcement and Restitution Act (ITERA) of 2008, under Title II, H.R. 5938 amends Section 1030(a)(7) of title 18, United States Code, to prosecute cyber-extortion. An offense is any of three threats, described subsequently, transmitted in interstate or foreign commerce with the intent to extort from any person any money or other thing of value. The threats include, (A) damage to a protected computer, (B) extract information from a protected computer without authorization or in excess of authorization or to impair the confidentiality of information obtained from a protected computer without authorization or exceeding authorized access, and (C) demand or request for money or other thing of value in relation to damage to a protected computer, where such damage was caused to facilitate the extortion.[19] The Act also provides for an offense under Section 1030 the forfeiture to the United States, (1) the personal property used or intended to be used to commit or to facilitate the commission of any violation of this section, or a conspiracy to violate this section, and (2) any property, real or personal, which constitutes or is derived from proceeds traceable to any violation of this section, or a conspiracy to violate this section.

16.1.4 Wiretap Act

The primary objective of the Wiretap Act [20], also referred to as "Title III," is to effectively protect the privacy of communications. While the original act addressed oral and wire communications, Congress amended it in 1986 to include electronic communications which naturally extends to computer network communications. The Wiretap Act has two purposes, namely, (1) to protect the privacy of oral, wire, and electronic communication, and (2) delineate a uniform basis the circumstances and conditions under which interception may be authorized.[20] While this section will be devoted to the first purpose of the Act, the reader is referred to 16.3.2 for some details on the second purpose.

Under the Wiretap Act, 18 USC §2511, while section 2511(1)(a) prohibits intercepting a communication, section 2511(1)(c) forbids disclosing an intercepted communication. Per 18 USC §2511(1)(a), "Except as otherwise specifically provided in this chapter any person who – (a) intentionally intercepts, endeavors to intercept, or procures any other person to intercept or endeavor to intercept,

[19] The DoJ's Prosecuting Computer Crimes Manual clarifies that this section applies to scenarios in which intruders threaten to penetrate a system, and encrypt or delete a database.

[20] S. Rep. No. 90-1097 (1968), reprinted in 1968 U.S.C.C.A.N. 2112, 2153.

any wire, oral, or electronic communication .... shall be punished as provided in subsection (4)." The law features five key elements, namely, (1) intentional, (2) interception, (3) contents, (4) wire, oral, or electronic communication, and (5) by use of a device. To qualify for punishment, the perpetrator's activity must be intentional, i.e., deliberate and purposeful, even if the individual did not specifically intend to violate Wiretap Act. Though not specified in the wording of the law, the interception must be contemporaneous, in order to distinguish this Act's application from that of the Electronic Communications Privacy Act's restrictions on access to stored communications. To qualify as interception, the acquisition must be of the contents of the communications, namely, the substance and meaning of the communications as opposed to the existence of the communications or transactional records about its existence. A gray area is whether a complete URL constitutes content or otherwise. Any network communication that is not carried by sound waves and does not contain characterizable human voice is labeled electronic and encompassed under section 2510(12). Human voice is covered by section 2510(2) and wired communications by section 2510(1) of the statute. For an acquisition to constitute an interception, it must be realized by an electronic, mechanical, or other device. The statute covers both computers and software running on a computer to intercept the communications.

16.2 Challenges Created by Computer and Network Crimes

Despite the well-developed substantive laws at the federal level that may be utilized to pursue cybercriminals, cybercrimes have created significant challenges for law enforcement. The challenges are not crime specific but appear in almost every type of cybercrime. In general, the challenges may be organized into three categories, namely, jurisdiction, masking techniques, and reporting. In addressing these challenges, this chapter focuses only on the legal and policy elements of the challenges; the technological elements have been addressed in Part II of the book.

16.2.1 Jurisdiction

The jurisdiction challenge permeates all of the cybercrimes discussed in this chapter. Before the advent of the Internet and multidimensional technologies, most crimes were local. In a given neighborhood in a specific city, an individual might break into a house and steal information or a person might take sensitive files from their employer without permission. The rules were mostly clear in that the city's official investigators would take the lead in pursuing the criminal, under the presumption that the suspect or his accomplices had to have been present in their city at one time. Computer networks have negated the presumption. Today, armed with a computer and a network connection, anyone can commit a crime halfway around the world without ever physically entering the jurisdiction of the crime scene. No longer does a criminal have to break into a house to steal information or wield a gun at a teller's face to rob a bank. Theft of information and money may be accomplished remotely, without the perpetrator ever leaving home. This "remote" attribute had allowed Onel De Guzman to create and release the Love Bug virus in his native Philippines and bring down networks around the world. Not only did he successfully release the virus; he could not even be prosecuted for the billions of dollars of damage he caused worldwide. By the same token, an warez site operator can remotely access foreign computers and use them as drop off points for illegal software.

Given that remote crimes is now a reality, we must address important jurisdictional issues. First, what is the definition of a crime scene? Is it the location of the victim, suspect, or that of the computer or network that has been used to perpetrate the crime? In general, experts believe that the crime scene must include the locations of both the victim and the suspect. In the US, jurisdiction also extends to the locations of the computer and network. As discussed earlier, the Patriot Act had addressed the jurisdiction issue through its definition of protected computer. By amending the definition to encompass computers even outside the territorial United States, as long as they affect "interstate or foreign commerce or communication of the United States," Congress had solved many of the potential jurisdictional issues relative to cybercrimes.

The key to the jurisdictional issue in prosecuting computer crimes is that most current statutes require an interstate or foreign jurisdictional hook [10]. Failure to establish the "interstate" basis for federal jurisdiction can lead to dismissal or acquittal. In United States v. Jones, 580 F.2d 219 (6th Cir. 1978), the Court affirmed acquittal in the wiretap case since the government failed to offer evidence that the telephone company had provided facilities for the transmission of interstate or foreign communications.

Absent evidence of a contrary intent, the laws of the United States are presumed not to have extraterritorial application. See United States v. Cotten, 471 F.2d 744, 750 (9th Cir. 1973). In 2001, as part of the USA PATRIOT Act, Congress revised both sections 1029 and 1030 to explicitly provide for extraterritorial jurisdiction in certain cases. The USA PATRIOT Act added the following language to 18 USC §1029(h):

(h) Any person who, outside the jurisdiction of the United States, engages in any act that, if committed within the jurisdiction of the United States, would constitute an offense under subsection (a) or (b) of this section, shall be subject to the fines, penalties, imprisonment, and forfeiture provided in this title if

1. The offense involves an access device issued, owned, managed, or controlled by a financial institution, account issuer, credit card system member, or other entity within the jurisdiction of the United States
2. The person transports, delivers, conveys, transfers to or through, or otherwise stores, secrets, or holds within the jurisdiction of the United States, any article used to assist in the commission of the offense or the proceeds of such offense or property derived therefrom

The USA PATRIOT Act also amended section 1030(e)(2)(B) to specifically include a computer "which is used in interstate or foreign commerce, including a computer located outside the United States that is used in a manner that affects interstate or foreign commerce or communication of the United States."

Other sources of extraterritorial jurisdiction may include 18 USC §7, which defines the special maritime and territorial jurisdiction of the United States, and 18 USC §3261-3267, which govern criminal offenses committed outside of the United States by members of the military and persons employed by or accompanying them. Extraterritorial jurisdiction can be found also on the basis of intended and actual detrimental effects within the United States.

With respect to intellectual property (IP) crimes, US copyright laws generally offer no extraterritorial effect. Thus, some copyright cases may not be brought in the United States, even when the victims are US nationals and companies and the infringed works are copyrighted in the US. In general, foreign countries protect US copyrights against infringement in their lands, similar to US domestic laws that protect foreign copyrighted works against infringement in the US.[21]

Second, who has the right to file a case relative to a cybercrime? In the event a hacker breaks into computer systems in multiple cities, clearly law enforcement in every affected city will launch an investigation and seek to prosecute the incursion. The city where the hacker is physically located may also desire to pursue the case. If the state and local laws had also criminalized the behavior, then local, state, and federal law enforcement agencies in the same city will all want to pursue the crime. At the present time, there are no precise rules on how such a criminal case should be pursued. In the US, coordination and cooperation exists on an ad hoc basis and relies on all law enforcement agencies working collaboratively to solve the crime. As expected, conflicts may and do arise and it would be critical to have a clear mechanism to resolve them. As a hypothetical example, if a hacker were to break into multiple government computers located in various districts around the country, it may be logical to have the case brought into the jurisdiction of Washington, DC, where the center of the government is located. There are no rules governing such efforts at the present time and the issue warrants an in-depth analysis for the future. It must be pointed out that a number of entities had been created over the past to coordinate law enforcement efforts. The Secret Service has established Electronic Crime Task Forces in a number of US cities to investigate different cybercrimes. The FBI's Cybercrime Squads, located in multiple cities, also put together special Task Forces for specific crimes to better utilize resources and avoid undue conflicts.

The Identity Theft Enforcement and Restitution Act of 2008 amends Section 1030(a)(2)(C) by removing the past restrictions that the conduct must involve an interstate or foreign communication. Under the Act, federal courts will be able to prosecute even when the victim and the cybercriminal reside in the same state.

---

[21] 17 USC §411(a).

16.2.2 Masking Techniques

Given Internet's permissiveness, cybercriminals will almost always try to hide their identity and their online activities. As explained in detail in Part I, the Internet offers anonymity and anonymous mechanisms through which cybercriminal can carry out their activities. A favorite approach is to launch their activities from a public location, including a library, copy store, or an Internet cafe, which renders it nearly impossible to track and trace them. We had also explained how legitimate services such as anonymizer.com [21] may be used by a cybercriminal to hide his or her identity. On the Internet, a cybercriminal may even hide his IP address by using a cloaking service, including cloak.com or other anonymizers, which "strip" all identifying information from an e-mail or other communications. The origin IP address can no longer be determined with certainty [21].

The US government painfully realizes the challenge of anonymity on the Internet [22]. As with anything, while the Internet is cybercriminal's favorite tool, anonymity on the Internet has also allowed lawful individuals to safely communicate with others, including Kosovo freedom fighters sharing information regarding government and military atrocities, domestic violence victims providing support and guidance to one another, and whistle blowers exposing dangerous environmental conditions without fear of retaliation from unjust authorities. In essence, anonymity's positive and negative attributes make it difficult to formulate meaningful regulation on the Internet. Law enforcement agencies must, therefore, seek alternative methods to locate cybercriminals.

In addition to hiding identity, a cybercriminal can exploit encryption, and steganography, and other technologies to hide his or her activities. Encryption, also known as cryptography, is the use of mathematical equations and keys to ensure secure communications between specific individuals. Just as encryption is critical to the success of e-commerce and banking activities and cannot be outlawed, cybercriminals can encrypt their data or communications, unabated, and hide their activities from law enforcement. This poses a unique challenge to law enforcement. Where an individual is suspected of wrong doing and there is probable cause for obtaining a search warrant or court approval for a wire-tap, encryption makes the effort practically useless unless law enforcement can successfully intercept and decrypt the criminal's activities. When modern public and private keys came into existence, more than a couple of decades earlier, Congress and law enforcement were involved in efforts to regulate encryption. For the most part, the efforts failed. Critics raised Constitutional violations of the proposed regulations, and argued that hindering technology would adversely affect e-commerce and new business initiatives. There were other technology-enabled practical difficulties.

In essence, steganography involves cleverly hiding a piece of information within another media, generally an artwork. It may be compared to hiding a needle in a haystack, which makes it very difficult to detect. In cyberspace, a piece of information is hidden in an electronic file, generally in unused memory locations. Thus, a viewer looking at a picture of a cat on a computer screen may fail to realize that a secret message is hidden in the file containing the image of the cat. Of course, special knowledge may be required to detect and retrieve the secret message. While a number of high-profile cases document the use of steganography, there is little data on the frequency with which cybercriminals employ this technology. In February 2001, Wired magazine ran a story suggesting that Bin Laden had used steganography to communicate with terrorist operatives around the world, hiding blueprints for proposed terrorists activities in seemingly innocent files [23]. To-date, it is unclear how formidable a challenge steganography has or will pose to law enforcement officials in the future.

Despite calls for government regulation of anonymous speech, Constitutional violations and other technology related difficulties have prevented laws against anonymity and masking techniques. Conceivably, the judicious use of procedural laws can effectively counteract the cybercriminals' use of masking techniques. For example, Congress may want to consider laws that authorize and govern the use of specific web bugs by law enforcement officials. A web bug is a graphic on a web page or in an e-mail message that is designed to identify who is viewing a website or a given e-mail. A web bug may extend a single pixel in size and viewed as invisible and undetectable [24]. Even where law enforcement is granted a court order to conduct a web bug, there are no specific laws governing its use. The closest law might be one that governs beacons, where a police officer can place a homing beacon on a suspect's car to track the individual. By enacting a specific law governing web bugs, Congress would be able to specifically dictate its deployment and use, authorizing law enforcement with a valuable tool to "unmask" cybercriminals.

16.2.3 Reporting

In Part I, we had already discussed the challenges contributing to the underreporting of cybercrimes.[22] It is believed that, even today, the officially reported rate is far below reality. By nature, we human beings perceive shame of being a victim of a cybercrime. This manifests at all levels. Within a company, victims do not come forward to report crimes. System administrators will often hide incidents from management for fear of losing their jobs or appearing less than diligent in their duties. Even management will refrain from reporting cybercrimes to law enforcement or other agencies from the fear of negative publicity or that the report will cast doubt on its competitiveness. There is also justifiable concern about stock prices and retribution from stockholders.

In addition to business concerns, companies often do not believe that law enforcement agencies will handle the incidents competently. There is justifiable fear that law enforcement agents may seize networks and servers, disrupt business operations, and take away control of their system. In truth, law enforcement agencies no

[22] The "Computer Crime and Security Survey" conducted by the CSI in collaboration with the San Francisco Federal Bureau of Investigation's (FBI) Computer Intrusion Squad.

longer come to the crime scene like the old-style cavalry and carry things away. Through the years, many federal agencies have developed expertise in computer forensics and analysis and can work with victims to ensure that their systems are minimally affected. Law enforcement agencies will often create a "mirror" of the attacked computer or computers, rather than removing the original and disrupting business. Of course, the exact procedure will be dictated on a case by case basis, defined by the facts of the crime.

Even where a company trusts law enforcement, there is fear that prosecutors will either not prosecute the case for any number of reasons or will publicize the case excessively for their own benefit and without regard to the impact on the business. Companies many also decide not to challenge the hackers or make their vulnerabilities known to third parties. In many cases, companies may not know precisely whom to call.

While the concerns are understandable, they are not insurmountable. While law enforcement agencies cannot promise companies that their identities will remain unknown forever, they can work with victimized companies to ensure that the identities are reasonably protected. At a conference in October 2002, co-sponsored by the DoJ and the Information Technology Association of America, each of two U.S. Attorneys assured executives of high-tech companies that prosecutors and investigators are willing to work to ensure a company's privacy. Roscoe Howard, U.S. Attorney for the District of Columbia, noted, "We can protect you where we can, and we will do that when it's within the law and the constitutional rights of the defendant. When we've got individuals (as witnesses) we want to keep off the stand, we just won't use them [25]."

The benefits from reporting cybercrimes to law enforcement are many. First, as good citizens, victims must report crimes to help law enforcement agencies better analyze the scope of the problem and formulate solutions toward the greater benefit of society. Furthermore, if a specific incident is one element of a chain of events or a bigger fraudulent scheme, prompt reporting might help law enforcement intercept the perpetrator and prevent additional crimes from occurring. As an example, where a few of the financial institutions are hacked and extorted for $50,000 each, law enforcement officials might be able to decipher a pattern, detect a weakness, and apprehend the cybercriminal. In contrast, if none of the banks come forward, there is little that law enforcement can do to prevent additional banks being victimized. In general, law enforcement agencies are better equipped to legally trace criminal activity. Where a hacker spans his activity through four or five different Internet Service Providers to confound the authorities, law enforcement agencies can use legal processes, including subpoenas, warrants, and wiretaps, to track the cybercriminals and their activities. For obvious reasons, this is generally beyond the means of a single company.

The ultimate decision whether a company will choose to report a cybercrime to law enforcement is dictated by a cost-benefit analysis. Recognizing this reality, there is a concerted effort within law enforcement agencies to reach out to companies before incidents begin to unfold. The FBI's InfraGard program, explained earlier in Chap. 10, epitomizes this effort. InfraGard is a partnership between private industry and the US government's FBI, developed to encourage the exchange of information between the government and the private sector. The National program was launched as a pilot program in 1996 in Cleveland and has since expanded to include over 72 chapters and hundreds of companies [26].

The Secret Service's Electronic Crimes Task Force also has successfully paired the private and public sectors to combat cybercrimes. The New York Electronic Crimes Task Force has been in existence for several years and has successfully brought industry, law enforcement, and academia together to share information and technical expertise. The Patriot Act mandated the creation of additional task forces around the country. As of the present, 23 more chapters have been created, including Boston, Charlotte, Chicago, Los Angeles, Miami, New York, San Francisco, Washington D.C., Las Vegas, and others and more are under development. For further details on the Electronic Crimes Task Forces, the reader is referred to [27].

16.3 Procedural Laws Addressing Computer and Network Crimes

In the first part of this chapter, we had focused on the "substantive" laws, which criminalizes select behaviors in cyberspace. We had seen how Congress had to amend many of these substantive laws and create new ones to ensure that criminal behavior was punished. Congress and policymakers also found it necessary to revise procedural laws and create new ones to govern the collection of evidence in cybercrime incidents. This section of the chapter provides a brief review of the procedural laws.

16.3.1 Computer and Network Crimes

In Theofel v. Farey-Jones in the 9th Circuit Court in San Francisco, California,[23] the court held that under the Stored Communications Act, 18 USC §2511 et seq., a party issuing a subpoena for e-mails from a defendant's ISP must limit the request in scope, time, and to the subject matter of the litigation. The Appeals court sided with the district court's finding that the massively overbroad subpoena issued by Farey-Jones was an egregious violation of Federal Rules. The district court had quashed the subpoena and imposed over $9,000 in sanctions against the defendants. The Appeals Court stated that the Stored Communications Act defines a criminal offense and includes an explicit mens rea requirement[24] and ruled that the defendants had acted

[23] United States Court of Appeals for the Ninth Circuit, No. 02-15742, D.C. No. CV-01-04166-MMC, Amended 17 Feb 2004.

[24] 18 USC §2701(a)(1).

in "bad faith." The plaintiffs-appellants also claimed that the defendants-appelles had violated the Stored Communications Act, 18 USC §2701 et seq.; the Wiretap Act, 18 USC §2511 et seq.; and the Computer Fraud and Abuse Act, 18 USC §1030. The district court had ruled that these federal statutes did not apply. The Appeals Court reversed the dismissal of the Stored Communications Act claim, affirmed the dismissal of the Wiretap Act claim, and reversed the dismissal with prejudice of the Computer Fraud and Abuse Act. The reasons were as follows.

First, the Wiretap Act, 18 USC §2511 et seq., does not apply since the Act applies only to "acquisition contemporaneous with transmission," not to stored e-mails. Second, although the subpoenaed e-mails were held by the ISP after they had been delivered to the recipients at least once and may appear to not to be in "electronic storage," the Appeals court determined that they had been stored for "purposes of backup protection."[25] The Stored Communications Act defines "electronic storage" as "(A) any temporary, intermediate storage of a wire or electronic communication incidental to the electronic transmission thereof; and (B) any storage of such communication by an electronic communication service for purposes of backup protection of such communication." Third, looking into legislative history, a passage form a 1986 report indicates that a committee intended that messages stored by a remote computing service would "continue to be covered by section 2702(a)(2)" if left on the server after user access.[26] Fourth, the subpoena's falsity transformed the defendants' access to the e-mails from a bona fide state-sanctioned inspection into private snooping. Fifth, like the tort of trespass, the Stored Communications Act protects individuals' privacy and proprietary interests, namely, users whose electronic communications are in electronic storage with an ISP or other communications facility. Sixth, although the ISP allowed the defendants access to the plaintiffs' e-mails under the subpoena, the subpoena itself was patently unlawful, implying that the defendants lacked "authorization" under section 2701. The subpoena was "not in line with the reasonable expectations" of the party granting permission, in this case the ISP, and that it was not "in any way related to [the system's] intended function."[27] Seventh, the ISP's consent, stemming from the defendants' deceptive subpoena, is tantamount to a hacker using someone else's password, even if obtained through guessing,[28] to break into a mail server and claiming that the server had authorized the access. Eighth, the Computer Fraud and Abuse Act provides a cause of action against one who, inter alia, "intentionally accesses a computer without authorization or exceeds authorized access, and thereby obtains ... information from any protected computer ..."[29] Ninth, although the district court believed that the Computer Fraud and Abuse Act does not apply to unauthorized access to a third party's computer, the Appeals Court determined

[25] 18 USC §2510(17)(B).

[26] H.R. Rep. No. 647, 99th Congress at 65 (1986).

[27] United States v. Morris, 928 F. 2d 504, 510 (2d Cir. 1991)

[28] Cf. Morris, 928 F. 2d at 510.

[29] 18 USC §1030(a)(2)(C), (g).

that individuals other than the computer's owner may be proximately harmed by unauthorized access, particularly if they have rights to data stored on it.

In United States (US) v. Comprehensive Drug Testing (CDT) in the 9th Circuit in Pasadena, California,[30] the court ruled against the government and issued a series of guidelines that the government must follow in its acquisition, handling, and processing of computer data. Key guidelines include, (1) Magistrates should insist that the government waive reliance upon the plain view doctrine in digital evidence cases, (2) Segregation and redaction must be either done by specialized personnel or by an independent third party. If the segregation is to be done by government computer personnel, it must agree in the warrant application that the computer personnel will not disclose to the investigators any information other than that which is the target of the warrant, (3) Warrants and subpoenas must disclose the actual risks of destruction of information as well as prior efforts to seize that same information in other judicial fora, (4) The government's search protocol must be designed to uncover only the information for which it has probable cause, and only that information may be examined by the case agents, and (5) The government must destroy or, if the recipient may lawfully possess it, return non-responsive data, keeping the issuing magistrate informed about when it has done so and what it has kept.

Following an investigation of the Bay Area Lab Cooperative (BALCO), the federal government had learned of ten players who had tested positive in the CDT program. The federal government, plaintiff-appellant, had secured a grand jury subpoena seeking all "drug testing records and specimens" pertaining to Major League Baseball in CDT's possession. In conjunction with Quest Diagnostics, Inc., a laboratory, CDT had carried out tests of the urine samples for drugs, collected from the players of Major League Baseball Players Association. While CDT was moving to quash the subpoena, the government obtained a warrant authorizing search of CDT's facilities in Long Beach. However, the warrant was limited to the records of the ten players as to whom the government had probable cause. In obtaining the search warrant, the government's affidavit explained the generic hazards of retrieving electronic data and sought broad seizure of computer records from CDT and for off-site examination and segregation of the evidence seized. Although the warrant permitted the government to examine all the data contained in the computer equipment and storage devices, and to attempt to recover or restore hidden or erased data, if any, it contained significant restrictions, compiled under Tamura procedures,[31] designed to ensure that data beyond the scope of the warrant would not fall into the hands of the investigating agents. The Cybercrime Lab of the DoJ had developed, as of August 2007, a detailed digital forensic analysis methodology to aid in the prosecutorial analysis [28]. The warrant required that the initial review and segregation of the data was not to be conducted by the investigating case agents

[30] United States Court of Appeals for the Ninth Circuit, No. 05-10067, D.C. No. MISC-04-234-SI, Filed 26 August 2009.

[31] United States v. Tamura, US Court of Appeals, Ninth Circuit, 694 F.2d 591, 10 Dec 1982.

but by "law enforcement personnel trained in searching and seizing computer data ("computer personnel")," whose job it would be to determine whether the data could be segregated on-site. These computer personnel – not the case agents – were specifically authorized to examine all the data on location to determine how much had to be seized to ensure the integrity of the search. Moreover, if the computer personnel determined that data did not "fall within any of the items to be seized pursuant to this warrant or is not otherwise legally seized," the government was to return those items "within a reasonable period of time not to exceed 60 days from the date of seizure unless further authorization was obtained from the court." In direct violation of the requirements of the warrant, the case agent "himself reviewed the seized computer data and used what he learned to obtain subsequent search warrants issued in Northern California, Southern California, and Nevada." Not only did the case agent brush aside CDT's offer to provide all information pertaining to the ten identified baseball players, he had deliberately suppressed this vital information in his affidavit. The Appeals Court ruled that "[t]he Government demonstrated a callous disregard for the rights of those persons whose records were seized outside the warrant." The court also ruled that omitting such highly relevant information is inconsistent with the government's duty of candor in presenting a warrant application. The government argued that it was not required to return any data it found showing steroid use by other baseball players because that evidence was in plain view once government agents examined the Tracey Directory in the seized computers. In rejecting the argument, the Appeals Court noted that the government has a powerful incentive to seize everything, more than what is authorized, which, thereafter, automatically becomes into plain view. Although not found in the Court's ruling, the federal agents had clearly exceeded their "authorization" and could also be held in violation of the Computer Fraud and Abuse Act. The court ruled that the government should, in future warrant applications, forswear reliance on the plan view doctrine. If the government does not consent to such a waiver, the magistrate judge should order that the seizable and non-seizable data be separated by an independent third party under the supervision of the court, or deny the warrant altogether. The court also ruled that when, as here, the government comes into possession of evidence by circumventing or wilfully disregarding limitations in a search warrant, it must not be allowed to benefit from its wrongdoing by retaining the wrongfully obtained evidence or any fruits thereof. Under its concluding thoughts, the Appeals Court recognizes that electronic storage and transmission of data is no longer a peculiarity or a luxury of the very rich; it is a way of life. Users can now choose to store data and information in electronic storage facilities at remote third-party locations, where it is intermingled with those of other users, making it difficult to retrieve without a thorough understanding of the filing and classification systems. This spurs law enforcement to seek broad authorization to examine electronic records, which creates a serious risk that every warrant for electronic information will become, in effect, a general warrant, rendering the Fourth Amendment irrelevant.

In Melendez-Diaz v. Massachusetts in the Supreme Court of the United States[32] the Supreme Court had ruled, 6-4, against the Massachusetts government and held that the admission of the certificates of state laboratory analysts as prima facie evidence had violated the petitioner's Sixth Amendment right to confront the witness against him. At the petitioner's state-court drug trial, the prosecution produced certificates of state laboratory analysts stating that the material seized by police and connected to the petitioner was cocaine of a certain quantity. Under Massachusetts law, the certificates were sworn to before a notary public and were submitted as prima facie evidence of what they asserted. The petitioner had objected, asserting that Crawford v. Washington, 541 U.S. 36 (2004), required the analysts to testify in person. The trial court disagreed, the certificates were admitted, and the petitioner was convicted. The Massachusetts Appeals Court affirmed, rejecting the petitioner's claim that the certificates' admission violated the Sixth Amendment. The Supreme Court asserts that The Sixth Amendment guarantees a defendant the right "to be confronted with the witnesses against him." A witness's testimony against a defendant is thus inadmissible unless the witness appears at trial or, if the witness is unavailable, the defendant had a prior opportunity for cross examination. The Supreme Court dismissed the argument that the analysts are not "conventional witnesses" (and thus not subject to confrontation) in that they "observe[d] neither the crime nor any human action related to it," for two reasons. First, there is no authority. Second, the argument would exempt all expert witnesses from confrontation. The respondent argues that the analysts' certificates emanate from "neutral scientific testing." The court rejects it, stating that forensic evidence is not uniquely immune from the risk of manipulation. The court cites a recent study conducted under the auspices of the National Academy of Sciences. The report states, "[t]he majority of [laboratories producing forensic evidence] are administered by law enforcement agencies, such as police departments, where the laboratory administrator reports to the head of the agency." Thus, a forensic analyst responding to a request from a law enforcement official may feel pressure – or have an incentive – to alter the evidence in a manner favorable to the prosecution. Confrontation is one means of assuring accurate forensic analysis. The court further notes that dispensing with confrontation because testimony is obviously reliable is akin to dispensing with jury trial because a defendant is obviously guilty. Clearly, the Supreme Court's opinion will weigh heavily on future forensic evidence in cybercrimes.

16.3.2 Real Time Transmission and Interception

When investigating cybercrimes, often, law enforcement official must intercept and capture the communications of criminals in "real-time," i.e., as the communications

[32] Melendez-Diaz v. Massachusetts, Certiorari to the Appeals Court of Massachusetts, Supreme Court of the United States, No. 07-591, Decided June 25, 2009.

are being sent and received. This is also referred to as "live" communications. For telephone systems, this implies listening and recording the human-to-human conversation as it occurs. In cyberspace, real-time interception includes the use of sniffers and keystroke loggers to capture e-mails and instant messages as they are composed and transmitted.

From the legal perspective, two forms of real-time communications are recognized, namely, wiretaps and pen/traps. Wiretaps focus on capturing the content of a communications, i.e., the actual words that are being written in an e-mail or the spoken words in a telephone. These may be intercepted and captured, i.e., recorded at an Internet Service Provider or on the hacker's computer. In the computing terminology, this is referred to as the payload. The Pen/Traps focus on collecting useful information related to the communications, other than the actual content or payload. This may include the "addresses," i.e., to and from for an e-mail. Pen/Traps may also provide the timestamp of a e-mail message, the port used by a perpetrator's computers, or other protocol related information.

To engage a wiretap on an e-mail account or a computer, law enforcement officials must obtain a wiretap order under the Wiretap Act, 18 USC 2510 et seq or satisfy one of three exceptions to allow them to intercept without an order. These exceptions have proven useful in the investigation of cybercrimes. The first, provider exception, 18 USC 2511(2)(a)(i), is a limited exception that allows system administrators to conduct reasonable monitoring to protect the provider's "rights or property" or when done in the normal course of employment while engaged in any activity which is a "necessary incident to the rendition of his service." The second, consent exception, 18 USC 2511(2)(c), allows for the interception of communications when a party to the communications "consents." In addition to a party explicitly stating, "yes, monitor my system," the exception might be satisfied if a company or agency has written consent forms signed by their employers or if networks are "bannered." Banners often appear as click-through on networks and imply the following, namely, (1) the user consents to monitoring while he or she uses the system, and (2) the individual acknowledges that he or she has no reasonable expectation on the network.

The 2001 Patriot Act added a third exception, namely authorizing law enforcement to intercept the communications of computer intruders without an explicit wiretap order. Prior to the Act, law enforcement could not proceed to monitor a system to apprehend a hacker without first obtaining permission from the company. This was contentious. Also, if law enforcement were to attempt to assist a company without first obtaining a wiretap order, it could trigger a violation of the Wiretap Act. In many instances, the provisions of the Wiretap Act were counterproductive. As an analogy, consider that a robber is attempting to break into a house. The owner is authorized to call the local police but then must stand back and watch the intruder successfully commit the crime. Intrusions occur with such speed that, often, it is detrimental for law enforcement to helplessly watch the intrusion progress while waiting for a wiretap order. The Computer Trespasser Exception, 18 USC 2511(2)(i), rectified this restriction by allowing law enforcement to intercept communications to or from "computer trespassers." The statute requires the perpetrator to be a "computer trespasser," i.e., an individual who accesses the network "without authorization" and "has no reasonable expectation of privacy." The statute is very clear in that the perpetrator must be an outsider for the exception to be invoked. The exception cannot be applied against any person known by the provider to have an existing contractual relationship with the provider for use of the system. The statute requires that the victim authorize the interception, the law enforcement official intercepting the communications must be acting under color of law, the communications in question must be relevant to an ongoing investigation, and only the trespasser's interceptions can be intercepted.

As with wiretaps, Congress created an exception to the Pen/Trap orders, 18 USC 3123, that require law enforcement to first obtain an order to use a pen/trap device for interception. The consent and provider exceptions exist for pen/trap orders, very similar to that for wiretaps. Furthermore, since pen/trap orders can have a "national" effect, the Patriot Act authorizes law enforcement to obtain an order to "trace" back the communications of a suspected individual.

The Pen/Trap statute, 18 USC §§3121-3127 [29], authorizes a government attorney to request a court to issue an order authorizing the installation of a pen register and/or trap and trace device if "the information likely to be obtained is relevant to an ongoing criminal investigation."[33] A pen register will record the outgoing addressing information, including the number dialed from a monitored telephone; and a trap and trace device will record incoming addressing information, including the caller ID. For communications utilizing the Internet Protocol, where headers contain both "to" and "from" information, a device that reads the entire header, minus the subject line in the case of e-mail headers, is both a pen register and a trap and trace device. It is commonly referred to as a pen/trap device. Per 18 USC §3127(3), a "pen register" is defined as "a device or process which records or decodes dialing, routing, addressing, signaling, information transmitted by an instrument or facility from which a wire or electronic communication is transmitted, provided, however, that such information shall not include the contents of any communication ..." The definition further excludes devices or processes used for billing or cost accounting.[34] A "trap and trace device" is defined as "a device or process which captures the incoming electronic or other impulses which identify the originating number or other dialing, routing, addressing, and signaling information reasonably likely to identify the source or a wire or electronic communication, provided, however that such information will not include the contents of any communication." The statute encompasses a wide variety of communications technologies, including non-mobile telephone, cellular telephone, Internet user account, e-mail account, or an IP address. Second, the definitions' inclusion of all "dialing, routing, addressing, [and/or] signaling information" encompasses virtually all non-content information in a given communication. Third, because the definitions of a pen register and a trap

[33] 18 USC §3122(b)(2).

[34] 18 USC §3127(3).

and trace device include both a "device" and a "process," the statute covers software as well as physical devices.

16.3.3 Stored Electronic Communications

In prosecuting crimes, often, law enforcement officials must recreate a crime, which requires them to trace the communications back to the source as well as gather evidence after the fact. In turn, this may require access to "stored electronic communications." The Electronic Communications Privacy Act (ECPA), 18 USC §2510 et seq governs access to stored communications. In 1996, Congress enacted the ECPA to strike a balance between the privacy needs of telecommunications users and the legitimate needs of government investigators. Per 18 USC §2701-09, ECPA prohibits individuals and entities from accessing or intercepting stored electronic communications belonging to others. The statute also explicitly details the requirements that law enforcement must satisfy in order to request service providers for different categories of stored information about subscribers. The wiretap provisions found in 18 USC §2511-2521 are considered a part of ECPA. This section is limited to discussions on stored communications; the real-time communications related issues have been addressed in Sect. 16.3.2.

ECPA also prohibits the disclosure of communications held in "electronic storage" by the service providers. "Electronic storage" is defined in 18 USC §2510(17) as any temporary, intermediate storage of a wire or electronic communication incidental to the electronic transmission thereof... (and) any storage of such communication by an electronic communication service for purposes of backup protection of such communication. The clause, "temporary" in the "electronic storage" definition is significant in that it implies that the communication is "in transit" and not yet arrived at its final destination.

Per 18 USC §2711(2), a "remote computing service" is defined as, "provision to the public of computer storage or processing services by means of an electronic communications system." An "electronic communications system" is, "any wire, radio, electromagnetic, photo-optical or photoelectronic facilities for the transmission of electronic communications, and any computer facilities or related electronic equipment for the electronic storage of such communications." The category of remote computing services includes data processing services, usenet services, and bulletin boards [30].

As we had noted earlier, restrictions were placed on when a subscriber's information may be disclosed by a provider. Depending on the type of information sought, ECPA placed complex requirements on law enforcement's search and seizure of information, which was protected by the statute. When crafting ECPA, Congress determined that specific types of information deserved greater privacy protections. The content of unread e-mails was deemed to need the most protection, while basic subscriber information did not deserve strict protection. As a result, investigators and prosecutors must carefully navigate different legal processes, in a complex and often baffling manner, to seek the information they require. While select information can be gathered with a subpoena, other material require a special order under 18 USC §2703(d), and specific content information can be obtained only with a search warrant. For details on how investigators may obtain real-time and stored information legally, the reader is referred to US DoJ's guidance document titled, "Searching and Seizing Computers and Obtaining Electronic Evidence in Criminal Investigations [31]."

In Warshak v. United States of America in the 6th Circuit in Cincinnati, Ohio,[35] the entire court of 14 federal appellate judges held, 9-5, that the preliminary injunction ordered by the federal district court that had enjoined the government from using 18 USC §2703(d) to seize the contents of "any personal email account []" belonging to Warshak or "any resident of the Southern District of Ohio" without "prior notice and an opportunity to be heard" be vacated and remanded because Warshak's constitutional claim is not ripe for judicial resolution. A panel of three judges of the 6th Circuit had previously upheld the ruling of the District Court. The Stored Communications Act, 18 USC §§2701-2711, authorizes the federal government to require Internet service providers to disclose the contents of "electronic communication[s]" of their customers in certain circumstances, including by way of an ex parte court order.[36] The government obtained two such orders in 2005 from a magistrate judge to search Steven Warshak's e-mails from NuVox Communications and Yahoo!. As required, the order were based on "specific and articulable facts showing that there [were] reasonable grounds to believe that the records or other information sought [were] relevant and material to an ongoing criminal investigation."[37] Also, the orders did not give Warshak immediate notice of the disclosures[38] on the grounds that it could seriously jeopardize the investigation. However, the magistrate judge ordered the government to delay the notice for 90 days and mandated that the "[o]rder[s] [be] sealed until otherwise ordered by the Court." When Warshak was finally given notice of the orders by the government a year later, he sued the government, seeking declaratory and injunctive relief. Among other complaints, Warshak alleged that 18 USC §2703(d) violated the Fourth Amendment on its face and as applied because the searches were based on a showing of less than probable cause and were not supported by a warrant. The court granted Warshak's motion. The court reasoned that Warshak would likely succeed on his Fourth Amendment claim because Internet users have a reasonable expectation of privacy in e-mails and because the orders authorized warrantless searches on less than probable cause. The entire Sixth Circuit court argued that per Article III, §2 of the US Constitution, the Constitution does not extend the "judicial power" to any legal question, wherever and however presented, but only to those legal questions presented in

[35] United States Court of Appeals for the Sixth Circuit, No. 06-4092; Appeal from the United States District Court for the Southern District of Ohio at Cincinnati, No. 06-00357 – Susan J. Dlott, District Judge; Decided and Filed 11 July 2008.

[36] Id §2703(d).

[37] JA 48,51; see 18 USC §2703(d).

[38] 18 USC §2703(b)(1)(B).

"Cases" and "Controversies." That is, a claim is not "amenable to ... the judicial process," when it is filed too early, making it unripe; when it is filed too late, rendering it moot; or when the claimant lacks a sufficiently concrete and redressable interest in the dispute, depriving the plaintiff of standing. The majority of the Appellate judges, namely 9, ruled that Warshak's claim is not "fit" for judicial review, citing that they have no idea whether the government will conduct an ex parte search of Warshak's e-mail account in the future. Given that Warshak has already been indicted and convicted by a jury, the possibility is exceedingly remote that the government will conduct another "ex parte" search of his e-mails. The minority of the Appellate judges, namely 5, dissent, stating that the case is ripe and that the majority opinion gives unwarranted deferential treatment to the government. They further argue that the government violated the terms of the Stored Communications Act by failing to notify Warshak 90 days after searching his e-mails. Also, the federal district judge and the original three-judge panel of the Sixth Circuit Court had concluded "that individuals maintain a reasonable expectation of privacy in e-mails that are stored with, or send or received through, a commercial ISP."[39] Brenner [32] writes that the federal government was taken by surprise when a federal judge and three court of appeals judges found that the Fourth Amendment does encompass e-mails. Since they had a weak case, the government chose to raise two procedural issues in hopes of getting the case kicked out without the court addressing the substantive issue. With the proliferation of new technologies and increasing government activities in the areas of (1) public surveillance through closed circuit TV, and (2) transactional surveillance such as access to banks, telephone, and other business records, Slobogin [33] believes that we need a new approach to the Fourth Amendment to limit the government's powers. He argues that Courts should recognize a Constitutional right to public anonymity because its absence will "promote conformity and an oppressive society." The governmental power to watch us in public can chill our speech, discourage our free spiritedness, and infringe upon our capacity for self-definition. Kerr [34] disagrees with Slobogin's proposed use of public opinion surveys to guide the courts in interpreting the Fourth Amendment, and recommends that Courts should tweak the law, not rework it from first principles. He believes that the existing framework of the Fourth Amendment protection already balances privacy and security and favors the approach of the New Jersey Supreme Court that requires state investigators to obtain a valid grand subpoena for IP addresses and bank records. While Kerr is justified in that the institutions will serve as the ultimate interpreters of the Constitution anyway, Slobogin's claim that the current Fourth Amendment was written a long time ago when today's massive surveillance capability of the government was unthinkable and his fear that government's watchful eyes will migrate into oppression are not entirely unfounded.

[39] Warshak, 490 F.3d at 473.

16.4 Investigatory Challenges

16.4.1 Jurisdiction

By updating a number of existing laws under the Patriot Act, Congress strengthened law enforcement's ability to meet the challenges posed by cybercrimes. Prior to the Patriot Act, the Pen/Trap statute, approved by numerous courts, contained language that appeared to restrict to telephone communications. The Pen/Trap order referred to being attached to a "line," implying that a physical device needed to be connected to a telephone line to intercept data. The Patriot Act changed the order to ensure that it applied to software, referred to line and other facilities, and generally ensured that other technologies were covered. The Patriot Act also permitted law enforcement to successfully trace back a communications beyond a single hop connection. Previously, a law enforcement official could obtain an order to trace communications only within his or her district. Where, as is often the case with the Internet, the communications transfers to another provider in a different district, the official would then seek assistance to obtain a pen/trap order for the second district. Clearly, if the communications required tracing back six or seven hops, an appropriate number of orders would be required, implying significant delay by which time the trail would go cold. To help track a cybercrime in a timely manner and apprehend the cybercriminal, the Patriot Act authorized law enforcement to obtain a single court order for a communications, regardless of the number of service providers spanned by the communications.

While the trap/pen order was "fixed" by the Patriot Act, other statutes might also need to be reviewed, analyzed, and brought up to par in the age of cyberspace. While investigating a cybercrime that spans across multiple jurisdictions, the current statutes relative to the use of wiretaps are not precise. Consider an IP investigation in Omaha, where investigators discover a hotmail account and have gathered sufficient evidence to warrant a wiretap. Key questions that arise include, should the wiretap be obtained in Omaha or in California where the hotmail facility is located? Does it matter if the wiretap "captures" the communications in California and then ships via digital wire to Omaha for review? Does it matter if the suspect is physically present in Omaha and that his or her only connection to California is the location of hotmail which can be accessed remotely anyway? While most law enforcement officials would seek the wiretap order in California, the statutes governing wiretap orders may need to be revised to permit a wiretap order request in the district where the investigation is being pursued. Such a revision would help immensely with investigations, especially with regard to assistance from the Internet service providers and provided better checks on the orders. The judge approving the wiretap is more in a position to be the vested in the actual investigation and more familiar with the individuals bringing the wiretap request before the Court.

Given that the issue of jurisdiction is already greatly aggravated by cybercrimes, the problem of "manufactured" jurisdiction is likely to surface in new forms in the future and cause serious complications. In United States v. Archer, 486 F.2d 670,

July 12, 1973, Second Circuit Court of Appeals, the Court rejected the federal government's claim that the three interstate and foreign telephone calls had brought the case within 18 USC §1952(a)(3), referred to as the "Travel Act." The court held that two of the three interstate/foreign phone calls, key evidence in the trial, were manufactured and deliberately planted by the federal government to prove jurisdiction under the Travel Act. As a result, the local bribery offense could not be transformed into a federal crime against the United States and the defendant could not be charged under the Travel Act, solely based on these phone calls. Spurred by the belief of rampant local corruption in the Queens district of New York, the federal government initiated an operation where one of the agents appeared to break a New York state law, got himself arrested, and then started to drop hints to the arresting officers that he might be interested in offering bribes to drop the case against him. While federal prosecutors did not have a definite suspect in mind when they launched their operation, their focus soon fell on the assistant district attorney of Queens, New York, Mr. Norman Archer. The court's findings may be organized into three parts. First, decency, security, and liberty demand that government officials must follow the same rules of conduct that bound the citizens. As the potent and omnipresent teacher, the federal government must teach citizens through its own example. Crime is contagious; if the government participates in breaking the law, it will breed contempt, resentment, and, ultimately, anarchy. Second, the sparse legislative history of the Travel Act, coupled with the lack of substantive debate in the House of Representatives and the Senate, requires the law to be carefully interpreted by the courts and scrutinize whether the evidence fits the intent of the law. The law had been enacted to curtail organized crimes and, more specifically, prosecute individuals who resided in one state and managed illegal activities in a different state, not to punish a person trying to fix a parking ticket by crossing a state line and offering a $10 payment to pay off the policeman. Third, although the federal government's actions may be understood to stem from the desire to root out serious local corruption that interferes with the effectiveness of Federal Criminal Laws, in this particular case, the Court noted that the federal prosecutors violated a number of New York state judicial and police processes before witnessing any evidence of federal crimes.

16.4.2 Venue

The US Constitution, article III, paragraph 2, clause 3, mandates that trial be held in the state and district where the crime was committed. The Federal Rule of Criminal Procedure 18, which implements the principle requires the court to set the place of trial within the district with due regard for the convenience of the defendant and the witnesses, and the prompt administration of justice. Absent from Rule 18, however, are many issues that arise in computer and network crimes, namely where the offense was committed and how to deal with crimes that span multiple states or even other countries. In recent times, different courts have elaborated on a few of these issues. First, when a defendant is charged with more than one count, venue must be proper with respect to each count. Second, if no single district has proper venue for all potential counts, prosecutors can either charge the defendant in multiple districts and seek transfer to a single district or bring all charges in one district and seek a waiver from the defendant. A defendant may also waive any objections to improper venue, either explicitly or by failing to object when the defect in the venue is clear.

The key challenge in determining venue in computer and networking crimes is that the different elements of the crime may be scattered widely in both space and time and may or may not coincide with the accused's actual presence. Section 1030(a)(2)(C) prohibits intentionally accessing a computer without or in excess of authorization, and thereby obtaining information from any protected computer. Logically, a crime would be considered committed at the location where the offender initiates access and where the information is obtained. Despite this clarification, there may be scenarios where establishing the exact location may be difficult. Of a more subtle nature is the location or set of locations where the impact of the cybercrime may be felt, even if the perpetrator had no intentions or even knowledge. In today's computers and networks, the connections and intricate interactions render it possible for a small perpetration at one location to exert a significant adverse impact at a far away location, at a different time, that defies understanding. For example, studies reveal [35] that a change in the bandwidth of a computer link near Anchorage, Alaska in a worldwide network quickly causes appreciable network congestion in the neighborhood of Washington, D.C.

With respect to intellectual property crimes, 18 USC §3237(a) allows crimes, "begun in one district and completed in another, or committed in more than one district, may be inquired of and prosecuted in any district in which such offense was begun, continued, or completed." In United States v. Tucker, 495 F.Supp. 607, 618 (E.D.N.Y. 1980), although the defendant resided outside the district, the Court held that the venue was proper for grand jury investigation into defendant's sales of counterfeit sound recordings because "middleman" in defendant's scheme resided, and purchaser was headquartered, in district.

16.5 Operational Challenges

Even with the most carefully crafted substantive and procedural laws in place, law enforcement agencies might still fail to keep ahead of the cybercriminals unless they are properly staffed, equipped, and trained. It is an unfortunate truth that law enforcement officials face formidable operational challenges, worldwide. Cybercrimes are intellectually highly sophisticated and require dedicated experts who can talk "geek," understand technology, and capable of keeping up with new technologies. Proper equipment to combat cybercrimes is a must. This requires continual updating of computers, networks, technology, and tools. Extensive training is required of all law enforcement officials. An agency cannot send an agent into a home or business to simply pick up a compromised computer and bring it back to the station for analysis. The agent must be capable of determining the type of computer, the underlying operating system, whether it is connected to a network where other evidence may reside, and whether it is booby trapped to destroy evidence upon sensing an effort to tamper with it. Additional challenges include the following:

- Lack of a coordinated effort where attacks are promptly reported, compiled, classified, and analyzed by a dedicated group of law enforcement agents who quickly develop effective solutions and transmit them to all who are affected.
- The inability of organizations to train and retain IT employees who are skilled in proactively defending the organizations' IT assets. Neglect and lack of challenges cause "brain drain," driving away many of the top IT employees. Too often, high turnover implies lost continuity and organizations with excellent defense at one time fall prey to simple attacks in the future.
- Consumed by the urgent problems of food, shelter, crime, education, etc., many countries cannot afford to take the issue of cybercrimes seriously. They do not enact proper laws for cybercrime that may exploit their land, water, or space, but otherwise leave them unharmed. As a result, law enforcement agents from advanced countries face impossible difficulties in tracing international cybercrimes and clever perpetrators are all too aware of it.
- While traditional crimes involve a very limited number of human actors, cybercrimes often involve gigabytes and even terabytes of data, which must be analyzed to uncover evidence of the crime. This poses an enormous challenge. It has been reported that many corporations leave their firewalls running for months but the gigabytes of data that are collected are never analyzed to determine if the corporate network had been scanned, attacked, or successfully penetrated. Corporations often purchase the most expensive firewalls or other security products, deploy it without even changing the factory set default password, and succumb to a false sense of security.

16.6 Technological Challenges

16.6.1 Diverse Business Environments

Three decades ago, the process for law enforcement to request information on a specific telecommunications user was straightforward. There was a single company with a single set of policies. Today, there is no longer a single monopoly and a single end-to-end communications may span over half a dozen carriers or more, located in diverse jurisdictions. Furthermore, the communications may be transmitted through different types of technologies including IP packets over optical fibers, microwave wireless, satellite frequencies, and electrical signals. The great diversity of carriers and technologies makes it very difficult to trace a single communication since several legal processes might be necessary to find its origin. Furthermore, if an attacker becomes suspicious and goes offline or successfully hides his tracks by using false information or stealing another's account, while law enforcement is "tracing" a communication, valuable source and destination data may evaporate. Given that different business models employ different techniques for retention and storage of data, it is conceivable for law enforcement to successfully trace one or two steps, only to find out that an upstream carrier has not retained the information, which is critical to continue the investigation.

16.6.2 Wireless

Over the past decade, wireless networking has popular, with governments, companies, and individuals setting up wireless local area networks (W-LANs) to remain connected to the Internet. Of the many types of W-LANs, a common configuration is an infrastructure wireless network, where an existing wired local area network is extended to "wireless" users. In this environment, an access point is connected to a wired Ethernet network, with the access point acting as a hub between the network and the wireless users. As a result, depending on the network configuration, individuals can freely roam around buildings, neighborhoods, campuses, and even blocks, while continuing to remain connected. W-LANs have grown to serve public areas, including airports, coffee shops, and hotels. By allowing users, both authorized and unauthorized, to remain mobile, WLANs pose significant challenge to law enforcement. A criminal may enter a network at a public access point and remain anonymous. Depending on the strength of the wireless signal, a sophisticated hacker may gain unauthorized access to a network through an access point, while remaining at a reasonable distance away. Attempts to trace back the hacker may lead to someone else's network [36], while the perpetrator will escape undetected. Sophisticated cybercriminals can either gain access to an open and unprotected W-LAN or install backdoor access points. As wireless technology proliferates, law enforcement's concern will deepen. Chapter 5 had described "warchalking," where cybercriminals and "war drivers" drive around and map wireless access points in a given neighborhood, noting buildings with public access or insufficient protections on their private WLANs, and post them on special websites [37]. The information is readily available for potential cybercriminals to access vulnerable networks.

16.6.3 Satellite-Based Telephony

Satellite-based telephony permits individuals to contact or be contacted virtually anywhere in the world, land or water. It poses a formidable challenge to law enforcement, given that both technology and laws to intercept the calls and identify their origin and termination points are limited. Satellite communications systems may be configured such that a specific customer's communications are processed entirely in a foreign facility, thereby complicating the investigation and prosecution of the criminal activity [38]. All communications and call related data will be subject to the laws of the country where the facility is located, obtaining which may range from very difficult to impossible, depending on the diplomatic relationship between the foreign country and the US.

References

[1] The Learning Channel. (2001, July 25). *Hackers: Computer outlaws*. Cable Television.
[2] A brief history of hacking.
[3] Keeney, J. C., Deputy Assistant Attorney General, Criminal Division, US DoJ. (1983, November 18). Statement before The Subcommittee on the Judiciary, citing two computer crime cases involving prosecutions under the wire fraud statute.
[4] H.R. Rep. No. 894, 98TH Cong., 2nd Sess. 1984, 1984 U.S.C.C.A.N. 3689. (1984).
[5] S. Rep. No. 432, 99TH Cong., 2nd Sess. 1986, 1986 U.S.C.C.A.N. 2479. (1986).
[6] US DoJ. Retrieved from http://www.cybercrime.gov/1030_anal.html and http://www.cybercrime.gov/PatriotAct.htm
[7] Retrieved from http://www.cybercrime.gov/tranPlea.htm
[8] Computer Crime & Intellectual Property Section (CCIPS), US DoJ. *Other network crime statutes* (pp. 77–91). Retrieved March 12, 2007, from http://www.justice.gov/criminal/cybercrime/ccmanual/03ccma.pdf-2007-03-12
[9] Liccardi, G. M. (2008). The computer fraud and abuse act: A vehicle for litigating trade secrets in federal court. In J. Marshall (Ed.), *Law school review intellectual property law* (Vol. 8, pp. 155–189).
[10] Computer Crime & Intellectual Property Section (CCIPS), US DoJ. *Prosecuting intellectual property crimes manual* (3rd ed.). Retrieved October, 2006, from http://www.cybercrime.gov/ipmanual/index.html
[11] H.R. Rep. No. 894, 98th Cong., 2nd Session, 1984, 1984 U.S.C.C.A.N. 3689. (1984).
[12] Retrieved from http://news.com.com/2100-1023-954591.html?tag=fd_top
[13] Retrieved from http://news.zdnet.co.uk/story/0,,t269-s2127714,00.html
[14] Electronic Frontier Foundation Media Release. (2002, February 6). *Security researchers drop scientific censorship case, government, industry claim DMCA not a threat to science.* Retrieved from http://www.eff.org/IP/DMCA/Felten_v_RIAA/20020206_eff_felten_pr.html
[15] Retrieved from http://www.cybercrime.gov/woodardIndict.htm
[16] Retrieved from http://www.cybercrime.gov/crimes.html#IXg
[17] Retrieved from http://www.ncvc.org/resources/statistics/references/index.html#74
[18] Consumers Union. (2009, January 7). *Notice of security breach state laws*. Retrieved from http://www.consumersunion.org/campaign//financialprivacynow/002215indiv.html
[19] Erin Nealy Cox. (2009, July/August). Data breaches have bred a patchwork of state laws. In *Executive Counsel* (Vol. 6).
[20] Computer Crime & Intellectual Property Section (CCIPS), US DoJ. *CCIPS prosecuting computer crimes manual* (p. 5). Retrieved March, 2007, from http://www.justice.gov/criminal/cybercrime/ccmanual/00ccma.html
[21] Businessweek. (2002, June 5). *Cloaking your movements in cyberspace*. Retrieved from http://www.businessweek.com/technology/content/jun2002/tc2002065_1287.htm
[22] Unlawful Conduct Report.
[23] McCullagh, D. *Bin Laden: Steganography master?* Retrieved from http://www.wired.com/news/politics/0,1283,41658,00.html
[24] Retrieved from http://www.privacyfoundation.org/resources/webbug.asp#1
[25] Hacking victims' ID to stay secret. Retrieved November 1, 2002, from http://www.cnn.com/2002/TECH/internet/11/01/reporting.hackers.ap/index.html
[26] Retrieved from http://www.infragard.net

[27] Retrieved from http://www.secretservice.gov
[28] Computer Crime & Intellectual Property Section (CCIPS), US DoJ. *Digital forensic analysis methodology flowchart (PDF)*. Retrieved August 22, 2007, from http://www.cybercrime.gov/forensics_chart.pdf
[29] Computer Crime & Intellectual Property Section (CCIPS), US DoJ. *CCIPS manual on electronic search and seizure*. Retrieved August 24, 2009, from http://www.cybercrime.gov/ssmanual/
[30] H.R. Rep. No. 99-647 (1986). (1986).
[31] US DoJ. (2002). Retrieved from http://www.cybercrime.gov/s&smanual2002.htm
[32] Brenner, S. (2008, July 12). *Warshak: 6th Circuit blinks*. Retrieved from http://cyb3rcrim3.blogspot.com/2008/07/warshak-6th-circuit-blinks.html
[33] Slobogin, C. (2007, November). *Privacy at risk: The new government surveillance and the fourth amendment*. Chicago, IL: University of Chicago Press. Retrieved from http://www.press.uchicago.edu/presssite/metadata.epl?mode=synopsis&bookkey=236643
[34] Kerr, O. S. (2009, April). Do we need a new fourth amendment? *University of Michigan Law Review, 107*, 951–966.
[35] Ghosh, S. (2002, April). *Principles of secure network systems design*. New York, NY: Springer.
[36] Brewin, B. (2002, July 15). *Watch out for wireless rogues*. Retrieved from http://www.computerworld.com/securitytopics/security/story/0,10801,72664,00.html
[37] Verton, D. (2002, August 14). *Mapping of wireless networks could pose enterprise risk*. Retrieved from http://www.computerworld.com/mobiletopics/mobile/technology/story/0,10801,73479,00.html
[38] Di Gregory, K. V., Deputy Assistant Attorney General, Criminal Division, US DoJ. (2000, September 7). Foreign ownership interests and foreign government ownership interests in the American Communications Infrastructure, statement before the U.S. House of Representatives Subcommittee on Telecommunications, Trade, and Consumer Protection Committee on Commerce.

Part VII
International Character of Cybercrimes

Chapter 17
International Dimensions of Cybercrime

Marc Goodman

In the networked world, no island is an island [1].

17.1 A Global Perspective on Cybercrime

If we ask ourselves the question, who cares about cybercrimes, the answer is far more involved than one might imagine. From the perspective of high technology, everyone should be concerned with the crimes in cyberspace, and this response would resonate with governments, businesses, and citizens in North America, Europe, Australia, Japan, and elsewhere.

In contrast, in the developing regions of the globe, including Africa, the Caribbean, the Middle East, and Asia, cybercrime appears to be of little significance. For all the time, attention, and money dedicated to cyberthreats in the developed world, few resources have been dedicated to combat cybercrime elsewhere. This is unfortunate, not only for the nations that are unprotected, but for all nations around the globe. In a world where every nation is wired and networked to one another, a criminal threat perpetrated on the network of one country can prove ruinous to a sovereign jurisdiction half way around the world. Moreover, the most technologically advanced societies are the most vulnerable and have the greatest amount to lose, often, as a result of the inability or unwillingness of developing countries to effectively detect, investigate, arrest, and prosecute cybercriminals.

The importance with which a given society treats cybercrimes appears directly related to the rate at which high technology has been adopted by the members of that society. Thus, in a technologically advanced city like Palo Alto, California, where mobile phones, iphones, laptops, and wireless networks rule the day, it would seem logical to be concerned about hackers and theft of proprietary data. In contrast, to a Masai warrior living in the Mara in Kenya, theft of proprietary data would be irrelevant and of no concern.

While nearly every nation has both telephone service and a connection to the Internet, the use and availability of these services to the general public is far from uniform. For example, there are more wired telephones in Manhattan than on the entire African Continent, although mobile phone usage is growing rapidly. While

S. Ghosh and E. Turrini (eds.), *Cybercrimes: A Multidisciplinary Analysis*,
DOI 10.1007/978-3-642-13547-7_17, © Springer-Verlag Berlin Heidelberg 2010

Manhattan in New York City has approximately two million residents, over 743 million people [2] call Africa their home. According to the United Nations (UN), 50% of the population on earth have yet to even make their first telephone call [3]. Thus, to understand the formidable challenge of a "global fight" against cybercrime, one must consider a number of sobering facts:

- In the United States, over 50% of all households have access to the Internet. In Africa, the figure is only 0.4% as per US estimates in 2001
- According to UNESCO, one billion adults are illiterate, worldwide, representing approx. 26% of the global population
- Nearly 30% of the world's population currently goes to bed hungry every night [4]
- According to the World Bank, three billion people on the planet subsist on less than $2 a day

Given these vast disparities in human development and health and technological progress, it is not surprising that there is little to no interest in cybercrimes in over 100 nations in the world. They are probably not even aware of the depth of the cybercrime problem. While the FBI and Scotland Yard may routinely occupy themselves with cybercrimes, police forces in other parts of the world have very different concerns and priorities. In India, police may be more occupied with dowry related crimes; in Tanzania, the smuggling in ivory products; in Riyadh, the enforcement of a moral code enshrined in Sharia Islamic law; and in Mexico, it may be trafficking in human beings. While cybercrime will arrive, sooner or later, in all nations around the globe, presently, it is of concern only in the 60 most developed nations. In these countries, cybercrimes have had a profound impact on law enforcement organizations charged with handling the offenses. In essence, the nature and scope of high technology crime, committed over global information networks, has required a paradigm shift in international policing.

17.2 The Globalization of Crime

Multinational corporations, including Toyota, Ford, Coca-Cola, Nestle, Siemen's, Sony, and McDonald's are recognized worldwide. They supply goods and services to the global marketplace and take advantage of the latest technology to improve efficiency and decrease operational costs. Criminal organizations have observed and analyzed these developments with great care and have adopted lessons from the corporate sector on how to forge strategic alliances to increase their worldwide access to new markets. Law enforcement organizations have discovered that even the most notorious criminal groups, including the Italian Mafia, Russian mob, Nigerian criminal enterprises, Chinese triads, Colombian and Mexican cartels, and the Japanese Yakuza are forging strategic alliances, networking, and developing new working relationships with each other and terrorist organizations in cyberspace. These global criminal networks deal in drugs, contraband, money laundering, trafficking in human beings, corruption of government officials, financial fraud, extortion, and other illicit money making schemes. Terrorist organizations are discovering new means of raising money, expanding their operations around the world, and creating a marketplace to purchase and sell sophisticated weaponry and other high tech equipment.

Criminal organizations have been cooperating with each other for a long time. The Colombian drug lords and Italian crime groups have been exploiting the West European drug market in the past and are now seen in New York City and Eastern Europe joining forces with the Russian group in drugs and financial crimes. Russian organized crime is spreading like wildfire. According to the Russian Interior Ministry (MVD), nearly 80% of Russian businesses are controlled or affected by organized crime. The former Director of the FBI, Louis Freeh, had noted that Russian organized crime has been detected in at least 58 foreign countries.

As organized crime groups become increasingly international in the scope of their activities, they are also less constrained by national boundaries. The new lowering of political and economic barriers allows them to establish new operational bases in commercial and banking centers around the globe. The willingness and capability of these groups to move into new areas and cooperate with local groups is unprecedented, magnifying the threats to stability and even the rule of law. In large portions of the globe where crime and corruption rule the day, the rule of law and government institutions is very much a foreign concept.

Former US president Bill Clinton summarized the problem of global crime syndicates in a speech on May 12, 1998, announcing a major initiative against international crime,

"... more porous borders, more affordable travel, more powerful communications, increasingly also give criminals the opportunity to reach across borders – physically and electronically – to commit crimes and then retreat before they can be caught and punished. Many Americans really don't realize the extent to which international crime affects their daily lives.

Cyber-criminals can use computers to raid our banks, run up charges on our credit cards and extort money by threats to unleash computer viruses.

Two-thirds of counterfeit US money is printed overseas. Illegal copying of our products costs us jobs and tens of billions in revenue. Spies seek important industrial secrets – and worse, materials to make nuclear, chemical and biological weapons. Up to $500 billion in criminal proceeds every single year-more than the GNP of most nations-is laundered, disguised as legitimate revenue, and much of it moves across our borders. International crime rings intimidate weak governments and threaten democracy. They murder judges, journalists, witnesses, and kidnappers and terrorists have attacked Americans abroad, and even at home with brutal acts like the World Trade Center bombing." The reference was to the first World Trade Center bombing in 1993.

Another frequent observer of the transnational crime phenomenon, US Senator, John Kerry of Massachusetts, has tried on many occasions to warn of the threat posed by international organized crime groups. Kerry chaired the Sub-Committee on Terrorism, Narcotics and International Operations of the US Senate Foreign Relations Committee. He noted,

"In strategy, sophistication, and reach the criminal organizations of the late twentieth century function like transnational corporations and make the gangs of the past look like mom-and-pop operations. ... Today's transnational criminal cartels use high-speed modems and encrypted faxes. They buy jet airplanes three or four at a time and even have stealth-like submersibles in their armadas. They hire the finest minds to devise encryption systems and provide the complex accounting procedures any multibillion-dollar empire requires. They engage the ablest lawyers to defend them, the craftiest spin-doctors to spiff their images in the media, the most persistent-and generous-lobbyists to influence legislative decisions. They retain retired intelligence officers from the world's best secret services to consult with them on security. Highly educated and well-trained scientists ensure quality control in the production of narcotics ... Crime has been globalized along with everything else except ... our response to it."

While President Clinton and Senator Kerry focused on traditional global organized crime groups such as the Russian Mob, the Italian Mafia, and Columbian Drug Cartels, there exists another international criminal organization, namely, organized criminal hacker groups. Although violent criminal organizations receive frequent press and film coverage and are more recognized by the society at large, in truth, international hacker organizations are every bit as menacing as their counterparts in the traditional crimes.

While a few of the hackers operate independently, the vast majority of them cooperate, practice, and learn from each another. There are known international syndicates of malicious computer hackers who work in unison and perpetrate a large number of different types of cybercrimes, ranging from unauthorized access of government information systems to massive financial frauds. Groups such as "Cult of the Dead Cow," "G-Force," and the "Chaos Computer Club" coordinate attacks and commit activists activities on an international scale using the Internet as their communications medium.

While society tends to think of traditional organized crime as distinct from high-tech criminals and hackers, there is evidence to suggest that the boundaries are blurring. Members of the Chinese triad groups and Japanese Yakuza are heavily involved in the theft of intellectual property on a global scale [5]. Counterfeit videos, music CD's, software, computer video games cost industry billions of dollars each year. The Russian mafia has been implicated in a vast array of cybercrimes, ranging from hacking into financial institutions to identity theft, credit card fraud, and extortion in cyberspace. Just as the traditional organized crime groups had hired experts in other areas to further their criminal enterprises in the past, today, they are turning to recognized criminal hacker organizations to open up new markets and improve their operational efficiencies.

17.3 A New Way to View Crime in the Global Village

Virtually all conventional crimes shared the attribute of locality. That is, a homicide committed in the Bronx section of New York City was very likely perpetrated by a suspect who lived in the area. Investigators would be virtually certain that the perpetrator had been in Bronx, physically, to commit the crime. Today, cybercrimes have shattered that assumption in that, for any given crime, the co-location of the suspect and the victim may no longer be taken for granted.

Rapidly advancing technology, including the Internet, now make it possible to commit a crime at any point on earth from anywhere in the world without ever physically entering the jurisdiction where the crime is committed. Thus, a hacking incident, financial fraud, or theft can take place entirely through the Internet without the suspect ever leaving his or her own home. This new development opens the door to tremendous transnational criminal opportunities. From a practical perspective, an investigator working in the 42nd Precinct in the Bronx are must not only consider potential suspects in the New York City but expand his net to include suspects in Tashkent, Tel Aviv, or Tokyo. In the past, police would often develop clues and leads about a perpetrator based upon physical evidence left at the crime scene. A diligent investigator could canvass the neighborhood to find out if anyone had observed the suspect in the area. In today's networked society, this is no longer true.

The physical distance between a criminal and his victim in the real world is lost in the cyberworld. No longer does a thief have to physically travel from Tashkent to Texas to commit a mere $500 burglary. Thus, conventional logistical and monetary impediments to burglary, namely the need for visas, passports, airplane trips, and border crossings, no longer apply. With fewer barriers today, both petty and organized criminals can target a whole new set of victims who had been previously unreachable. The trend will only accelerate, given the increasing scope of advancing technology. Just as corporations have benefited from the global economy, cybercriminals are poised to make a huge expansion in their business.

Since Sir Robert Peele established the world's first professional police force, London Metropolitan Police, in 1829, little had changed in the nature of the conventional crimes. A homicide committed in London during the time of Charles Dickens time is not very different from a homicide committed today. Guns, knives, explosives, and poison have changed little over time and, as a result, police officers and prosecutors have developed an arsenal of well tested tools and techniques to handle traditional crimes. Burglaries, homicides, auto thefts, and other "non-high-tech crimes" usually leave behind "real-world" tangible evidence, which helps police track down the suspects. Over the decades, experienced investigators have become adept at searching and locating physical clues including blood- and paper-trails. However, when it comes to hunting and tracking "data trails" in cybercrimes, the accumulated experience in law enforcement is little to nil.

The world has been accustomed to dealing with objects based on atoms. We can see, touch, and feel such objects, including a collection of Shakespeare's plays or an Elvis Presley music recording. In the middle of the twentieth century, something changed. With the advent of computer technology, electronic bits were born. As Nicholas Negroponte writes, "a bit has no color, size, or weight, and it can travel at the speed of light." It is the smallest atomic element in the world of information [6]. Despite the absence of physical properties, bits can represent atom-based objects or analog forms of information. Speech, text, music, photographs, video, books, and even money can all be represented in a digital format.

From a criminal's perspective, the new nature of the object of theft, namely, electrons, bits, and bytes, is perfectly suited for international theft and exploitation. It is an attractive option for criminals, worldwide. If one were to rob a bank or an armored car of $2 million dollars in cash, transportation and storage of the paper currency would pose a formidable challenge. The cash would weigh a thousand pounds and would be hard to physically carry away from the bank and even more difficult to hide under a mattress on in the backyard. In cyberspace, money has no physical weight. The theft, transportation, and storage of electron-based stolen money, or other goods for that matter, is easy. Also, there are no additional difficulties whether one steals $1 billion dollars versus $1,000, implying that the potential for loss of huge amounts of cash and other cyber goods is enormous.

Most of the restrictions placed by Sovereign governments around the world have instituted systems including immigration control, customs checks, and border patrol, to restrict the movement of criminals and contraband. Immigration departments carefully screen passports and visas, checking against watch lists and databases of suspect criminals developed by law enforcement worldwide. All of these are rendered totally irrelevant in cyberspace. Consider that for an Australian jewel thief to commit a crime in Canada, he would have to cross a Canadian border. However, if the same thief plans to defraud a hypothetical company, say, jewels.com.ca out of the diamonds sold online, physical travel would not be a necessity. A shipment of cocaine from Bogota to Miami might be intercepted though elaborate warning and intelligence systems developed by the US Customs. Child pornography sent through traditional mail from Amsterdam to Bern might be inspected by Swiss Customs. But who would be responsible for inspecting the "child pornography bytes" as they flow over the Internet from the Netherlands to Switzerland? While the local customs can intercept a million dollars in cash, carried from New York to the Cayman Islands, in a money laundering scheme, a criminal agent passing through any of the world's airports with a million dollars of "currency" on an electronic smart card would never be stopped. Few, if any, customs officials are tuned to the issues related to cyber-smuggling.

While criminals have been quick to adapt new technologies, law enforcement has moved relatively slowly. There are a number of reasons, the primary one being limited funding and competing priorities [7]. Moving even slowly is the pace of the law itself. While criminal conduct represents a fairly well defined body of substantive law in most jurisdictions around the world, the state of international law is much more in question.

17.4 The Networked World

As computers in different nations are increasingly being interconnected through telecommunications networks, it is influencing how we communicate, share information, conduct business, entertain, educate ourselves, and even commit crime. Today, information is widely distributed both within and without an organization. Outside the protected corporate intranet, information is downloaded by employees working at home and client sites and shared with joint venture partners. Clearly, hackers, competitors, and disgruntled employees may obtain access to this information and commit all kinds of mischief. They may steal confidential information, alter critical data, or even disable a company's vital networks. Ironically, the moment an individual or organization connects a computer system to the global information network, the company's front door is rendered wide open to criminals around the globe in the world of cyberspace.

For many multinational organizations, while the proprietary information may be centrally located on a single, well-protected computer server, the latter may, in turn, be connected to thousands of other computer systems spread across the globe. Each and every one of these attached computer systems is a vulnerability in that any individual who connects to a system via remote login may range from a legitimate user, student, business person, and computer enthusiast to a small time neighborhood thug, organized crime, saboteur, or even a foreign intelligence agent.

Today, computer systems and networks have established a new infrastructure. Not only has society come to critically depend on it, it has also become fundamental to our way of life. Publicly switched telephone systems, air traffic control, police, fire dispatch centers, electric grid, gas, water utility companies, banking, health care institutions, national defense, civilian aviation, and others all rely heavily on the new infrastructure. Even military data, trade secrets, and hospital patient records are increasingly being placed into computer networks, implying that their protection is vital. Yet, the task is exceptionally challenging.

17.5 The Love Bug and International Cybercrime: A Case Study

The brief and destructive role of the "Love Bug" virus and computer worm represents a unique case study of the legal challenges faced by police and prosecutors in their pursuit of cybercriminals. The virus was created and launched in the Philippines. it appeared in Hong Kong on 11 May 2000, rapidly spread around the world, and destroyed files and stole passwords [8, 9]. The claim that the damage was widespread is an understatement. Within hours, the computer worm had spread [10] to the offices of the German newspaper Abendblatt in Hamburg, where system administrators watched in horror as the virus deleted 2,000 digital photographs in their picture archive. In Belgium, ATMs were disabled, leaving citizens without cash. In Paris, France, cosmetics maker, L'Oreal, lost its e-mail servers, as did other businesses throughout the Europe. As much as 70% of the computers in Germany, the Netherlands, and Sweden were disabled. Ford, Siemens, Silicon Graphics and Fidelity Investments were all affected. Even Microsoft was so seriously affected that it decided to sever the outside e-mail links coming into its Redmond, Washington headquarters.

Governments were not immune to the virus. In London, the Parliament shut down its servers before the Love Bug's assault actually arrived. On Capitol Hill in Washington, D.C., crippled e-mail systems forced an atypical silence in the halls of Congress. In the US, the Love bug infected 80% of all federal agencies, including both the Defense and State departments, leaving them temporarily out of e-mail [10] contact with their international outposts. The virus corrupted no fewer than four classified, internal Defense Department e-mail systems. The virus affected NASA and the CIA [11], raced around the entire world in 2 h, three times faster than its Melissa predecessor [10]. The virus was estimated to have affected at least 45 million users in more than 20 countries [12], inflicting a damage between $2 and 10 billion [13]. As explained in Part III of the book, it is always difficult to precisely compute the harm inflicted by a cybercrime [14].

Virus experts traced the "Love Bug" to the Philippines. Using information supplied by an Internet Service Provider, agents from the Philippines' National Bureau of Investigation and the US FBI identified individuals suspected of creating and disseminating the "Love Bug." Then, they ran into wall with their investigation. The Philippines had no cybercrime laws, implying that creating and disseminating a virus was not a crime. Law enforcement encountered great difficulty convincing a magistrate to issue a warrant to search the suspects' apartment. Obtaining the warrant took several days, which allowed the suspect ample time to destroy key evidence [15]. When authorities finally executed the warrant and seized evidence, analysis revealed that Onel de Guzman, a former computer science student, was responsible for creating and disseminating the "Love Bug." The police seized telephones, wires, computer disks, and computer magazines from de Guzman's apartment [16, 17]. Philippine law neither criminalize hacking nor the distribution of viruses, so officials struggled with whether de Guzman could even be prosecuted. Law enforcement finally charged him with theft and credit card fraud, but the charges were dismissed as inapplicable and unfounded.

De Guzman could not even be extradited to other countries that have laws against cybercrimes, including the US, for prosecution. Extradition treaties explicitly require "double criminality," i.e., the act must be viewed as a crime by both the extraditing nation and the nation seeking extradition. The conduct attributed to de Guzman was a crime in the eyes of the US, not the Philippines. Despite billions of dollars of damage and hundreds of thousands of primary and secondary victims in dozens of countries, the responsible individual could not be brought to trial. No one has ever been prosecuted for the damages inflicted by the "Love Bug."

Law enforcement officials are paralyzed against cybercriminals unless nations institute laws to criminalize cybercrimes. Without such laws in every nation, given the international reach of cybercrimes today, prosecution of cybercrimes is impossible. On the surface, establishing laws against cybercrimes may appear simple and straightforward. In reality, it is far more difficulty, for three reasons. First, should the scope of the laws in any given nation be restricted to outlawing activities including hacking and virus dissemination or extend into crimes perpetrated against other individuals and their property, including cyberstalking and cyberterrorism? Second, should the laws be written very narrow and specific to cybercrimes? That is, given that fraud is already outlawed in a nation, should new laws be written to specifically criminalize computer-initiated fraud or fraud perpetrated on a computer? While the first and second reasons are intra-nation in nature, the third challenge focuses on the international element, namely, how a nation's laws against cybercrimes, or lack thereof, may impact on other countries. The Philippines' failure to enact cybercrime legislation was certainly inadvertent. Nonetheless, it implied that a citizen was able to inflict untold damage to other countries but without any consequences for his actions. Although the Philippines hurriedly adopted legislation outlawing certain types of cybercrimes, including the creation and dissemination of viruses [18, 19], such reactionary behavior must be superseded by a thoughtful and concerted effort, worldwide.

While Western governments are making steady progress to combat cybercrimes, in many nations, governments face far more serious and immediate problems and cybercrimes are the least of their concerns. Poverty, illiteracy, lack of health care, food, and water implies that cybercrimes cannot be but a low priority. The situation cannot continue forever and affluent governments, worldwide, must recognize the reality. In a networked world, one can no longer turn a blind eye to the lack of infrastructure in another nation. We are all tied together and an "us versus them," mentality is obsolete. The more modern and technologically advanced a nation, greater is its dependency on advanced critical information infrastructures and higher its consequent vulnerability to global cyberthreats. Though affluent governments can request, lecture, and beg developing nations to pay attention to cybercrimes, it is likely to be entirely useless. On occasions, well-resourced nations have used their national and international development programmes to try and make a difference on cybercrime issues in Africa, Latin America, and Asia. Unfortunately, few of these efforts have had any lasting impact. While a few police investigators may have been trained, often they have chosen to leave shortly thereafter to pursue more lucrative careers in the private sector. On other occasions, donated international computer equipment went missing or were sold by corrupt local officials. Clearly, in order to truly impact cybercrime in the developing world, a long-term, robust, and committed global strategy will be required.

It may be worthwhile to seek lessons from a previous effort to limit global money laundering activities. More than two decades ago, money-laundering havens were widespread. From the Cayman Islands to the Isle of Mann, bank secrecy provisions helped create offshore financial havens where drug dealers, smugglers, and deposed dictators could safely hide their stolen wealth and proceeds from illegal financial transactions. To combat the growing threat of the international money laundering organizations, the G-7 created the Financial Action Task Force (FATF) at the Economic Summit in 1989. The FATF, comprised of 26 countries, the European

Commission, and the Gulf Cooperation Council, is dedicated to promoting the development of effective anti-money laundering controls and enhanced cooperation in counter-money laundering efforts among its membership and around the world. The FATF had engaged in explaining the benefits of defeating money laundering to relevant entities, threatened sanctions, provided extensive training programs, and offered development aid. We propose that affluent nations engage with developing nations to ensure a minimum standard of cybercrime enforcement so as to protect the national security and information infrastructure of all nations. We also propose that appropriate legal and investigative structures be put in place now before the next generation of cybercriminals and cyberterrorists get the upper hand and begin to perpetrate even more disruptive and pernicious attacks upon society.

17.6 International Law and Cybercrime

As the present time, cybercrime is an ill-defined term and includes a wide range of criminal activities and issues. Unlike traditional crimes, including murder, rape, and robbery, whose definitions have been refined over the millennia, there are no universally accepted definitions of computer crime, high technology crime, and cyberfraud. Each of these terms have different meanings to criminal justice professionals around the world. Clearly, for a specific activity to be considered a crime, it must be proscribed in criminal statues and penal codes, i.e., a nation's legislative body, such as Congress in the US must specifically pass a law to render the activity illegal. Today, many sovereign nations lack specific prohibition for criminal acts involving a computer. The fine line between a criminal activity and anti-social behavior in the online world is not agreed upon universally.

To combat cybercrimes, nations must modernize both their substantive and procedural laws. As explained in detail in Part V, substantive laws specifically proscribe behaviors and address murder, rape, robbery, and hacking; while procedural laws refer to issues such as search and seizure, jurisdiction, extradition, data interception, and methods of international cooperation. Nations, worldwide, must not only create substantive laws to prohibit malicious acts in cyberspace, but specify the exact manner and methods through which law enforcement can cooperate, gather evidence, arrest, and pursue prosecution, nationally and internationally.

While a strong framework of cybercrime penal law is an absolute requirement for effective action against cybercriminals, equally important is updated procedural law, which will authorize the issuance of warrants to search and seize tangible evidence [20], including documents, books, papers, and other tangible objects. Since the prosecution of cybercrimes usually requires collecting and analyzing intangible evidence, the omission can be a serious problem for investigators [21]. Therefore, sovereign nations must evaluate their procedural laws governing evidence gathering and analysis and amend it, if and as necessary, so it does not suffer from the past limitations [22].

In the remainder of this section, we will focus on three key elements of international cybercrime laws, namely jurisdiction; potential challenges to extraditions stemming from conflicts between the laws of sovereign nations; and search and seizure of evidence.

17.6.1 Jurisdiction

Over the past several hundred years, since most crimes were committed by nationals belonging to a specific jurisdiction, there was little need for the law to consider the prosecution of foreign nationals and need for extradition. With the advent of ships, trains, automobiles, and airplanes, international travel increased dramatically and the law was confronted with criminals from one nation committing an offense and fleeing to a different nation, thereby raising new questions about national sovereignty and extradition. Thus, long before computers became an everyday fact of life, it was common for traditional criminal cases to raise issues of jurisdiction.

Historically, a majority of the difficult jurisdictional problems had stemmed from a conflict of laws between two or more countries, namely, where a specific activity is considered legal by one country but held illegal in another nation. A second source of jurisdictional problems arise when either an accused is located in a country X (say) but the victim resides in a different nation (say Y); or the accused and victim belong to the same jurisdiction but the criminal evidence is found abroad. Foe example, key questions may arise, does France have the right to request the return of a French citizen who had fled to Morocco; should the Moroccan government turn over the accused to the French government for a crime allegedly committed in France; or what steps may the French government undertake, other than declaring war, if Morocco were to fail to produce the accused?

The answers to many of the complex questions that arise are generally provided by diplomats, law enforcement officials and prosecutors who develop well-recognized methods for obtaining and providing legal assistance. The most logical approach to addressing the issues is through voluntary cooperation between the respective governments, i.e., where governments agree to assist one another in an international criminal investigation. When such cooperation is absent or not easily available, sovereign nations can seek the help of both Mutual Legal Assistance Treaties (MLATs), which are often negotiated on a country-by-country basis, and the Letters Rogatory process.

MLATs are bilateral treaties, negotiated between countries to create a formal mechanism for cooperation in matters of international crimes. MLATs contain outlines of procedures for formal communications between the "central authorities" of the respective nations and for gathering evidence in a foreign nation. MLAT's are used to facilitate the issuance of subpoenas, interviewing of witnesses, and for the search and seizure of evidence. The US is party to over 44 bilateral MLATs. In the US, requests for information pursuant to an MLAT are handled by the DoJ's

Office of International Affairs which forwards US requests to foreign governments and receives similar requests from foreign law enforcement authorities. Thus when a rape occurs in Paris and the suspect flees to Casablanca, there are formal mechanisms through which France may seek extradition of the suspect in Morocco. While these processes are time consuming and often contain limitations on the type of assistance that may be received, they represent a starting place for matters involving international crimes. In cybercrimes, time is of the greatest essence since computer logs, the key source of evidence, are often retained only for days and weeks, at most. A significant delay in cooperation, typical in the traditional approach to requesting international legal cooperation, is highly detrimental to a successful investigation and prosecution of a cybercrime.

Letters Rogatory provide a mechanism for nations to share and request criminal information in the absence of a MLAT. The Letters Rogatory process involves one country's judicial authority writing a formal request to the counterpart authority in a different country for legal assistance with a single specific criminal activity. In the US, the Letters Rogatory process is authorized under Title 28 USC, §1781-82. A major disadvantage of a Letters Rogatory is that the nation receiving the request is under no obligation to comply. The nation may choose to help out of comity and international goodwill but it is under no obligation. The process requires extensive coordination between the DoJ and State Department/Foreign Affairs Department and, as expected, it is more time consuming and less efficient than the MLAT. As with MLAT, the Letters Rogatory is of little value in cybercrimes.

For cybercrimes, especially where the Internet is involved, the need to extend the jurisdiction to more than one physical location is almost guaranteed. The investigation and prosecution of the crime must be carried out at multiple jurisdictions. Even in a relatively simple case, say, where two neighbors in a given Chicago neighborhood exchange child pornographic materials over America Online, the investigation will not only include Chicago, Illinois but extend into Virginia, where America Online's computer server is located through which the messages may have been routed. Key questions arise, namely, whether the crime scene is Chicago or Virginia or both and should the investigation be led by the Chicago Police Department or Loudin County Sheriff's Office? It is no surprise that an international cybercrime may become utterly confusing. Consider that a Latvian hacker, living in Germany, breaks into and hijacks a computer system in Buenos Aires and compels it to launch an attack on the student information service center at the University of Toronto. A judicious resolution of who among the law enforcement of Latvia, Germany, Argentina, and Canada will lead the investigation, collect evidence, initiate prosecution, and submit request for extradition is critical to the successful prosecution of the criminal. For further details, the reader is referred to a report from an extensive Internet jurisdiction project, conducted by the American Bar Association's Business Law Section's Cyberspace Committee and presented at the Annual meeting in London [23].

17.6.2 Extradition and Potential Conflict of Nations' Laws

Under extradition, one nation hands over an accused individual to stand trial for an offense in a different country. Extradition is generally governed by existing extradition treaties between the corresponding nations. Extraditable offenses tend to be serious in nature and often punishable by more than 1 year in prison. Many countries, as a matter of principle, will not extradite their own citizens, regardless of the treaties.

In principle, for one government to deliver an accused to another government for prosecution, "dual criminality" must exist. That is, the suspect's offense must be viewed illegal in both jurisdictions. Otherwise, extradition cannot be granted. This is logical. As an example, consider that in many regions of the world, where strict Islamic law or Sharia constitute their criminal code, women are required to dress modestly in public, including the covering up of their faces and heads. If a US actress from Hollywood were to unwittingly wear a short sleeve shirt while in transit in an Saudi Arabian airport and then return to Los Angeles, should the US agree to extradite her to Saudi Arabia to face a criminal charge, for which there is no equivalent offense in the US?

Conversely, if a US citizen were to speak out publicly in favor of Nazism, it would be protected under the US Constitution. In France and Germany, however, such behavior would be prohibited and is against their national law. If the German authorities were to request the FBI to arrest and extradite a US citizen for promoting Nazism, the FBI would be hard-pressed to cooperate. How can the US extradite an individual for an activity, which though criminalized by a law in Europe, is protected by the Constitution? The principle of dual-criminality is precisely focused on protecting the citizens of one nation against the laws of another. While the concepts of jurisdiction and extradition are hardly new, the proliferation of the Internet has brought these issues into new light.

In many regions of the world, including North America, Western Europe, Australia, there exists a substantial amount of substantive criminal law that allows for the investigation and prosecution of high-tech crime. In many regions of Asia, the penalties for cybercrimes are more stiff than in the US. However, there exists many nations in the world today where cybercrime regulation is totally missing. Only 60 nations of the United Nations have enacted some form of laws against cybercrimes. Clearly, extradition has become a real battleground.

17.6.3 Search and Seizure

In many nations around the world, individuals are guaranteed the right to privacy and freedom from unnecessary government intrusion in their lives, as stipulated in the respective Constitutions. The United Nations Declaration of Human rights and the US Constitution explicitly enumerate the rights of individuals toward these goals. Under the 4th Amendment of the US Constitution, the government is prohibited from engaging in any unreasonable search of an individual, his home, or place of business without proper cause and without an order issued by a court. Thus, in a traditional burglary investigation, police must generally obtain a court order and a warrant from a judge before entering and searching the home of a suspect for evidence of the crime, including the stolen goods or tools and implements used to commit the burglary.

Search and seizure issues in traditional crimes are complex and have always been the subject of much debate and legal wrangling in the courts. Questions are often raised as to what evidence should be admitted, what evidence suppressed, did the police act properly in obtaining the evidence, and was the proper court order obtained from the appropriate court? While these matters are already very complicated in the "real world," the level of complexity does not even begin to approach the multifarious nature of the issues involved in cyberspace. The combination of looking for evidence in the virtual world along with the international scope of these investigations implies a high degree of expertise necessary to ensure that any evidence obtained will be admissible in front of a competent judicial authority.

In the US, the DoJ has developed a guideline, several hundred pages long, addressing electronic search and seizure issues at the national level [24]. At the international level, the complexity can be overwhelming. Key questions and issues must be resolved. Representative questions may include the following. Can investigating authorities in a given country obtain data, as evidence, from abroad, through an interconnected computer system, directly? Can data be obtained from a publicly available source and used as evidence? Can data as evidence be obtained from private systems or data banks with the consent of third parties who have the right to access the data in the foreign country, without first seeking judicial authority or permission from the foreign country? How was the evidence from a foreign jurisdiction obtained? Can the French government seeking key information from an AOL computer server located in Virginia serve a subpoena to AOL France and compel them to produce the evidence? If the police in China had tortured a suspect until he provided his password, would such evidence be admissible under German law which clearly prohibits coercive behavior? The questions and issues raised are not hypothetical; they are the emblematic of the conundrums faced on a daily basis by the international cybercrime investigators.

Given the extreme limitations associated with the formal channels of international cooperation, particularly timeliness, investigators may be tempted to conduct a transborder electronic search of a networked computer physically located in a foreign jurisdiction, without first waiting for permission and formal assistance from the corresponding law enforcement authorities.

Unilateral cross-border searches in cyberspace are unauthorized and controversial at the least. They represent potential violations of sovereignty of the corresponding nation. Critics warn that unilateral cross-border searches are likely to set a dangerous precedence in that they will encourage other countries with significantly different laws and interests to search computers belonging to a bordering nation, without prior authorization. It is unclear what type of conflict such perpetrations would trigger. Consider as an example that China was searching criminal information on an individual, discovered it on a computer server physically located in Japan, and downloaded the evidence over the Internet, without appropriate permission from the judicial authority in Japan. A question will arise immediately, has China violated the sovereignty of Japan? Clearly, if such an act of perpetration were carried out in the real world, namely China determines that a Japanese citizen holds key evidence in a criminal matter, sends one of their policeman to Tokyo to abduct the individual, and bring him back to China, it would most likely trigger a declaration of war by Japan.

In a widely publicized case, law enforcement of a specific country had carried out a search of foreign computers without first seeking approval through the usual mutual assistance channels. The case was tried in the courts in multiple states of the US. It involved the FBI carrying out a search of a Russian national's computer, physically located in Russia. The FBI was seeking evidence in a string of hacking and extortion cases against US companies. Fearing that the evidence may be destroyed by the suspect's associates in Russia, the FBI lured the suspect to the US and used a keystroke logger to capture his password while he accessed his own computer in Russia. The FBI then used the stolen password to access the Russian computer, downloaded the data, and then asked a US court to issue a warrant authorizing a search and seizure. In at least two of the trials in two different states, the accused had moved to suppress the evidence. He had argued, among other things, that the unilateral search had violated the search and seizure law both in Russia and the US. Both courts denied the motion, one of which explained that (1) the FBI investigators were not bound by Russian search and seizure law and that (2) the protection against unreasonable search and seizure in the US Constitution does not apply to searches and seizures of non-US persons conducted outside the US. The case remains controversial to say the least. In response to the FBI's actions, the Russian Federal Security Service initiated criminal proceedings against FBI Agent Michael Schuler, charging him with illegally obtaining evidence in Russia and for unauthorized access to a Russian computer system [25]. Ironically, while law enforcement in the US and Russia are engaged in a bitter fight against each other, cybercriminals can walk away from prosecution. The incident demonstrates the many unresolved issues relative to international cybercrime investigations [26] and appears to confirm that the preferred route is to seek legal assistance from foreign law enforcement through the appropriate channels.

17.7 International Efforts to Combat Cybercrime

The greatest challenge to tracking an international cybercrime in progress and subsequent investigation and prosecution, is the extreme narrow time window within which the investigation must commence. Once an effort to trace a suspect IP packet reveals that the key evidence is held by an ISP in Buenos Aires, Argentina, what steps may an investigator in the US initiate to obtain an immediate snapshot of the information flow and later obtain it for prosecution. Other challenges include

(1) where does a local investigator turn to when he or she realizes that the suspect is inconveniently located in Kazakhstan? or (2) how does an investigator in Atlanta, US get the police in Sydney, Australia, interested in pursuing a cybercrime case. Clearly, there is no single, "one size fits all" approach to address every cybercrime situation. Each case will require unique tools and distinct set of contacts for successful prosecution.

Fortunately, the past two decades had witnessed a number of positive developments. Many nations have begun prohibiting unlawful access to computer systems in the 1980s and early 1990s. The national efforts were further strengthened by several international organizations including the Organization for Economic Cooperation and Development (OECD), Council of Europe (COE), G-8, European Union, United Nations [27], and the Interpol, which recognized the inherent crossborder reaches of cybercrime, the limitations of unilateral approaches, and the need for international harmony in legal, technical, and other areas.

17.7.1 The Organization for Economic Cooperation and Development (OECD)

With the headquarters located in Paris, France, the OECD [28] includes more than 30 member countries, which share a commitment to democratic government and the market economy. OECD member countries come together to discuss, develop, and refine economic and social policies. Members compare their experiences, seek answers to common problems, and coordinate domestic and international policies as they increasingly become necessary in the globalized world.

The OECD was the first organization to launch a comprehensive inquiry into the problems of criminal law as applied to cybercrimes in the international scene. In 1983, a group of experts recommended that the OECD undertake an initiative to harmonize the European computer crime legislation [29, 30]. The problem was studied between 1983 and 1985 and produced a report in 1986 titled, "Computer-related Crime: Analysis of Legal Policy." The report surveyed existing laws and reform proposals, compared substantive laws around the world, and recommended that countries consider prohibiting and penalizing a minimal list of serious abuses [31]. The reported list includes:

1. The input, alteration, erasure and/or suppression of computer data and/or computer programs made willfully with the intent to commit an illegal transfer of funds or of another thing of value
2. The input, alteration, erasure and/or suppression of computer data and/or computer programs made willfully with the intent to commit a forgery
3. The input, alteration, erasure and/or suppression of computer data and/or computer programs, or other interference with computer systems, made willfully with the intent to hinder the functioning of a computer and/or of a telecommunication system

4. The infringement of the exclusive right of the owner of a protected computer program with the intent to exploit commercially the program and put it on the market
5. The access to or the interception of a computer and/or telecommunication system made knowingly and without the authorization of the person responsible for the system, either by infringement of security measures or for other dishonest or harmful intentions [32]

The OECD report is significant from two perspectives. First, it outlined a minimal set of computer and network abuses that can potentially harm all nations. Second, the OECD recommendations, known as "soft law," is a set of non-binding instruments, which gives nations time to reflect and adopt good policies on their own accord. Attempts to impose rules on sovereign nations are generally met with resentment and reactions.

17.7.2 The United Nations

In 1948, the UN established its first office to fight international crime. Today, the UN is well positioned to play the role of an impartial organization, where all nations can work cooperatively to address increasingly important international problems including those posed by organized crime.

Building on OECD's report, the UN convened the Eighth United Nations Congress on the Prevention of Crime and the Treatment of Offenders in 1990 to address the international legal challenges posed by cybercrime. The Congress generated a resolution calling for all Member States to intensify their efforts to combat cybercrime by modernizing their national criminal laws and procedures and bring it on par with the high tech crimes, creating new laws and procedures where necessary, improving computer security and prevention measures, and promoting the development of a comprehensive international framework of guidelines and standards for preventing, prosecuting, and punishing computer-related crime in the future [33,34]. The resolution also called for forfeiture or restitution of illegally acquired assets resulting from the commission of computer-related crimes.

In 1995, the UN published the Manual on the Prevention and Control of Computer-Related Crime [35], which examined the phenomenon of computer crime, substantive criminal law protecting the holder of data and information, substantive criminal law protecting privacy, procedural law, crime prevention in the computer environment, and the need and avenues for international cooperation. In the manual, the United Nations recognized [36],

"The international element in the commission of computer crime creates new problems and challenges for the law. Systems may be accessed in one country, the data manipulated in another and the consequences felt in a third country. Hackers can physically operate in one country, move electronically across the world from one network to another and easily access databases on a different continent. The result of this ability is that different sovereignties, jurisdictions, laws and rules will come into play. More than in any other transnational crime, the speed, mobility, flexibility, significance and value of electronic transactions profoundly challenge the existing rules of international crime law."

The UN manual not only addresses the global threat posed by cybercrime but all crimes that easily cross national boundaries. Recognizing that organized crime had become too widespread for any single nation to combat on its own, UN member nations joined forces to propose the UN Convention Against Transnational Organized Crime [37]. The Convention establishes a common framework for harmonizing different legal systems that exist in each country, and highlights the importance of a unified, legally-binding instrument to overcome problems traditionally encountered in international cooperation and mutual assistance situations.

The UN has undertaken two additional initiatives to combat transnational cybercrimes. First, in April of 2000, the UN dedicated an entire division of their 10th UN Congress on the Prevention of Crime and the Treatment of Offenders, held in Vienna, Austria, to crime prevention and crimes related to the computer network. A technical workshop held during the Congress addressed topics in computer crime and a number of recommendations were put forth for further consideration by the UN. Second, in 2000, the UN Asia and Far East Institute for the Prevention of Crime and the Treatment of Offenders (UNAFEI), surveyed 185 UN members and queried whether they have "amended their substantive criminal law in order to make it apply to all kind of noxious or otherwise illicit behavior that can be committed by means of, through or against computer systems and networks" [38]. The survey questionnaire sought information on a number of different categories of cybercrime. Only 37 nations responded, indicating that many nations, worldwide, do not consider the topic important. The survey also highlighted the differences between different nations' approach to high tech crime. In most countries, child pornography is not very precisely defined in criminal law [15]. Countries differed in the way their criminal law defined a "child." In Germany a child is a person "under the age of 14 years," while in Norway a child is anyone under the age of 16, and in Sri Lanka, a child is anyone under the age of 18 [13]. The laws in Finland, France and Iceland, do not define a child by physical age for the purpose of applying laws criminalizing child pornography [13]. Clearly, the differing definitions of a child across nations will inevitably frustrate investigators pursuing international child pornography cybercrimes. As expected, UN tends to move forward very, very slowly. Often, international treaties can take decades to create and ratify. Nonetheless, UN's work in combating international cybercrimes is critical to the long term health of the civilization.

17.7.3 The Group of 8 (G-8)

The Group of 8 (G-8) was formed at an economic summit in France in 1975 and comprises of the eight leading industrialized countries including the United Kingdom, Canada, France, Germany, Italy, Japan, Russia, and the United States. At the annual summit in 1996 in France, the Heads of State adopted a number of recommendations targeting international crime, including electronic crime. Subsequently, a G-8 Subgroup on High-Tech Crime was established in January 1997. Since its creation, the Subgroup (WGUCI 2000) has carried out the following activities:

- Established a 24 h/7 day a week network of international contacts within the G-8 and other interested countries for high-tech crime emergencies
- Hosted an international computer crime conference in 1998 for law enforcement personnel of the G-8
- Reviewed G-8 legal systems relative to high-tech crime, including efforts to bridge a number of the gaps
- Worked on enhancing G-8's abilities to locate and identify criminals who use networked communications

In 1997, the Justice and Interior Ministers of the G-8 met in Washington and adopted ten principles to combat High-Tech Crime:

1. There must be no safe havens for those who abuse information technologies
2. Investigation and prosecution of international high-tech crimes must be coordinated among all concerned States, regardless of where harm has occurred
3. Law enforcement personnel must be trained and equipped to address high-tech crimes
4. Legal systems must protect the confidentiality, integrity, and availability of data and systems from unauthorized impairment and ensure that serious abuse is penalized
5. Legal systems should permit the preservation of and quick access to electronic data, which are often critical to the successful investigation of crime
6. Mutual assistance regimes must ensure the timely gathering and exchange of evidence in cases involving international high-tech crime
7. Transborder electronic access by law enforcement to publicly available (open source) information does not require authorization from the State where the data resides
8. Forensic standards for retrieving and authenticating electronic data for use in criminal investigations and prosecutions must be developed and employed
9. To the extent practicable, information and telecommunications systems should be designed to help prevent and detect network abuse, and should also facilitate the tracing of criminals and the collection of evidence
10. Work in this area should be coordinated with the work of other relevant international fora to ensure against duplication of efforts [39]

The Justice and Interior Ministers also adopted an action plan, where they to Combat pledged to "review our legal systems to ensure that they appropriately criminalize abuses of telecommunications and computer systems and promote the investigation of high-tech crimes" [40].

In May 2000, the G-8 held a cybercrime conference to discuss "how to jointly crack down on cybercrime" [41]. The conference, which brought together nearly 300 judges, police officials, diplomats and business leaders from the G-8 nations, drafted an agenda for a follow-up summit to be held in July 2000 [42]. At the summit, the G-8 issued a communiqué which declared that it would "take a concerted approach to high-tech crime, such as cyber-crime, which could seriously threaten security and confidence in the global information society. The G-8 efforts are ongoing and they have created useful tools for investigators and prosecutors working on global high technology crime matters. Specifically, the G-8's points-of-contact network, working 24/7, allows members from the G-8 and other nations to get in touch with experienced cybercrime investigators in different countries on an immediate basis under emergency situations. To date, nearly 30 nations have participated in the G-8's points-of-contact network. While the G-8's efforts are commendable, the benefits are limited to a handful of nations and fails to reach the large majority of the countries in the world.

17.7.4 The Council of Europe

The Council of Europe (COE) is an international organization established following WW II by a few of the Western European countries. Located in Strasbourg, France, COE features a pan-European membership of 41 countries, including the Baltic states, Russia, and Turkey. Its primary mission is to strengthen democracy, respect for human rights, and the rule of law throughout its member states. The COE has approved two recommendations, the first in 1989 and then in 1995, encouraging individual governments to modernize their laws to meet the challenges of cybercrimes.

From 1985 to 1989, the Select Committee of Experts on Computer-Related Crime of the COE debated cybercrime related issues and drafted Recommendation 89(9), which was adopted on 13 September 1989 [43]. The 1989 recommendation emphasized the importance of quick and adequate response to the newly emerging challenges of cybercrime and noted that the crimes are transborder in nature, requiring harmonization of the laws and their practice and improved international legal cooperation. It further emphasized the need for international consensus in criminalizing specific computer-related offenses. In the guidelines for the national legislatures to review and enhance their laws, the recommendation specified (1) a "minimum list" of cybercrime offenses that must be prohibited and prosecuted by international consensus and (2) an "optional list" that enumerates prominent offenses on which international consensus would be difficult to reach. The "minimum list" included computer fraud, computer forgery, damage to computer data, computer sabotage, unauthorized access, unauthorized interception, and unauthorized reproduction of a protected computer program or topography.

In 1995, the COE adopted its second cybercrime related Recommendation No. R (95)13 from the Committee of Ministers and delivered it to the member states. The COE report presented detailed principles that should guide the member states and their investigating authorities in the field of information technology. The principles addressed the topics of search and seizure, technical surveillance, obligations to co-operate with the investigating authorities, electronic evidence, use of encryption, research, statistics and training, and international cooperation. The COE document addresses investigations of both cybercrimes and traditional crimes where evidence may be found or transmitted in electronic form. The 1989 report had focused primarily on substantive law, while the 1995 document concentrated on legal procedural issues.

In 1997, the COE's European Committee on Crime Problems (CDPC) created a new Committee of Experts on Crime in Cyberspace (PC-CY) [44]. The PC-CY Committee was asked to examine "in light of Recommendations No R (89) 9 and No R (95) 13" the problems "of criminal law connected with information technology," including, inter alia, "cyberspace offenses and other substantive criminal law issues where a common approach may be necessary for the purposes of international cooperation." The PC-CY Committee was also assigned the task of drafting "a binding legal instrument" to deal with these issues [45].

Building on the Recommendations No R (89) 9 and No R (95) 13, and the PC-CY committee's work, the COE took one of the most significant steps forward in the fight against global cybercrimes. In November 2001, the COE's 43 member states and "partner countries," namely, Canada, Japan, South Africa, and the United States, completed the first ever binding, multilateral treaty on cybercrime at a convention ceremony held in Budapest, Hungary [46, 47]. The preparation leading up to the convention was a long and hard process; it took 27 drafts over 4 years before the final version, dated 25 May 2001, was submitted to the European CDPC [48]. The treaty was signed by 31 member countries, plus the four partner countries on April 2002 [49]. The primary goal of the treaty, noted in the Preamble, was to "pursue, as a matter of priority, a common criminal policy aimed at the protection of society against cybercrime, inter alia by adopting appropriate legislation and fostering international cooperation." The treaty was organized into three sections, namely, substantive law, procedural powers, and international cooperation. These sections were aimed at:

- Harmonize substantive criminal law by setting out the elements of various computer crimes and computer-related offenses
- Assist law enforcement agencies in the investigation of cybercrime cases and cases involving electronic evidence
- Establish a rapid and effective system for international cooperation in relation to such cases

17.7.5 Other Fora and Interpol

While the COE's treaty on cybercrime has had the greatest number of participants, a number of regional cooperative organizations have been studying international issues relative to cybercrime, including the European Union, Organization of

American States, Commonwealth Secretariat, Gulf Cooperation Council, and the Asia-Pacific Economic Cooperation Forum. These fora have provided guidance in understanding the problems, yet much work remains to be done especially with respect to developing nations.

Since 1990, the International Criminal Police Organization (Interpol) has been very active in cybercrime. Founded in 1926, Interpol serves law enforcement organizations by sharing intelligence and providing investigative support across national boundaries. According to its mission statement, the organization "exists to help create a safer world ... to provide a unique range of essential services for the law enforcement community to optimize the international effort to combat crime." The Interpol Secretariat and its headquarters are currently located in Lyon, France, and features more than 178 participating members [50].

In 1990, Interpol created its first working group on cybercrime matters, the European Working Party of Information Technology Crime. In 1995, Interpol held its First International Conference on Computer Crime [50], confirming law enforcement's serious concern with cybercrimes. At the conference, participants were especially concerned with the lack of a worldwide mechanism to address the crimes effectively and efficiently. Interpol's approach has been to harness the expertise of its members in the field of Information Technology Crime (ITC) through the vehicle of a 'working party,' consisting of the Heads or experienced members of the national computer crime units. The working parties reflect regional expertise and are located in Europe, Asia, the Americas, and in Africa.

Within each of Interpol's member nations, a National Central Bureau (NCB) is responsible for passing along requests for assistance to the corresponding government. In the US, the NCB is located in Washington, D.C., and is coordinated by the DoJ. Law enforcement personnel in the US can contact the NCB to have their requests officially transmitted to Interpol headquarters in Lyon, France. The Interpol Secretariat General would then route the request to the appropriate law enforcement in the foreign country. The system has worked fairly well for many years. However, it has been criticized for being slow and cumbersome. Given the global focus of the organization, budget constraints, and constantly evolving technologies, Interpol has been slow to keep pace with the world of high technology crime.

A number of national law enforcement organizations have also stepped in to ensure that their national police interests have strong representation in foreign countries. The FBI has established a Legal Attaché program (LEGAT), wherein it posts FBI agents at United States embassies abroad to interact with the local law enforcement. The Australian Federal Police, German Bundeskriminalamt (BKA), and the Royal Canadian Mounted Police, and others have similar programs. While these efforts have proven very successful in general criminal matters, most international law enforcement delegates have little to no particular expertise in high technology cybercrimes. Nonetheless, they serve as and important point of contact for global cybercrime investigations.

17.8 The Importance of Building International Consensus on Cybercrimes

The disparate legal approaches across nations, coupled with the radically different nature of cyberspace relative to normal jurisprudence can lead to widespread confusion and frustration among people and businesses. An average citizen abiding by the laws of his or her own country may abruptly find themselves subject to prosecution in a different country, where the laws are different [51]. The conflict in the laws can lead to most peculiar situations. Consider, for example, that CompuServe in France decides to take down a Nazi web site in the US cyberspace because of its offensive content, not for any violation of CompuServe's terms of service. CompuServe officials may abruptly find themselves sued in the US for violating the site operators' First Amendment rights. In contrast, if CompuServe in the US were to fail to take down a similar Nazi web site in the French cyberspace, assuming no violation of the terms of service, CompuServe officials may be sued in France for violating the French national laws. Cybercriminals can take advantage of this confusion by hopping around the world, exploiting gaps in criminal laws, and committing offenses with little fear of being detected and prosecuted by authorities.

The networked and interconnected nature of cyberspace coupled with the emergence of cybercrime and the enactment of new laws make it imperative to achieve consistency in international criminal prohibitions. The simplest solution would consist in creating a single code of law governing cybercrimes, valid throughout the world, regardless of the laws of individual nations [52]. The solution is not viable at the present time. No nation is inclined to surrender their own laws in favor of international cybercrime laws.

The alternative is to create a framework, consisting of a set of principles, that each country can utilize to analyze their existing laws for traditional offenses [53] and amend them to meet the challenges of cybercrimes. The idea is one of defining consensus cybercrime offenses, which, as we had explained earlier, had been the cornerstone of the COE's treaty. The notion of consensus cybercrime offenses may appear oxymoron in that nations fundamentally differ in what they define as intolerable conduct, which demands society's harshest sanctions. On the contrary, there is a great deal of consistency, across geography and time, in how countries delineate behaviors that are outlawed [54]. The consistency is founded on the function of criminal law, which must maintain an acceptable level of order within any society [55]. Social order is synonymous to maintaining integrity of key vital interests, including the safety of the individual; security of property; stability of the government; and the sanctity of specific moral principles.

The ease with which we can converge on a consensus will depend on whether we can draw accurate analogy between traditional and cybercrimes. Human civilization has had familiarity with conventional crimes for millennia. Thus, it would be much easier to devise consensus cybercrimes that deal with malum in se offenses, including burglary, larceny, and property damage than with offenses such as pornography and gambling because the definitions of the former will be far more consistent across national boundaries than the latter. Building on existing legal concepts renders the process far more efficient and effective; attempting to enact new laws from scratch is a very time consuming and inefficient, especially since the technology and the corresponding threat is rapidly evolving. Although we have made good progress in protecting us against cybercrimes than three decades ago, we have far to go, especially with developing nations. Until and unless every country prohibits the consensus cybercrime offenses, let alone develop an internal capacity to investigate and respond technologically, all other nations will be at risk.

While formal channels for information exchange exist, they can be very slow to respond. We had already seen that time is of essence in cybercrimes, given that evidence is highly perishable and dependent on short-lived computer logs. Cybercrimes can occur in a fraction of a second. In contrast, extradition, evidence preservation orders, and mutual legal assistance treaties can take lot longer. At the present time, a complete global directory of cybercrime points of contact around the world is utterly lacking. Given that the majority of countries around the world have no cybercrime legislation, bringing cyber criminals to justice can be excruciatingly difficult. Though technologically advanced countries are more vulnerable to cybercrimes than others, in the end, the entire world suffers. A concerted effort is urgently needed through which financial, legal, linguistic, and public policy issues associated with global cybercrime investigations must be overcome in order that law enforcement organizations can continue to protect the public from serious and emerging criminal threats.

17.9 Conclusion

Any nation that is connected to the Internet today may incur the wrath or greed of a cybercriminal anywhere in the world. Unless steps are taken now to ensure that all governments around the world have a modicum of capacity to respond cyberthreats, all nations will suffer. Just as money laundering havens had developed in the previous century, so too may "data havens," where cybercriminals will launch their attacks with virtual impunity. One might ask, how would a rogue nation become a haven for cybercrimes. The answer is twofold, namely, either by design or default. Many of the former Soviet republics are already de facto havens, not de jure [56], stemming from the absence of penal law to prosecute cybercrimes; lack of cybercrime investigative expertise, technical knowledge, and forensics [57]; and reluctance to assist law enforcement officials seek and apprehend cybercriminals operating within their borders. In one instance, Russian authorities repeatedly ignored FBI requests for assistance in apprehending Russian hackers who were breaking into the computers and networks of US companies in an extortion scam [56]. Should a rogue nation intend to serve as a cybercrime haven, it may adopt any number of approaches. First, it may simply refuse to participate in any extradition treaties involving cybercrimes. Second, it might direct its law enforcement officials not to cooperate with officials from other countries seeking evidence of cybercrimes against their own citizens. Third, it might frustrate the application of extradition treaties by refusing to outlaw select or all cybercrime offenses [56]. While an extradition haven would certainly outlaw hacking, cyber-theft and cyber-extortion to protect its own citizens from the depredations of cybercriminals, it might craft these prohibitions so that they did not encompass acts committed within the haven territory but that were directed at citizens of other nations. Fourth, with a little imagination, a rogue nation may establish a mechanism, wherein cybercriminals can vector their criminal activities through their country in such a way that the offenses are untraceable, regardless of the physical location of the criminal. In essence, the offenses will become invisible and law enforcement officials elsewhere would run into dead ends. In a practical sense, this is equivalent to non-extradition of the native offenders as well as foreign criminals. This technique is already in use today in that many nations forbid their ISPs to maintain activity logs.

Although the idea of "data havens" may sound a bit far-fetched, it is already emerging in a disguised form. Realizing the strong human desire to gamble and that gambling is outlawed in most countries [58], a small group of nations are actively seeking online gambling server farms to physically locate their equipment and operations within their borders. To outrun the competition, often this group of nations will lower the taxes assessed on the casino profits [59]. They view online casinos as an excellent source of revenue which, as one source noted, represent "earnings which are dollar-based and generated from outside the economy and jurisdiction" which hosts the casino [60]. They charge exorbitant licensing and application fees to approve online casinos, far exceeding those assessed for other commercial activities [61]. Similar to the high-seas pirates of the eighteenth century and the American copyright pirates of the nineteenth century, nations that host online casinos in the twenty-first century are eager to reap economic benefit by letting casinos prey on the citizens of other nations, where gambling may have already been outlawed.

In cyberspace, a haven no longer has to be associated with a conventional country or even physical land; it may be "virtual country," similar to The Dominion of Melcheznik that had already been created. A ship on the high seas or a platform built 500 miles off the coast of Australia can easily support a server farm that evades current legal regimes and host cybercrime activities in international waters. The haven might even be an aircraft or drone flying over international waters, carrying out processing and networking while airborne and erasing all hard drives before landing, thereby rendering any forensics recovery impossible.

Cybercrime confronts the world with a problem that no nation has had to address in the past, namely, the permeability of all national borders. In the past, crime had been a "real world" phenomenon which required the commission of an overt act or omission. By definition, it had a limited geographical reach and idiosyncratic criminal laws were sufficient to protect a nation's citizens from harm. Cybercrimes have negated the simplicity. The growth of the Internet serves to favor the cybercriminals. As more and more of the earth's six billion people get connected to the Internet from all corners of the world [62] and their information becomes available online, the frequency and impact of cybercrimes will increase. In a networked world, no island is an island anymore.

It must be pointed out that, through a variety of sources, we now know that many terrorist organizations, including al Qaeda, have been using the Internet to coordinate, plan, and perpetrate attacks against the world. The attacks of 11 September 2001 have been a wake-up call for many who had associated hackers and child pornographers with cybercrimes. Increasingly, international criminal organizations are migrating many of their criminal enterprises online and incorporating technology into their operations. When Wall Street Journal reporter, Daniel Pearl, was kidnapped by Pakistani radicals, the first indication of the kidnap arrived via e-mail in the form of a ransom note.

No matter how challenging and complex, cybercrimes are not beyond the reaches of society. Cyberspace is neither the first nor the only policy domain which lies beyond the control of a single nation. International air traffic control, the law of the sea, and militarization of space have required concerted international cooperation and agreement. We will point out, however, that the time to prepare for the impact of global high technology crime is not when terrorists threaten to kill hostages under a 24-h deadline. The world must work proactively now to prevent future crimes and protect the global population from this new menace of the twenty-first century.

References

[1] Cyber Crime ... and Punishment? Archaic Laws threaten global information. In *McConnell International*. Retrieved from http://www.mcconnellinternational.com/services/cybercrime.htm

[2] Columbia Encyclopedia (7th ed.). Retrieved from http://www.encyclopedia.com/html/A/Africa.asp

[3] United Nations Educational, Scientific and Cultural Organization. Retrieved from http://www.unesco.org/webworld/news/2001/010706_ecosoc.shtml

[4] United Nations Food and Agricultural Organization. *The State of Food and Agriculture 2001*. Retrieved from http://www.fao.org/DOCREP/003/X9800E/x9800e07.htm#P3_00

[5] Glasser, J. (2000, February 7). The software sopranos: Organized crime targets the booming high tech black market. *US News & World Reports*.

[6] Negroponte, N. (1995). *Being digital*.

[7] Goodman, M. D. (1997). Why the police don't care about computer crime. *10 Harvard Journal Law & Technology, 465*, 468–469. Retrieved from http://jolt.law.harvard.edu/articles/10hjolt465.html

[8] Students Named in Love Bug Probe. In *APBNEWS.COM*. Retrieved May 20, 2000, from http://www.apbnews.com/newscenter/internetcrime/2000/05/10/lovebug0510_01.html

[9] Thomas, R. (2000, May 12). *Love bug virus is no herbie*. Retrieved from http://www.thepbj.com/051200/a19.htm

[10] Grossman, L. (2000, May 15). Attack of the Love Bug. *Time Europe*. Retrieved from http://www.time.com/time/europe/magazine/2000/0515/cover.html

[11] Experts Call for 'Anti Love-Bug' Computer Czar. In *APBNEWS.COM*. Retrieved May 11, 2000, from http://www.apbnews.com/newscenter/internetcrime/2000/05/11/lovebug_congress0511_01.html

[12] Philippine Investigators Detain Man in Search for 'Love Bug' Creator. In *CNN.COM*. Retrieved May 8, 2000, from http://www.cnn.com/2000/TECH/computing/05/08/ilove.you.02/

[13] Clark, M. (2000, May 13). Love bytes. In *PC Review*. Retrieved from http://www.mg.co.za/pc/2000/05/13may-lovebug01.htm
[14] Menzies, C. (2000, June 20). Love bug was just first bite by a very dangerous virus. *Financial Review*. Retrieved from http://afr.com/reports/20000620/A19850-2000Jun19.html
[15] Philippines' Laws Complicate Virus Case. (2000, June 7). *USA Today*.
[16] Waiting for 'Love' Suspect. In *ABCNEWS.com*. Retrieved May 8, 2000, from http://204.202.137.113/sections/tech/DailyNews/virus_000508.html
[17] Suspect Charged in Love Bug Case. In *WIRED NEWS*. Retrieved June 29, 2000, from http://www.wired.com/news/lovebug/0,1768,37322,00.html
[18] 'Love bug' Prompts New Philippine Law. *USA Today*. Retrieved June 14, 2000, from http://www.usatoday.com/life/cyber/tech/cti095.htm
[19] Republic of the Philippines. (2000, June 14). Eleventh Congress – Second Regular Session, Republic Act No. 8792. Part V §33.
[20] D.C. Super. CT. Rules Crim. Pro. 41(h).
[21] Council of Europe. (2001, February 14). Draft explanatory memorandum to the draft convention on cyber-crime 171.
[22] Model Code of Cybercrime Investigative Procedure, Article VII. Retrieved from http://www.cybercrimes.net/MCCIP/art7.htm
[23] American Bar Association's Business Law Section's Cyberspace Committee. Retrieved 2000, from http://www.abanet.org/buslaw/cyber/initiatives/jurisdiction.html
[24] US DoJ. *Federal guidelines for searching and seizing computers*. Retrieved from http://www.cybercrime.gov
[25] Russians Accuse FBI Agent of Hacking. Retrieved August 16, 2002, from http://www.theregister.co.uk/content/55/26715.html
[26] Lemos, R. (2001, May 1). *FBI 'hack' raises global security concerns*. Retrieved from http://news.cnet.com/news/0-1003-200-5785729.html?tag=prntfr
[27] United Nations. (1994). International review of criminal policy: United Nations manual on the prevention and control of computer-related crime. *CNET.com*.
[28] Retrieved from http://www.oecd.org/about/general/index.htm
[29] Schjolberg, S. *The legal framework – Unauthorized access to computer systems §I*. Retrieved from http://www.mossbyrett.of.no/info/legal.html#foot
[30] Sieber, U. (1998). *Legal aspects of computer-related crime in the information society* (pp. 20–21). Retrieved from http://europa.eu.int/ISPO/legal/en/comcrime/sieber.doc
[31] United Nations. (1995). *United Nations manual on the prevention and control of computer-related crime §II(C)(2) – ¶117*. Retrieved from http://www.uncjin.org/Documents/EighthCongress.html
[32] United Nations. (1995). *United Nations manual on the prevention and control of computer-related crime §II(C)(2) – ¶118*. Retrieved from http://www.uncjin.org/Documents/EighthCongress.html
[33] Sieber, U. (1998). *Legal aspects of computer-related crime in the information society* (pp. 164–165). Retrieved from http://europa.eu.int/ISPO/legal/en/comcrime/sieber.doc
[34] Eighth U.N. Congress on the Prevention of Crime and the Treatment of Offenders. (1990, September 4). Doc. A/CONF. 144/L. 11, Section 2.
[35] United Nations. (1995). *United Nations manual on the prevention and control of computer-related crime*. Retrieved from http://www.uncjin.org/Documents/EighthCongress.html
[36] United Nations. (1999). *International review of criminal policy – United Nations manual on the prevention and control of computer-related crime*. Retrieved from http://www.ifs.univie.ac.at/~pr2gq1/rev4344.html
[37] United Nations. *United Nations convention against transnational organized crime*. Retrieved from http://srch1.un.org/plweb-cgi/fastweb?state_id=1026942645&view=unsearch&docrank=12&numhitsfound=509&query=Convention%20Against%20Transnational%20Organized%20Crime&&docid=2368&docdb=pr2000&dbname=web&sorting=BYRELEVANCE&operator=and&TemplateName=predoc.tmpl&setCookie=1

[38] United Nations. (2000, April 4). *UNAFEI report, overview of the criminal legislation addressing the phenomenon of computer-related crime in the United Nations member states*. Retrieved from http://www.rechten.vu.nl/~lodder/papers/unafei.html
[39] Meeting of the Justice and Interior Ministers of The Eight, Communique Annex, Washington, D.C. Retrieved December 9–10, 1997, from http://www.cybercrime.gov/principles.htm
[40] Meeting of the Justice and Interior Ministers of The Eight, Communique Annex, Washington, D.C. Action Plan to Combat High-Tech Crime, Item #3. Retrieved December 9–10, 1997, from http://www.cybercrime.gov/action.htm
[41] Group of Eight Meets to Discuss International Cooperation on Cybercrime. In *Adlaw by request*. Retrieved May 22, 2000, from http://adlawbyrequest.com/international/G8Cybercrime.shtml
[42] Blueprint to Fight Cybercrime. Retrieved May 15, 2000, from http://www.wired.com/news/print/0,1294,36332,00.html
[43] Council of Europe. (1989). *Recommendation No. 4 (89) 9 of the Committee of Ministers to Member States on Computer-Related Crime*. Retrieved from http://cm.coe.int/ta/rec/1989/89r9.htm
[44] Council of Europe. (1997, February 4). 583RD *Meeting of the Ministers' Deputies, Appendix 13*. Retrieved from http://www.cm.coe.int/dec/1997/583/583.a13.html
[45] Council of Europe. (1997, February 4). 583RD *Meeting of the Ministers' Deputies, Appendix 13 §4(c)*. Retrieved from http://www.cm.coe.int/dec/1997/583/583.a13.html
[46] Council of Europe. (2002). *Convention on cybercrime – Budapest, 8.XI.2001(ETS No. 185)*. Retrieved from http://conventions.coe.int/Treaty/EN/CadreListeTraites.htm
[47] Council of Europe. (2001, November 14). *Opening for signature of the first international treaty to combat cybercrime in Budapest*. Retrieved from http://press.coe.int/cp/2001/840a(2001).htm
[48] Council of Europe. (2001, May 25). *Committee of experts on crime in cyber-space, explanatory memorandum to the draft convention on cyber-crime* (pp. 7–15). Retrieved from http://conventions.coe.int/Treaty/EN/cadreprojets.htm
[49] Retrieved from http://conventions.coe.int/Treaty/EN/searchsig.asp?NT=185&CM=&DF=
[50] Retrieved from http://www.interpol.int
[51] League Against Racism and Antisemitism v. Yahoo!, Inc., No. RG: 00/05308 (County Ct. of Paris). Retrieved November, 2000, from http://www.kentlaw.edu/perritt/conflicts/yahooparis.html
[52] Secretary-General, U.N. Commission on Crime Prevention and Criminal Justice. (2001). *Conclusions of the study on effective measures to prevent and control high-technology and computer-related crime, 10th Sess., Item 4 at 15, U.N. Doc. E/CN.15/2201/4*. Retrieved from http://www.odccp.org/adhoc/crime/10_commission/4e.pdf
[53] §II(A), supra (cybercrimes consist of using computer technology to commit new types of crime and to commit traditional crimes in new ways).
[54] Compare Indian Penal Code (1860) with American Law Institute, Model Penal Code (1962). Retrieved from http://www.indialawinfo.com/bareacts/ipc.html
[55] The Code of Hammurabi. Retrieved from http://www.yale.edu/lawweb/avalon/hamframe.htm
[56] Brunker, M. (2001, May 30). Cyberspace evidence seizure upheld. *MSNBC*.
[57] Ciluffo, F. J., & Johnson, R. J. (1997, Sept/Oct). Corruption in the Kremlin. *International Police Review, reprinted by Global Organized Crime Project*. Retrieved from http://www.csis.org/goc/ao971001.html
[58] National Centre For Academic Research Into Gaming. (1999, August). *Project South Africa – Internet gaming and South Africa: Implications, costs, opportunities 7–8* (pp. 22–23). Retrieved from http://www.gamingtech.com/news/report.doc
[59] Rose, N. (2000, November). Gambling and the law: The future legal landscape for Internet gambling. *Fourth annual internet symposium on Internet Gambling Law and Management*. Retrieved from http://www.gamblingandthelaw.com/antigua.html

[60] National Centre For Academic Research Into Gaming. (1999, August). *Project South Africa – Internet gaming and South Africa: Implications, costs, opportunities 9* (pp. 22–23). Retrieved from http://www.gamingtech.com/news/report.doc

[61] National Centre For Academic Research Into Gaming. (1999, August). *Project South Africa – Internet gaming and South Africa: Implications, costs, opportunities 23* (pp. 22–23). Retrieved from http://www.gamingtech.com/news/report.doc

[62] Global Internet Statistics. (2002, March 31). *Global Internet statistics: Sources & references*. Retrieved from http://www.global-reach.biz/globstats/evol.html

Chapter 18
Formidable Challenges Posed by Cybercrimes

Sumit Ghosh

Throughout the previous chapters, we had explained how computers and networks are relentlessly pushing deeper and deeper into each and every aspect of all human endeavors. We had also seen how every computer and network, whether at home, deployed in businesses, or integrated into the national infrastructure are susceptible to attacks, without exception, both from the outside as well as from within. In this chapter, we will focus on three critical areas of human activity; examine the precise role that computers and networks play in them; assess the potential impacts of cybercrimes in these areas; and analyze their far-reaching consequences. These three areas serve to underscore the formidable challenge that cybercrimes pose to humanity. We will also examine two other formidable challenges that may be potentially posed by cybercrimes.

We are used to the idea that, in general, the impact of a traditional crime will reverberate in society for a reasonable but limited period of time. Also, after sufficient time has passed following an incident, the adverse consequences are possibly behind us. This thinking serves as the foundation of the principle of the statute of limitations. While cybercrimes, in general, challenge this thinking, the field of electronic medical records is one specific area, where cybercrimes may be so formidable that their impact in society may truly extend for indefinite time.

In the previous chapters, we had observed how the Internet, uniformity in computer hardware, and software monoculture had made it possible for malicious code to infect millions of computers, at extreme speed. This, in turn, affected millions of computer users as well as the general public living in advanced nations, where computers and networks control much of the infrastructures. Nevertheless, a non-trivial population of the world that either did not own computers or lived in non-computerized nations, had been largely unaffected by malicious code or cybercrimes. With a conceivably new manifestation of money that is about to dawn on the horizon, cybercrimes are poised, for the first time in our civilization, to extend their web of influence over virtually every human resident in the world, cutting across cultures and nations. Cyberattacks aimed at money and currency directly can threaten the very fabric of our organized societies and represent a formidable challenge to our collective well being. There is a second, equally formidable threat posed by cyberattacks against money. We had seen in Chap. 1 that the DoJ's current criminal justice system and the USA Federal Sentencing Guidelines both work primarily with the

S. Ghosh and E. Turrini (eds.), *Cybercrimes: A Multidisciplinary Analysis*,
DOI 10.1007/978-3-642-13547-7_18, © Springer-Verlag Berlin Heidelberg 2010

extent of monetary damage caused by a cybercrime. Where money and currency, the very basis of determining whether or not an act is a cybercrime, is itself manipulated, the criminal justice system will unquestionably fail to carry out its mission.

At this juncture in our history, we must admit that education, beyond everything else, constitutes the heart of our modern civilization. For the foreseeable future, education will continue to define and redefine the very nature of our society. While teaching and learning can occur anywhere, schools, universities, and academic institutions represent today's educational infrastructure. For a number of reasons, including economic efficiency and failure to understand the essence of knowledge, education is increasingly becoming online, where the traditional mode of teachers and students interacting with each other, in person, is being replaced by their mere online presence. This, in turn, necessitates their authentication through computers and networks, which inevitably opens up the door to mischief as well as cybercrimes with exceptionally serious consequences.

To the average person, it may appear puzzling why all of a sudden so many of the issues which had been routine all these past thousands of years are becoming critical. In truth, it is not that today's problems are new or unique; they have been around for as long as there have been intelligent life forms on earth. It is simply this that today, with computers and networks, the efforts to masquerade and impersonate someone else are rendered extremely easy. We no longer rely on people-to-people authentication. Instead, we are representing human beings in the computers and databases through identifiers, which are essentially indirect pointers and references, expressed through strings of 0s and 1s. If these identifiers are based on biometrics and DNA and even if were to discover a uniquely distinguishable property of each and every human being, the corresponding strings of 0s and 1s may be duplicated or altered with great ease. There is an even deeper reason but is beyond the scope of this book. It will suffice to say that the perception of the benefits of using computers and networks are so immense that we are willing to tolerate the consequent hazards and challenges.

18.1 Electronic Medical Records and Cybercrimes

For a given patient undergoing a specific medical diagnosis, therapy, or treatment or a series of related treatments, a conventional medical record is a documentation of the key details of the medical event on paper. An electronic medical record (EMR) is the exact same documentation, except that it is stored in the form of 0s and 1s on an electronic media, such as a magnetic hard drive, CD-ROM, DVD-ROM, USB drive, etc. Conceptually an EMR is no different than a paper record; however, the convenience of storage and ease of transmission of an EMR offers the promise that, for any given patient, all past EMRs from different health care providers may be consolidated into a single electronic medical book (EMB), located in a cyberspace repository, and made available very quickly to any attending physician during subsequent medical events.

The first serious use of EMRs in the USA occurred in the early 1990s, when a handful of medical organizations, no more than half a dozen hospitals and health care facilities, began to compile patient medical records in electronic form. One such facility was the CIGNA HMO clinic in Chandler, Arizona, with whom the author had worked extensively on the research topic of medical continuity of care. The author's research group, supported by the National Library of Medicine, and CIGNA physician, Dr. Peter Churgin, had analyzed over 90,000+ patient EMRs, acquired over a 3 year period, to yield scientific findings [1, 2] on the quality of medical care which would have been, otherwise, very difficult.

18.1.1 Vulnerability of EMRs

To assess whether EMRs are vulnerable and to gain insights into the whys and hows of their vulnerabilities, we will first quickly review the traditional practices. Presently, different health care providers and hospitals hold patient data. While a few concerned individuals may archive their own family's paper medical records in their personal vaults, for the vast majority of the population, their medical records are in paper form and geographically distributed. This has, inadvertently, rendered a systematic and widespread physical attack on EMRs very difficult and a very low probability of successful compromise of all medical data. In contrast, however, as soon as a majority of all USA citizens' medical data is consolidated in EMBs and archived in cyberspace, the temptation for hackers and cybercriminals to wage attacks on the medical data would be far too immense for them to ignore. Furthermore, along the lines of Dan Geer's monoculture argument, explained in Chap. 9, hackers are likely to successful in bringing about widespread damage to the EMBs.

As we had seen across the chapters in this book, especially under Part II, any information in cyberspace is vulnerable. Given enough time, any and every password and authentication, no matter what, can be successfully broken by a determined perpetrator. There is a simple yet profound reason. Even if there were to exist an algorithm underlying the generation of an encryption or password and that the secret is known only to the inventor(s) and no one else, there is no power inherent in all of mathematics and the sciences that can guarantee that another individual will be forever successfully precluded from discovering the secret. Once the password or authentication mechanism is broken, the perpetrator can release all EMBs quickly and widely across cyberspace, implying a tremendous loss to all.

There is another, subtle aspect to EMRs' vulnerability, the source of which lies in the fact that the multidimensional nature of authentication, generally associated with physical medical records in the real world, is replaced through a uniform authentication approach in cyberspace. For instance, paper records including birth certificates encapsulate a style of handwriting that it unique to a specific physician or provider. Even if the record was typed on a keyboard or dictated, the style of the composition including the idiosyncratic choice of words can uniquely point to the physician author of the record. The quality and size of paper, folds and crease marks, dogears, depth of indentation from pressing hard while signing, and any additional marks and watermarks on the paper can also serve to authenticate a medical record. If there were any attempts to tamper with a medical record, such as overwrites, use of whiteouts, and "trash marks" from copying on a Xerox machine [3], a paper record or that on another material will preserve it best. All of the associations and potential identification marks may be discarded when the information is transformed and transferred into a string of 0s and 1s in the EMR, and lost forever.

EMRs can be attacked at the moment and at the point they are first created, at the storage facility in cyberspace where they are archived, and while they are enroute over the network to attending physicians at the time of medical need. EMRs can also be retrieved from cyberstorage and transmitted to researchers for the purpose of scientific analysis, legal investigations, and other reasons. The legal tradition in the USA has been that an EMR can be shared with other individuals for a legitimate purpose provided that the name and other identifying numbers and marks of a patient have first been removed. However, analysis by the author has revealed that this precaution may not necessarily be sufficient to guarantee privacy and prevent mischief.

18.1.2 Consequences of EMRs Compromises

At first glance, the concept of consolidated patient EMBs is extremely attractive. An attending physician will have quick access to the patient's near-complete medical history and, in theory, he/she can analyze the data to infer the best diagnosis and therapy. The EMB will contain the patient's age; vaccinations; blood type; pulse, heartbeat, blood pressure, white blood corpuscle count, fingerprint; retina scan; palm print; hair type; DNA sequence; allergic reactions to drugs; history of past medical procedures including surgeries, mamograms, CATscans, MRIs, and fMRIs; and previous incidences of diseases including asthma, diabetes, etc. Given our current scientific thinking that a human body is a highly sophisticated machine, the more parameters we can measure about the operation of the constituent internal organs, the greater our knowledge on the internal state of the machine. To health care administrators and policy makers, the citizens' EMBs offer a bird's eye view of the health of the entire nation, from which one can deduce the national productivity, anticipated medical expenses in the future years, what common diseases warrant greater medical research, and even how to anticipate and develop potential techniques to thwart upcoming epidemics and pandemics.

Underlying this elation, however, lurks an equally immense danger. For a given patient, the EMB contains virtually all information to identify him or her uniquely, at least in the cyberworld. If the EMB is stolen, altered, or cloned, the person's true identify can be seriously jeopardized. To understand how, consider the following. When an individual's credit card number is stolen, the corresponding bank can cancel the card and issue a new one with a new set of numbers to the consumer. Also, with periodically changing expiration dates and addresses, etc., the useful life of a given credit card is generally limited to 2–3 years. If an individual's social security number is compromised, the social security administration, following an investigation and successful finding, can issue a new number. Increasingly, all organizations in the USA are being forbidden to use the social security numbers, except in the most serious situations. Now, if a person's EMB is compromised, no amount of legislation by any government, monetary compensation, nor efforts by law enforcement agencies can restore the damage, ever. There are no known scientific and safe ways to change a person's blood type, white blood corpuscle count, or DNA sequence. One a patient's EMB is compromised, it is lost forever. For a large number of citizens, society may never learn of their true identity with certainty. It may be very difficult to be sure if society's leaders are imposters or who they claim to be, leading to dangerous consequences. Details of birth records can be altered, with profound consequences to a family's as well as a nation's security and future well being. An enemy nation with a long-range plan can infiltrate into the core leadership of a prosperous neighbor and lead the country to destruction. Clever perpetrators and deranged but otherwise brilliant scientists can analyze EMBs to find potential vulnerabilities and exploit them to bring selective harm to the corresponding individuals. For a rich patient afflicted with leukemia requiring bone marrow transplant, organized crime can explore EMBs, identify an appropriate victim, and either coerce the individual to donate the needed bone marrow or pursue a far more destructive course of action. The deliberate design of synthetic poisons and toxins to selectively target a family, race, or group of people with a shared biological or genetic characteristic, will pose an unthinkable challenge to society's peaceful existence. Cyberspace offers the potential for such efforts to be executed with immense precision and surreptitiousness, capable of defeating all known forensic techniques. For obvious reasons, we can only describe here a few of the potential threats of EMB compromise. The true scope of the potential consequences is limited only by our imagination and can never be predicted a priori by anyone with absolute certainty. No one, absolutely no one, will be immune from these dangers. For, as we had stated earlier, every individual without exception is represented in cyberspace by a string of 0s and 1s and the computer does not care to distinguish an important leader from an ordinary citizen.

18.1.3 Far-Reaching Benefits of EMRs?

In Sect. 18.1, we had enumerated the immense benefits that can potentially flow from the availability of EMBs. To bring to fruition the potential benefits, however, several practical obstacles must be addressed.

- First, there is an implied assumption in the theory that the availability of the EMB for a patient containing all past EMRs will help an attending physician render superior diagnosis. While the author joins most medical scientists in sharing this belief intuitively and although there may be anecdotal evidence, absent in the scientific literature is a comprehensive and systematic study that provides scientific proof of the theory. Exceptions notwithstanding, we do not presently have EMBs for individuals in the age group of 45–80, extending all the way back to their birth. Clearly, information such as whether a patient's vaccinations are up-to-date, if available in the EMB, are important and helpful. However, these represent simple scenarios. Furthermore, it is just as equally possible for an attending physician to derive from the patient's EMB a wrong inference, leading to misdiagnosis and possible death. There is a growing belief among policy makers and elected government officials that EMRs and EMBs will save money [4]. This is unproven, at best, by any scientific measure, and could be false per current practices. For a nation to undertake a serious and expensive effort to compile EMBs for every citizen [4], a scientific study is absolutely critical. Otherwise, the project may need to be abandoned halfway.

- Second, as further evidence of the need for a scientific analysis, it is presently unclear whether a patient EMB should be organized chronologically or through medical events, what elements must be included in an EMR with the future in mind, and what are the limits of the theory. A logical organization is likely to bear profound impact on an attending physician's comprehension of the patient's medical state. In lung pathology, for instance, images of a patient's tissue samples are presently obtained and interpreted using default white balance settings of the microscope and, as a result, they are generally archived in the patient's files with no further mention of the white balance settings. The future may witness significant advancement [5] in inferencing, where precise knowledge of the white balance setting may be critically necessary.
- Third, presently, a patient's EMB contains little to no links to the EMBs of his or her close relatives. This may be of paramount importance in many medical conditions. In rare cases, one may find within a patient's EMB a set of unverified, self-reported statements indicating whether a medical problem has occurred in the patient's family tree. However, such connections are generally accidental and do not reflect a conscious attempt on the part of a medical facility.
- Fourth, given the daily pressures, desire to make efficient use of their time, and past anecdotes of patients' wrong foot being operated or wrong kidney being removed, few physicians will understandably possess the patience to read through the entire EMB. Anecdotal evidence points to an average interaction time of 5 min between patients and physicians in 2009, down from 15 min that had been assessed in 1995 [1]. Furthermore, there is a vast difference between possessing a EMB, reading it, and understanding the contents against the backdrop of the present medical condition on one hand, and analyzing the EMB to draw timely inferences that will make a positive impact on the patient's quality of care on the other hand. There is no question that a few dedicated and gifted physicians will make very good use of EMBs. For the vast majority of the cases, however, the question is whether the potential for immense abuse will outweigh the meager advantages stemming from the mandatory compilation of EMBs.
- Fifth, it would be unwise not to expect government bureaucrats at the State and Federal levels to pass mandates requiring physicians to read the patient EMBs prior to every medical procedure. This may be unwise and impractical to realize.

While the governments may believe that imposing uniform standards will lead to higher quality, we must remember two fundamental limitations with standards: (a) A standard is a double-edged sword. While it is likely to proliferate, promote business, and provide huge benefits initially, over the long run, mediocrity will creep in and innovation will be stifled, eventually sinking the overall discipline to the lowest common denominator. A system driven by standards quickly becomes mindless and will push away intuitive, creative, and insightful physicians; (b) Standards do not logically imply the pursuit of excellence.

- Sixth, to derive the maximum gain from the EMBs, the medical community, with assistance from policy makers and all citizens, may consider embarking on an ambitious program to uncover deep insights and hidden medical connections between the different constituent organs and the overall well being, starting from a deeper and holistic analysis of the medical conditions recorded in patient EMBs. By definition, insights transcend established scientific norms, may take a significantly different position from the traditional medical establishment, and may not be amenable to immediate explanation by current medical, scientific, and mathematical understanding. The value of insights is beyond measure. Developing extra-logical connections is synonymous to classic associativity which comes from diverse experience and rare intuition and cannot be easily taught in any standard curriculum. It will require an entirely new thinking in medical diagnoses and a new educational architecture, far beyond the current practice in medicine. We may remind ourselves that knowledge is not reflected by the number of books that are available; the true value of knowledge lies in how one can envision the unseen connections and uses them to solve an immediate challenge. We may be well advised to actively seek the help of the most enlightened, progressive, and gifted physician healers, worldwide, and begin to address this exceptionally important problem.

18.1.4 A Formidable Challenge to EMRs and EMBs?

According to the tradition in the USA, patients' rights comprise of two key articles. First, a patient's medical records are owned wholly and legally by the patient and neither by the government nor any other organization. Second, no medical record, once written and entered into a patient's file, cannot be altered for any reason. Thus, a medical record is "permanent" in every sense of the term. Even if a typo or error were to be subsequently discovered, necessitating correction, a new record must be created, referencing the previous error, and appended to the previous record. Despite the laws, perpetrators in the past had made attempts to alter the paper records, as had been highlighted in the classic movie, The Verdict. As has been the norm, paper records involve a number of people handling them and illegal alteration assumes the form of overwriting, use of whiteouts, coercing others to lie, etc., all of which leave behind traces of physical evidence. Thus, paper records offer a limited number of natural impediments to alterations. In contrast, EMRs and ECBs in cyberspace can be altered with such unbelievable ease and incredible speed that the notion of a "permanent" medical record may be considered negated for all practical purposes. If governments were to take away the citizens' choice and require the use of EMRs and EMBs, the mandate is likely to constitute the greatest threat to all patients, today and in the future. As we had stated earlier, no one's EMB is immune from tampering, whether a common citizen or that of society's leaders.

18.2 EM-Money and Cybercrimes

18.2.1 The Origin of Money

Although the first manifestation of money in the form of metal coins has been traced back to 700 BC Lydia, in present day Turkey, history does not tell us who invented the concept of money. While commodities such as grain, meat, clothing, and others can be and had been used directly for barter, the conception of money as a common vehicle through which the value of all commodities may be expressed reflects that money is not a real product but an abstract idea, in essence, a uniform measure of worth and value. Thus, the fundamental characteristics of money would include:

1. Everyone would want it at all times
2. It is not perishable
3. It holds its value in time and across as many neighborhoods as possible and that its reach in space and time is increasing

With respect to its manifestation in the real world, the unit of money must possess the following attributes:

- It is exclusive, i.e., its form is limited
- It is very difficult to create, synthesize, or find
- It holds together for a reasonably long time

18.2.2 The Evolution of Money

Beginning with the coins made from base metals, the manifestation of money gradually took on the form of precious metal coins, namely gold and silver coins, which rendered the value of the coins relatively independent of the issuing nation or government and, therefore, imparted them longer life. Gradually, sovereign nations began producing gold-backed paper currencies, where the value of a paper currency note was not only assured by the issuing nation but guaranteed in gold, i.e., upon demand, the nation would produce and repay the bearer of the currency note with the stated amount in gold. This had been true in Kuwait as recently as 2002. Today, for a number of different reasons, most nations have resorted to "fiat" currency notes, where the exact value is declared by the government as legal tender and enforced by its laws, police, and military power, if and where necessary. The word "fiat" is adopted from its Latin origin, meaning, let it be done. Thus, while the paper on which a currency bill is printed may not have any intrinsic worth, the government stands behind the stated value; there are no other explicit guarantees. Although the removal of the gold and silver backing renders a currency without obvious support and potentially weak, it may have been driven by the desire to promote economic expansion and wealth creation, far beyond the cumulative monetary currency notes that may be printed in strict accordance with the total value of authentic gold and silver bullion held by a given nation's vaults. Nations have argued that the net productivity of their citizens more than assures the integrity of their currency notes. As a logical downside, the desire for economic well being for all citizens may be surreptitiously subsumed by unexpected emergencies, unusual national priorities, or excessive greed of the financial stewards and policy makers, leading to an uncontrolled and overprinting of currency notes. When exposed, the obvious result would be a falling trust in the value of the currency, eventually leading to a downward spiral and total collapse of the currency.

18.2.3 Characteristics of Future Money

The author believes that the economic and financial crisis precipitated in 2008–2009 is pushing the world toward a new form of currency and that we have arrived at a threshold, poised to witness the dawn of a new and logical manifestation of money. Before we present the proposed details of this new manifestation which we will label electromagnetic money (EM-money), we will first review the problems and challenges and, second, identify the necessary attributes of EM-money. We will note that although credit and debit cards, electronic wallets, Internet-driven mail and electronic cash [6] and, more fundamentally, the USA Federal Reserve-style debt or bank loans [7–9] allude to electronic money, in reality, they constitute an illusion. It is merely an entry in a computer, solely for the purposes of book-keeping; fictitious; and it does not correspond to any real money that is saved after having been first earned through effort and hard work, physical or mental. Fundamentally, the credit and debit cards and the Federal Reserve-style debt and credit do not require a computer; they may be and have been realized through paper-based ledgers for millennia. In contrast, a fundamental requirement of EM-money is an underlying computing engine and networked computing system. A few of the problems of the traditional money include:

- Although money is conceptually abstract, to-date, its manifestation has been physical, assuming the form of metal coins and paper. While paper currency notes are lighter in weight, easy to store, and offer many more practical conveniences than metal coins, both are subject to physical theft as well as wear and tear. There is no provision for a currency bill to reflect its legitimate owner and, as a result, one who possesses a bill is its owner by default. Traditionally, theft of currency bills and coins have proven very challenging for law enforcement, given the saying, possession is nine-tenths of the law.

- When private individuals or organizations enter into covert transactions, utilizing government issued currency notes and coins, for the purposes of tax evasion, money laundering, gambling, and other illegal pursuits, it is very difficult for governments and authorities to track them.
- According to history, periods of stable economic activity have generally been characterized by a currency backed by gold and precious metals. In the modern world, nearly all sovereign currencies were backed by gold until 1913. In the history of the USA, the dollar had always been backed by gold until the support was removed in 1971. The theory was that gold backing represents a constriction to an expanding economy and that there is not enough authentic gold, as opposed to composite base materials masquerading as real gold, to account for the world's potential economic worth in terms of production, infrastructure, and other financial and non-financial business activities. The absence of gold backing ushered the era of FIAT currencies and the USA dollar as the world's reserve currency.
- It is generally agreed that any nation's government must print and place into circulation adequate FIAT money, in the form of currency notes and coins, in order to facilitate the nation's business activities. Furthermore, the total money supply at any given time instant must be supported by the nation's broadest measure of wealth. This would include the assets including authentic gold and precious metals reserves and natural resources; roads, bridges, tunnels, and other infrastructure; and the productive capacity, that would include factories, industries, and the produced goods in demand. Of great importance is the fact that the government should not print excessive money for it would inevitably drive the currency's worth less and less, eventually rendering it worthless. The most well known incident in history is that of the Weimar Republic of the 1920s. When a government prints massive quantities of currency notes without any support and this act is eventually exposed, the reference value of money is lost. As a result, commodity prices become arbitrary, which is generally followed by social chaos. With currency in the form of physical paper bills and coins, today, it is a challenge to detect whether a government has been engaged in printing excessive money and even more difficult to determine an exact measure of the money oversupply. In 2008–2009, there is widespread belief that every national government is secretly engaged in printing uncontrolled quantities of money but it has been very difficult to prove with certainty. There is justifiable fear that this may result in the catastrophic destruction of all currencies, worldwide, which would be followed by unprecedented social and economic chaos.

18.2.4 EM-Money: A New Manifestation of Money

Clearly, logic dictates the development of a new manifestation which will significantly increase the transparency of money supply and ownership from every perspective.

We propose the development of an abstract data structure in the computer, termed EM-money, and a few associated functions or procedures to ensure that its precise worth, integrity, and legitimacy are maintained at every instant of time. EM-money will represent the first abstract realization of money in this civilization and will be logically consistent with the fundamental nature of money, which, as we had described earlier in this section, is abstract. Under this proposal, for any nation, every currency bill, except the ones with low denominations, will exist only in cyberspace, i.e., in the computers of the nation's financial system. The cost to produce EM-money would be significantly less. All physical manifestations of money including paper bills and metal or plastic coins will cease to exist. The details of the financial system, including the nature of the EM-money computing engines, hardware, software, and networking; authentication and security; required training of the human operators; ownership and access rules for the different components, etc. are beyond the scope of this book and will be described elsewhere. Also, whether and how credit and debt may be expressed as special cases of EM-money will be described elsewhere. We will limit our focus here only on EM-money's key attributes that are pertinent to the theme of this book.

For each and every EM-money currency bill, the financial systems' sphere of the cyberspace will contain a unique instance of a data structure and the associated functions. The structure will include a comprehensive number of distinct fields, a few of which includes a unique identifier for the bill itself, denomination of the currency bill, identifier of the current owner of the bill, history of all previous owners of the bill, country of origin, identification of the legitimate institution of the financial system where the currency bill had originated, date of origin of the bill, identifier of the institution where the bill is presently being held, and list of factors that provide the backing of the currency. EM-money will facilitate the following:

- Unlike today's money, the proposed EM-money is intelligent and accurately reflects the current economic conditions of the corresponding nation at every time instant. Traditional currencies based on paper and metal coins are inert and dumb in that they are completely unaware of their true owner and may be easily stolen and used by anyone. Under EM-money, a bill can only be used in a transaction by its legitimate current owner. Every EM-money currency bill will contain the history of transactions that it had encountered since its creation. Traditional currencies are also static in that the values printed on their faces never changes and, at times, fail to reflect their current worth. At best, this is very confusing. For example, the one-ounce, 99.99% pure USA gold Buffalo coin displays a face value of $50 but is traded at over $1,100 in December 2009.
- The occurrence of physical theft of money, especially violent bank holdups and robberies would be obsoleted, permitting law enforcement to focus their energies elsewhere.
- All transactions between individuals, businesses, and institutions will be on record, rendering them transparent and subject to verification at any time. The occurrence of shadow transactions in today's society, involving the use of the proverbial "black money" will be rendered difficult, but not impossible.
- When a EM-money currency bill is first created at the instruction of a nation's government and introduced into the financial system, the name of the country

will be listed as the first owner of the bill. It is expected that as economic activity progresses, an individual or business will become the subsequent owner of the bill through a transaction. Thus, at any time instant, the nation's net money supply in the system [10], reflected by the cash in the system, bank checking accounts, bank savings accounts, jumbo CDs, and institutional money funds; and the exact fraction of the total money owned by the government will be transparent to the citizen-taxpayers of the nation and other international watchdog groups. Any occurrence of excessive "money printing" will be quickly detected by the money computing engines associated with the EM-money, orders of magnitude faster than any errant government official or policy maker can even begin to physically manipulate the currency. Any EM-currency that is hidden from the system can obviously be dismissed and treated non sequitur and all consequent adverse consequences may be morally and legally repudiated by the citizen-taxpayers, while international investors can take appropriate actions.

- The intelligent attribute of EM-money may also manifest in the fast and precise computation of a sovereign currency's strength, relative to a non-sovereign, international reference currency, in terms of the nation's authentic gold and precious metals reserves, agricultural and industrial productivity, national savings rate, oil and mineral deposits, population and consumption rate, and other pertinent factors established through international dialogue, agreements, and protocols. The computation of a given currency's worth will be automatic, immediate, impersonal, and objective, orders of magnitude faster than the ability of rogue nations and errant policy makers to begin to manipulate foreign exchange rates. EM-money will greatly facilitate the practical decoupling of the world reserve currency from that of any sovereign nation, while rendering the transparency of the foreign exchange rate. This, in turn, may prevent a recurrence of the currency crisis of 2008–2010, triggered by the falling value of the US dollar as the current world's reserve currency. While a given nation's internal turmoil or immediate economic difficulties may cause its currency, relative to the reference currency, to go down in worth for any reason, the direct impact on other sovereign currencies of the world may be kept at a minimum. Lacking the kind of transparency promised by EM-money, world citizens are likely to slowly but gradually refuse every sovereign FIAT currency today, printed in paper or base metal, regardless of whose picture is on the face, the denomination, words, calligraphy, etc.

18.2.5 Formidable Challenges to EM-Money

Notwithstanding the unprecedented potential offerings of EM-money, if it were to become reality, it would be subject to two formidable cybercrimes. First, sophisticated and determined cybercriminals, if unabated, can target select nations and manipulate their financial systems to wreck economic havoc and disrupt the nations' well being. The manipulation may be immense, causing huge swings temporarily in the value of the currency, and it may be brought about at a great speed. A calculated attack may induce a high frequency oscillation in the world's currencies, bringing international business to a screeching halt. An assault on EM-money would be equivalent to simultaneous attacks on hundreds of companies' financial health and even all law enforcement agencies, worldwide, may not be equipped to deal with the problem. Second, as explained in Chap. 1, the classification of an act as a cybercrime and the sentencing guidelines both rely on the prosecution successfully proving the extent of the monetary damage caused by the perpetration. This founding basis for prosecuting cybercrimes may be defeated by perpetrators through successfully manipulating the nation's currency. In essence, the cybercriminals' plan would destroy the reference, without which the justice system would become blind and arbitrary. To understand the incredibly powerful role of reference, consider the following, hypothetical scenario. If a powerful and errant organization were to engage in the underhanded manipulation of the price of gold, the purpose being to erase the monetary reference provided by gold over the past 6,000 years, it will lead to fraudulent numbers for inflation; true prices of commodities, goods, and services; workers' wages; GDP, etc.

18.3 Student Academic Records, Online Education, and Cybercrimes

Analysis of history reveals an unmistakable trend throughout time, namely, that great economic regions have been forged through education and learning. Deeper understanding of mathematics and science had led to the wheeled chariots, weapons for self defense as well as to hurl at the enemy at a distance, robust dwellings, bridges to span bodies of water, and new materials such as bronze to construct durable agricultural implements and weaponry. The industrial revolution that took root in Manchester and Liverpool emerged from an understanding and mastery of steam engines and precision pistons, while the Silicon Valley revolution stemmed from a deep understanding of differential metal junction behavior and the mastery of the transistor and, subsequently, logic gates and computers. According to the ancient sages, while the past can never become the present, it does give rise to the future. So, our future will very likely follow the same trend and it would not be an error to look forward to the dawn of the next great economic region.

Clearly, any threat to our education and learning would be tantamount to a formidable challenge to our future well being. So serious is this issue that when the United States of America was founded in the late 1700s, the wise founding fathers and founding mothers had noted that the education and banking functions of the individual states should never be usurped by the Federal government. They had put in place key controls, which we are now dismantling without even pausing for a moment to try to understand their original intent. Today, universities are the most visible representations of our belief in the power of education. We expect our institutions of learning to produce new ideas and principles, which the industries will subsequently use to develop new products and services for the advancement of society. If and when they fail, the very purpose of the universities will be lost. Our industries will become void of new products and services, leading to an inevitable dark age. We have placed our entire faith in our universities to impart new knowledge and thinking to our future generation and to cultivate ethics and trust in the young minds so as to guide their use of powerful knowledge. If universities fail to carry out the entrusted tasks or worse, where they begin to promote distrust and engage in teaching how to circumvent ethics, the purpose of universities is also lost. The adverse long-term impact on our civilization would be incalculable and beyond description.

18.3.1 Relocating Universities into Cyberspace

In theory, if we were to relocate, either deliberately or inadvertently, the primary functions of our institutions of learning into cyberspace, the universities' primary mission and objectives would immediately come into the field of view of the cybercriminals. The potential adverse impacts of cybercrimes in education would be unthinkable.

Although scholars would travel far and wide to seek out and learn from the great teachers since time immemorial, the present idea of online learning started in the 1990s and have increasingly gained momentum as a viable alternate to the traditional university system, which required students and teachers to engage in face-to-face activities. While online learning may assume many faces, in general, teachers do not have to physically meet the students at a given time and place to impart learning. Instruction may be imparted through virtual classrooms in cyberspace, either synchronously or asynchronously, without the teachers and students ever physically leaving their homes. Today, in 2010, online education is becoming very attractive, given the need to curb the escalating university budgets, ever increasing tuition costs, and the ancillary costs of transportation to and from school, paying for room and board in the vicinity of the university, etc. Today, both government-supported and privately-funded universities are facing tremendous pressure to reign in their runaway budgets and many individuals in academic leadership positions are openly discussing "a new model of funding education," where the traditional university programs would be dissolved and replaced with online programs. Clearly, virtual classrooms may be brought into people's homes, implying the potential for tremendous efficiency. The need to find room and board in the vicinity of a school, transportation, mental pressure of being away from home for extended periods of time, etc. would all be eliminated.

In addition to instruction delivery online, instruction materials may be archived in cyberspace; admission and acceptance of students into academic programs may be carried out completely online; assessment of a student's learning including examinations can be accomplished online; grades may be posted by faculty examiners on the universities' computers and retrieved by students remotely; and student academic records, transcripts, and diplomas may all be archived in cyberspace and delivered to potential employers online.

18.3.2 The Vulnerabilities of Education and Learning in Cyberspace

It is hard to believe that anyone, even cybercriminals, would be tempted to attack learning and that there could even be problems lurking underneath online education. The simple reason is that knowledge is power, not metaphorically, but in the most literal sense. Not only is knowledge extremely powerful, it is the ultimate power in this world. Anything and everything in this universe, without exceptions, can be controlled through knowledge, which is generally acquired through education and learning. There may be other techniques to acquire knowledge, insights, and wisdom without involving the traditional forms of learning but they are very difficult. To the cybercriminals, the temptation to acquire power and control through attacking learning is too strong to ignore. A few of the potential weaknesses of online education, that may be exploited by cybercrimals include the following:

- Under online education, teachers, students, and administrators are all uniformly reduced to identifiers, in the form of strings of 0s and 1s. To the students, the teacher is a mere identifier in cyberspace, just as the students appear as identifiers to the teacher. The only way to ascertain that an individual X is who he or she claims to be is through the usual authentication techniques, which, as we have seen throughout the book, are not difficult to compromise. As a result, regardless of the claims and advertisements, trust in online education will be broken from time to time, guaranteed. The teacher can never be certain of the true identities of the students, just as the students can never be sure whether the instructor is the genuine person or an impersonator.
- A logical question arises namely, why should the students care whether the instructor is genuine as long as the university certifies the online teacher and promises to award them the diplomas at the conclusion of the courses and the program? Today and in the future, education and learning will increasingly focus on quality, i.e., the students' ability to analyze unknown situations and not merely memorize and regurgitate. We have computers, networks, robots, and online search engines that are capable of storing in memory and regurgitating all known facts, information, and knowledge upon demand, millions of times faster and with far greater precision than any human being. What will be worth learning in the future is how to analyze, think, and understand independently, which can only be learned from genuine teachers. Those students who successfully learn the art of learning will be in great demand in the future; all others, in contrast, would be obsoleted by computers and robots.
- In today's environment, one might wonder whether it really makes any difference to the teacher whether or not a student is genuine, as long as he or she has been admitted, the tuition is being paid, and is making regular progress. The prevalent thinking is that any student is entitled to any education, provided the individual is "qualified," desires the education, and is willing to pay the required tuition, regardless of the individual's ethical and moral character. The delivery of instruction must be impersonal and objective, regardless of the student's expressed or

hidden intentions on how he or she intends to employ the knowledge gained. This thinking is diametrically opposite to the ancient paradigm in India, where a guru would often train and test a disciple repeatedly over many years before imparting to him or her knowledge and skills that encapsulated great powers. In theory, today, plagiarism and cheating in examinations by students are not accepted by any university. In practice, however, the situation is a lot more clouded and is unduly influenced by funding and economics. Thus, a university is very likely to teach a paying student how to take off and fly a Boeing 747 passenger airliner but not care if the student openly admits that he is not interested in learning how to land the jet aircraft. We now know how the hijackers caused untold damage during the September 11, 2001 terrorist attacks. If education is power, as we had stated earlier, clearly it would be important and necessary to assess how that power is likely to be utilized in society by the recipient. Consider the following anecdote. In the 1937–1942 time frame, Prof. John Vincent Atanasoff and Clifford Berry had invented and designed the first Atanasoff-Berry Computer (ABC) at Iowa State College. A colleague from University of Pennsylvania, Dr. Mauchly, came to Atanasoff in 1941, pretending to be fascinated with the computer and desiring to learn how Atanasoff had built the computer. Unaware of Mauchly's hidden sinister intentions, Atanosoff invited Mauchly to stay at his home for a week and explained the details of his invention over countless hours. According to history, Mauchly would go ahead and along with Eckert make a copy of Atanasoff's ABC computer design at University of Pennsylvania, call it ENIAC, and claim it as his own invention, until a patent infringement lawsuit subpoena compelled him to appear in USA Federal court in 1973. He testified, under oath, that he barely knew of Atanosoff's invention, never had any discussions with him, and saw the ABC machine with its cover on. The court [11] found Mauchly guilty of stealing Atanasoff's invention and of lying and invalidated the ENIAC patent. The damage that Mauchly had caused to the issue of trust among academicians continues to reverberate to this day. Today, any attempt at forging a collaboration is viewed with great distrust by all concerned parties, and the focus invariably shifts onto documenting who contributed what rather than a free exchange of ideas toward solving the challenging problem. An ancient Indian legend portrays an amusing story in which an evil person, Bhamasur, had once prayed to God Shiva for a very long time. Pleased with his devotion, God Shiva appeared before him and asked him to choose a boon. Bhamasur asked that whenever he would choose to place his hand on top of another person's head, the latter would be immediately reduced to ashes. As soon as God Shiva granted him the boon, presumably teaching him the exact Sanskrit mantra, the individual wanted to verify his power by placing his hand on God Shiva's head. The story has an interesting end and it epitomizes the fact that individuals with evil tendencies will often pretend to be students, desiring to learn and serve society. In reality, their plan all along is to abuse the power gained from the knowledge and cause wanton destruction. Thus, imparting learning and education to individuals with questionable character and unethical dispositions may constitute an open invitation to disaster. While education and learning have been prone to vulnerabilities since time immemorial, the proliferation of online learning will facilitate cybercriminals to exploit the weaknesses including breaking into the online admissions facility with incredible ease, speed, and impunity.

- Until we discover a superior system, grades earned in individual courses and the overall transcript of a student represents his or her academic achievement in a given academic program. In determining whether or not to hire a graduate, private companies, public institutions, and government organizations utilize the transcript as a key criterion to assess qualification. Clearly, grades and transcripts are of great importance to society and ensuring their accuracy and integrity are of primary concern. Increasingly, grades are recorded online by the instructor, viewed by the students online, and granted access to potential employers by the university administration. Virtually every aspect of a student's total academic experience, including the academic record, attendance, transcript, program details, course details, recommendations, etc. are located in cyberspace. As with any other information in cyberspace, the academic information is susceptible to attacks by cybercriminals. Students may be assigned high grades in courses held in high demand by industry, even though the students were not enrolled and the courses never offered by the university. The manipulation of transcripts, either targeting a single individual or en masse can permanently damage institutions' credibilities, destroy graduates' reputations, and create widespread disruption in hiring and economic progress. Of greatest concern is the potential for a calculated, long-term manipulation of grades and transcripts leading to an excessive supply of graduates all with seemingly outstanding transcripts and society's failure to distinguish between excellence and mediocrity. The consequence may be a failure of leadership, down the road, in virtually every aspect of society, leading to its downfall and disintegration. The manipulation may be conceived and carried out by a lone perpetrator; a determined group; rival universities, domestic as well as international; or it may be self-inflicted for reasons even stranger than fiction.
- The most troubling concern with transferring a significant component of the traditional education and learning entirely into cyberspace is the potential for serious and permanent damage to society, which may be realized through a well-calculated attack, deployed over a long period of time in the most subtle and surreptitious manner. Such an attack would be exceptionally difficult to detect. We will enumerate only a few of the possibilities and note that perpetrators will be limited only by their imagination. First, instructional materials in cyberspace may be intercepted during delivery to the students and altered very gradually, steadily pushing successive cohorts of students toward a destructive goal that is diametrically opposite to the founding principles of the given university or nation. Since the archived instructional material is not touched, detecting the attack would be challenging. Second, educational foundations, anonymously hiding in the cyberspace, may begin making philanthropic awards for scientific discoveries, initially starting out with noble goals but slowly altering the criteria in order to push the scientific efforts toward weaponization and forcible control of the general population. Given enough time, money, and patience,

the foundations may completely dominate all scientific pursuits and lead society down the wrong path, robbing us of our ethics and trust in humanity. Third, under the pretext of concern for the students' mental health, accreditation bodies might gradually dilute the requirement for analytical mathematics, eventually eliminating trigonometry and complex analysis from the programs. After all, with sophisticated calculators available, why should students be burdened with the need to understand the subtle intricacies? Over time, the accreditation bodies would be guaranteed to achieve their goal of a future national workforce, totally unprepared and non-competitive in the coming age of computing-based transdisciplinary science and engineering. Fourth, assume that a majority of the legislators of a state or a nation have been sold the idea that all students must learn a single computer programming language, say Z. This would represent great cost savings to the nation in terms of requiring a single uniform computer hardware and software environment, fewer instructors to teach computer science at the universities, fewer books, and any programmer may be assigned to any project. What more could one desire? To ensure compliance, the authorities may gradually outlaw the pursuit of any other programming language, declaring it as a blasphemy to even criticize the tiniest deficiency in Z. While the legislators would be wildly successful in achieving their goal, cybercriminals would have a field day, utilizing a fundamental attribute of computing not modeled in Z, to attack and shut down the computer system of the entire state or nation. Of greater concern is that the entire workforce would be completely outdated overnight when an entirely new kind of computing engine is invented, opening up whole new ways to solve far more challenging problems than can be presently imagined. The scenarios presented here are not new. Similar events have occurred in the past. The Catholic Church had tried very hard to dissuade Galileo from his revolutionary idea of the earth revolving around the sun by offering him teaching positions and facilitating his research. The Church authorities had successfully plunged the entire population of Europe into scientific ignorance for more than a thousand years. However, they had underestimated Galileo's stubborn faith in scientific inquiry and curiosity. What is new today is the incredible ease and efficiency with which vast and destructive changes may be perpetrated through cyberspace in very short time.

- The recent article written by Mark Graham and titled, In Law Schools, Grades Go Up, Just Like That, published in the New York Times, 21 June 2010, raises two significant concerns. First, the grades have been altered retroactively for an indeterminate number of years into the past; this destroys all references and defeats any future attempt to assess the degree of grade inflation or when it had been commissioned. Second, the decision was kept deliberately hidden until it was leaked by students and others.

18.3.3 Summary

It is undeniable that beneath the expectation of inexpensive and affordable online education and all of the promised savings lurks a severely dark downside. Education is the key to any society's survival and it ultimately rests on trust. Since trust is easily broken in cyberspace, cybercrimes pose formidable challenge to education, learning, and, ultimately, the very existence of society.

18.4 The Concept of Witnesses and Cybercrimes

The concept of witnesses is fundamental to the criminal justice system and has played a critical role in our civilization from time immemorial. A credible witness can help resolve the truth by establishing the causality, i.e. distinguishing the cause from the effect, namely, who did to whom first and what, etc. From the discussions in the preceding section, in sophisticated cybercrimes where an intent is transformed into a sequence of steps through the use of inanimate robots and computers alone, the absence of any other human being in the process renders the notion of witnesses essentially irrelevant. No other human being may be ever aware of what had been accomplished by the mastermind cybercriminal. In general, given the incredible speed of computers and networks, humans beings can rarely serve as credible witnesses in the cyberworld. Conceivably, another computer, say B, is capable of witnessing the crime, i.e., observing the progress of the crime committed by computer, say A, in its native resolution of time. This would, however, compel us to trust computer B, which may bring us to a circular argument. How do we know for certain that B had not already been attacked and compromised? There are other serious technical challenges in correctly establishing a causal chain of event in distributed systems, beyond the scope of this book. The reader is referred to [12] for further details.

Computers and networks pose yet another challenge to the concept of the witness. To understand it, consider the fact that there is a great disparity in the reaction time of different animals. When a building is about to be demolished through a controlled explosion, as soon as the dynamite is charged, pigeons that might be resting on the structure sense the flash and begin to fly away to safety. Their sensors and reaction time are even faster than human beings. In contrast, a snail, walking near the building about to crash, will go about its business, literally oblivious to the dynamically changing environment. The snail reaction time is so slow that its sensors and brain fail to register fast activities. Given that we, human beings, have slow reaction time, computers and networks can trick our perception and cause us to believe an activity as having already occurred, when it fact it never came to transpire, and vice versa. Human beings have an additional quality, that of sensing the motion of a foreign object, when, in truth, there is nothing in our brain that physically moves in relation to the external object. The combination of the eye, brain, and memory and the physical limitations of all three components impart to us this unique ability. Through the innovative use of computers, conceivably, an operational brain can be successfully tricked into believing a sequence of activities as true and compelled to infer erroneous cause–effect relationships. There is no absolute reference of time in our brain, so past, present, and future are all relative for every individual. It has been documented in psychiatric medicine that severe injury to the brain, caused by concussion, viral attacks, or natural degeneration can lead to a warped perception of time that moves backward and forward erratically or the complete loss of ability to sense motion.

18.5 The Scope and Gravity of Cybercrimes

With computers and networks becoming integrated into every human endeavor, both at the individual and societal levels, the geographical scope of cybercrimes will gradually extend to every corner of the earth, while its influence in time will last well into the future. Logically, any future crime will inevitably encounter at least one computer, implying that all future crimes will be classified as cybercrimes. Unlike in the past, where an ordinary criminal could bring harm to a limited number of people, today, a cybercriminal can cause physical harm to millions of people with very little physical effort and at extreme speeds by attacking the environmental life support, electric grid, infrastructure including water and food supply, nuclear power plants, medicine stockpile, and all others in ways, limited only by imagination. On 3 December 1984, the Union Carbide pesticide plant in Bhopal, India, incurred an accident in which a poisonous gas, methyl isocyanate, leaked from an over-pressurized storage tank. The gas leaked into the atmosphere at dead of night, spreading a blanket over a good part of the city, and literally suffocating people while they were fast asleep. More than 15,000 people perished in a matter of hours and over the next few years, an additional 50,000 people either died, become blind, or permanently disabled. Although the event was classified as an accident, stemming from human negligence, a similar incident or much worse can just as easily be accomplished today at any chemical plant in the world by a determined cybercriminal from a remote corner of the earth.

The cybercrime issue can potentially become a grave problem, worldwide. This stems from an unexpected and unintended effect of computers and networks on our civilization. Beginning in the 1980s, computers and networks have been steadily making inroads into manufacturing, bringing enormous efficiencies and helping us enhance individual productivity. Since the 1990s, the rise of productivity, worldwide, has turned exponential. Economists such as Batra [13] have attributed this phenomenon to the rising wage-productivity gap across all nations, which first disturbs the equilibrium between demand and supply and, second, brings economic chaos. Sociologists such as Reich [14] believe that computers and networks are reshaping the new economy and eliminating many of the traditional jobs. In the new landscape, the labor market appears as a three-tiered workforce, with knowledge workers at the very top; followed by production workers in factories and offices carrying out simple, repetitive tasks; and the third layer, occupied by workers providing personal service in retail outlets, hotels, and hospitals. According to Reich, who served as the Secretary of Labor of the USA in the 1990s, scientists, engineers, lawyers, and others who occupy the first tier, are the symbolic analysts who manipulate information to solve problems. Reich also observes that knowledge workers are few but growing both in number and in wealth, while more and more workers from the middle layer are being pushed away by computers either into the first or third tiers, and the wages in the third tier are falling. A wide chasm is being created between the tiers.

In examining the issue from the discipline of cybercrimes, while Reich's observations and predictions may represent a gross oversimplification, let us assume for the sake of argument that the basic premise is correct. That is, given their precision, speed, untiring efficiency, and reliability, computers, networks, and robots will increasingly replace more and more workers in tier 2. An undeniable consequence is that computers and networks will not limit their challenge to the tier 2 workers alone. Very quickly, the chasm will spiral out of control and consume the knowledge workers, giving rise to smaller and still smaller groups of individuals who will trip their failing peers, all the way to the bottom. The transformation would occur with exponential speed, facilitated by the fact that knowledge, intelligence, and creativity are fractal [15]. When all is said and done, most people will find themselves in the bottom tier, while the top tier would consist of very, very few individuals, the elite of the elite, with exceptional understanding of the subtleties of computers and networks and will easily succeed in managing, operating, and controlling the entire world's affairs through the use of computers and robots. They would not need anyone else and may even enjoy the support of everyone. As long as the tiny elite adheres to ethics and altruism, civilization would enjoy an indescribable golden age. In contrast, should these individuals lose their conscience, fall victim to their dark side, and decide to perpetrate a cybercrime, they can potentially bring a halt to all progress for a considerably long period of time.

With computers and networks, one can conceivably formulate a cybercrime that is spread out so far (in time) and wide (geographically speaking) that it may literally lie beyond everyone else's imagination. One can also formulate a cybercrime that is so fast that it can blow away even our collective imagination. In the experience of the author, knowledge, intelligence, and creativity are fractal, implying that amazingly new principles and sub-principles will continue to be discovered by individuals. Consider the following, impossible appearing facts, but already found in Nature. While the AIDS virus, one billionth in size to a human being, can take 20+ years to kill an individual, the hantavirus can kill a healthy young person in 24 h and the neurotoxins from a box jellyfish can kill an adult healthy swimmer in less than 120 s.

References

[1] Citro, R., Ghosh, S., & Churgin, P. G. (1997, September). A fundamental metric for continuity of care: Modeling and performance evaluation. *IEEE Transactions on Information Technology in Biomedicine, 1*(3), 189–204.

[2] Citro, R., Ghosh, S., & Churgin, P. G. (1998, September/October). Administration of modeling and evaluation of continuity of care in a representative staff model health maintenance organization. *M.D. Computing, 15*(5), 298–306.

[3] Retrieved December 17, 2009, from http://www.handwritingexpertconsultant.com/borrowing_from_oneself.htm

[4] Worthen, B. (2009, August 4). New epidemic fears: Hackers. *The Wall Street Journal*.

[5] Allen, T., Veeramachaneni, A., & Ghosh, S. (2008, October 12–17). Computer-aided image analyses of immunostained tissue sections: Preliminary findings from an interdisciplinary investigation. *Megaron Athens International Conference Center, Athens, Greece*. Retrieved from http://www.iap2008.com

[6] Anderson, H. (1997, February). Money and the Internet: A strange new relationship. *IEEE Spectrum, 34*(2), 74–76.

[7] Federal Reserve Bank of Chicago. (1991). *Modern money mechanics: A workbook on bank reserves and deposit expansion*. Federal Reserve Bank of Chicago, P. O. Box 834 Chicago, IL 60690-0834.

[8] Brown, E. (2007, July 3). *Dollar deception: How banks secretly create money*. Retrieved from http://www.webofdebt.com/articles/

[9] The Daily Eagle, Montgomery, Minnesota: February 7, 1969. (1993, June 3). A landmark decision. In P. Cook (Ed.), *Reprinted in P. Cook, "What Banks Don't Want You to Know*. Retrieved from http://www9.pair.com/xpoez/money/cook

[10] Williams, J. *Shadow statistics*. Retrieved from http://www.shadowstats.com

[11] US District Court E.R. Larson. (1973, October 19). Findings of fact, conclusions of law and order for judgement, file No. 4-67 Civ. 138, Honeywell Inc. vs. Sperry-Rand Corp. and Illinois Scientific Developments Inc. Technical report, US District Court, District of Minnesota, Fourth Division.

[12] Ghosh, S. (2003, September). *Algorithm design for networked information technology systems: Principles and applications*. New York, NY: Springer.

[13] Batra, R. (2008, April 24). *The new Golden Age*. New York, NY: Palgrave Macmillan.

[14] Reich, R. (2005, December 17). The new rich–rich gap. *CommonDreams.org*.

[15] Ghosh, S., & Lee, T. (2010, May). *Intelligent transportation systems: Smart green approach to infrastructure design* (2nd ed.). Boca Raton, FL: CRC Press.

Part VIII
Mitigation of Cybercrimes

Chapter 19
Increasing Attack Costs & Risks and Reducing Attack Motivations

Elliot Turrini

This chapter explains why cybercrime mitigation should adopt a three-prong approach: raise attack cost [1], increase attack risk, and reduce attack motivation. The term, "attack cost," encapsulates the efforts and resources that an attacker must harness to commit the cybercrime. The term, "attack risk," means the probability that a cybercriminal will experience negative consequences from an attempted attack, including (1) physical injury, (2) monetary penalties, (3) loss of liberty through apprehension, incarceration, and probation, (4) social stigma leading to the loss of social standing, peer approval, economic opportunity, and other opportunities, and (5) psychological pain associated with conscience, namely guilt and shame. The term, "attack motivation," represents the cybercriminal's inner drive to conceive and execute a cyberattack, and it consists of two elements: (1) anticipated reward, i.e., expected economic, social, or psychological benefits, and (2) needs, i.e., the criminal's individual circumstances and preferences. Stigler [1] refers to attack costs and attack risks together as "costs of production of offenses." He views criminal activities from a economic supply and production perspective, where offending activities are synonymous to supply, while the demand is generated by society. Thus, wallets and office funds are invitations to the pickpockets and embezzlers, respectively. The costs of production of the crimes include the efforts of the offenders plus the penalties imposed by society. Thus, the crime industry will pivot around an operating point, governed by the composition of the criminals and the cost of producing offenses.

The approach springs from a critical analysis of the complexity of crime prevention in general; the unique nature of the cybercrime environment, explained in Chap. 1; the psychology of the cybercriminal, discussed in Chap. 14, and the findings of research into crime prevention. We will emphasize at the outset that we need continuing scholarly and objective research to critically assess this complex issue. The rationale underlying this chapter pivots around two key premises:

1. Behavioral science research has proven that raising attack costs and risks and reducing attack motivation are often more effective in preventing traditional crimes than the criminal justice systems' traditional deterrence
2. The traditional approach to deterrence ("traditional deterrence") is less likely to be effective against cybercrimes than against traditional crimes

S. Ghosh and E. Turrini (eds.), *Cybercrimes: A Multidisciplinary Analysis*,
DOI 10.1007/978-3-642-13547-7_19, © Springer-Verlag Berlin Heidelberg 2010

19.1 Behavioral Science Research and Traditional Deterrence

19.1.1 The Criminal Justice System, by itself, does not Adequately Prevent Crime

Research has shown that, in general, the criminal justice system by itself fails to prevent a socially adequate quantum of traditional crime [2–4]. The overwhelming evidence lies in the overcrowded prisons and repeat offenders. The principal reasons for the failure include the following:

- Potential offenders generally do not know the law
- They fail to accurately perceive that the expected cost for a violation outweighs the expected gain
- They are unable to make rational choices in favor of their self-interest
- They encounter low risk of punishment for the contemplated offense
- They never fully understand the true cost to them of the potential punishments

The failure should be examined in the light of the two key attributes of the criminal justice system, namely, (1) the criminal justice system relies on traditional deterrence as its primary crime prevention mechanism, and (2) traditional deterrence has limited effectiveness in preventing crime. Clearly, from time to time, the criminal justice system succeeds in preventing crimes by apprehending the attackers before the actual execution of the crime. However, this is infrequent, serendipitous, and it does not even constitute its main goal. The primary focus of the criminal justice system is traditional deterrence, which is founded on the "influence by fear," and attempts to create a coercive and pervasive social atmosphere where, "potential offenders decide to refrain from committing criminal acts due to a fear of apprehension and punishment [3]." Clearly, it assumes criminals as "rational actors," who think logically, seek to maximize the benefits from their crimes, and minimize the consequences and costs. As expected, traditional deterrence fails to grasp the notion of martyrs, kamikaze attempts, and suicide bombers. Research shows that, in general, non-violent criminals and those seeking monetary rewards are more than likely to qualify as rational actors. It is logical to assume that cybercriminals, generally drawn by monetary greed, may be classified as rational actors.

At its very core, traditional deterrence [2] is based on five basic assumptions about the criminals. First, individuals are aware that criminal and social punishments may be imposed on them for committing the contemplated act, namely, the crime. Clearly, if an attacker in unaware of the potential negative consequences, traditional deterrence fails. Second, attackers take into consideration the probability i.e., the likelihood, that they will be apprehended and punished for the crime. In general, higher probability of apprehension inhibits crime, while a lower likelihood of being punished will promote crime. Third, individuals can accurately estimate the total discomfort that the punishment will inflict on them, if apprehended. The total discomfort may include monetary penalties, loss of liberty, and social stigma and it must be perceived by the criminal as significant and severe. Otherwise, traditional deterrence will fail. Fourth, the potential criminal can accurately compute the benefits of the contemplated activity, including the economic, social, and psychological rewards. The higher the net reward from the commission of the crime, the greater the motivation and lower the deterrence effect. Fifth, the cost benefit analysis will clearly convince the potential criminal that the punishment is far too severe relative to the reward and that the criminal activity is not worthy of pursuit. In the event the total rewards outweigh the net punishment, traditional deterrence fails [5], as would be logically expected. Missing in the analysis in [2] is the criminals' inability to comprehend the benefits of punishment.

Two of the leading researchers and legal commentators, Robinson and Darley [2], have argued that the traditional deterrence's assumptions are flawed. They claim that, "potential offenders do not know the law, do not perceive an expected cost for a violation that outweighs the expected gain, and do not make rational self-interested choices." They further argue that, "the possibilities of deterrent effect are weakened by the difficulties in establishing a punishment rate that would be meaningful to potential offenders;" "the perceived probability of punishment is low, to the point where the threatened punishment is commonly not thought to be relevant to the potential offender;" and that a "delay between violation and punishment can dramatically reduce the perceived cost of the violation." Robinson and Darley [2] believe that, when they were writing, the probability of being apprehended and punished for robbery in the US, at best, was 1% [3]. Viewed rationally, crime often does pay. In summary, the commentators suggest that in general, traditional deterrence has failed to bear "any major impact" on crime.

19.1.2 Why Does Anyone Obey the Law: Social Stigma and Conscience?

The undeniable limitations of traditional deterrence raise a logical question, namely, why does anyone obey the law? Stated differently, "[g]iven the weak deterrent threat [from the criminal justice system] ... why do the vast majority of those free in society still act in a way consistent with the law" [4]? The quick answer is that "people obey the law (1) because they fear the disapproval of their social group if they violate the law [referred to herein as social stigma], and (2) because they generally see themselves as moral beings who want to do the right thing as they perceive it (referred to herein as following ones conscience)" [6]. "In social science, these two factors are referred to as (1) compliance produced by normative social influence [referred to herein as 'social norms'], and (2) behavior produced by internalized moral standards and rules [referred to herein as 'conscience']" [4]. Thus, social stigma and a person's own conscience, i.e., internalized moral standards, may offer more effective mechanisms to prevent crime.

19.1.3 Need for a Holistic Crime Prevention Approach

Despite the limitations of traditional deterrence, the legal community has not called for a radical restructuring of the criminal justice system – nor is it likely to do anytime soon. Most experts acknowledge that the criminal justice system plays an important, although limited, role in preventing crime. In looking for alternative crime inhibitors, research indicates that, for efficiency and effectiveness, "[c]rime prevention must utilize the wide range of ideas and abilities found throughout society" including, "[c]ommunity planning, architecture, neighborhood action, juvenile advocacy, security planning, education, and technical training." The research also emphasizes the need for (1) concerted public and private crime prevention strategies, and (2) the use of all available regulatory methods, including environmental and social norms. In other words, crime prevention requires a holistic approach.

19.1.4 Need to Target Cost, Risk, and Motivation

Current research indicates that increasing costs and risks and reducing motivation offer significant promise toward preventing crime. Strategies that target effort, risk, and reward [7] to prevent crime are termed "situational crime prevention," which describes "measures (1) directed at highly specific forms of crime (2) that involve the management, design, or manipulation of the immediate environment in as systematic and permanent way as possible (3) so as to reduce the opportunities for crime and increase the risks as perceived by a wide range of offenders [7]." According to leading researchers, situational crime prevention [8] has four objectives, namely, (1) increase perceived effort, (2) increase perceived risks, (3) reduce anticipated rewards, and (4) induce guilt and shame [9]. Its main premise is that, "deviant activity can be seen as a result of converging factors that influence opportunities for and the decision to commit crime. Actions that limit those choices, therefore, hold the potential to reduce crime ... "

Similar to traditional deterrence, situation crime prevention assumes that potential attackers are "rational actors," in that their decision, "whether to commit an offense [is] based on an array of inputs, including the effort involved, the potential payoff, the degree of peer support for the action, the risk of apprehension and punishment, and the needs of the individual [7]." Situational crime prevention recognizes that environmental changes can make "offending less attractive to potential offenders," and that "offenders seek out or respond to places, times, and potential victims that offer the least risk [7]." Although criminals do not always make rational decisions, as we had stated earlier, there is no question that criminals generally carry out a cost benefit analysis in some form when deciding whether to commit a crime. Under these circumstances, providing information on the costs, risks, and benefits to potential criminals is very important for it may bear substantial influence on criminal behavior, positive or otherwise. Research on information flows to criminals have led to the routine activities theory, which notes that the "source of information upon which an offender bases decisions, whether consciously or unconsciously, comes from the daily routines of the individual [7]." Under this theory, "the daily activity of individuals results in the convergence of motivated offenders with suitable targets in the absence of guardians." Furthermore, "[i]ncreasing mobility in society serves to bring targets and offenders together with greater frequency than ever before. Both the opportunity and choices for offending are enhanced [7]."

19.1.5 Summary

In summary, traditional deterrence is insufficient – by itself – to prevent a socially appropriate level of crime. Current research reveals the need for a comprehensive approach toward crime prevention, combining situational crime prevention and facilitating the flow of critical information to potential attackers.

19.2 Impact of Traditional Deterrence on Cybercrimes

Although there is no conclusive statistical data, anecdotal evidence, including the CSI/BFI survey, suggests strongly that traditional deterrence is even less effective in preventing cybercrime than traditional crime. At present, our cybercrime prevention efforts are derived predominantly come from the criminal justice system, augmented by the indirect regulatory efforts explained in Chap. 15. Also, the bulk of the crime prevention resources are allocated to traditional deterrence, although regulators have begun to recognize the need for alternative strategies. In the remainder of this section, we will examine the premise that a deficiency in the punishment probability, lack of social stigma for committing computing crimes, and the abundance of vulnerable targets have reduced traditional deterrence's ability to prevent computing crime and fostered a significant increase in cybercrime.

19.2.1 Research into Traditional Deterrence

Researchers in crime prevention have found that the effectiveness of traditional deterrence is a function of three factors, (1) certainty, i.e., the probability of being punished, (2) celerity, i.e., the swiftness with which the punishment is meted out, and (3) severity, i.e., the nature and extent of the punishment. While more study is warranted, researchers note that the certainty of punishment has the strongest deterrent effect, especially in the area of monetary or economic crimes [7]. They also note that an increase in social stigma associated with apprehension has a stronger deterrence effect than a corresponding increase in the severity of legal sanctions. Clearly, a high probability of apprehension and greater social stigma would be highly effective at preventing crime. In reality, however, today's cybercrime apprehension probability is low and the social stigma associated with a cybercrime conviction is not great. A convicted cybercriminal may even get a bump in earning potential because of the publicity related from his or her "cyber prowess."

19.2.2 Low Apprehension Probability for Cybercrimes

As explained in Parts I and II, even unsophisticated computing criminals can achieve almost perfect anonymity, making it very difficult for law enforcement to apprehend them. The presence of substantial evidentiary and investigatory impediments, described in Chap. 16, also works in favor of the cybercriminals.

19.2.3 Minimal Social Stigma from Computing Crimes

Historically, crimes have been associated with darkness, implying that the veil of ignorance of the perpetrators' undesirable activities by members of the society had been the greatest weapon of criminals. As long as they can commit their crimes without others' knowledge, the criminals can operate with total impunity and without fear of any social stigma. By its very nature, the operations in cyberspace are highly symbolic and, therefore, not easily visible to the members of society.

Cybercrimes pose four challenges to the issue of social stigma. First, the anonymity offered by the computer systems and the Internet symbolizes the veil of darkness, which not only facilitates but encourages cybercrimes. Second, cybercrimes are highly symbolic and complex, rendering their perpetration difficult to understand by the average citizen. Without a straightforward understanding, typical members of society are prone to be easily confused, especially by the criminals' clever accomplices. Third, cybercrimes can occur so quickly, in time, and with such near-perfection that, they appear beyond belief of most people. Fourth, exceptions notwithstanding, the traditional belief is that highly intelligent people cannot be totally unethical. However, it is an undeniable fact that superior intelligence will facilitate more subtle cybercrimes to be conceived and executed. Even though highly intelligent individuals may be initially drawn to cybercrimes out of sheer intellectual challenge, it may quickly spin out of control and focus on wanton destruction and selfish personal gains.

19.2.4 Abundance of Vulnerable Targets

Intuitively, the abundance of vulnerable targets in cyberspace is likely to entice criminals to commit crimes. There is undeniable evidence in history of a societal tendency to explore ways to defeat and exploit new technologies. Given the abundance of vulnerable targets, those who had pursued cybercrime related activities were often successful. This created a positive feedback loop and increased the propensity to commit computing crimes. There is, however, a deeper and more complex reason, involving the flow of cost, risk, and reward information and its influence on cybercriminals. In Chap. 14, we had explained that while a few individuals are inclined, i.e. predisposed to committing crimes, many others exhibit a strong aversion to crime which arises from an internalized moral standards referred to as conscience. Bounded by these two extremes, the majority of the individuals in any society fall somewhere in the middle. This majority are opportunists, constantly assessing the cost, risk, and reward of engaging in a cybercriminal activity. Consider the well-known fact that it is common for taxpayers to assess the risks and rewards of cheating on a tax return. Many individuals who are otherwise law abiding citizens choose to cheat on their taxes. This approach of continually assessing the cost, risk, and reward of an activity may have contributed to the increase in cybercrimes.

A common trait among all potential criminals is that their decision whether to commit a crime is strongly influenced by the flow of cost, risk, and reward information. Clearly, factors including economic need, psychological issues, namely, jealously, rage, etc., and drug and alcohol use influence the decision to commit a criminal act. Furthermore, we should not separate the choices of whether to commit a crime from that of the type of crime committed. The separation would be artificial since the choices often occur simultaneously. In essence, for every individual, criminal options are generally limited by each person's abilities, knowledge, skills, and information on the costs, risks, and rewards of the crime.

A logical extension of the routine activities theory, discussed earlier in this chapter, may be expressed as follows. When new information reveals an abundance of vulnerable targets, more people will begin to consider whether to attack the targets. They absorb the widely available knowledge about the vulnerability of any technology into their constant cost, risk, and reward analysis exercise.

When the Melissa virus spread around the world in March 1999, the media devoted significant resources to cover cybercrimes. The trend continues to this day with newspapers featuring cybercrime related articles frequently. This publicity unwittingly motivates the cybercriminals who derive satisfaction from others reading about their accomplishments in the media. The notoriety also increases the cybercriminal's reputation and standing within the underground community. The articles routinely mention the low cost of attacks and low risks of being apprehended. As a result of the flow of information relative to the low cost of attack and low probability of apprehension over a substantial period of time, in general, criminals have been emboldened and cybercrimes have been on the rise. Conceivably, it may have even increased the proclivity of the general public toward cybercrimes.

As expected, individuals react differentially to the information, depending on their proclivity toward crime, goals, knowledge, and skills. Consider a scenario where two individuals, I_A and I_B, are both equally inclined to commit cybercrimes for the purpose of monetary gain. While I_A is computer illiterate, I_B possesses average computing skills. For I_A and I_B, the decision whether to commit a cybercrime will be dictated by a complex function, whose inputs will consist of their knowledge, skills, and the available information on the costs, risks, and rewards. If I_A is an otherwise accomplished con artist, the cybercrime related information might have little effect because he or she might not perceive cybercrime as a more profitable enterprise than his current fraudulent schemes. A relevant factor is I_A's switching costs, namely, the effort and resources that would need to be mustered to successfully commit a cybercrime. However, where the switching costs are minimal and I_A realizes that the commission of a cybercrime will likely generate substantial reward, especially given the large number of vulnerable targets, logic would dictate turning to cybercrimes. As we had presented in Part II, the easy availability of automated, point and click, cybercrime tools has significantly reduced both the cybercrime attack costs and the switching costs for traditional criminals. The result is the undeniable, rapid proliferation of cybercrimes in society.

Consider an example from the field of enforcing the speeding laws of the country. In the past, a police car would give chase to a speeder, catch up with the driver, and then apprehend him or her. As speeders began to use high speed cars, law enforcement had to update the police cars, making them capable of sustaining high speeds for longer periods of time. In essence, by improving the cooling element of the engines, the newer police cars would continue the chase while the speeder's car would begin to overheat and malfunction. Exceptions notwithstanding, today, most drivers pull over when they see the flashing lights behind them. In the mid 1990s, when the photo radar was introduced in Phoenix, a large number of average citizens were issued citations for exceeding the posted speed limits without the police ever giving chase. The tickets carried a penalty of around $100. For a while, the program appeared to be wildly successful. The cameras, fitted onto police cars, would detect a speeding car, snap a picture of the license plate, and send a citation to the driver's home via regular mail. Very quickly, a piece of knowledge proliferated among ordinary people that by placing a piece of transparent plastic over the license plate, the police cameras would yield a hazy picture, from which it would be difficult to accurately decipher the license plate. Without the precise numbers on the license plate visible in the picture, the offending vehicle could no longer be traced. While the piece of plastic cost only a few dollars, the installation required only simple tools and could be easily accomplished in less than an hour. Most important, it was completely legal. The use of this simple device skyrocketed.

19.2.4.1 Reasons Underlying Abundance of Vulnerable Targets

- By definition, computing involves the use of arithmetic and logic to process and transport information at very high speed. Thus, computers are increasingly utilized in every societal function and are fast becoming ubiquitous. Clearly, armed with an understanding of the computing process, a perpetrator can adversely influence one or more computers and disrupt select societal functions, either for personal gain or to carry out irrational destructive tendencies.
- By nature, computing is synonymous with flexibility, which is manifested through devices, including floppy disk drives, CD-Rs, DVD-Rs, USB drives, etc., that

offer convenient transfer to and from the computers. This convenience also represents a vulnerability, present in every computer.

- The offer of anonymity on the Internet and the abundance of easily available attack tools renders all computers and networks as vulnerable targets. They also serve to tempt many otherwise law-abiding citizens to engage in cybercrimes for personal gain or mischief. The temptation is greatly aggravated by the low probability of apprehension, ease of launching the attack, and strong likelihood of success in perpetrating the crime.
- The effort and resources required to commit a cybercrime are substantially less than for traditional crimes. In general, effort refers to the combination of mental energy and time necessary to implement the attack. Consider, for example, the attack cost to physically burglarize a house. An individual must expend time and mental energy to select a target, choose the appropriate attack technique, implement the attack, and extract the benefit by either using or selling the bounty. Clearly, greater the time and the intensity of thought required to commit the crime, the higher the costs and the criminal act becomes less attractive to the criminal. The resources refer to the external items that the potential burglar would need, including money, tools, accomplices, information on the target, and the techniques to attack. Information on the presence of guard dogs, types of alarm systems deployed, tools to pick the locks and disable the alarm would be necessary. The burglar would need accomplices to carry the stolen items, drive the getaway car, and keep surveillance on any watchful neighbor or police patrol. Again, the greater the demand for attack resources, less attractive the target. In contrast, with cybercrimes, computers provide most of the effort and resources, by virtue of their tremendous speed of processing, rendering cybertargets attractive.
- The objective of a cyberattack can be classified into two broad categories, namely, (1) information theft, destruction, and alteration, and (2) interference with the normal operation of the computing technology, including DDoS. Under the first category, attackers may target select computer systems from which they may derive personal gain and the damage is generally localized. In contrast, under the second category, a significant number of key computers and networks may be attacked, damaging a nation's critical infrastructure and adversely affecting millions of people. The opportunity to cause widespread wanton destruction is often too strong an enticement for cybercriminals to ignore (think about the publicity generated by these cybercrimes), rendering the key computers and networks of any nation's critical infrastructures as attractive targets.
- As explained in Part II, the current tendency of homogeneity implies the use of identical hardware and software modules in every computer. While this uniformity offers speed and convenience, its contribution toward an abundant supply of vulnerable targets is overwhelming. The incredible successes of Code Red, Nimda, and I Love You malicious codes, explained in Chap. 3, stem directly from the homogeneity attribute. Consider another example, an unfortunate incident that occurred at a national brokerage firm in March 2002. A disgruntled system administrator used his administrative access privileges to install a destructive

program on 1,500 personal computers, nationwide, that were used to facilitate stock trading. The destructive program deleted all files in the target computers. The same administrative privileges that had been created to facilitate control of all of the 1,500 computers from a single point was successfully exploited by the perpetrator to delete all files in all 1,500 computers at an incredible speed.

- The incredible speed with which computers and networks have been embraced by society coupled with the lack of embedded security in the underlying hardware and software have introduced tremendous vulnerabilities. This has not only led to an explosion of cybercrimes, which we are witnessing today, but the potential for even more crimes as computing becomes more prevalent. Even if superior quality hardware and software modules were to be developed in the future, the continued use of legacy systems will ensure the presence of a severe weak link in the cyber-infrastructure. Furthermore, as the "convenience overshoot" tells us, industry (without further prompting and incentives) might not produce sufficiently secure computing hardware and software.

19.2.5 Summary

In summary, given that traditional deterrence appears to bear a minimal effect on cybercrimes, we must seek superior alternatives through which we can (1) raise attack costs and attack risks and (2) reduce motivation to attack.

19.3 Relative Effectiveness of Raising Attack Costs and Attack Risks and Reducing Attack Motivation

The pursuit of raising attack costs and attack risks and reducing attack motivation all assume a foundation of conscience and social stigma. Any effort at architecting innovative systems in cyberspace that are very hard to defeat and circumvent will increase the cost of attack and reduce cybercriminals' motivation to plan and execute attacks. Analogies from history include constructing fortresses on hilltops and surrounding them with thick and high walls. Furthermore, if the systems are designed to accurately detect any attempt to attack, preempt the attack, and accurately identify the perpetrator, then publicly exposing the cybercriminals will bring social stigma. This may serve as a far stronger and effective deterrent than possibly legal sanctions [7]. Social rejection is likely to trigger an appeal to one's own conscience, which gives it great potential for crime deterrence. Given the presence of an internalized sense that cybercrime violates the moral standard, the individual is likely to experience a silent, psychological pain. The result may be a lasting transformation into a cyber-ethical person.

There are two important assumptions here. First, the architecture is dynamic, evolving, and always anticipating and ahead of any schemes that perpetrators may conceive. This will require the confluence of the most intelligent, creative, and ethical minds of society as the architects and watchdogs of cyberspace. Second, social stigma requires that the significant bulk of the members possess a steady internal moral compass; that justice is fair, impartial, and genuinely free of any hypocrisy; and that absolutely no one is above the law.

Ideally, governments and legal experts will soon grow to appreciate that traditional deterrence in general has limited effect; that, relative to cybercrimes, its limited effect is even weaker; and that because of the growing integration of computing technology in every aspect of society and its endemic vulnerabilities, we need a holistic approach to cybercrime. When used as intended, computing technologies offer tremendous societal benefits – ranging from improved health care to renewable energy. But, when controlled for nefarious purposes, these same computing technologies can wreak havoc, causing untold social harm. Never before – except arguably in the arena of weapons of mass destruction – have so few (referring to cybercriminals) with so little resources (just a computer and internet access) had amassed the ability to cause such great harm. Imagine if the Melissa virus had deleted all the information on all of the infected hard drives. The cybercrime problem must be taken very seriously, and it requires an approach that goes far beyond the traditional approach to crime.

References

[1] Stigler, G. J. (1974). The optimum enforcement of laws. In G.S. Becker & W.M. Landes (Eds.), *Essays in the economics of crime and punishment*. New York, NY: Columbia University Press.

[2] Robinson, P. H., & Darley, J. M. (2003). The role of deterrence in the formulation of criminal law rules: At its worst when doing its best. *Georgetown Law Journal*, 949–1002.

[3] Clarke, R. V. (Ed.). *Crime prevention studies, 1,3,5*, 124.

[4] Robinson, P. H., & Darley, J. M. (1997, Winter). The utility of desert. *Northwestern University Law Review, 91*, 453–459.

[5] Shavell, S. (1985, October). Criminal law and the optimal use of nonmonetary sanctions as a deterrent. *Columbia University Law Review*, 1232–1262.

[6] Braithwaite, J. (1995). Inequality and republican criminology. In J. Hagan & R. Peterson (Eds.), *Crime and inequality* (pp 283–284). Palo Alto, CA: Stanford University Press.

[7] Clarke, R. V. (Ed.). (1993/1994/1996). *Crime Prevention Studies, 1,3,5*, 159.

[8] Clarke, R. V. (1980, April). "Situational" crime prevention: Theory and practice. *The British Journal of Criminology, 20*(2), 136–147.

[9] Clarke, R. V., & Homel, R. (1997). A revised classification of situational crime prevention techniques. In S.P. Lab (Ed.), *Crime prevention at a crossroads* (pp 150–151). Cincinnati, OH: Anderson Publishing.

Part IX
Future of Cybercrimes: Who Will Have the Last Word?

Chapter 20
Nature of Cyberattacks in the Future

Sumit Ghosh

Given society's increasing dependence on networked systems, it is clear from their past occurrences that cybercrimes pose serious threats to our long-term welfare. This chapter focuses purely on the technical nature of cyberattacks. It examines the current relationship between networked systems and cybercrimes, analyzes the nature of the relationship from a fundamental engineering perspective, and explores systematically where and how future advances in networked systems might influence the evolution of cyberattacks, even inadvertently giving rise to new forms of cybercrimes. Historical data reveals that technological advances in engineering systems design, including communications and transportation, were often accompanied by lack of foresight, thereby inadvertently opening doors to new forms of vulnerabilities following deployment. The greater the extent of the advancement, the deeper the potential chasm and more severe the damage incurred when a clever perpetrator successfully exploits the weaknesses. For example, when the Bell Telephone System employed human operators to switch telephone calls in the early 1900s, anonymous and unauthorized long distance calls were a rarity. As soon as automatic switching equipment replaced human operators, "phone phreaks" [1] discovered a serious flaw in the system. First by simply whistling or using a toy whistle and later through utilizing a tone generating blue box, one could break into the signaling control and dial long distance calls, unauthorized.

This chapter is organized as follows. Section 20.1 introduces the most basic principles underlying networking to help us understand the whys, whats, and hows of attacks directed at networks. Sections 20.2 and 20.3 present a detailed analysis of networking from two perspectives, uncovering in the process, some serious concerns about IP. Section 20.4 argues the need to pursue a new direction in network design for the future and lists a few recommendations and new approaches towards secure networked system design. Last, Sect. 20.5 reviews the fundamental attributes of cyberspace and what direction society may choose to travel toward a happy and prosperous future.

S. Ghosh and E. Turrini (eds.), *Cybercrimes: A Multidisciplinary Analysis*,
DOI 10.1007/978-3-642-13547-7_20, © Springer-Verlag Berlin Heidelberg 2010

20.1 The Engineering Fundamentals of Networked Systems

To facilitate understanding, this paper begins with a simple yet fundamental and complete picture of networked systems. Any networked system consists of three basic elements – nodes, transport links, and control algorithms. While the nodes appear in the public in the form of terminal devices such as the telephone handset for voice communication, computer terminals on which electronic messages are typed and received, or automated teller machines where financial transactions are initiated, their more complete and powerful form consists of the high-performance telephone switching systems housed in telephone stations, powerful routers located in the back office closets, control centers that govern the operations of trains, planes, and nuclear reactors, and highly reliable servers in the financial institutions and the Federal Reserve banks. Although the copper cables, belonging to telephone and telegraph companies, and the line-of-sight microwave and wireless towers of the cell phone industries are visible in the open, the optical fibers and line-of-sight laser and microwave links employed by the Internet service providers (ISPs) are generally out of sight of the ordinary public. The control algorithms constitute the invisible force, are the least tangible of the three elements, and reside in the hardware and software programs of the entire system.

Conceptually, the nodes represent computing engines that encapsulate the ability to execute computationally intelligent software programs. Throughout history, computing needs were supplied by the human brain. This extended into the early 1900s when human operators supplied the intelligence required for telephone switching. Since their conception in the mid 1900s, computers have continued to supply computing power, faster and more reliably and precisely than the average human brain. Since any two communicating devices must be separated by a finite geographical space, regardless of how small or large the actual distance, the energy representing the communication must cross this space, thereby requiring a transmission media. The forms currently in use include copper cable, optical fiber, wireless, laser-link, etc. The control algorithms constitute the underlying decision-making and help realize the overall intent and functions of the system. In its true form, a control algorithm is an abstract idea that is realized utilizing the tangible resources of the system. Thus, in a simple telephone system, the control algorithm finds and establishes, where possible, a path from the caller to the callee while in a complex financial network, the system ensures that the correct payer account is debited and the exact same amount credited to the payee account. In general, every node performs two distinct functions – route packet traffic and provide computing power for executing the underlying control algorithms. Over the past decades, while nodes and links have experienced phenomenal growth, our understanding of control algorithms have evolved the most and it holds the key to immense innovation in the future. In the future, control algorithms will be increasingly distributed, fast executing, and highly powerful. As an example of the subtle power of control algorithms, consider the following real-world example. Authorities would like automobile drivers to slow down in front of a school, while in session, to prevent children from getting hurt when they accidentally run into the street and the oncoming vehicle's high speed precludes it from stopping in time. One child has been hurt and there had been a number of near misses. The authorities first try posting speed limits on the side of the street but they are ignored. They then try to place the signs in the middle of the pavement but to no avail. The authorities seek assistance from the police department and an officer patrols the area for a limited time, giving out a few tickets, but as soon as the officer leaves, the situation is back to square one. The authorities also realize that while the event has strained their relationship with the residents of the neighborhood, the cost to permanently station the officer at the school is prohibitive. At this time, an individual, say A, comes up with an idea, one whose constituent components involve different elements of the system. The person reasons that current automobile suspension systems are not designed to react well under abrupt discontinuities in the pavement. The car and the driver would receive a medium jolt causing a highly unpleasant experience but no serious damage. A reasons that the pavement in front of the school could be re-engineered, a set of two or three discontinuities, of increasing width, inserted into the pavement, and metallic strips placed into these discontinuities such that they may be raised or lowered electrically. The strips are lowered to open up the gaps in the pavement while the school is in session and raised to make the pavement uniform when school is out. The technology is mature and has been used in draw bridges and elsewhere for decades. Under these circumstances, speeding drivers would be compelled to slow down on their own to avoid the discomfort and the authorities would achieve their safety goals, economically and without confrontation. Thus, the success of the control algorithm stems from a solid understanding of the properties of automobiles and pavement systems, knowledge of driver behaviors, and the conception of a mechanism that successfully exploits these knowledge pieces to achieve the objective.

20.2 Potential Advances in Networked System Stemming from its Fundamental Nature

From Sect. 20.1, it follows that any networked system is fallible to the extent that one or more of its three fundamental elements are vulnerable. Clearly, improvements in networking will also center around these three elements and the most logical enhancements include the following:

- *Bandwidth increase*: The speed with which information is carried by the transport links is captured by the notion of bandwidth. Clearly, to transport a greater volume of information and faster, greater bandwidth is desirable. To meet the increasing demand, greater number of optical fibers may need to be installed along existing conduits or higher capacity blue and UV laser may be deployed. Future technologies may even include lasers operating at X-ray, α-particle, and γ-ray frequencies, pushing the carrier frequencies to even higher limits. Though necessary and useful, increased bandwidth incurs an inherent weakness. Under attack and during the phases of detection and recovery, a very large number of packets may be lost in a short time, posing a significant challenge. While highly sophisticated attacks may cause unprecedented damage, even a simple, hit-and-run type attack, capable of disrupting the systems for a very short period, can cause appreciable damage while eluding detection.

- *Geographic proliferation of networking*: Since sharing constitutes a fundamental attribute of networking [2] and as it holds the potential to facilitate innovation among the citizens of the world [3], it is both logical and inevitable that networking will undergo extensive proliferation, touching individuals in every corner of the world, transcending even into deep space. Under these conditions, network vulnerability will increase sharply. For, attacks may now be launched from anywhere in the vast network, even far away remote locations. Also, the difficulties in controlling and managing such widely-dispersed networks may serve as encouragement for the perpetrators. Furthermore, if hackers are able to design lightning-fast attacks, a topic that will be discussed subsequently, the implications on our current ability to detect, identify, and contain such attacks, are grim.
- *Increase in the number of network users*: Spurred by the attribute of "sharing," the future will very likely witness a large increase in the number of network users. Under these circumstances, networks will require a sharp increase in the level of personnel support for management functions, thereby increasing the risk from insiders. The sheer numbers of personnel and users will imply significant challenges to authentication and non-repudiation.
- *Innovation in service types*: As a consequence of proliferation, future networks are likely to witness new and highly sophisticated types of services, beyond the current schemes that are based on bandwidth reservation, quality of service (QoS) attributes, etc. The new services are likely to constitute attractive targets because they tend to utilize specialized knowledge of the network's resources and perpetrators may exploit such knowledge to synthesize attacks tailored to specific services and users [4], causing significant harm while rendering the attacks hard to detect and localize their origins.
- *Transfer of executable code*: The idea of transporting executable code through the network has recently experienced rapid proliferation, bringing with it tremendous advantages. In essence, an executable code containing elements specifically designed and incorporated at node A is transported from A to node B where it is subsequently and immediately executed. Upon execution, B perceives an image and interacts with this interface, as intended by A, without possessing any a priori, detailed knowledge of A's design. Presently, network manufacturers and researchers [5] are pursuing this concept in the context of remote network configuration and management and it is likely that the level of interest will continue to remain high. Underlying this promise, however, is a serious vulnerability with far reaching adverse consequences. The threat stems from the fact that computer viruses consist of a string of 1s and 0s, are indistinguishable from any highly useful executable code segment, and there are virtually no known scientific principles that can guarantee any system protection from their first attack [6]. As in nature, where in a conflict between a venomous snake and a scorpion, the first

one that successfully strikes deals a fatal blow to the other, a carefully designed computer virus can completely wipe out a system during its first attack, denying the system any second chance to recover.

- *Continued use of IP networking principles*: Notwithstanding the technologies of classic telephony, ISDN, and the more recent ATM, TCP/IP networking has continued to dominate the evolution of networks over the last three decades. It also underscores the bulk of today's Internet. The November 21, 2001, request for information (RFI) for the design and deployment of GOVNET [7], intended to provide critical Government functions, clearly mandates it to be a private IP network. Careful analysis reveals two key properties of TCP/IP networking that underlie current networking products as well as the thinking among industry practitioners. The first property is the store-and-forward concept whose advantages include the fact that the exact route for any packet is dynamic, i.e. unknown a priori, and that different packets, even corresponding to the same message, may assume different routes, thereby enhancing security. In many of the current IP routers, to save on computation, the routing tables are deliberately left unchanged for long periods of time. As a result, many if not all packets of any given message may adopt the same route, thereby sacrificing a basic, security enhancing premise of the IP protocol. The second key characteristic is the classic end-to-end reasoning [8] that argues that, regardless of a specific weakness of the intermediate nodes, reliable communication between two end points, A and B may be achieved through executing high level protocols. Thus, where the intermediate nodes suffer from transmission related errors, the high-level protocol, TCP, solves the problem by repeated transmissions, initiated and controlled by the end points. Also, where the intermediate nodes are untrustworthy, secure communication between A and B may be achieved through encryption. A key difficulty with TCP is that its inherent retransmission capability also constitutes a potential weakness and perpetrators have successfully flooded the network, causing buffer overflow, severe congestion, and ultimately network failure. Furthermore, TCP's consumption of the valuable computational resource is an inherent performance limiter. Should TCP continue to be employed in future networks, hackers may exploit this weakness even more. Difficulties with sole reliance on encryption have been documented in [4]. To ensure security, the GOVNET RFI further requires that the network features limited connectivity and prohibits any interconnection or gateways to the Internet or any other private and public network. A serious concern with this requirement is that it contradicts a fundamental attribute of networking, namely sharing [2], and, as a result, GOVNET can quickly become obsolete and abandoned, even by the very users it is expected to serve. The following is a related scenario described by a security firm at the management of technologies (MOT) symposium [9]. To enhance its computer security, a high-tech company attempted to discourage its employees from using modems on company phone lines by converting its entire telephone system to digital. At the same time, the number of requests for FAX lines increased dramatically and it was later revealed that employees had connected their modems to the analog FAX lines to get their "job done." While users rely on information accessed through the network in order to complete their tasks, the exact location of an information source may never be predicted with absolute certainty, a priori. Internet II and Next Generation Internet (NGI) had been launched to compete with one another and succeed the current Internet [10]. Both Internet II and NGI were designed to be identical to the Internet except for employing faster fiber links and the list of expectations included no congestion and unlimited bandwidth for all users. Except for increasing the address space, adding a "scope" field for multicast addressing, and providing support for encryption-based authentication, integrity, and confidentiality, the latest version of the Internet protocol, IPv6, is identical to the traditional Internet protocol, IPv4. The NSF-sponsored workshop on Ultra Large Networks [11] noted the disarray in which Internet II had fallen, stemming from lack of use, and it was the majority feeling that Internet III is not needed as Internet II proved that it is not necessary. The most recent IETF's security specification [12] states that "solutions need to work end-to-end without depending on services in the middle," thereby confirming IETF's belief in the end-to-end reasoning, and advocates the use of ciphers and public–private key system – Diffie-Hellman or RSA, to achieve security on the Internet. There is yet another potentially serious problem with GOVNET. When a system that has been completely closed and isolated for maximal security is attacked from within, often, the result may be unimaginable damage. As an analogy, consider the recent flooding of the Mississippi river in the Midwestern states of the USA, when volunteers frantically piled sand bags to raise the height of the levies on both banks. However, as the weather worsened, rainfall inland continued to accumulate since the levies blocked their drainage into the river. As a result, all homes in the town were flooded. The same levies that were being faithfully raised to secure the town from the rising waters of the Mississippi ironically turned into seeds of destruction. As a second analogy, the most prestigious and fastest train in India, Rajdhani express, had an unprecedented record of security. For each of the air-conditioned compartments, the conductors dutifully locked every window and door shut, not just to keep the inside cool but shut out dust, bandits, and unauthorized people. However, On September 9, 2002, when the "up" train fell into the river Dhave [13], the same locked windows and doors turned into death traps for the passengers inside as they could not be opened by rescuers from the outside.

There is widespread optimism in the scientific community [14] that the solar system will be richly colonized within the next one hundred years. Given the relatively slow speed of space travel, a deep space network (DSN) will play a crucial role in space colonization. In discussing NASA's Interplanetary Network (IPN) project, Charles [15] notes that future plans for the IPN are to integrate local networks on Earth, other planets or moons, or even a space station or spacecraft, using traditional Internet protocols with a network that uses special long-haul, deep space protocols [15]. Robert Durst and others at MITRE Corporation have been working on a communication protocol to extend Internet communications into space. They present extensions to the TCP protocol for space communications [16]. However, DSNs are characterized by extreme latencies. For example, despite the potential for minor errors in store and forward routing in IP networks, the consequence is minimal since message transport times on earth range in the milliseconds. In contrast, the propagation delay from Earth to Mars ranges from 3 to 20 min and a minor error in forwarding a packet may have severe consequences, especially for remote control. Thus, if DSNs are based on TCP/IP in the future, they will be highly susceptible to attacks.

- *The role of control algorithms in the evolution of networked systems*: A key attribute of networked systems is the complex set of interactions between the constituent entities that are encapsulated by the underlying control algorithm. While the absolute timing of the interactions are very important, the relative timings are far more critical and challenging. Historical analysis of the evolution of networking and networked systems reveal the lack of a comprehensive set of principles and systematic experimental techniques to guide the synthesis of accurate control algorithms. Leading researchers from the top telecommunications companies [17] have expressed their serious concern over the occurrence of inconsistencies and failures in the context of "feature interactions" and the present inability to understand and reason about these events. For example, while private telephone numbers are successfully blocked from appearing on the destination caller id screens under normal operation, as they should, these private numbers are often unwittingly revealed during toll-free 800 calls [18]. As a second example, despite the telephone subscriber paying a monthly fee for the "caller id" service, incoming phone calls from the outside including even those initiated by the local telephone service provider, often show up as "out of area" on the consumer's caller id display. At the NSF-sponsored workshop on Ultra Large Networks [11], the general consensus among the leading experts on networking was that the Internet is not truly understood and its successful growth remains a mystery. Other experts have started to comment, privately and publicly, that the "Internet is far too complex to secure" [19]. At the MOT symposium [9], it was observed [20] that "buggy" code is responsible for security holes. While it is true, it only reflects the tip of the iceberg. A far deeper cause is little or no understanding of the interactions between high-level software and the underlying hardware at their interface. Moreover, any number of software patches, layered on top on an ill defined interface will not only fail to address the problem, worse, the additional layers will unnecessarily increase the computational burden and severely diminish system performance. For example, in a university campus, the use of firewalls and intrusion detection is extensive, resulting in emails typically requiring up to 3 h to reach building B from building A that are a mere 400 feet apart. Clearly, it is faster to walk for 5 min and deliver the message in person. In the sub-discipline of buffer management, an important area in network design and research, virtually all of the publications represent studies, either based on analytic modeling or simulation, of the behavior of proposed techniques for a single switch [21]. Clearly, a single switch network is not realistic. Lawson [22] traces the origin of the complexity in the computer industry to the deployment of "compromised" hardware design for all types of computing leading to the demand for unprecedentedly complex system software which, despite involving thousands of code developers, was never completely understood. To meet the increasing demand for sophisticated services, future systems must employ even more complex control algorithms. Thus, a complete understanding is imperative to harden systems from potential attacks and prevent serious failures.

- *Attacks Directed against Networking Elements*: In contrast to the past and current virus attacks against computer installations and user machines, perpetrators in the future are likely to direct their attacks against the networking elements. Potential reasons for this shift in focus are threefold. First, given the growing sophistication, range, and operational speed of the switches and routers, any disruption of the networking elements will cause far more widespread damage than attacking user machines individually. Second, given that the network providers are increasingly attracted to transferring executable code from network management centers to remote network switches for dynamic node reconfiguration or dynamic services deployment, perpetrators will find it irresistible to design viruses to attack the switches. Third, current practice and thinking in the industry is that network management centers may safely exchange control and status signals with the remote nodes through the same channels that carry user traffic. This greatly increases the vulnerability and, if the present thinking persists, widespread network disruption is likely in the future.
- *Electric Power Line as a Serious Vulnerability*: Since electric power constitutes the life-support of all computers today and as this trend is likely to continue into the future, the power line constitutes a serious vulnerability. The ability of current operating systems to shut down power to the underlying hardware, under user directive, has proved highly useful, especially when it comes to an uninterruptible power supply initiating a safe shutdown following a power outage. However, this feature also underscores serious threats. First, perpetrators may design viruses designed to initiate shutdown during critical activities and camouflage them to appear as a system crash, thereby eluding detection. Second, attacks may target and corrupt the system BIOS, thereby rendering the node temporarily unusable. Serious attacks may consist in reprogramming the BIOS, recovery from which will require the motherboard to be repaired or the BIOS replaced, implying a complete and prolonged shutdown. Third, viruses may initiate repeated shutdowns, even improper transient shutdowns, throwing the underlying hardware into a meta-stable state and causing damage to its internal components. Fourth, it is conceivable for a clever perpetrator to design a virus that will systematically shut down a node following every effort to turn in back on. Fifth, it is not entirely inconceivable for a team of determined perpetrators to transmit a virus infected signal, disguised in the form of a traditional power surge, over the power line into the nodes at homes and business offices. We exclude the potential use of the physical power lines to carry networking signals [23]. The attackers may get help from tapping into the control signals that are also sent over the power lines by the power generating companies to dynamically divert power to different power consuming substations. The great number of nodes that are likely to succumb to this attack renders the threat very severe.
- *Blindingly Fast Viruses*: To-date, most virus designs have targeted high-level application programs that execute slow due to their significant code lengths.

Since viruses piggyback on the host program and execute every time the host program is executed, current viruses execute relatively slow. Thus, when the Nimda virus would attack a node, one could observe the folders steadily stripped off their constituent files, in real time. In the future, sophisticated viruses that are designed to "jump" from the host application program to the core operating system, are entirely conceivable. In biology, the notion of a virus jumping from one animal species to another has been confirmed. Since the core functions are highly efficient compact code fragments that execute frequently and quickly, the virus will execute blindingly fast.

- For decades, it had been a routine practice to test the random access memory (RAM) of a computer along with the presence of other devices connected to the CPU and system bus when the machine was powered ON. Following a successful completion of the test, the operating system and other applications would be loaded, thereby rendering the computer operational. For computers manufactured a decade earlier, for RAM sizes of 144 megabytes (144 MB), the testing procedure would require approximately 28 s, which was significantly less than the time it took to load the operating system and other essential applications. Once a computer is already in operation, say it is either controlling the flight of a Boeing 747 over the Pacific Ocean, running a nuclear reactor, guiding a spacecraft in deep space, or pumping the anti-lock brakes of a car hurling down a steep and windy street in San Francisco, the speed of information exchange between the CPU and RAM is incredibly fast and memory testing becomes impractical, let along the danger that tampering with the memory would lead to erroneous results and the computer crashing with disastrous consequences. Today, in 2009–2010, many of the commercial operating systems vendors claim that from the time a desktop or laptop computer is powered ON, their operating systems are successfully loaded within 30 s. These computers may feature a massive 4 gigabytes (4 GB) of RAM, which would require approximately 800 s or 13 min to test the entire memory. Clearly, the traditional practice of memory testing has been eliminated to enable machines boot up faster and mitigate our impatience. Unfortunately, it also represents a significant vulnerability for computers and networks, and opens the door wide open to innumerable attacks with very serious consequences.
- *"Cloaked" Mobile Communications Devices*: While both mobile- and satellite-phones employ wireless technology and can move about freely within the area of coverage, they are governed by the principle of circuit connection or virtual circuit connection, implying that the infrastructure system is ever aware of the source and destination end units while a voice call or computer-to-computer call is in operation. This is necessary for the calls to be properly billed and revenue collected from the users. Even in computer-based Skype phone calls, which are free of charge, the Skype system must be aware of the location of the end users in order to properly route the audio and video packets over the Internet. In contrast, a new type of device is likely to appear in the near future, where the system will no longer be able to detect the origin of a voice call, rendering the task of tracking such calls exceptionally difficult. Subsequently, even newer devices will emerge, where the system will no longer be able to detect the destination

of a voice call. This will imply cloaking or invisibility, i.e., the communications network infrastructure will totally fail to detect the many voice calls that may be underway inside it.

20.3 Long-Term Innovations in Networked Systems

Networked systems are here to stay, the underlying reasoning is simple and profound. Networked systems reflect human civilization's core objectives – (1) acquire information on appropriate channels through interaction with other individuals on a need-to-know basis and (2) execute decisions on an individual or collective basis to (3) accomplish a desired goal or purpose. These objectives bear a direct one-to-one correspondence with the three basic elements of networked systems stated earlier. Thus, as the discipline of networked systems matures and increasingly becomes integrated into society, demand for greater efficiency and widespread benefit will spur revolutionary innovations. This section focuses on a few conceptual ideas that are original and possibly revolutionary but yet untested.

20.3.1 Generalized Networks

Increasingly in the future, networks will include both stationary and mobile nodes. In the resulting generalized network, while a few nodes may constitute the core, a set of nodes may aperiodically join and leave the network. For greater cooperation and efficiency, every node may even participate in route computation, discovery, and other important networking functions. A generalized network of the future may span terrestrial nodes as well as nodes orbiting around the earth, space stations, switches on other planets, and even space ships en-route in deep space. This desire for great efficiency and usefulness also renders such networks vulnerable to impersonation by perpetrators, leading to a potential breakdown in privacy and accountability. To eliminate the weaknesses, designers must carefully synthesize the underlying control algorithms. A thorough understanding of the principles of asynchronous distributed algorithms [24] followed by insights into the proposed algorithms obtained through modeling and asynchronous distributed simulation [25], may be of immense help.

Since wireless communication can either be radio based or employ direct line-of-sight microwave or laser, generalized networks are susceptible to computer viruses forcibly injected from the outside. A remote perpetrator may direct a strong beam at a target, overwhelm the local signal, and force a virus infected signal that may eventually disrupt the system. Current versions of cellular phones, for example, are susceptible to severe damage by viruses transported over the ether. It is pointed out that, unlike a biological virus that is tiny yet based on matter and must necessarily reach the target physically, i.e. either through direct contact or airborne, a computer virus can assume the form of pure electromagnetic energy and is not subject to the same restrictions.

The USA military is increasingly embracing the concept of precision weapons such as the recently tested massive ordnance air blast (MOAB) bomb, and the intelligent hovering missiles, drones, and robotic tanks of the future, that focus on intercepting wireless signals from the global positioning satellites to calibrate their present positions and guide themselves to the target precisely. Such weapons are highly susceptible to directed viruses that can not only cause the weapon's programming to be severely disrupted but even reprogrammed, en-route, to force it to turn back to the launch site and detonate.

20.3.2 Strictly Inanimate Networked Systems

Although any network must ultimately be in the service of mankind, the concept of a "strictly inanimate networked system" has been motivated by the observation that most system break-ins, approx. 90%, are caused by insiders. Then there are human errors, stemming from fatigue and lack of understanding, and unintentional leakage of critical system information resulting from employees succumbing to "social engineering" tactics by clever perpetrators. There is yet another reason cited to keep human beings away from networks, namely operational speed. Given that human beings are slow and impatient, their reaction times around 0.25–0.5 s, in contrast to computer operational speeds governed by GHz clock rates, i.e. execution cycle time of one-billionth of a second, any interaction invariably slows down networks dramatically. Therefore, whenever possible, network functions must be handled entirely by inanimate robots and computers, and kept off-limits to human operators. Clearly, while human beings may not be removed entirely from the process of network design, network operation and management constitute ideal candidates for automation. Conceivably, one can envision a future, where networks, upon design and deployment, permit no direct interface with human beings. The network itself schedules tasks, allocates resources, analyzes its integrity, checks connectivity, initiates self-healing [26] in the event of failures, etc. All interactions with such networks occur through inanimate robots and computers that serve as the controlling gates, task schedulers, and watchdogs. All valuable data, information, and procedures – whether related to medical, financial, trade secrets, etc. are maintained by inanimate entities, beyond direct access and manipulation by human operators. When an individual or organization with the proper authorization requires access to a specific information, the request is submitted to a computer or robot which first verifies the authorization, analyzes any potential conflicts, and then schedules the request to be processed. For high efficiency, the computational and network resource requirements of the request must be substantial.

Despite their obvious advantages from the perspective of security, strictly inanimate networked systems underlie serious potential problems. First, while an inadvertent system design flaw is clearly conceivable, during operation, the defect may interact with other system characteristics in unknown ways. Under a fully automated operational mode, before the error is detected, user data and information may be irreparably damaged and the network elements rendered uncontrollably haywire. Second, given the huge complexity of networked systems, an unscrupulous network designer may easily and surreptitiously leave behind backdoor traps and subtle susceptibilities that may be enabled and disengaged at will, years later. Third, the probability is very high that such systems will completely defy any attempt to develop a reasonably accurate analytic model. Assuming today's design techniques are translated into the future, unchanged, any serious malfunction or catastrophic failure of the automated network will provide very little insight into the causes of the failure. Fourth and most severe, if and when a perpetrator launches a virus, its interactions with the automated network may take on a new life, unknown even to the virus designer. Worse, if multiple viruses are launched, their convoluted interactions may yield a behavior that is unprecedented and beyond imagination. Without human beings to slow down the network, the unplanned and undesirable interactions will operate blindingly fast. The resulting damage may either be very extensive or the attack may be sustained over such long periods of time that it permanently alters the nature of information and brings about unforeseen societal changes. Fourth, in the event that portions of the networked system are detected to have gone berserk and it has been decided to shutdown those units down for repair, one may encounter severe difficulty in attempting to disable the illegal activities. During operation, the system may have autonomously modified the connectivity and routing algorithms through self-healing, making it difficult to determine the true source of the problem. In essence, the source of the attack is internal although it may be triggered by an external event or attack. Conceivably, in the future, the notion of self-healing may be extended to the network autonomously "reaching out" and choosing power receptacles or turning on backup power generators for most efficient, uninterrupted operation. Under these circumstances, turning off suspected network components may pose an enormous challenge.

20.3.3 Highly Interlinked Networked Systems

To provide for the growing need of highly sophisticated services and for efficiency in our daily activities, networks from different areas will be increasingly integrated in the future. As an example, a giant intelligent transportation network is clearly conceivable in the future, one that integrates the airline network, railway network, public transit system network, and taxi network. The thinking is that, while enroute, any traveler may continuously replan the route to the destination, taking into account current information on any expected delays stemming from accidents and incidents, etc. or unexpected changes in personal matters. As a second example, the benefits of integrating the cell phone network with a home automation network and the national power grid, are immense. An Arizona resident returning home ahead of schedule from New York may utilize the cell phone to remotely turn on the home

A/C a few hours prior to his expected arrival, turn on the swimming pool pump having recently learned of a dust storm in Phoenix, and instruct the computer to turn itself on after the house has cooled down below 74°. Already, in parts of the USA, the water company utilizes unused telephone lines in homes to remotely read the water meter, thereby interconnecting the telephone and water services network. Also, electric power generating companies transmit control signals to dynamically divert power to different cities over the same high tension lines that carry the high voltage electricity. In the post 9–11 era, there is an increasing desire to develop a homeland security networked system that will coordinate the different federal, state, and local agencies to meet any future threat to the nation.

While the benefits of increased connectivity are limited only by our imagination, so are the threats and attacks that a perpetrator may conceive and develop. For a highly interlinked networked system to be successful, the underlying control and coordination algorithm must be accurate, i.e. it must generate correct results under every conceivable interaction between the elements of the interacting networks. Where the algorithm is less than sound, a perpetrator may cause a disproportionately high degree of damage by exploiting the tremendous resources of all of the networks combined. In the homeland defense scenario, a weak control and coordination algorithm may enable a smart perpetrator not only to cause confusion and panic but to turn the networks' resources into a self-destructive weapon. To understand whether and how this is at all possible, consider the following example [27] from biology. The human immune system has evolved a highly sophisticated defense mechanism, in essence an algorithm, against foreign microbes, over hundreds of thousands of years. A number of different types of specialized cells, T-cells, white blood corpuscles, etc., numbering in the hundreds of thousands, constantly patrol up and down the bloodstream, searching out and attacking foreign microbes and destroying them whenever possible. By most measures, the algorithm is exceptionally successful for it has continued to successfully defend billions of human beings against millions of different types of microbes over the last hundreds of thousands of years. However, it has recently come to light that a tiny humble hantavirus has learned not only how to penetrate the defense mechanism but to bring about complete self-destruction. The mechanism it employs is fascinating. The tiny hantavirus enters the human body through the skin and propagates towards the lungs, easily slipping through the thin walls of the blood vessels lining the air sacks. Before the virus can do any discernible damage, the antibodies have detected the invader and quickly give chase, forcing their way through the blood vessels in the lungs. In the process, however, their much bigger size forces the blood vessels to rupture, and plasma leaks into the air sacks, causing death within hours from respiratory failure.

The importance of a carefully synthesized coordination and control algorithm was recently underscored in a simulated attack, carried out in Denver [28], to measure the country's level of preparedness against a bioterrorism attack. To mobilize the maximum resources under an attack, all relevant federal, state, and local agencies were involved. As the exercise unfolded, while the communication between members of the same agency intensified, as expected, the overall decision making process broke down, causing tremendous casualties and widespread panic. For every major decision, over one hundred people from the different agencies had to be brought into a massive conference call for consultation. While some of the workers were on the surface with wired telephones, others used cordless or satellite phones, and yet others used cell phones while in underground bunkers. The conference call frequently broke down, resulting in the lack of right decisions and ultimately, confusion.

Furthermore, a highly intelligent and dedicated perpetrator of the future may carefully analyze the coordination and control approach of a massively interlinked system and develop a sophisticated attack by utilizing (1) enormous computing power from distributed processors, (2) knowledge of asynchronous distributed algorithms, and (3) testing and refining the attack through modeling and simulation.

The most serious threat to the highly interlinked networked systems in the future may come from coordinated attacks that are likely to be extremely effective while remaining elusive. For quick response in an emergency, in the future, the railway network, telephone network, intelligent transportation system network, FAA network, FBI network, immigration and naturalization network, air defense network, coast guard network, police network, and hospital network, are more than likely to be all interlinked. Underlying every timely interaction between the networks is the concept of an event, a key attribute of which is the notion of time. Given that the networks are dispersed over a wide geographical area, algorithms must be put in place to ensure proper time synchronization for consistent and accurate results. A coordinated attack on the clocks through the use of high energy electromagnetic pulses (EMPs) may cause disruption, even for a short period of time, causing unexpected, possibly unthinkable losses. The phenomenon of timing discrepancies with seriously adverse consequences is not new, there have been numerous inadvertent occurrences in the past. In the accidental downing of two USA military helicopters during the Gulf war by a USA fighter [29], timing discrepancy caused two critical pieces of information to be flipped erroneously – (1) the radar image is a friend, and (2) the radar image is unknown, possibly an enemy.

Consider a hypothetical coordinated attack within the financial industry. A team of perpetrators design and launch a virus that recognizes files with financial records in them, surreptitiously changes a few of the facts and figures at random just prior to the initiation of the backup process, and then restores the figures to their original values at the conclusion of the backup routine. Since the backup routine handles thousands of files, it possibly cannot check the integrity of every individual file prior to saving it on the backup media. Since the on-line records are unaffected, regular audit checks do not detect the anomaly. By design, the virus executes surreptitiously over a very long period of time, thereby adversely affecting the backup records at several levels and destroying any chance of the correct figures from ever being reconstructed through correlation, later. The viruses may even be customized for each bank and financial institution so as to defeat any attempt to recognize a discernible pattern, thereby diffusing any suspicion of a coordinated attack. The last phase of the coordinated attack consists of an assault on the main on-line computer system and every concurrently running secondary unit, either through an explosive device or by manipulating the grid that provides electric power to the machines.

Thus, not only are the on-line records destroyed but the backups, at every level, have been corrupted, causing confusion, panic, and unforeseen difficulties.

To test the protection of the nation's critical infrastructure, two exercises, the first, code-named Black Ice held in Salt Lake City in November 2000, and the second, code-named Blue Cascades, held on June 12, 2002 in Portland, Oregon, revealed the following. The effects of a major terrorist attack or natural disaster could be made significantly worse by a simultaneous cyberattack [30].

The October 14, 2002 terrorist attack in Bali, Indonesia, may have been planned as a coordinated attack. Immediately following the disaster, it was reported that the cause was a single powerful bomb. Soon thereafter, it was revealed that there were two explosions. The first, a small one, was detonated inside the club which caused the panicked patrons to huddle outside in an alley behind the building. With a high concentration of people in the alley, a much more powerful bomb was then exploded by the terrorists, causing extensive death and damage.

20.3.4 Quantum Entanglement Technology for Packet Transport?

The notion of "entanglement" [31] in quantum mechanics refers to the fact that when two quantum particles – A and B, in our universe, are entangled, they share the same destiny regardless of the physical distance between them. That is, whatever occurs to A will happen to B, simultaneously. The phenomenon has already been experimentally verified. Clearly, entanglement occurs at speeds in excess of the speed of light, transcending the limits set by the special theory of relativity. However, even though B undergoes a change at time t (say), corresponding to the change experienced by A at that instant, an observer O_B located near particle B may not possess instantaneous knowledge, all by itself, of the fact that the cause of B's transformation is indeed particle A. For this, another observer, O_A, near particle A must send a message by any conventional means to observer O_B. Thus, although particles A and B may experience exact changes instantaneously, information flow between A and B is still bound by the speed of light. From the perspective of information security, quantum entanglement offers an unprecedented new capability. We can subject particle A to a transformation locally and upon successful completion of the transformation of A, observer O_A sends a conventional message to observer O_B. The actual change experienced by A can be viewed as an important message. This message, however, is never propagated by conventional means. Only a simple communication from observer O_A to O_B asking the latter to read the state of particle B, is propagated over a copper cable, optical fiber, wireless, direct laser, etc. Upon reading the state of B, observer O_B can extract the degree of change experienced by B and determine its meaning by referring to a table, jointly developed between O_A and O_B earlier. Thus, given that the actual message is manifest in the form of a transformation of A, strictly performed locally, the need for encrypting a packet in transit is eliminated. Furthermore, even if a perpetrator were to steal the table or intercept and read the simple communication from O_A to O_B, little harm would come from it. However, there is a serious difficulty with this approach. A perpetrator can easily cause complete disruption by intercepting and destroying the simple communication. Observer O_B would be denied knowledge that A had been attempting to communicate with it. Other forms of attacks are also conceivable. In the teleportation experiment that validated quantum entanglement, the research team led by Zeilinger [31] had obtained entangled photons by splitting a UV laser pulse through a parametric down-converter crystal and then directed the photons to O_A and O_B. Clearly, a perpetrator can hijack photon B and masquerade as observer O_B. Worse, by performing manipulations and measurements on photon B, prior to those conducted by observer O_A, the perpetrator may surreptitiously affect observer O_A's observations and measurements. The perpetrator can also duplicate the experimental setup, masquerade as O_B, and send a bogus entangled photon to O_A.

20.3.5 Fundamental Insight into the Nature of Security

Careful analysis reveals that, from theoretical principles and practical considerations, 100% security in any networked system may not be achievable. The underlying reasoning may be traced to the inherent characteristics of human nature, namely limited memory, impatience, susceptibility to fatigue, easily bored during repetitive tasks, and the desire to maintain full control over every system design. Consider, for example, the issue of password-based access control. For obvious reasons, a password must consist of a finite number of characters, presumably between 5 and 9, so one may commit to memory. Any longer sequence of characters may be easily forgotten and would require it to be written down, implying a vulnerability. Given today's fast computers, even a brute force approach to breaking a password would yield quick results. Thus, one precautionary measure, used in practice, limits the number of password attempts for a given user account to 3 or 4 after which, the user account is locked out and must be reset by the systems manager with access to the root account. This measure, however, cannot be extended to the root account. For then, a perpetrator will repeatedly attempt to logon to the root account, making sure that the bogus passwords fail, and lock out the root account, from which the system may not ever be recovered. Therefore, by design, the system must tolerate an indefinite number of logon attempts to the root account. This constitutes a fundamental vulnerability for, in time, any password cracking program will invariably break the system.

Although the discipline of mathematics categorically denies a network from ever gaining a 100% security status, the situation is far from bleak. Through engineering principles, a pragmatic secure network to carry out society's critical functions is realizable.

20.4 New Approaches to Secure Networked System Design for the Future

This section briefly presents a few key suggestions and new approaches that may assist in secure network design in the future. It is pointed out that even the consensus report from the National Research Council on networking research [32] recommends the aggressive pursuit of new ideas under the three M's – measurement of the Internet, modeling of the Internet, and making disruptive prototypes.

- Develop superior network node hardware architecture including distributed switching fabric and buffers to offer superior reliability and defeat performance attacks [4]. Develop superior programming language principles and derive robust code [6] to defeat perpetrator's attempts to alter the execution semantics and manipulate the network node computing engines.
- Augment the concepts of store-and-forward and end-to-end reasoning with other networking principles, presented in [4]. It is pointed out that the recent breakthrough – a deterministic $O((log\ n)^{12})$ time algorithm for testing if a number is prime [33], poses a fundamental challenge to the computational intractability that had constituted the main defense of cryptography.
- Utilize the principles of asynchronous distributed decision-making algorithms [24] to develop accurate control and coordination algorithms for complex networked systems.
- Test, refine, and experimentally study a proposed networked system design through modeling and simulation prior to developing and deploying a complete prototype. Specifically, develop accurate behavior-level models of proposed networked system designs, synthesize a simulation employing asynchronous distributed event-driven techniques, and then execute the simulation on a testbed of loosely-coupled parallel processors that closely resembles reality. While the approach is scientific and unquestionably economical, it has the potential to eliminate serious design errors, possibly preventing catastrophic failure and irreparable damage during its operational life.
- The designers of a secure networked system must be fully committed and determined to develop an accurate solution, not a good enough one, even if that means falling behind schedule or cost overruns, within reason. For, not only will a well designed system last 100–200 years but any compromise or imprecision may imply irreparable loss in the future or the failure to prove the guilt of perpetrators beyond reasonable doubt.
- Examination of history reveals that courageous individuals as well as perpetrators were able to discover fatal weaknesses, in otherwise highly fortified systems though comprehensive analysis. Often, the attacks that had successfully exploited these vulnerabilities were blatantly simple. For example, in ancient Asia Minor, Alexander of Macedonia clashed with Darius, emperor of the mighty Persian empire. In their first battle, Alexander and his army of 15,000 faced Darius with his army of over 45,000. According to the prevailing rules of military engagement, Alexander should have withdrawn in the face of superior numbers to avoid

a crushing defeat. However, brash, in his early twenties, a novice, and bent on revenge for earlier humiliating Greek defeats, Alexander decided to engage in battle. He noticed that Darius had employed a number of archers, a sign of weakness in that era and embarked on an unprecedented strategy. Leaving behind the bulk of his army in charge of his generals, Alexander charged at the head of an elite group of 5,000 Macedonian Republican Guards, focusing straight for Darius. Observing the battle from his location in the middle of his own army, the seasoned veteran Darius quickly recognized Alexander's single-minded focus on capturing him. Fearing for his life, Darius fled the battlefield, leaving the Persian army in complete disarray and eventual defeat. Consider a second example. Fast forwarding to our century, in the late 1960s, despite employing thousands of engineers and scientists to develop a highly sophisticated telephone system, phone phreaks [1] were able to use a simple toy whistle found in Captain Crunch cereal boxes to break into the system and initiate unauthorized long distance calls. At the time, Bell Telephone Systems had employed in-band signaling wherein the control signals were transported along the same wire that carried voice. From the security perspective, this was a fundamental design flaw, one that had to be corrected later by installing a physically distinct signaling network. Consider a more recent occurrence as the third example. In the mid to late 1990s, a major oil company stated publicly that it was developing a secure wireless network rated at GB/s, at an enormous cost, to transfer billions of bits of data from ship to shore, obtained from the ocean bed exploration for oil. Lacking a holistic approach, the planners had overlooked a simple fact that these billions of bits would be subsequently processed down to a few hundred bytes and ultimately expressed in the form of maps and charts of the ocean floor which, in turn, would help engineers decide whether or not to drill the ocean floor. Clearly, the processing may be carried out locally on the ship, using desktop or laptop computers and the few hundred bytes of processed information easily sent to the corporate laboratory through inexpensive and existing secure wireless links.

Clearly, the greatest threat to any networked system comes from an intelligent individual or a team, dedicated to harm the system. The most logical and, perhaps, the only recourse lies in the designers expending serious effort to uncover any flaws and errors in the system design, before the perpetrators find them, through holistic thinking and simulation, both prior to developing the prototype and after the system is deployed. Furthermore, it may help to maintain a fine line of distinction between individual hackers who are tempted by the challenge to discover vulnerabilities in highly fortified system and organized perpetrators motivated to cause meaningless harm to others. Should individual hackers, who tend to draw a line when it comes to causing real harm to people, be severely prosecuted, we may never find out system vulnerabilities until a perpetrator strikes a severe blow and it is too late to prevent a catastrophic meltdown. In a strange sort of way, without clever hackers earnestly at work, the discipline of networked systems may quickly suffer from complacency, arrested progress, and become unexciting and lifeless.

20.5 Who Will Have the Last Word in Cybercrimes?

To grasp their scope and full potential, cybercrimes may be correctly viewed as a collection of all of the crimes ever committed over the past 3,000 years of human history, only amplified a billion times or more through every possible permutation and combination and at every conceivable resolution of time.

At its core, cybercrime is the ultimate intellectual battle of the minds. The battlefield is the abstract mental plane, even though the manifestation occurs in the physical world. In the battle, one party plays the role of the cyberattacker, while the other serves in the adversarial role of the cyberdefender. Exactly who is on the side of Truth and who is unrighteous becomes blurred after a while and everything boils down to a matter of perspective. To understand this strange dichotomy, consider an ancient Indian philosophy, which states, for anything and everything in this universe, without exception, there is always an opposite or anti. The statement has both troubled and inspired the author. It appears to corroborate the notion of fractal intelligence we had introduced earlier, where, the deeper we dive into our pursuit of knowledge, the more we realize the subtle and finer forms of knowledge. The distinctions that we may have held very firmly at a given level appears to blur at the finer level, yet we gain tremendous clarity and profound understanding. For example, in a debate whether Nature is analog or discrete, we can begin with our own galaxy, the Milky Way. Although it appears continuous and analog to the naked eye, a powerful telescope will reveal that there are countless yet discrete stars, many with their own solar systems. When we focus our attention to any given planet of a solar system, we find it continuous, similar to our earth. Yet, when we examine the earth with a fine microscope, we find it is made of countless number of discrete particles. Each particle again appears continuous and analog until we pull out an even more powerful microscope. Then we discover that the particle is made up of uncounted number of discrete sub-particles, each exceptionally tiny. This continues, ad infinitum, and it teaches us that whatever appears analog is actually discrete, and vice-versa. It all depends on the resolution of the perspective. It follows from the Indian philosophy and from the fractal nature of intelligence that there can never be a permanent winner in the battle for cyberspace. One party can win for a short while but soon its reign will come to an end when the adversary discovers an even deeper principle. This is guaranteed. Jules Verne had stated, what one person can dream, another can build. Although Verne may had referred to physical objects such as submarines and spaceships, the principle can be equally extended to the abstract world of cyberspace. Furthermore, just as an idea can be constructive and beneficial to humanity, another idea can be equally destructive. Under our present adversarial system of thinking, of which the criminal justice system is the by-product, control will oscillate back and forth between the cybercriminals and cyberdefenders, with consequences that will be primarily destructive and pointless. If society is to survive and prosper, we must respect everyone's inalienable right of free will, i.e., withhold the temptation to control others, and pursue the path of harmony through ethics, compassion, caring education, and understanding, which has been the message across all of the chapters of this book.

References

[1] The Learning Channel. (2001, July 25). *Hackers: Computer outlaws*. Cable Television.

[2] Pillalamarri, S., & Ghosh, S. (2001, June 11–15). The impact of source traffic distribution on quality of service (QoS) in ATM networks. *Proceedings of the IEEE International Conference on Communications* (pp. 2855–2859).

[3] Lessig, W. (2001). *The future of ideas: The fate of the commons in the connected world.* New York, NY: Random House.

[4] Ghosh, S. (2002, April). *Principles of secure network systems design.* New York, NY: Springer.

[5] *Annual international working conference on Active Networks*. Retrieved December 4–6, 2002, from http://www.iwan2002.org

[6] Ghosh, S. (2002, Feb/Mar). Computer virus attacks on the rise: Causes, mitigation, and the future. *Financial IT Decisions 2002 (Vol. 1), a Bi-Annual Technology Publication of the Wall Street Technology Association, Red Bank, New Jersey.* Retrieved from http://www.wsta.org; ISBN 1-85938-369-6, 1:16–17.

[7] General Services Administration. (2001, November 21). *Request for information – GOVNET.* US Federal Government.

[8] Voydok, V. L., & Kent, S. T. (1983, June). Security mechanisms in high-level network protocols. *ACM Computing Surveys*, 135–171.

[9] Management of Technologies Symposium. (2002, October 22–24). *Guarding your business: Enterprise architectures for security.* Retrieved from http://attila.stevens–tech.edu/motsymposium

[10] Swartz, J. (1997, July 28). PAGE ONE – Need for speed spawns 2 internetlets. *San Francisco Chronicle*. Retrieved from http://www.sfgate.com/cgi–bin/article.cgi?file=/chronicle/archive/1997/07/28/MN20332.DTL

[11] *NSF sponsored workshop on ultra-large networks: Challenges and new research directions.* (2001, Nov 18–20).

[12] Schiller, J. I. (2002, July 1). *IETF security specification – Designing secure protocols.* Retrieved from http://www.ietf.org

[13] Editorial. *The Rajdhani Disaster*. Chandigarh, India: The Tribune. Retrieved September, 2002, from http://www.tribuneindia.com/2002/20020911/edit.htm

[14] Lange, L. (1999, January). The Internet technology 1999 analysis and forecast. *IEEE Spectrum, 36*(1), 35–40.

[15] Charles, J. (1999, September). Technology news: Interplanetary network aims for the stars. *IEEE Computer, 32*(9), 16–19.

[16] Durst, R. C., Miller, G. J., & Travis, E. J. (1997, October). TCP extensions for space communications. *Wireless Networks, 3*(5), 389–403.

[17] Private communications with Dr. Al Aho. (2001, December) *Vice President of Research.* Murray Hill, NJ: Bell Labs, Lucent Technologies.

[18] Private Communications with Gottfried Luderer. (2002, January). *Emeritus ISS Chair Professor*. Electrical Engineering Department, Arizona State University, Tempe, AZ 85287.

[19] Schneier, B. (2001, August). *Code Red Worm.* CRYPTO-GRAM, Counterpane Internet Security, Inc. Retrieved from http://www.counterpane.com

[20] Bellovin, S. (2002, October 22–24). Realistic security. *Guarding your business: Enterprise architectures for security, Management of Technologies Symposium.* Hoboken, NJ: Stevens Institute of Technology. Retrieved from http://attila.stevens–tech.edu/motsymposium

[21] Bonde, A., & Ghosh, S. (1994, August). A comparative study of fuzzy versus "fixed" thresholds for a robust queue management in cell-switching networks. *IEEE/ACM Transactions on Networking, 2*(4), 337–344.

[22] Lawson, H. W. (2002, June). Rebirth of the computer industry. *Communications of the ACM, 45*(6), 25–29.

[23] Held, G. (2006). *Understanding broadband over power line*. Boca Raton, FL: CRC Press.

[24] Ghosh, S. (2003, September). *Algorithm design for networked information technology systems: Principles and applications*. New York, NY: Springer.
[25] Ghosh, S., & Lee, T. (2000). *Modeling and asynchronous distributed simulation: Analyzing complex systems*. Piscataway, NJ: IEEE Press.
[26] Kawamura, R., Sato, K., & Tokizawa, I. (1994, Jan). Self-healing ATM networks based on virtual path concept. *IEEE Journal on Selected Areas in Communication, 12*(1), 120–127.
[27] Public Broadcasting Service, KNME-TV, Albuquerque, New Mexico.. Dangerous friends, friendly enemies. In *Intimate strangers: Unseen life on Earth*. Retrieved from http://www.pbs.org/opb/intimatestrangers/, Aired February 26, 2000
[28] Channel 13, New York City. (2001, November 16). *Bioterrorist attack: who gets vaccinated?* Public Broadcasting Service. Retrieved from http://www.pbs.org/wnet/religionandethics/week511/cover.html, Show 511.
[29] CNN Primenews. (1994, August 24). Defense Department Finding, Pentagon. In *Reporter Jamie McIntyre*, Cable Network News, Atlanta, GA, USA.
[30] Verton, D. (2002, July 8). Exercise exposes vulnerabilities. *Computerworld*. Retrieved from http://www.computerworld.com/industrytopics/energy/story/0,10801,72532,00.html
[31] Mullins, J. (2001, February). The topsy turvy world of quantum computing. *IEEE Spectrum*, 42–49.
[32] CSTB: Annual Convening on Research Horizons. (2001, January 23–24). *Looking over the fence at networks: A neighbor's view of networking research*. National Research Council Consensus Report. Retrieved from http://www7.nationacademies.org/project_researchhorizons.html
[33] Agrawal, M., Kayal, N., & Saxena, N. (2002, August 6). *PRIMES is in P*. Retrieved from http://www.iitk.ac.in/infocell/announce/algorithm

Introducing the Authors

Stewart A. Baker is a partner in the law firm of Steptoe & Johnson in Washington, D.C. From 2005 to 2009, he was the first Assistant Secretary for Policy at the Department of Homeland Security. His law practice covers matters of homeland security, cybersecurity, data protection, and foreign investment regulation. During 2004 and 2005, Mr. Baker was General Counsel of the Robb-Silberman WMD Commission investigating intelligence failures prior to the Iraq war. Mr. Baker has also been General Counsel of the National Security Agency and Deputy General Counsel of the Education Department. He clerked for Justice Stevens on the Supreme Court and Judge Coffin on the First Circuit.

Alan Boulanger is the Senior Security Architect at BlueRISC – a provider of innovative cryptographic hardware/software solutions to the computing and mobile markets. Prior to joining BlueRISC, Mr. Boulanger spent 11 years conducting information security research at the IBM TJ Watson Global Security Analysis Laboratory. His research interests include cryptography, network security, intrusion detection and remediation, applied penetration testing techniques, data forensics, telephony security, and emerging threat analysis. Mr. Boulanger has authored several research papers, articles, and holds information security related patents. As part of his research, Mr. Boulanger has provided award winning information security related expertise to the business community and to the US Secret Service, FBI, and other federal agencies.

Michael Caloyannides earned his PhD in Electrical Engineering, Applied Mathematics and Philosophy from Caltech. He worked at top technical levels for 15 years in the aerospace industry, followed by another 14 years as chief scientist for an agency of the US government during which time he was awarded the coveted Scientist of the Year award plus five separate certificates of Exceptional Accomplishment. He then worked as Senior Fellow for Mitretek Systems (now Noblis, Inc.), and is now with TASC Inc. He has also been an adjunct professor of computer science for George Washington University and Johns Hopkins University for a number if years. He has published two books on computer security as a sole author, and countless papers. He has lectured throughout the Far East, as well as in Dubai and the US. He has a US patent on high speed modem design. He has been a member of the board of IEEE's Security and Privacy magazine, where he authored a monthly column for the first two years of its existence. His hobbies include scuba diving and piloting airplanes; he is a licensed commercial, multiengine instrument pilot.

Michael Erbschloe's career has been mostly focused on the analysis of the economics of information technology, public policy relating to technology, and the process of utilizing technology in reengineering organizations. Over the last 25 years he has held positions in private consulting firms, government organizations, and research institutes. Michael has taught at several colleges and universities and has designed technology-focused. He received an M.A. in Sociology from Kent State University and a B.A. in Sociology from Webster College. Michael has authored thousands of articles for a wide variety of publications in the computer and business press. These articles focused primarily on the future of technology and the impact of technology on societies. He has also authored several books including: Physical Security for IT Managers (Elsevier Science); Trojans, Worms, and Spyware (Elsevier Science); Implementing Homeland Security in Enterprise IT (Digital Press); Guide to Disaster Recovery (Course Technology); Socially Responsible IT Management (Digital Press); Information Warfare: How to Survive Cyber Attacks (McGraw Hill); The Executive's Guide to Privacy Management (McGraw Hill); and Net Privacy: Implementing an e-business Privacy Plan (McGraw Hill). He was a founding member of the National Cyber Security Alliance (NCSA) which focuses on computer security awareness. As a member of the High Tech Crime Investigators Association (HTCIA), he contributed to their primer to guide business people on how to work with law enforcement agencies in dealing with computer crimes. Michael contributed to efforts of the National Science Foundation (NSF) and the American Association of Community Colleges (AACC) in developing computer and network security curriculums. He was served on the Board of the COMDEX Conference and chaired the Future of Technology conference track.

Emily Q. Freeman is Executive Director for Technology and Media Risks for Lockton International and Specialty Broking Services in London. She has been a principal drafter of cyberspace and technology insurance products. She has also been a senior consultant for risk analysis of operational risk and applications utilizing computer networks and the Internet. She has had brokerage background in London and the United States, as well as an underwriting background. She has been responsible for large insurance and risk management programs, and served as a technical advisor on coverage and underwriting matters. She was Vice President at National Union/AIG involved with underwriting and management of technology and cyber risks. Ms. Freeman also led the e-business practice at Marsh. Prior to 1998, she was a marketing manager at Sedgwick and a member of the executive committee of the Sedgwick Technology Group. Ms. Freeman began her career with Industrial Indemnity, a unit of Crum & Forster Group, in San Francisco as a casualty underwriter. A graduate of the University of California, Ms. Freeman also was a Distinguished Graduate of the Associate Underwriting Program of IIA. She holds the Associate in Risk Management (ARM) and Associate in Underwriting (AU) professional designations. Ms. Freeman has been a frequent speaker on cyber risks, technology, outsourcing, intellectual property, and other related risk and insurance issues. She has authored articles for a number of business and finance publications, including Washington CEO, Financial Executive, IRMI, Risk Management, Riskvue.com, and The John Liner Review. She has authored a chapter for a book on Cyber Security and Cyber Terrorism, and recently completed a major article on outsourcing and contractual risks. Ms. Freeman has been an expert guest on CNN's World News and National Public Radio's All Things Considered, and has been interviewed on matters relating to the identification and management of e-business risk by The New York Times, The Wall Street Journal, American Banker, Fortune, The Associated Press, Bloomberg Business News, CFO, Infoweek, Wired, Treasury & Risk Management, Business Insurance, National Underwriter, Risk & Insurance, Washington Post, and numerous other leading business/financial, technology and general news media outlets.

Dan Geer's milestone achievements include the X Window System and Kerberos (1988), the first information security consulting firm on Wall Street (1992), convener of the first academic conference on electronic commerce (1995), the "Risk Management is Where the Money Is" speech that changed the focus of security (1998), the Presidency of USENIX Association (2000), the first call for the eclipse of authentication by accountability (2002), principal author of and spokesman for "Cyberinsecurity: The Cost of Monopoly" (2003), co-founder of SecurityMetrics.Org (2004), convener of MetriCon (2006-8), and author of "Economics & Strategies of Data Security" (2008).

Prof. Sumit Ghosh received his B.Tech. degree (1980) in electrical engineering from the Indian Institute of Technology at Kanpur, India, and his M.S. and Ph.D. (1984) degrees from the Computer Systems Laboratory (joint EE and CS departments) at Stanford University, California. Sumit's industrial research training has been at Bell Labs Research (Holmdel, New Jersey), Fairchild Advanced Research and Development Labs (Palo Alto, California), and Silvar-Lisco (Menlo Park, California). He has held academic positions at Brown University, Arizona State University, and Stevens Institute of Technology, and is currently at University of Texas at Tyler. He is the recipient of the 2004 IEEE Computer Society's Technical Achievement Award, a Fellow of the Society for Design and Process Science (SDPS), and has been elected in 2008 to serve as President of SDPS, the leading society for transdisciplinary research and education. He is the primary author of six reference books: Hardware Description Languages: Concepts and Principles (IEEE Press, 2000); Modeling and Asynchronous Distributed Simulation of Complex Systems (IEEE Press, 2000); Intelligent Transportation Systems: New Principles and Architectures (CRC Press, 2000); Principles of Secure Network Systems Design (Springer-Verlag, 2002); Algorithm Design for Networked Information Technology Systems: Principles and Applications (Springer-Verlag, 2003); and Intelligent Transportation Systems: Smart, Green Approach to Infrastructure Design (Second edition, CRC Press, 2010). He is co-editor of the book, Guarding Your Business: A Management Approach to Security (Kluwer Academic Publishers, 2004). He has written 95+ transactions/journal papers, 120 refereed conference papers, and presented keynotes at major international conferences. Sumit's PhD dissertation inspired the founding of USAF's VHDL effort, now a industry standard; his pioneering research on a fundamental framework for network security constitutes the cornerstone of NSA's Network Rating Model; and his research in networking has been adopted in the key elements of the ATM Forum's secure PNNI protocol.

Mark D. Goodman (photograph not available) has extensive international experience on matters relating to cybercrime, cyber-terrorism and information security. Since 1999, Mr. Goodman has worked in a variety of capacities with INTERPOL, the International Criminal Police Organization, headquartered in Lyon, France, where he serves as the Senior Advisor to the organization's Steering Committee on Information Technology Crime. Mr. Goodman frequently consults with global policy makers, security executives and industry leaders on technology-related transnational security threats and has worked in more than fifty countries throughout the Middle East, Africa, Europe, Latin America and Asia. In addition to chairing two of Interpol's global cybercrime conferences, Mr. Goodman has participated in numerous specialized high technology crime projects for the organization, ranging from the investigation of E-Commerce crime to live data forensics. Mr. Goodman currently chairs INTERPOL's working group on Crime in Virtual Worlds and is helping to coordinate a global law enforcement response to the real-world threats posed by these cutting-edge developments in virtual communities. In 2009, Mr. Goodman was asked to serve as member of the United Nation's Office on Drugs and Crime Expert Working Group on Transnational Organized Cybercrime. Moreover, in 2007, Mr. Goodman was nominated by the Secretary General of the United Nations International Telecommunications Union (ITU) to serve as a member of his High Level Experts Group on Global Cybersecurity (HLEG). HLEG serves as a global multi stakeholder think tank for the United Nations and is tasked with the analysis of new security challenges as well as the development of strategic solutions for both the Secretary General and for United Nations member states. Mr. Goodman is also the founding officer-in-charge of the Los Angeles Police Department's Internet Unit, LAPDOnline. A veteran police officer, he served with the LAPD for over a decade in a variety of positions including patrol, vice and investigations. Mr. Goodman holds degrees from Harvard University and the London School of Economics and Political Science. Goodman also served as a Visiting Fellow at both Stanford University's Center for International Security and Cooperation and the Hoover Institution.

Jessica Herrera-Flanigan is a partner in the Monument Policy Group and also a Senior Fellow at the George Washington University Homeland Security Policy Institute. Prior to joining Monument in 2008, Jessica served as the Staff Director and General Counsel for the House Committee on Homeland Security. Jessica has also served as Senior Counsel at the Computer Crime & Intellectual Property Section, Criminal Division, of the U.S. Department of Justice, where she focused on technology issues and led the Section's cybercrime investigation team. She was one of the government's leading experts on critical infrastructure protection, CFIUS, and electronic evidence gathering. She also served as vice-chair on the U.S. Delegation to the Organization for Economic Cooperation and Development ("OECD") Experts Group on international information security and represented the United States on security and privacy issues at Asia-Pacific Economic Cooperation ("APEC") and the Organization of American States ("OAS"). Jessica also was a Special Assistant U.S. Attorney working on fraud and public corruption cases in the U.S. Attorney's Office in Washington, D.C. Prior to her government service, Jessica worked at Crowell & Moring LLP in Washington, D.C., where she practiced communications/media, intellectual property, and energy law. She received her JD from Harvard Law School and her BA with distinction in American Studies from Yale University.

Marcus K. Rogers, Ph.D., CISSP, CCCI, DFCP, is the Director of the Cyber Forensics Program in the Dept. of Computer and Information Technology at Purdue University. He is a Professor, Faculty Scholar, and Fellow of the Center for Education and Research in Information Assurance and Security (CERIAS). Dr. Rogers is a member of the quality assurance board for (ISC)2's SCCP designation, the International Chair of the Law, Regulations, Compliance and Investigation Domain of the Common Body of Knowledge (CBK) committee, Chair – Ethics Committee Digital & Multimedia Sciences Section – American Academy of Forensic Sciences, and Chair – Certification Committee Digital Forensics Certification Board. Dr. Rogers is the Editor-in-Chief of the Journal of Digital Forensic Practice and sits on the editorial board for several other professional journals. He is also a member of other various national and international committees focusing on digital forensic science and digital evidence. Dr. Rogers is the author of numerous book chapters, and journal publications in the field of digital forensics and applied psychological analysis. His research interests include applied cyber forensics, psychological digital crime scene analysis, and cyber terrorism.

Paul B. Schneck is Chairman and was previously CEO & President of Rembrandt IP Management, LLC, a patent enforcement firm. Prior to that Schneck was Vice President and CTO of Veridian, a 7,500-person professional services firm. Earlier in his career Schneck was a Fellow at Mitre Corporation and its spin-off Mitretek. He was Founding Director of the Supercomputing Research Center, formed to provide the National Security Agency with orders of magnitude increases in its mission computing capability. The Center introduced processing-in-memory (PIM) computing and developed the SPLASH reconfigurable computer. Schneck served as Director of Information Sciences at the Office of Naval Research, responsible for the Navy's computing research programs. He began his career at NASA, first at the Goddard Institute for Space Studies where he headed a team that wrote an OS for the IBM 360, 370 and Amdahl mainframes (including dual-processor configurations) that far exceeded the speed and flexibility of then-contemporary systems. Schneck was also responsible for the development of early "vectorizing" and "parallelizing" compilers. Schneck is a Fellow of the IEEE and of the ACM. He is a Member of the British Computing Society and is a Chartered Engineer (UK). Schneck holds two fundamental patents, 5,933,498 and 6,314,409 in digital rights management. He is the author of "Supercomputer Architecture," published by Kluwer in 1987, as well as numerous book chapters. Schneck received his Ph.D. from the Courant Institute of Mathematical Sciences, NYU, and his M.S. and B.S. from the School of Engineering and Applied Science, Columbia University.

Melanie Schneck Teplinsky is an associate with the law firm of Steptoe & Johnson LLP in Washington, D.C. Her work in the firm's Telecom, Internet & Media group has involved a wide array of cybersecurity and data protection issues. Ms. Teplinsky also has written and spoken extensively on information technology law. Prior to joining Steptoe, Ms. Teplinsky worked on information technology policy issues in the Executive Office of the President, dividing her time between the Office of Science and Technology Policy and the Office of Management and Budget's Office of Information and Regulatory Affairs, Information Technology Branch. Ms. Teplinsky began her career in 1991 as an analyst at the National Security Agency and continued her technical work at the Institute for Defense Analyses' Center for Communications Research. She later authored an internal government white paper outlining United States encryption policy options while working in the Computer Security Laboratory at the National Institute of Standards and Technology and studied network technologies at the Center for Information Strategy and Policy at Science Applications International Corporation. Ms. Teplinsky clerked for the Honorable Judge Rya W. Zobel, U.S. District Court, District of Massachusetts upon graduation from Harvard Law School and is a 1995 Harry Truman National Scholarship winner.

Richard A. Stanley, Ph.D., PE, CISSP is Vice President of Wheeler Associates, Limited, a technology and educational consulting firm outside Boston, which specializes in custom information security solutions. He has over 35 years experience with telecommunications, information processing, and security systems, and has directed research in those areas for both the US Government and in the private sector. Among the research activities he has directed have been the development of the Ada computer programming language, a secure wireless data network for trading on the floor of the New York Stock Exchange, a state of the art communications system for peacekeepers in the Middle East, and a series of research projects on ad hoc computer networking for the United States Army. He has lived and worked all over the United States and Canada and also in Europe, Asia, and Africa. He is a Registered Professional Electrical Engineer in the Commonwealth of Massachusetts and a Certified Information Systems Security Professional. Dr. Stanley is a member of the New York Electronic Crimes Task Force and the New England Electronic Crimes Task Force. He often speaks at professional gatherings, and holds appointment as an adjunct professor at Worcester Polytechnic Institute, where he teaches topics in electrical engineering and computer science. He is also the author of five books, many professional papers, and the holder of several patents.

Elliot Turrini is the CEO and Founder of CollaborativeHealth ("CH"), which is using entertainment, break through behavioral science, and cutting-edge technology to make achieving good health easier and more enjoyable. He is a member of the board of directors of the American Council on Exercise. From 2004 to 2007, Elliot was the EVP of a 300 employee IT services firm, where his responsibilities included strategy, leadership, marketing, managing all legal issues, and overseeing finance. From 2003 to 2004, Elliot practiced law with McElroy, Deutch, Mulvaney & Carpenter in N.J. From 1995 to December 2002, Elliot served as an Assistant U.S. Attorney for the District of N.J., where he was the Computer and Telecommunication Coordinator and prosecuted high-tech and IP criminals including David Smith for disseminating the Melissa Virus. Elliot received a B.A. from Yale in 1987 and a J.D. Summa Cum Laude from Seton Hall University School in 1992, where he was an Articles Editor for the Law Review. He is the former law clerk to the Honorable Morton I. Greenberg, United States Court of Appeals for the Third Circuit.

Index

Printed in the USA
CPSIA information can be obtained
at www.ICGtesting.com
CBHW071544221124
17885CB00003B/127

9 783642 135460